SPRINGER SERIES
IN PERCEPTION ENGINEERING

Series Editor: Ramesh Jain

Springer Series
in Perception Engineering

P.J. Besl: *Surfaces in Range Image Understanding*

J.L.C. Sanz (ed.): *Advances in Machine Vision*

Paul J. Besl

Surfaces in Range Image Understanding

With 141 Illustrations

Springer-Verlag
New York Berlin Heidelberg
London Paris Tokyo

Paul J. Besl
Staff Research Scientist
Computer Science Department
General Motors Research Laboratories
Warren, MI 48090-9055
USA

Series editor
Ramesh Jain
Electrical Engineering
  and Computer Science Department
University of Michigan
Ann Arbor, MI 48105
USA

621·367
BES

Library of Congress Cataloging-in-Publication Data
Besl, Paul J.
    Surfaces in range image understanding / Paul J. Besl.
      p. cm. — (Springer series in perception engineering)
    Rev. ed. of the author's thesis (Ph.D.)—University of Michigan,
  1986.
    Bibliography: p.
    ISBN 0-387-96773-7
    1. Image processing.   I. Title.   II. Series.
  TA1632.B47   1988
    621.36'7—dc19   88-12249

Camera-ready text prepared by the author using T$_{\rm E}$X software.
Printed and bound by R.R. Donnelly & Sons, Harrisonburg, Virginia.
Printed in the United States of America.

9 8 7 6 5 4 3 2 1

ISBN 0-387-96773-7 Springer-Verlag New York Berlin Heidelberg
ISBN 3-540-96773-7 Springer-Verlag Berlin Heidelberg New York

To Betsy and Sophie

Series Preface

Three major problems with machine perception research are: many techniques are useful only in extremely limited domains and tend to yield fragmented rather than unified theories, many techniques commit to particular interpretations of the data much too early, and most research literature presents either a theory, an algorithm, or application results but seldom are all three effectively presented. Paul Besl's dissertation, which is published here as the first book in the series on *Perception Engineering*, addresses all these problems and is a very significant contribution to the emerging field of Machine Perception. This book presents a solid, unified view of digital image analysis based only on mathematical surface concepts and an algorithm for obtaining useful segmented image descriptions. Experiments on numerous images, acquired using different sensors for widely different scenes, using a fixed set of input thresholds, show the robustness of this approach. Besl's dissertation presents a unique rigorous approach in machine perception that *works well* on real images.

In regard to wide applicability and unification of theory, the data-driven, surface-based segmentation algorithm, discussed in this book, is effective in segmenting range images, intensity images, and edge images and is even generalizable to higher-dimensioned image data. Region growing based on variable-order function fitting is used to obtain a precise, general, compact, symbolic representation of the original image. The final image description evolves gradually as a function of the spatial properties of the data; there is little bias imposed by preconceived notions of what the data should look like.

His work has already influenced several researchers in the field and will be one of the most influential research in early processing in machine perception systems. Moreover, this dissertation demonstrates that like established fields of science, mathematical theories can be applied to practical problems in machine perception by a careful analysis of the problem. I am very happy to start the series on *Perception Engineering* with a book that represents the spirit behind the series so well.

Preface

Perception of surfaces plays a fundamental role in three-dimensional object recognition and image understanding. The general purpose image segmentation algorithm presented in this book is based on three-dimensional surface geometry and has been applied successfully to range image and intensity image segmentation and reconstruction problems.

A range image explicitly represents the surface geometry of objects in a given field of view as an array of range values and invites processing based on surfaces. Previous research in range image understanding had limited itself to extensions of edge-based intensity image analysis or to interpretations in terms of polyhedra, generalized cylinders, quadric primitives, or convex objects. If early visual processing algorithms were not committed to interpretation in terms of restrictive, domain-specific, high level models, the same algorithms might be incorporated in different applications with minimal effort.

A general approach has been developed for processing digital images to obtain a high quality, information preserving, accurate, intermediate level description consisting of graph surface primitives, the associated segmented support regions, and their bounding edges. Only general knowledge about surfaces is used to compute a complete image segmentation and reconstruction. The digital image segmentation algorithm consists primarily of a differential geometric, visible invariant pixel labeling method based on the sign of mean and Gaussian curvatures and an iterative region growing method based on variable order surface fitting of the original image data. The high level control logic of the algorithm implementation is sequential, but all low level image processes can be executed on parallel architectures. This surface based image analysis approach has been successfully tested on a wide variety of range images and intensity images. Details of both surface and edge description algorithms based on the dimension-independent "sign-of-curvature" paradigm are described.

Acknowledgements

This book is a corrected, revised, updated, and reformatted version of the author's Ph.D. dissertation *Surfaces in Early Range Image Understanding* completed at the University of Michigan, Ann Arbor in 1986.

The author thanks R. Jain for his extraordinary enthusiasm, optimism, ideas, insight, encouragement, and guidance during the research that helped lead to the development of many ideas in the text. The efforts and contributions of the members of the author's doctoral committee, L. Maloney, R. Haralick, T. Weymouth, and T. Mudge, are also gratefully acknowledged. Many conversations with others have helped to refine the ideas in this thesis. The author would particularly like to thank L. Watson, M. Micallef, P. Eichel, R. Sarraga, D. Chen, and J. Callahan for their helpful comments on various aspects of this work. My appreciation is also expressed to D. Thomas and K. Gilbert. And special thanks go to my wife, Betsy, for her continual understanding, patience, and support.

Several organizations have also helped to make the dissertation and this book possible. The author acknowledges the past support of the International Business Machines Corporation, the DeVlieg Machine Tool Company, the Air Force Office of Scientific Research, and the Robot Systems Division of the Center of Robotics and Integrated Manufacturing at the University of Michigan. The author also acknowledges the software contributions of the Structural Dynamics Research Corporation and the range image data contributions of the Environmental Research Institute of Michigan and Prof. T. Henderson from the University of Utah. Finally, the author thanks General Motors Research Laboratories and N. Muench, G. Dodd, S. Holland, and R. Tilove for encouraging the further development of these ideas in industrial applications.

Paul J. Besl

Table of Contents

Chapter 1

Introduction

1.1 Perception, Surfaces, and Range Images

The goal of a machine perception system is to automatically interpret the information in physically sensed signals, such as sound, light, radar, or pressure signals, in a useful way for a given application. Researchers have attempted with limited success to use digitized signals from various sensors to endow digital computers with the abilities to hear, see, and touch so that machines can intelligently interact with an uncertain, dynamic environment. Whereas automated speech recognition techniques attempt to understand one-dimensional (1-D) signals in terms of a natural language structure, computational vision research attempts to use two-dimensional (2-D) signals to determine the geometric structure of corresponding three-dimensional (3-D) scenes. Each data point in a digitized 2-D signal is discrete in the two x,y spatial directions and in the level z of the sensed quantity. Such 2-D signals are usually processed as a large matrix of integers. Each matrix element, or *pixel*, has a row/column location and a value representing the sensed physical quantity. In machine perception, it is useful to view a large matrix of this type as a *digital surface* because the sensed values at each pixel can be considered as noisy samples of an "analog surface" $z = f(x, y)$. Digital surfaces are more commonly known as *digital images*. Figure 1.1 shows a 20x20 matrix taken from a larger digital image and the corresponding digital surface view of the same data. The digital image might have been an intensity image, a range image, a tactile image, or some other type of image; it is not possible to tell from the numbers themselves. The final interpretation of such images depends, among other things, on what the z values at each pixel mean and how they are processed. The image processing algorithms of computer vision systems depend on how the signal is viewed by the data analyst as well as the meaning of the pixel values. For example, the signal in Figure 1.1 might be treated primarily as a statistical entity with a mean and standard deviation or as a geometric entity with surface shape.

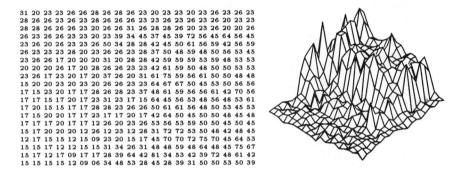

```
31 20 23 23 26 26 28 26 28 26 23 20 23 23 20 23 26 23 26 23
28 26 26 23 26 23 28 26 26 26 23 23 26 23 26 23 26 20 23 23
28 28 26 26 26 23 20 26 26 31 26 28 28 26 20 23 26 20 20 26
26 23 26 26 23 23 20 23 39 34 45 37 45 39 72 56 45 64 56 45
23 26 20 26 23 23 26 50 34 28 28 42 45 50 61 56 59 42 56 59
26 23 23 23 28 20 23 26 26 23 28 37 50 48 59 48 50 56 53 45
23 26 26 17 20 20 20 31 20 28 28 42 59 59 59 53 59 48 53 53
20 20 20 26 17 20 28 26 26 23 23 42 61 59 50 48 50 50 53 53
23 26 17 23 20 17 20 37 26 20 31 61 75 59 56 61 50 50 48 48
15 20 20 23 20 23 20 26 26 23 23 64 67 67 50 45 53 50 56 56
17 15 23 20 17 17 28 26 28 23 37 48 61 59 56 56 61 42 70 56
17 17 15 17 20 17 23 31 23 17 15 64 45 56 53 48 56 48 53 61
17 20 15 15 17 17 28 28 23 26 26 50 61 61 56 48 50 53 45 53
17 15 20 20 17 17 23 17 17 20 17 42 64 50 45 50 50 48 45 48
17 17 17 20 17 17 12 26 20 23 26 53 56 53 59 50 50 45 50 45
15 17 20 20 20 12 26 12 23 12 28 31 72 72 53 50 48 42 48 45
12 17 15 15 12 15 09 23 20 15 17 45 70 70 72 75 70 45 64 53
15 15 17 12 12 15 15 31 34 26 31 48 48 59 48 64 48 45 75 67
15 17 12 17 09 17 17 28 39 64 42 81 34 53 42 39 72 48 61 42
15 15 15 15 12 09 06 34 48 53 28 45 28 39 31 50 50 53 50 39
```

Figure 1.1: A 2-D Signal Viewed as a Matrix and a Digital Surface

Digital intensity images (also known as brightness, luminance, or irradiance images) have been studied in image processing and computational vision for over twenty-five years and have received significantly more attention
than any other type of digital surface in machine perception. Nonetheless,
many other digital images, such as tactile, radar, infrared, scanning electron
microscope, ultrasound, and X-ray have also been analyzed with the goal
of automated interpretation. Digital *range images* (also known as *depth
maps*) can be created using a number of different active or passive range
sensing methods [Jarvis 1983]. A range image is a large matrix of distance
measurements from the sensor coordinate system to surface points on objects in a scene. The image quality and the speed of image acquisition of
range imaging sensors has steadily improved to the point that high-quality
8-bit 128x128 registered range and intensity images can be produced by
commercially available sensors at a rate of more than one frame per second. Many active optical range imaging sensors, including some with frame
rates faster than one frame per second and others with higher than 8-bit
range resolution, are described in Besl [1988]. As discussed in Chapter 2,
range images are unique in a mathematical sense among all other types of
2-D signals for scene analysis in that they directly approximate the physical surfaces of objects in scenes. Quantitative surface geometry can be
directly extracted from high-quality, high-resolution range images whereas,
in other kinds of images, the surface structure of a scene must be inferred
indirectly from the sensor data regardless of the resolution or quality.

People are remarkably proficient at the qualitative visual inference and
perceptual organization processes required for image interpretation regardless of image type and quality. The human visual system is able to discover
continuity, smoothness, regularity, and spatial coherence in noisy image
data and to organize pixels into important regions even when *a priori*
knowledge about the meaning of the image data is lacking. In contrast, it
has proven to be quite difficult to program computers to perform similar

visual tasks in a general purpose manner. When a machine vision system is successfully applied to a particular problem, one is fortunate if that same system can be applied to a significantly different problem without a major development effort. Why should such a discrepancy in perceptual capability and flexibility exist when computers can easily outperform people in many other tasks that people find difficult or tedious? A large part of the answer lies in the differences between the amount and the variety of *knowledge* that can be stored and accessed by each. People can interpret a wide variety of images using poorly understood, high-level visual mechanisms and a vast storehouse of quickly accessible knowledge. Current computer vision systems are limited to particular application domains where relevant knowledge can be organized in a form compatible with existing computer software and hardware. High-level mechanisms are still extremely primitive in comparison to human capabilities and tend to get slower instead of faster as the amount of flexible knowledge is increased.

There are numerous easily observed examples of "high-level" knowledge at work in visual perception. Consider a simple image in which a shadow falls across a visible smooth surface. A person perceives the smooth surface as a single geometric entity. If the same image were given to a computer vision system, it would probably find a dividing line that separates the brighter part of the smooth surface from the darker part in the shadow. In order to correctly *segment* the image near the shadow boundary into image regions that correspond to physical scene surfaces, high-level world knowledge is clearly needed to correctly infer scene surface structure from the intensity image structure. High quality range images are potentially very useful in that higher-level, domain-specific knowledge is not required to segment a scene into its component physical surfaces because the component surfaces of the scene are explicitly represented by the collection of range measurements. Only generic information about surfaces is required to organize range image pixels into spatially coherent surface primitives. It is interesting to note that speech signals and tactile images are more similar to range images than intensity images because they contain explicit information about audio frequencies and skin pressure, quantities that are directly useful to interpretation tasks. In contrast, brightness and color contain surprisingly little explicit geometric information about the 3-D world that we perceive. Of course, higher level knowledge is still required for any signal type in order to establish with reasonable certainty the meaning of the various parts of the signal by relating them to known structures in a domain model. For example, object level knowledge is required to decide which surfaces in a range image belong to which objects.

The 2.5-D sketch and the intrinsic image paradigms proposed by Marr [1976,1982] and Barrow and Tenenbaum [1978,1981] respectively seek a range image as the primary intermediate output from early visual processes operating on an intensity image. In these paradigms, the range image along with the intensity image from which it was derived and other computed quantities provide input to higher level, goal-driven, domain-specific modules that perform interpretation, object recognition, and image understanding. But some researchers have doubted the importance of range images in visual perception perhaps because the widely accepted paradigms do not state exactly how range images should be used. For example, Witkin and Tenenbaum [1983] made the following statements:

> Even if a depth map could be reliably obtained, how would it be used? [p. 493]

> Being just an array of numbers, it is difficult to think of tasks that a depth map directly supports. [p. 493]

> ...recognizing objects requires that the depth data first be organized into larger structures corresponding, for example, to continuous visible surfaces. Although perhaps better defined, this process is a great deal like that of segmenting a brightness image. [p. 493]

> However, all the fundamental difficulties due to noise and low contrast edges remain. Range contributes incrementally, in much the same way as color; it adds a dimension that simplifies some decisions, but certainly does not make segmentation trivial. [pp. 493-495]

> Although depth maps can be helpful, it is not obvious that they are helpful enough to deserve their present stature as a central goal of vision. [p. 495]

It is true that raw range images in their full dimensionality are just a list of numbers representing distance measurements and cannot directly support high-level image interpretation processes without some type of perceptual organization, such as segmentation. And it is certainly true that range image segmentation is not trivial; most intensity image segmentation problems are also encountered with range images. However, it is premature to dismiss range image analysis merely because range images are currently not helpful enough to image understanding efforts. Range information provides a basic, fundamental contribution toward the goal of understanding 3-D shape, which is required for general-purpose object recognition and image understanding. Given the results of Chapter 7, it appears that range image understanding research may provide a useful basis for pixel grouping operations that might also assist intensity image understanding efforts. Also, many high-level object recognition issues must be confronted in image understanding research regardless of whether range, intensity, or some other type of images are being used as sensor input. If working with range images simplifies the framework for solving difficult object recognition problems, then insightful ideas for solutions to intensity image problems might be more readily obtained.

1.2 Low-Level vs. High-Level Processing

Extracting useful information from digital surfaces is a difficult *signal to symbol transformation* problem. Computational processes that use the pixel values themselves or transformed pixel values are known as *low-level, early,* or *signal* processes. Processes that use properties of *groups of pixels* are known as *high-level, later,* or *symbolic* processes. These terms are relative, of course. The level of two higher level processes may be compared in terms of the amount of grouping and/or the "meaningfulness" of the groups. For example, a sentence is a higher level entity than a word even though both are groups of alphabetic symbols.

A series of low-level and high-level processing steps are typically required to extract useful information from digital images. Low-level processes are predominantly data-driven whereas the highest level processes are mainly model-driven. Since high-level model-driven processes and low-level data-driven processes must interact to provide complete system capabilities, any successful algorithm must include a transition between low and high level processing. It is unclear exactly how or where this transition from data-driven to model-driven processing should take place in computer vision. High-level knowledge can be used directly in low-level processes, but this tends to severely limit the scope of applicability of such approaches unless the interface between the low-level processing algorithms and the high-level knowledge base is designed in a flexible, modular manner. As a general principle, data-driven perceptual processes should be developed to the highest possible level, which will depend on the type of sensor data, before domain-specific high-level information is used. In range image analysis, data-driven processes can yield surface-level information about a scene before a transition to high-level, object model information is needed.

Closely associated to the question of interactions between low-level and high-level processes are the fundamental problems related to local and global digital surface properties. For example, a small neighborhood around a pixel may appear to be flat locally even though it is actually part of a curved surface. On the other hand, if any noise is present, a small neighborhood may appear curved even though the corresponding physical surface is flat. Mathematical reasoning can provide good insights into the computation of local properties. However, as one begins to combine local properties into global ones, existing mathematical analysis techniques become much less clear about the methods that should be used for image understanding. In Chapter 3, it is shown that local properties of digital surfaces can be described using concepts from the differential geometry of smooth surfaces. In Chapter 4, function approximation is used to describe global properties of the data.

The function approximation approach to describing global properties brings with it the fundamental grouping problems encountered when fitting models to noisy data from unknown statistical populations. When a collection of sample data points have been drawn from a known population, there are straightforward procedures for fitting models to the data that assume that random measurement errors are responsible for all inconsistencies between model and data. However, collections of sample data points are often obtained where no *a priori* information is available concerning how these points are grouped or from which population the points are drawn. Attempts to fit models to this type of data must account for systematic grouping errors as well as random measurement errors. When this situation occurs, various clustering and segmentation algorithms can be applied based on a uniformity criteria satisfied by the data points from a given population. The Ransac technique of Bolles and Fischler [1981] is one example of an iterative algorithm that can be used for such purposes. Some basic concepts from that approach are used in the surface-based image segmentation algorithm described in Chapter 4. The theory of robust statistics [Hampel et al. 1986] also formally addresses these issues, but has not yet been applied to vision problems perhaps owing to the relatively expensive computational requirements.

Computer vision and machine perception are characterized by the need to address these basic dichotomies in the processing of digital surfaces: signals vs. symbols, data-driven vs. model-driven algorithms, low-level vs. high-level processes, local properties vs. global properties, and measurement errors vs. grouping errors. Specific ideas for addressing these issues are discussed throughout the text.

1.3 Data-Driven Range Image Analysis

The problem: **Given** a large matrix of numbers that represent noisy samples of the range from a sensor focal plane to the physical surfaces of unknown objects in a real-world scene, **segment** (partition, organize) the digital surface matrix into surface primitives that will be useful to higher-level application-specific algorithms without making any domain-dependent assumptions about specific objects, object classes, or applications.

The motivation for attempting to solve this isolated, component problem is given by way of two example problems. Consider an autonomous vehicle with a range imaging sensor that is attempting to navigate intelligently on its path through a largely unknown world. The vehicle has relatively limited knowledge about the 3-D world. It is assumed that one cannot afford to pre-define and store all known object shapes in the vehicle's on-board computer. That is, it is assumed that all possible boulders, holes, road surfaces, trees, telephone poles, earth terrains, vehicles, and buildings cannot be digitized or modeled to create a detailed, deterministic, object-model database. It is also assumed that technology will remain limited enough in the near future that computers will not be capable of human-like abilities to understand, conceptualize, and move about in unfamiliar, changing surroundings. Yet, this vehicle must "understand" and navigate in its environment as well as possible using relatively qualitative, abstract notions about roads and obstacles. Range image pixel values may be directly useful for simple processing, but a higher-level description is necessary to make intelligent, automated decisions about road smoothness, obstacles, and other objects in the field of view of the vehicle's range imaging sensor. This description should be useful for identifying all kinds of surfaces: horizontal, vertical, flat, curved, kinked, and textured surfaces, regardless of the viewpoint from the vehicle. An algorithm that can provide a piecewise-smooth surface representation for arbitrary range images could certainly be useful for such a vehicle.

Next, consider a non-mobile factory robot equipped with a range imaging sensor. It inspects component parts and/or assembles larger systems of parts, but is not given these parts in a rigidly constrained fashion: the parts may be in a jumbled pile in a bin, oriented randomly on a conveyor belt, or spread out on a table. A 3-D understanding of part shape is desired owing to the tendency of the parts to be scattered about in various orientations and to the need for inspecting all surfaces of the part before attaching the piece to the assembly. In this more limited domain, it is feasible to build a database of 3-D object models that completely describe and specify all allowable part shapes. This information is used to inspect the part and to determine location and orientation parameters of the part when it is in an unknown position in the robot's field of view. In this scenario, it is desirable to compute features of parts that are invariant to viewpoint transformations. The ability to compute a piecewise-smooth surface description of a part without being constrained to a particular set of objects would be useful for a general-purpose vision system.

What do these two applications of range imaging have in common? Both cases require scene surface descriptions from range images that describe visible surface shape independent of viewpoint. The descriptions should be at a higher representational level than the original data in order to avoid working with hundreds of thousands of range values directly. That is, some type of data compression is desired. For example, a list of fewer than a hundred surface regions or edges would be much easier to handle. The high-level scene surface structure description must be processed at another even higher level that depends on the application domain to derive information useful to that application.

The two examples above and many applications would benefit from a technique for converting raw image data into a higher-level format that combines local data properties into more global data properties. If a range image is thought of as a signal (a 2-D signal as opposed to a more conventional 1-D voltage vs. time signal), and if descriptions of the image signal are viewed as symbols, then this is an example of a *signal to symbol transformation* problem. Two commonplace signal-to-symbol processes are discussed to draw several important analogies.

When people listen to speech, a sound signal (air pressure as a function of time) is converted into an internal nervous system signal by the human ear. That internal signal is eventually grouped into sound primitives (phonemes), which are then grouped into words and sentences. The sounds associated with the letters 'r' and 'c' cannot be distinguished on the basis of instantaneous samples or even small groups of samples of either the internal or external signal. These signals must be observed *over time* to identify symbolic sound primitives. That is, individual signal samples must be *grouped* together to form symbolic primitives. The sound primitives themselves have no intrinsic meaning, i.e., no higher level interpretation other than an 'r' or 'c' sound. Meaning is only assigned to groups of sound primitives (groups of symbols) within the context of a specific language.

Similarly, when people observe a scene, a light signal (photon count as a function of frequency and two spatial parameters) is converted into an internal nervous system signal by the human eye. This internal signal is eventually grouped into symbolic visual primitives, which are then grouped into objects (groups of symbols). The visual primitives associated with the cylindrical body and the handle of a coffee cup cannot be distinguished on the basis of individual samples or even small groups of samples of either the internal or external visual signals. Signals must be observed *over space* to identify visual primitives, or in other terms, pixels must be grouped into symbolic visual primitives. Again, the visual primitives themselves have no intrinsic meaning of their own. Meaning is only assigned to groups of visual primitives within the context of an almost universal "visual language" structure based on three-dimensional reasoning capabilities.

Range images can be interpreted visually by people when range is encoded as brightness on a display monitor. Range image signals consist of noisy estimates of scene depth as a function of two spatial parameters. A signal must be organized into spatial primitives first before higher level processes can accept it for interpretation. Once these spatial primitives have been identified, they can be grouped at a higher level into meaningful objects in a manner depending on the application. For example, an autonomous vehicle might have a simple qualitative world model consisting of roads, obstacles, and other objects if it is only interested in maneuvering to stay on the road and avoid obstacles. The factory robot might have a very specific quantitative world model because it is interested in determining exact part position and verifying part integrity.

At an abstract level, biological sensor systems accept external physical signals as input, transform signals to new internal signals, convert the new signals into symbolic primitives, and then group the symbolic primitives into higher level symbols (groups of symbols) that permit the association of meaning within the context of a specific domain. In machine perception, the same sequence of operations applies. Let signal A be an ordered collection of N data samples (pixels). These data samples are transformed into signal B, another set of N data samples, which represents signal A.

In a biological perception system, signal A could be the external signal and signal B, the internal signal. In a machine perception system, let the transformation of signal A to signal B represent all signal (image) processing operations that maintain the same dimensionality of the signal. Next, a *grouping operation* segments (partitions) the set of N pixels in signal A into a set of M disjoint groups (regions) where $M << N$. This set of M groups represents the early levels of symbolism, or perceptual organization of the data. The symbolic primitives (regions) at this level do not permit or require the attachment of meaning. Later in the perceptual process, meaning (an interpretation) is attached to L groups of symbols, which are also symbolic entities ($L < M << N$). This is represented as follows:

Signal A $\rightarrow$ Signal B $\rightarrow$ Symbol $\rightarrow$ Groups of Symbols $\leftarrow$ Meaning

In the context of the proposed approach to range image understanding, signal A represents the set of N pixel values in a range image. It is converted to a set of N local surface type labels, known as the surface curvature sign map, the HK-sign map, or the surface type label image. These local surface type labels enable the grouping of pixels into M surfaces, which are the basis symbols in this example. Meaningful groups of surfaces are later recognized as L objects by a higher-level process. The subsequent chapters focus on the process of taking raw signal data (a range image) and converting it to intermediate level symbolic primitives (smooth surface regions) using only general principles.

Although one cannot logically prove that early vision should always be a data-driven process, there are many advantages to data-driven low-level processing for flexible vision systems. If one chooses to directly involve domain-specific, high-level information and world models in the early stages of the signal-to-symbol process, it may be difficult to use the same system for other purposes than that for which it was designed. Imagine needing three different eye-brain systems for reading, walking, and eating. If an early vision module of a vision system relies only on general principles in identifying symbolic primitives in the signal, that module should be applicable in any situation where those general principles apply. For example, 'r' and 'c' sounds can be recognized independent of the words or the language in which they are used. Consider the additional difficulty in learning a new language in which none of the normal sounds of alphabetic letters are used. For flexibility and adaptability, the raw data and its properties should be the driving factor in early vision processing algorithms, not high-level models.

Successful visual perception involves interaction between model-driven and data-driven processing stages at some level in a vision system. It is critically important to the performance and flexibility of the system how and when these stages are combined, what type of information is used at each stage, and how it is used. With range images, it is appropriate to apply primarily data-driven processes until a piecewise-smooth surface description of the image is obtained. This surface-based data description could then be matched against a set of surface-based object models, as in Fisher [1986] for example. An autonomous vehicle might use a qualitative, surface-based object model in which roads are long, almost flat, roughly horizontal surfaces that are wider than the vehicle itself. An intelligent factory robot might use quantitative, surface-based object models to verify that a slanted machined surface on a part is flat to within a specified tolerance and has holes drilled at prespecified locations. If the same data-driven image segmentation algorithm could be used in these two applications, it would also serve as an generic basis for solving many other problems.

1.4   Qualitative Algorithm Description

The items above have attempted to explain the motivation for developing an application independent, data-driven algorithm to create a symbolic surface primitive description of an image. The subsequent chapters form a case study in the design of a surface-based image segmentation algorithm based on a piecewise-smooth surface model and a mixture of mathematics and heuristics. The algorithm consists of three stages and involves an intermediate high-dimensionality signal domain and an intermediate low-dimensionality symbol domain. The input to the algorithm is any digital image that exhibits the *surface coherence property* discussed in Chapters 2 and 4. The surface coherence concept may be briefly expressed by noting that a range image of a piecewise-smooth surface with double precision pixel values and no added noise is completely coherent if the smallest smooth surface region is represented by at least a minimum number of pixels, e.g. 30. In comparison, an image of random noise is completely non-coherent. The accuracy and usefulness of the algorithm's output is directly related to the spatial coherence of the input. Moreover, a method for estimating the surface coherence of the input image automatically is described.

The final output of the image segmentation algorithm is (1) the smooth surface primitive list containing 2-D region data, 3-D graph surface equations, 2-D region boundary equations, and fit errors, (2) the segmentation plot showing the various surface primitive regions, and (3) the digital surface reconstructed from the smooth surface primitive list that allows the human observer to visually evaluate the approximation quality of the surface primitives. This final output contains much more information than just the 2-D region descriptions available from most image segmentation algorithms published in the literature. It is a rich (information-preserving) description that allows one to reconstruct an image representation of the coherent surfaces in an image.

Figure 1.2 provides a reasonably detailed overview of the three-stage digital surface segmentation algorithm. Chapter and section numbers indicate where the details of each processing step can be found. The non-

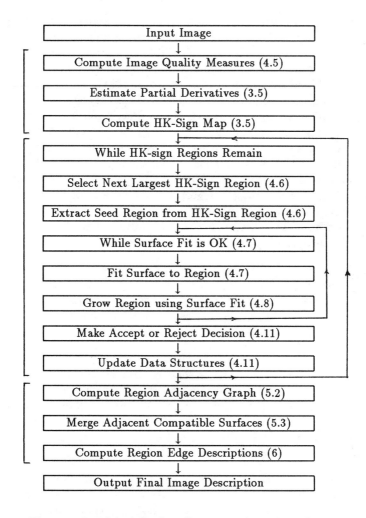

Figure 1.2: Digital Surface Segmentation Algorithm

iterative first stage of the algorithm (1) estimates the noise variance in the image to see if surface coherence condition is satisfied, (2) smooths the image retaining the fractional part of pixel values, (3) estimates the partial derivatives of the smoothed digital surface, and (4) computes the surface curvature sign image in which each pixel is labeled according to its fundamental surface type based on neighboring pixel values.

The iterative second stage of the algorithm (1) isolates connected regions of pixels of the same surface type, (2) finds small, maximally interior, highly reliable seed regions where the connected region pixel values are noisy samples from the same spatially coherent, underlying surface of a given fundamental surface type, and (3) performs an iterative, region growing procedure on each seed region based on variable-order surface fitting to obtain simple, spatially coherent, graph surface primitives and a set of 2-D region descriptions which complement each other. This region growing stage is described with pseudo-code in Appendix G.

The non-iterative third stage of the algorithm (1) combines the 2-D region descriptions to obtain a unified region description for each surface, (2) computes a region adjacency graph, and (3) merges compatible, smoothly joining, adjacent surface primitives into larger smooth surface regions yielding a final smooth surface segmentation of the image. The surface segmentation algorithm is a mixture of high-level sequential and low-level parallel computations. Moreover, the algorithm has been applied successfully to both range images and intensity images.

The primary strengths of this image analysis algorithm as opposed to other approaches in the literature are enumerated:

1. An approach for grouping pixels in digital images based on the surface coherence predicate is provided. In range images, arbitrary curved surfaces are isolated and represented as being curved, and flat surfaces are isolated and represented as being flat in the context of the same algorithm as determined by the data, not by restrictive high level models.

2. Depth discontinuities and orientation discontinuities between surfaces in a scene become well defined in the algorithm's output representation by means of the surface approximation mechanisms used by the algorithm. The occluded and occluding surfaces of range discontinuities are isolated, and convex and concave orientation discontinuities are also distinguished [Sugihara 1979].

3. Region boundaries conform to whatever arbitrary four-connected region structure is present in the data. There are no problems with the blocky boundaries of window-based split-and-merge segmentation techniques. Convex regions are not required.

4. A parallel region growing technique allows non-adjacent regions of the same surface to be grouped together based on shape similarity during image segmentation, not afterward.

5. A noise-free piecewise-smooth image reconstruction is produced by the algorithm indicating its noise cleaning abilities.

6. The iterative region growing process exhibits reasonable convergence properties. The average number of iterations is approximately seven and almost all regions converge in under fifteen iterations.

7. It is possible to determine a fixed set of input thresholds that yield excellent performance across a wide variety of range and intensity images. Moreover, it is also possible to define these thresholds in terms of image noise estimates such that the thresholds adapt from image to image.

8. Although the coefficients of graph surface primitives are not viewpoint independent, viewpoint independent surface characteristics are used and surface primitive shape properties are relatively insensitive to viewpoint transformations.

9. The exact same sign-of-curvature paradigm for surface shape description is also applicable to edge shape description and to multidimensional image segmentation and description. The method is applied to region boundaries to identify linear and curved portions and to provide parametric edge descriptions.

Later chapters substantiate the above list of claims by means of theoretical arguments, detailed algorithm descriptions, and experimental results on real data. The algorithm is not claimed to be a foolproof, hands-off segmentation technique, and it is not claimed that the image segmentation problem has been completely solved, but the current algorithm has worked successfully on over 95% of the more than sixty images processed. Rather, an interesting set of simple ideas have yielded an encouraging set of results that point in what appears to be a fruitful direction for early image understanding research.

1.5 Overview

This text addresses several interrelated topics in varying amounts of detail. Figure 1.3 shows the hierarchy of the subjects of interest and lists the relevant chapter numbers for each. The main emphasis is on digital surface characterization and image segmentation. Chapter 1 has introduced the reader to the data-driven image analysis problem and to the basic approach used in the surface based segmentation algorithm. A literature review of surface characterization and image segmentation research prior to 1986 is presented in the next section to conclude this chapter.

In Chapter 2, a system level approach to range image analysis, and image analysis in general, is taken. The object recognition problem and the digital surface segmentation problem are defined and a solution approach for object recognition in range images based on surface characterization, surface segmentation, and surface matching is proposed. Surface characterization and image segmentation are then subsequently addressed in a framework that involves no application specific knowledge, only knowledge of surfaces.

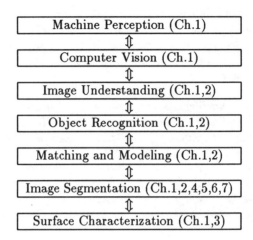

Figure 1.3: Hierarchy of Machine Perception Subjects by Chapter

In Chapter 3, visible-invariant quantities from differential geometry are used as digital surface characteristics. Relevant concepts for curves and surfaces are reviewed with an emphasis on qualitative concepts, and several theorems are stated in support of the choice of mean and Gaussian curvature as basic visible-invariants. Methods for estimating the necessary partial derivatives of the digital surface are also discussed. Experimental surface characterization results are presented.

In Chapter 4, surface curvature sign characteristics are used by an iterative region-growing method based on variable-order surface fitting. This method computes polynomial graph surface equations $z = f(x, y)$ and three complementary region descriptions of the lowest level surface primitives as a segmentation of the digital surface. In Chapter 5, methods for combining region descriptions into a single description and for merging adjacent surface primitives that join smoothly along their separating boundary are presented. This step is necessary, in general, to group surface primitives that jointly represent meaningful smooth surfaces of a complicated shape. For scenes consisting of only basic surface types, this processing step is not required. In Chapter 6, it is shown that the surface curvature sign concepts for surface description reduce to a sign of curvature method for edge description that is useful for describing region boundaries. In this way, surface primitives are specified by graph surface equations and by the equations of "trimming" curves that bound the support region of the graph surface.

In Chapter 7, the experimental results of the surface-based image segmentation algorithm are displayed and critiqued. The algorithm is applied to several intensity images indicating that the digital surface approach is general enough to be used for other types of images. In Chapter 8, a summary is given, and future research directions are outlined. Several appendices are included to review technical points mentioned only briefly in the chapters.

1.6 Literature Review

How should high-dimensionality range images be processed to provide a complete low-dimensionality image description that preserves the visual information in the image and that is useful to high-level 3-D object recognition and image understanding algorithms? In answering this question, the two central topics of this text, surface characterization and image segmentation, are naturally encountered. This section briefly reviews other research in these areas prior to 1986. The 3-D object recognition literature is reviewed in [Besl and Jain 1985] [Chin and Dyer 1986] whereas computational approaches to image understanding are reviewed in [Brady 1982].

1.6.1 Surface Characterization Review

A *range image processing* algorithm is an algorithm for processing digital range images to obtain some type of useful information, such as edge maps or planar region descriptions. A *surface characterization* algorithm is an algorithm that is capable of describing many different types of digital surfaces based on shape. Hence, the class of range image processing algorithms contains the class of surface characterization algorithms. Range image processing and surface characterization algorithms are reviewed below along with several related papers.

Duda et al. [1979] discussed the use of registered range and reflectance images to find planar surfaces in 3-D scenes. A *sequential* planar region extraction procedure was used on range and reflectance images obtained from a amplitude-modulated imaging laser radar [Nitzan et al. 1977]. Reflectance images are different than intensity images in that shadows cannot occur because the source and detector are located very close to each other, but they have a very similar appearance. *A priori* scene assumptions concerning man-made horizontal and vertical surfaces motivated their procedure. First, horizontal surface regions of significant size were segmented and removed from an image using a filtered range histogram. Second, major vertical surfaces were extracted from the remaining scene data using a Hough transform method. Third, arbitrary planar surfaces are identified with the help of reflectance histogram data. All large planar surfaces are segmented and labeled in this manner. All unlabeled regions correspond to range discontinuities, non-planar regions, or small planar regions not found in the three main processing steps above. Their technique worked well on three test scenes, but many *a priori* assumptions have been used. This was one of the earliest papers to use registered range and intensity images for scene analysis.

Milgram and Bjorklund [1980] presented a different approach to planar surface extraction from range images created by an imaging laser radar. Their system was planned for vehicle navigation. A spherical coordinate transformation converts slant range, azimuth angle, and elevation angle sensor data into Cartesian x, y, z data before image processing (see Appendix D). For each Cartesian coordinate range pixel, a plane is fitted to the surrounding 5 x 5 window, and (1) the unit normal vector, (2) the plane position variable, and (3) the planar fit error are computed. *Connected components* of pixels that satisfy planarity constraints are formed into planes. After region growing, a complete list of planes is built. This plane list, a symbolic scene description, is compared with a reference plane list to determine the sensor position relative to a stored scene model. Experimental results are discussed for four real range images and two synthetic range images displaying different viewpoints of the same building site. Their method is a more straightforward approach to planar surface extraction than that of Duda et al. [1979] because *a priori* assumptions are avoided.

Henderson [1983] developed a method for finding planar faces in lists of xyz points, a range data format different from the range image format discussed above. First, a list of 3-D points are received from a range imaging sensor. To handle multiple range images, points are transformed into a single object-centered coordinate system using transformation data recorded during range data acquisition [Henderson and Bhanu 1982]. Such transformations can destroy the regular matrix grid structure of single view range images if surfaces from different views overlap, requiring an xyz list format for the data. These points are first stored randomly in a list with no topological connectivity information. The points are then organized into a 3-D tree structure requiring $O(N \log N)$ time where N is the number of points. Second, each point's neighbors are determined with the aid of the 3-D tree, and the results are stored in a 3-D spatial proximity (nearest neighbor) graph. Third, a spiraling sequential planar region growing algorithm, known as the three-point seed method [Henderson and Bhanu 1982], creates convex planar faces using the spatial proximity graph as input. The union of these planar faces form a polyhedral object representation extracted directly from the range data. Several processing steps mentioned above are required because of the xyz list format of the input data. If working with a single view, point neighbors are given explicitly in a digital range image format. This method can be used either for range data segmentation or object reconstruction, and it also works on dense range data or a sparse collection of points. Curved surfaces are approximated by many polygons.

Wong and Hayrapetian [1982] suggested using range image histograms to segment corresponding registered intensity images. All pixels in the intensity image that correspond to pixels in the range image with range

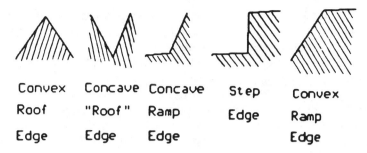

Convex	Concave	Concave	Step	Convex
Roof	"Roof"	Ramp	Edge	Ramp
Edge	Edge	Edge		Edge

Figure 1.4: Edge Types of Interest in Range Images

values not in a certain range are set to zero, segmenting all objects in that particular range for object points outside that range. Segmentation tricks like this can be useful in specific applications, but they do not work in general.

Reeves et al. [1985] extended their previous work in moment-based 3-D shape analysis to include range moments of range images. Single-object, pre-segmented, synthetic range images of aircraft were classified using silhouette moments, range moments, and a combination of both types of moments. It was shown that this set of images was best characterized by the combination of range and silhouette moments. Although good results were obtained, this method relies on global object characteristics and cannot be expected to provide reasonable results if objects are partially occluded.

Gil et al. [1983] demonstrated the usefulness of combining intensity and range edges from registered range and intensity images to obtain more reliable edge information.

Langridge [1984] reported on an investigation into the problem of detecting and locating discontinuities in the first derivatives of surfaces determined by arbitrarily spaced data. Neighborhood computations, smoothing, quadratic variation, and the biharmonic equation are discussed. The techniques are useful for detecting roof edges in range images.

Inokuchi et al. [1982] presented an edge/region segmentation ring operator for range images. The ring operator extracts a 1-D periodic function of range values that surround a given pixel. This function is transformed to the frequency domain using an FFT algorithm for either 8 or 16 values. Planar-region, step-edge, convex-roof edge, and concave-roof edge pixels (see Figure 1.4) are distinguished by examining the 0th, 1st, 2nd, and 3rd frequency components of the ring surrounding that pixel. These pixel types are grouped together, and the resulting regions and edges are labeled. Experimental results are shown for one synthetic block's world range image. The ring-operator method computes roof edges fairly well at planar surface boundaries on high quality data. Inokuchi and Nevatia [1980] discussed another roof edge detector that applied a radial line operator at step edge corners and followed roof edges inward.

Mitiche and Aggarwal [1983] developed a noise-insensitive edge detector based on a probabilistic model that accounts for range measurement errors. The computational procedure is as follows: (1) Step edges are extracted first from a range image using standard techniques. (2) For each discrete image direction (usually four) at each pixel, a roof edge is hypothesized. For each hypothetical roof edge, two planes are fitted to the immediate neighborhood of the pixel, and the dihedral angles between these planes are computed. (3) Pixels are not considered further if all dihedral angles are less than a threshold. A Bayesian likelihood ratio is then computed, and the most likely edge direction is chosen. If the dihedral angle for the chosen direction is not large enough, the pixel is also disregarded. (4) All remaining pixels are passed through a non-maxima suppression algorithm that theoretically leaves only the desired edge pixels. This method can handle large amounts of noise in the data because the system is biased by its internal model to look for horizontal and vertical edges.

Lynch [1981] presented a range image enhancement technique for range data acquired by a 94 GHz (3.2mm) radar. In the special case of such systems with a very shallow (nearly horizontal) line of sight, a very strong depth gradient always exists in a range image. This gradient makes it very difficult for people to interpret such range images using a typical 8-bit display device. Two types of *1-D high-pass* filters are derived, discussed, and applied to an example scene to create an intensity image that is easier to interpret on a video monitor than the original range image. Such approaches distort the shape information in range images making them undesirable in connection with geometric analysis.

Sugihara [1979] proposed a range image feature extraction technique for edge junctions similar to the junction features used by Waltz [1975] and others for intensity image understanding. A junction dictionary of possible 3-D edge junctions is implemented as a directed-graph data structure and is useful in aiding 3-D scene understanding. Unlike intensity image edges, range image edges are classified as *convex, concave, obscuring, or obscured* without additional higher level information from surrounding image regions. That is, junction knowledge is not necessary for line categorization. This categorization is used to predict missing edge segments. Since several junctions are only possible when two or more objects are in a scene, junction information can be used to segment the range image into different objects. A system is described that uses range discontinuities (step edges) and junctions for complete scene segmentation. It is limited by the constraint that every vertex is connected to at most three faces.

Several papers have discussed range image processing techniques for the detection of cylinders in range data [Agin and Binford 1973] [Nevatia and Binford 1973] [Popplestone et al. 1975] [Bolles and Fischler 1981]. The most relevant of these to the surface based segmentation algorithm is [Bolles and Fischler 1981]. They present the Random Sample Consensus (Ransac) technique for fitting models to noisy data containing a large percentage

(20% or more) of non-normally distributed errors. Such errors occur, for instance, when fitting a plane to a set of points where most points do belong to the plane, but some points are from other nearby surfaces and other points are just sporadic outliers. Linear least-squares techniques are effective for filtering normally distributed measurement errors, but do not handle non-normal outlier errors very well. They proposed a two-step process where (1) initial estimates of model parameters are computed to eliminate outlier errors, and (2) an improved fit is computed by applying standard smoothing techniques to the pre-filtered data. For example, the Ransac approach to circle-fitting is to select three points at random from the data, compute the circle passing through those points, and count the number of other compatible points in the data that are within the expected measurement error threshold. If there are enough compatible points, then least-squares smoothing is applied to the three initial points and all other compatible points. If not, another set of three points is selected and the process is repeated. If the number of trials exceeds a preset threshold, then the process is terminated for that data set. The Ransac technique was applied to finding ellipses, and then cylinders, in range images from an active triangulation light stripe range imaging sensor. Although this method is slower than normal regression methods, the model parameters are insensitive to outliers. The approach to surface fitting advocated in Chapter 4 is similar to the Ransac approach, but seed points for surface fitting are not selected at random and the surface model is allowed to change depending on the data.

Dreschler and Nagel [1981] proposed the use of Gaussian curvature to find corner points in intensity images, which is equally valid for finding range image corner points. They computed Gaussian curvature using the 5x5 window operators of Beaudet [1978] to estimate the necessary partial derivatives. Gaussian curvature for surface characterization is computed using a similar approach in Chapter 3.

Most of the research above in the range image processing category is limited to searching for particular structures in the data, such as planes, cylinders, edges, and vertices. More general surface characterization techniques that allow flexibility in the shapes of surfaces are now reviewed.

The Gauss map of differential geometry and Gaussian curvature (the derivative of the Gauss map) have been treated in a discrete form as surface normal orientation histograms, known as Extended Gaussian Images (EGI's) [Horn 1984]. The EGI of a surface in 3-D is a 2-D orientation histogram of the distribution of normal vectors on the surface. This orientation histogram approach provides unique rotationally-invariant shape description for convex objects [Little 1983] [Minkowski 1897], but does not maintain this property for non-convex objects as shown in Figure 1.5. The EGI concept was extended by Ikeuchi et al. [1983] so that each discrete view of a non-convex object has its own orientation histogram, but this produces a voluminous object description. Two EGI's from different sur-

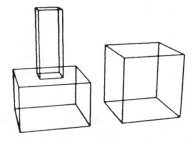

Figure 1.5: Two Objects with the Same Basic EGI Representation

faces are compared using a template matching approach. For example, with
240 triangular solid angle bins on the unit sphere, 720 hypotheses must be
tested. Since the EGI approach requires only surface orientation information, photometric stereo may be used to obtain sensor data for input to the
EGI algorithm. Object surface regions are assumed to be pre-segmented
by another process in most EGI approaches.

Liang [1987] recently proposed an extension of the EGI approach. Since
saddle-shaped negative Gaussian curvature surfaces are not uniquely characterized by Gaussian curvature alone, he proposed that a 4-vector orientation histogram be computed instead of the scalar EGI orientation histogram. He states a theorem that if a diffeomorphism from one umbilic-free
surface patch to another umbilic-free surface patch preserves the Weingarten mapping matrix (discussed in Chapter 3) at each point, then the
diffeomorphism is necessarily an isometry, and therefore the two surface
patches have the same shape. Hence, given a saddle-shaped surface patch,
which is necessarily free of umbilic points, (1) the maximum principal curvature, (2) the minimum principal curvature, and (3-4) two of the three
components of the maximum curvature principle-direction unit vector are
computed and recorded as a 4-vector in the appropriate surface-normal
orientation bin. Two components of the principle-direction unit-vector
determine the third component, and one principal direction vector and
the surface normal vector determine the other principal direction. Hence,
both principal curvatures, both principal directions, and the surface normal vector are represented in the 4-vector orientation histogram. Coarse-
to-fine EGI-type matching algorithms (Bhanu and Ho [1987]) can be used
to match the 4-vector histograms. In addition, he discusses the fact that
zero Gaussian curvature surface patches map to curve and point entities
on the Gaussian sphere. If digital surfaces can be adequately segmented
into positive, negative, and zero Gaussian curvature surface patches, then
standard EGI, 4-vector EGI, and Gaussian sphere curve and point matching algorithms can theoretically provide general purpose surface matching.
Only results for synthetic surface patches are presented so it is not clear
how well the proposed method works on real data.

Faugeras et al. [1985] at INRIA used an approach that is similar to the EGI approach in its dependence on surface normal information and its assumption that object surface regions have been pre-segmented by another process. Planar patches are isolated in xyz range data using a region growing approach described below. Rotational matching on planar surface normals of the object surface is performed using a *quaternion*-based algorithm that finds the best-fit rotation parameters to align a set of planar normal vectors. Quaternions provide a method for solving a three-variable non-linear least squares problem using a 4x4 matrix eigenvalue problem. A slightly faster singular value decomposition (SVD) method [Golub and VanLoan 1983] can be used to compute the best orthogonal matrix, which is usually the same as the rotation matrix generated by the quaternion method under typical conditions, but may be a reflection matrix under degenerate or very noisy data conditions. The mathematics for quadric surface set matching is also described. A working object recognition system has been developed based on this approach. It also allows one to automatically build object models of parts from range images. The EGI and INRIA approaches are both able to characterize any piecewise planar surface in a way that is amenable to matching algorithms. Curved surfaces are represented by many planar facets.

Faugeras et al. [1983] developed a region-growing algorithm for segmenting range data into planar or quadric patches. They state the segmentation problem as follows: Given a set of 3-D points, determine the minimum number of regions of the data points such that each region is approximated by an *algebraic* surface of degree 2 (a quadric) to within some fit error threshold. The region growing algorithm is the following: (1) Find the pair of adjacent regions with the smallest fit error less than a threshold for the merged pair. Merge the pair. (2) Repeat until no further merges are possible. Selecting breakpoints for curves and breakcurves for surface is a major problem in shape segmentation. Region merging is explicitly prevented across lines of high curvature that are computed first using a separate approach. Attention is also given to the problem that least-squares quadric surface fitting does not yield a fit error that corresponds to the RMS distance of the data points from the fitted surface. Their algorithm is similar to that presented by Dane [1982]. Results are shown for the Renault auto part, which is also shown in Chapter 7 as well as many other papers in the literature [Henderson 1983] [Bhanu 1984].

Early researchers [Shirai and Suwa 1971] [Popplestone et al. 1975] have processed range data by analyzing small surface regions and then linking regions with compatible characteristics into surfaces. This technique is discussed as it appears in Oshima and Shirai [1983]. They addressed object recognition and the processing of range images from a light-stripe range imaging sensor. Range images are processed as follows: (1) range pixels are grouped into small planar surface elements, (2) surface elements are merged into elementary regions that are classified as either planar or curved (spherical, cylindrical, conical), (3) curved elementary regions are merged into consistent global regions that are fitted with quadric surfaces, and (4) a complete scene description is generated from global region properties and relationships between these regions. Elementary region features are based on the best-fit *planar* region and its boundary and include the following quantities: perimeter; area; peround; minimum, maximum, and mean region radii around the region centroid; and the standard deviation of the radii of the boundary. Region relationships are characterized by the distance between region centroids, the dihedral angle between best-fit planes, and the type of intersection curve between the regions. This surface characterization was used as input to a higher-level view-dependent matching algorithm that recognizes objects.

Medioni and Nevatia [1984] employed a surface curvature-based description of range images. They proposed the following curves for surface shape description: (1) zero-crossings of the Gaussian curvature (2) zero-crossings of the maximum principal curvature, and (3) the maxima of the maximum principal curvature. This set of differential geometric shape descriptors is a subset of or can be derived from the descriptors that are computed in Chapter 3. These curves are computed by smoothing a range image with a large window and by using simple 1-D derivative windows to compute directional derivatives. This 1-D derivative approach can provide good localization, but is more sensitive to noise than the 2-D window derivative operators used in Chapter 3.

Snyder and Bilbro [1985] discussed difficulties in processing and segmenting range images. Their segmentation approach is as follows: (1) Determine points of high surface curvature first, e.g. the edges and vertices of polyhedra, (2) Perform connected-component analysis on the remaining points to determine regions where the surface curvature changes smoothly, and (3) Group high-curvature (boundary) points with associated regions. They made the following important points: (a) Local geometric features of range images are sensitive to quantization noise, (b) Surface normals and surface curvature (mean and Gaussian curvature) are useful for range image segmentation, and (c) The chain rule should be used to evaluate spatial derivatives whenever the range image projection is not orthographic.

Ittner and Jain [1985] took a different approach to surface curvature characterization based on clustering and local surface curvature measures computed from normal vector estimates. Range data points are assumed to be in the xyz form used by [Faugeras et al. 1985] [Henderson 1983] [Bhanu 1984] and are first clustered (segmented) into groups based on 3-D coordinates and surface normal vectors using a mean square error criterion. The groups of range data points are then characterized by six separate surface curvature estimates, including mean and Gaussian curvature, the principal curvatures, average normal curvature, and the principal curvature ratio. Their methods for estimating surface curvature are different than the 1-D and 2-D window methods encountered in other research. Although excellent results have been obtained with this method, the segmentation does not generate the same type of global surface descriptions described in Chapter 4 and shown in Chapter 7 because point coordinates and mean square error are used in the clustering algorithm. Hoffman and Jain [1987] extended this approach and used it for object recognition [Hoffman 1986].

Brady et al. [1985] used differential geometric features to describe surfaces, but they concentrated on lines of curvature, asymptotes, bounding contours, surface intersections, and planar and spherical umbilic surface patches. By relying on surface curves to describe surface shapes, the curvature primal sketch work of Asada and Brady [1986] could then be used for *planar* curve shape description of surface curves, like lines of curvature and asymptotes. One problem with this approach, as pointed out in [Ponce and Brady 1985], is that lines of curvature are generally not planar. Another problem is that, because every surface curve of each surface is processed individually by the Curvature Primal Sketch algorithm, the method is computationally intensive. One hour running times on a Lisp machine for 128x128 range images have been mentioned. They compute principal curvatures and principal directions and then link principal directions at each image pixel into lines of curvature. A Surface Primal Sketch is proposed that combines information on significant surface discontinuities. This description is very general and rich (information-preserving), but the final image description includes an excessive amount of information for simpler surfaces when it may not be necessary. Experimental results for a light bulb, a telephone receiver, a coffee mug, and an oil bottle are quite good. The 3-D axis of symmetry of cylindrical bodies can be recovered by fitting circles to the lines of curvature.

Vemuri et al. [1986] presented a technique that fits tension splines to x, y, z range data and then classifies surface points as parabolic, elliptic, hyperbolic, spherical umbilic, and planar umbilic based on the spline surfaces. They do not segment the data before they perform surface fitting except to test if a discontinuity runs through a fixed window. Experimental results are shown for a polyhedron, a cylinder, a balloon, and a light bulb.

Nackman [1984] described a method for view-dependent surface description using critical point configuration graphs (CPCG's). Critical points are isolated from each other except in degenerate circumstances. Nondegenerate critical points of surfaces are local maxima, local minima, or saddle points. If critical points of a surface are identified as the nodes of a graph, and the connecting ridge and valley lines (zero crossings of the first partial derivatives) are considered the arcs of a graph, a surface is characterized by its critical point configuration graph. Slope districts are the regions bounded by graph cycles. Two important theorems about these graphs are presented: (1) only eight types of critical points are possible: peaks (local maxima), pits (local minima), and six types of passes (saddle points); (2) only four non-equivalent types of slope districts are possible. All surfaces have a well-defined characterization as the union of slope dis-

trict regions where each region belongs to one of four basic slope district
types. This characterization approach is a generalization of techniques for
describing 1-D functions $f(x)$. In the 1-D case, only two types of non-
degenerate critical points exist: local maxima and local minima. Between
these critical points are intervals of constant sign of the first derivative.
Slope-districts are generalizations of these intervals. Nackman mentioned
curvature districts determined by the *sign* of the mean and Gaussian curvature of a surface, but did not explore them in the context of range image
analysis. This work is related to his research in generalizing the symmetric
axis transform for 3-D objects [Nackman 1982].

Haralick et al. [1983] discussed topographic classification of digital surfaces. They reviewed seven earlier papers on the subject by various authors,
and their ten topographic labels are a superset of all labels used previously:
peak, pit, ridge, valley (ravine), saddle, flat (constant), slope (planar), convex hill, concave hill, and saddle hill. At each pixel in an image, a *local
facet model* bicubic polynomial surface is fitted to estimate the first, second, and third partial derivatives of the surface at that pixel. Other types
of functions were tested by Watson et al. [1985]. Once the derivatives have
been estimated, the magnitude of the gradient vector, the eigenvalues of
the 2x2 Hessian matrix, and the directional derivatives in the directions of
the Hessian matrix eigenvectors are computed. These five scalar values are
the input to a function table that produces the pixel classification. Pixel
classification forms groups of pixels of a particular type. The topographic
primal sketch is proposed for use with intensity image digital surfaces because of the invariance of the pixel labels to monotonic transformations of
gray levels, such as changes in brightness and contrast. It is also useful for
range images, but more than half of the pixel labels are not invariant to
arbitrary changes in viewpoint, which is of course not really a concern in
intensity image analysis. This approach to surface characterization is similar to the approach discussed in Chapter 3, but differs significantly with
respect to viewpoint invariance properties. A more detailed comparison of
these two methods is found in [Besl and Jain 1986].

Lin and Perry [1982] investigated differential geometric surface shape
description using a piecewise-planar surface triangularization. When a surface is decomposed into a network of triangles, many features are can be
computed using their discrete coordinate-free formulas for surface area,
Gaussian curvature, aspect ratio, volume, and the Euler-Poincare characteristic. The formula for Gaussian curvature is interesting because explicit
estimates of first and second partial derivatives are not needed and the formula is coordinate-system independent, reflecting the isometric invariance
properties of the Gaussian curvature (see Appendix B). Integral Gaussian
curvature, integral mean curvature, surface area, volume, surface area to
volume ratio, integral curvature to the n-th power, and genus (or handle
number) are given as scalar values characterizing the shape of a surface.
No experimental results were given, but Besl et al. [1985] used several of

the described features, such integral mean and Gaussian curvature, to aid in classifying intensity images for inspection of solder joints.

Peet and Sahota [1985] used surface curvature measures of image texture for discriminating biological cell nuclei in gray-scale intensity images. Given an image or subimage, they computed 17 different surface curvature averages based on local quadratic surface fit using a 3x3 window: (1) principal curvature difference, (2) maximum absolute value principal curvature, (3) minimum absolute value principal curvature, (4) minimum principal curvature, (5) maximum principal curvature, (6) absolute value of the minimum principal curvature, (7) absolute value of the maximum principal curvature, (8) mean curvature, (9) Gaussian curvature, (10) sum of absolute value principal curvatures, (11) difference of absolute value principal curvatures, (12) the number of elliptic points, (13) parabolic points, and (14) saddle points, and (15) the number of peak points, (16) pit points, and (17) flat points. The results for discrimination tests were not impressive, but the first two surface curvature averages did appear to improve the performance of an existing system. Based on experience in using similar features to classify solder joint quality, 3x3 windows on 8-bit data generally produce extremely poor surface curvature results if any noise is present in the image, even just quantization noise, and if no smoothing is done. Thus, it is not surprising that only two such curvature measures proved to be worthwhile. Larger window sizes are needed.

Hebert and Ponce [1982] proposed a method of segmenting range images into plane, cylindrical, and conical primitives. Surface normals are computed at each range pixel using the best-fit plane in an NxN window. These normals are mapped to the *Gaussian sphere* where planar regions become very small clusters, cylinders become unit radius semicircles, and cones become smaller radius semicircles. This orientation histogram is known as the extended Gaussian image, or EGI, as discussed above. A Hough transform algorithm detects these circles and clusters. Regions are refined into labeled, connected components.

Sethi and Jayaramamurthy [1984] investigated surface classification using characteristic contours. The input is a needle map of surface normals. A characteristic contour is defined as the set of points in the needle map where surface normals are at a constant inclination to a reference vector. The following observations were made: (1) the characteristic contours of spherical/ellipsoidal surfaces are concentric circles/ellipses, (2) the characteristic contours of cylindrical surfaces are parallel lines, and (3) the characteristic contours of conical surfaces are intersecting lines. These contours are computed for all normals using 12x12 windows. The identity of the underlying surface for each window is computed using a Hough transform on the contours. A consistency criterion is used to handle noise effects and the effects of multiple surface types within a given window. This approach is similar to that of Hebert and Ponce [1982] above. Classification results are discussed for synthetic 40x40 needle maps of adjacent cones and cylinders.

Tomita and Kanade [1984] generated range image scene descriptions using an edge detection approach. Gap (step) edges and corner (roof) edges are detected and linked together. Surfaces are defined by the closed boundary of edges. All edges are assumed to be linear or circular, and all surfaces are assumed to be planar or cylindrical (conic). Smith and Kanade [1985] and Hebert and Kanade [1985] used similar approaches for describing range images.

Bolles et al. [1983] and Horaud and Bolles [1984] also relied completely on roof edges and step edges for characterizing the properties of range images with their 3DPO system. The system groups edges into coplanar clusters and searches for circular arcs in these clusters. The main emphasis of this work is on special feature detection, such as dihedral edges and corners. Excellent part position determination results have been achieved for range images of a parts bin containing one type of industrial part.

Herman [1985] extracted a detailed polyhedral object description of range images also using an edge detection approach. Edges, which may be occluding, convex, or concave, are computed to create a line drawing using a Hough transform. These line segments are refined to eliminate gaps so that 3-D planar faces may be formed.

Potmesil [1983] developed an algorithm for generating 3-D surface models of solid objects from multiple range image projections. Although this work emphasizes the integration of range information obtained from known multiple views for object reconstruction, it is of interest to range image understanding because it treats the basic problems of surface matching and surface representations for vision. He fitted a sheet of parametric bicubic patches to a range image to describe its shape. These rectangular surface patches are recursively merged into a hierarchical quadtree structure where a surface patch at each level approximates the shape of four finer resolution surface patches. Evaluation points at surface control points and points of maximum surface curvature are used to manipulate the surface patches for matching purposes, and therefore, constitute a surface description. Excellent experimental results for a turbine blade and a car model were obtained by the object reconstruction algorithm. Potmesil [1987] presents a similar algorithm based on octrees.

Marimont [1984] described a representation for image curves, which is a simplification of similar surface ideas in Chapter 3. The curve representation was "designed to facilitate the matching of planar image curves with planar model curves, and the estimation of their orientation in space despite the presence of noise, variable resolution, or partial occlusion" and is based on the curvature function computed at a predetermined list of scales, or smoothing filter window sizes. For each scale, the zeros and the extrema of curvature are isolated as knot points and stored in a knot list with a tangent direction and a curvature value for each knot. These knot points have the following properties:

1. The zeros of the curvature of a 3-D plane curve almost always project to the zeros of the curvature of the corresponding projected 2-D image curve.

2. The sign of the curvature value at each point does not change within an entire hemisphere of viewing solid angle. The pattern of curvature sign changes along a curve is invariant under projection up to a global sign change except in the degenerate case when the viewing point lies in the plane of the curve.

3. Points of maximum curvature of 3-D plane curves project to points that are very close to points of maximum curvature of the projected 2-D image curves. The relationship between these points is stable and predictable depending upon viewpoint. Moreover, the relative invariance of these points increases as the curvature increases. Ideal 3-D corners almost always project to ideal 2-D corners.

The algorithm is outlined as follows: (1) The image curve data is smoothed at multiple scales by Gaussian filters and fitted at each scale with a continuous curve parameterization in the form of composite monotone-curvature splines. (2) Curvature extrema (critical points) are extracted at each scale and stored in a list. (3) Dynamic programming procedures are used to construct a list of critical points that is consistent across the range of scales. (4) The integrated critical point information from the image curve is matched against the computed critical point information for the plane curve model. Related work on multiple scale curve matching has been done by Mokhtarian and Mackworth [1986].

1.6.2 Image Segmentation Review

Image segmentation is the partitioning of pixels in a 2-D image into connected regions that possess a meaningful correspondence to object surfaces in the 3-D scene represented by the image. This definition appears to say that an image cannot be segmented without specific knowledge of possible object surfaces and image formation. It is generally acknowledged that, in the absence of special purpose object features, it is difficult to recognize objects in an image unless the image is already segmented. Given the difficulty of the segmentation problem, many computer vision algorithms have been constrained to limited domains. As researchers have attacked the problem from many angles, the volume of literature on image segmentation has grown so large that is cannot be adequately reviewed here. Instead, a chronological review of image segmentation survey papers is presented that contains references to exemplary articles that represent the categorization of segmentation methods advocated in that survey.

After Zucker wrote the first segmentation survey paper in 1976, which concentrated on region growing techniques, the literature has seen about one new segmentation survey paper per year for the last ten years. Zucker [1976] is still an excellent reference on region growing perhaps indicating a lack of significant developments since then. The general mathematical definition of segmentation, given by Horowitz and Pavlidis [1974], was used in this survey paper and is given in Chapter 2. Zucker classifies region growing schemes into the following categories:

1. Regional Neighbor Search Schemes: Images are divided into small cells. Neighboring cells are joined if statistically compatible to form labeled image segments until no joinable neighbors are left [Muerle and Allen 1968].

2. Multiregional Heuristic Schemes: Connected-component regions of nearly constant intensity are formed. "Phagocyte" and "weakness" heuristics are applied sequentially to remove weak boundaries between adjacent regions [Brice and Fennema 1970].

3. Functional Approximation and Merging Schemes: Image strips are approximated by piecewise linear functions. Compatible pieces of image strips are merged to form image segments [Pavlidis 1972].

4. Split and Merge Schemes: A pyramid or quadtree data structure is used. Image quadrants are recursively divided into smaller quadrants until sufficiently well approximated constant valued quadrants are obtained. Compatible, adjacent smaller quadrants are merged. Similar squares are grouped to form irregularly shaped regions [Horowitz and Pavlidis 1974].

5. Semantic-based Schemes: Connected regions of nearly constant intensity are formed. *A priori* domain-dependent knowledge about an image is used to maximize the probability that the image is correctly segmented. The probability of all correct region interpretations and all correct region boundary interpretations is maximized [Feldman and Yakimovsky 1974].

Zucker also discusses the critical issues of threshold selection, order dependence, partitioning, and global initialization.

Riseman and Arbib [1977] view the main goal of the initial stages of processing in visual systems as segmentation, which is defined as "a transformation of the data into a partitioned image with the parts in a representation which is more amenable to *semantic* processing." They divide all segmentation approaches into two broad categories: (1) edge formation approaches, which focus on differences in image data, and (2) region formation approaches, which focus on similarities. They describe the edge formation tools of (a) spatial differentiation [Hueckel 1973] [Davis 1975], (b) nonmaxima suppression [Rosenfeld and Thurston 1971], (c) relaxation [Rosenfeld et al. 1976], and (d) edge linking. Region formation approaches are divided into (a) region growing under local spatial guidance [Brice and Fennema 1970], (b) semantic-guided region merging [Feldman and Yakimovsky 1974], (b) histograms for global feature analysis [Ohlander 1975], and (c) spatial analysis of feature activity [Hanson et al. 1975]. This lengthy survey includes detailed accounts of many approaches.

Rosenfeld and Davis [1979] pointed out the critical importance of the underlying image model assumptions to the performance and the limitations of image segmentation techniques. Statistical image models, such as first-order gray level probability density models, random field models, and time series models, are reviewed in addition to several spatial structure image models. They informally examine the use of image models to predict performance of given segmentation methods and to help design new segmentation methods. The discussion was limited to 2-D scenes to avoid three-dimensional issues. Segmentation techniques were not categorized in this survey since Rosenfeld and Kak [1976] had already presented discussions of (a) thresholding, (b) edge detection, (c) region growing, (d) border following, (e) spectral signature classification, and (f) template matching techniques for segmentation in the first edition of their textbook.

Kanade [1980] presented a model of image understanding that is jointly model-driven and data-driven, and points out that region segmentation methods may have three different goals depending on the levels of knowledge used by the method:

1. **Signal**-level segmentation methods use cues from the image domain only, and are therefore limited in what they can achieve by the properties of the image domain.

2. **Physical**-level segmentation methods use cues from the scene domain by using physical image-formation knowledge about how scene domain cues transform into image domain cues.

3. **Semantic**-level segmentation methods use semantic, physical, and signal level knowledge to compute an entire image interpretation in terms of an instantiated model.

Kanade categorized existing signal-level schemes as (a) region growing by spatial criteria [Muerle and Allen 1968] [Brice and Fennema 1970] [Pavlidis 1972], (b) region segmentation by global spectral distribution [Prewitt and Mendelsohn 1966] [Tsuji and Tomita 1973] [Ohlander 1975], and (c) combined usage of spatial and spectral information [Milgram 1977] [Rosenfeld 1978]. Semantic region segmentation schemes are discussed but not categorized [Barrow and Popplestone 1971] [Feldman and Yakimovsky 1974] [Tenenbaum and Barrow 1976]. Physical knowledge processing schemes are also reviewed [Horn 1977] [Woodham 1977] [Barrow and Tenenbaum 1978] [Kanade 1981]. Note that *image domain cues are scene domain cues* in the range image segmentation problem because scene geometry is captured in image geometry.

Fu and Mui [1981] categorize signal level image segmentation techniques into (1) characteristic feature thresholding or clustering, (2) edge detection, and (3) region extraction. The emphasis of the survey is on techniques in categories (1) and (2). Zucker [1976] is referenced followed by a brief survey of region techniques, which are divided into merging, splitting, and split and merge approaches. The Horowitz and Pavlidis [1974] definition of segmentation as given in Chapter 2 is again used as in Zucker [1976]. It is mentioned that despite the extensive research into segmentation, very little is known about how to compare algorithms and how to measure segmentation error besides the percentage of misclassified pixels criterion [Yasnoff et al. 1977]. Thresholding algorithms are divided into statistical and structural methods. The statistical thresholding methods [Weszka 1978] are divided into global ([Prewitt and Mendelsohn 1966]), local ([Ohlander 1975]), and dynamic algorithms. Structural thresholding techniques, such as [Tsuji and Tomita 1973], are not categorized further. Numerous clustering algorithms from the pattern recognition literature are reviewed for image segmentation. Edge detection techniques are categorized as parallel or sequential [Davis 1975]. Parallel edge element extraction techniques are subdivided into spatial frequency filters, gradient operators, and function approximation techniques. Edge element combination techniques (edge linking) are subdivided into heuristic search, dynamic programming, relaxation, and line and curve fitting.

DiZenzo [1983] has written a comprehensive review of image segmentation at the signal level. The main contribution of this survey is that it is more up-to-date than previous surveys and it is written in an introductory style. Many current topics are discussed, such as random-field image models, the sloped facet model, surface fitting, quadtrees, and relaxation methods. The main subject divisions in this survey article are (1) image models, (2) labeling of pixel collections, (3) pixel labeling, (4) edge detection, and (5) region-based split-and-merge methods using quadtrees.

Mitiche and Aggarwal [1985] presented a review of conventional image segmentation techniques, which stress region extraction and edge extraction approaches, to provide a basis for discussion of novel information-integrating segmentation techniques. They stress the importance of *integrating sensor data over time from many different sensors*, such as intensity, thermal, and range imaging sensors. Motion cues in each sensing modality can contribute to segmentation along with static cues from each sensor. By combining several sources of information, better segmentation results can be achieved than those possible from any single source.

Haralick and Shapiro [1985] divided signal-level image segmentation techniques, viewed as clustering processes, into the following categories:

1. Single-linkage region growing schemes: Individual pixel values used for similarity measurement.

2. Hybrid-linkage region growing schemes: Neighborhood pixel values used for similarity measurement.

3. Centroid-linkage region growing schemes: Individual pixel values are compared to mean of growing region to determine similarity measure.

4. Measurement space clustering schemes: Histogram analysis guides spatial clustering via image thresholding.

5. Spatial clustering schemes: Histograms guide region growing techniques.

6. Split and merge schemes: Pyramid data structures and homogeneity measures are used to split inhomogeneous image quadrants into four smaller quadrants. Small regions are merged based on similarities.

This survey is unique in that it applies several different segmentation techniques from the literature to the same image, an F-15 bulkhead image, to compare the performance of different algorithms. They note how similarity tests in the various algorithms can be made more rigorous by using statistical tests, such as the F-test, at given levels of significance.

The two past approaches to intensity image segmentation that are most similar to the approach described in Chapter 4 are now reviewed. Pavlidis [1972] posed the image segmentation problem as an optimization problem in functional analysis. He sought a set of approximating functions defined over regions that partition the image. He chose to divide the image into N thin strips. Each image strip is then approximated by one-dimensional piecewise-linear functions over the J segments of each strip. Adjacent segments in different strips are merged if the slopes of the segments are sufficiently close to one another. The merging continues until no further merges are possible. This work evolved from previous work in waveform segmentation using piecewise linear functions. It is possible to reconstruct a representation of the original image from the piecewise-linear approximations used to segment the image. This approach attempts to solve an inherently 2-D problem by decomposing it into two 1-D problems that can be solved separately, one after the other. Although an excellent idea for the computer hardware at that point in time, the approach is limited by its 1-D framework and its use of piecewise-linear functions.

Haralick and Watson [1981] developed a global facet model for intensity image processing that provides a unified framework for addressing edge detection and region growing. A *facet* is a connected region of pixels with a local surface fitted to the pixel values in that region. A flat-facet model is a piecewise constant representation of an image, and a sloped-facet model is a piecewise planar representation. The facet iteration algorithm is a provably

convergent relaxation algorithm that partitions any arbitrary image into
facet regions and creates a noise-cleaned version of the image. Although it
was not specifically designed as an image segmentation algorithm, it does
segment an image into homogeneous facet regions. The basic concepts of
the algorithm are summarized: Each pixel in an $N \times N$ image that is
more than $K/2$ pixels from the image boundary lies in K^2 different $K \times K$
windows. Each of these K^2 windows may be fitted with an approximating
polynomial surface of order M. One of these windows will have a minimum
surface fit error. New value of the pixel is set to the value of the minimum-
fit-error surface at that point. The iterative process converges in a few
iterations leaving a noise-cleaned image of facet regions. The borders of
the facet regions form a segmentation of the image.

Haralick and Watson [1981] showed results for 3x3 windows applied to
a house scene from the University of Massachusetts. It was concluded that
the sloped-facet model is a good model for the interior of regions, but is
not as good for edges. The strengths of this approach are its mathematical
properties: the algorithm is provably convergent, and since it is parallel,
it possesses no order dependence in the way the segmented regions are
derived. Several weaknesses are that (1) features smaller or thinner than
3x3 windows are significantly degraded, (2) slanted, high contrast edges
become blocky in the output image, (3) too many facet regions are formed,
and (4) one must select the window size K and the surface function order
M depending on how one wants the algorithm to perform. A later paper
by Pong et al. [1984] discusses segmentation results using a facet model
region grower based on property vectors. Good results were obtained on a
complex aerial scene. Many similar ideas are involved in this approach.

One major problem in computer vision that is not as prevalent in the
physical sciences is the difficulty in making objective comparisons between
new and old algorithms and their results. It has not been easy to share digital images, processed results, or computer vision software largely owing to
the variety of incompatible computer systems used by different researchers
and the inherent difficulties in transferring large sets of data between such
systems. There is a definite need for image processing and computer vision
standards in the areas of image formats, processed results formats, and
source code so that research can progress more smoothly by avoiding du-
plication of effort. For example, the Alvey computer vision consortium of
universities and industries in the United Kingdom adopted the convention
that all source code would be written in the C programming language and
designed to run on generic Unix workstations. Without at least sharing
images and processed results, each research group must reimplement algorithms based on sketchy information in the literature in order to evaluate
the performance of new algorithms relative to past results.

The fundamental issues in image segmentation have centered around
the regions vs. edges, uniformity vs. contrast, signal vs. semantics, and
statistical vs. structural controversies. In the terminology of these surveys,

the digital surface segmentation approach described in Chapter 4 is a *function approximation and merging* method although it is quite different than any existing approaches in that category. It might also be considered a *hybrid-linkage/centroid-linkage region growing* scheme, but again it is not similar to any existing techniques. It has little in common with segmentation techniques based on histograms, edge detection, or split-and-merge algorithms.

Although differential geometric approaches to range image analysis and function approximation methods for image segmentation are not new, the combination of surface characterization based on differential geometry and region growing based on variable-order surface fitting appears to be a novel technique for image segmentation that has proven to be robust in numerous experiments as documented in Chapter 7. Subsequent chapters provide a case study of the development of the digital surface segmentation algorithm.

Chapter 2

Object Recognition and Segmentation

Both the ability to organize signal samples into symbolic primitives and the ability to recognize groups of symbolic primitives are necessary for machine perception. Just as a person must identify phonemes to form words to understand a sentence, a computer vision system must identify 3-D surfaces belonging to 3-D objects to understand a 3-D scene. That is, surface segmentation and object recognition are fundamental tasks in image understanding. Although the goal is to devise a data-driven algorithm that extracts surface primitives from images without knowledge of higher level objects, a systems approach is taken and the entire problem is examined first before attempting to solve a part of it.

2.1 Three-Dimensional Object Recognition

Three-dimensional (3-D) object recognition is not a well-defined term as one might expect. A brief survey of the literature on this subject demonstrates this point [Roberts 1965] [Guzman 1968] [Shirai and Suwa 1971] [Sadjadi and Hall 1980] [Wallace and Wintz 1980] [Ikeuchi 1981] [Douglass 1981] [Brooks 1981,83] [Casasent et al. 1982] [Fang et al. 1982] [Oshima and Shirai 1983] [Sato and Honda 1983] (see surveys [Besl and Jain 1985] [Chin and Dyer 1986]). The research efforts represented by this list have relatively little in common. Several schemes handle only single, pre-segmented objects while others can interpret multiple object scenes. Some systems perform only 2-D processing using 3-D information. Other approaches require objects to be placed on a turntable during the recognition process. A few methods even require that intermediate data is provided by the person operating the system. Many techniques have assumed that idealized data will be available from sensors and intermediate processors. Others require high-contrast or backlit scenes. Most efforts have limited the class of recognizable objects to polyhedra, spheres, cylinders, cones, generalized cones, or a combination of these. Many papers fail to mention how well the proposed method can recognize objects from a large set of objects, e.g. at least fifty objects, that are not customized to individual algorithms. Therefore, a reasonably precise definition of the rigid object recognition problem is given. A brief outline of several human visual system capabilities is given to motivate the definition of a computer vision problem.

The real world that we see and touch is primarily composed of rigid solid *objects*. When people are given a new object they have never seen before, they are typically able to gather information about that object from many different viewpoints. The process of gathering detailed object information and storing that information is the *model formation* process. Once we are familiar with many objects, we can normally identify them from any *arbitrary viewpoint* without further investigation. People are also able to identify, locate, and qualitatively describe the orientation of objects in black-and-white photographs. This basic capability is significant to computer vision research because it involves the spatial variation of only a single intensity parameter within a rectangular region corresponding to a single static view of the world. Human color vision is more difficult to analyze and is typically treated as a *three*-parameter color variation within a large, almost hemispherical solid angle that corresponds to a continually changing viewpoint.

If it is assumed that automated visual processing is to be done on digital computer hardware, then the sensor data must be compatible with the hardware. The term *digitized sensor data* refers to a matrix of numerical values, which may represent intensity, range, or any other parameter, and associated auxiliary information concerning how that matrix of values was obtained.

This list of human capabilities and the constraint on the form of the input data motivates the following model-based definition of the autonomous single arbitrary view, rigid 3-D object recognition problem:

1. **Given** any collection of labeled solid rigid objects:

    (a) Each object may be examined as long as the object is not deformed.

    (b) Labeled models may be created using information from this examination.

2. **Given** digitized sensor data corresponding to one particular, but arbitrary, field-of-view of the real world as it existed during the time of data acquisition; **given** any data stored previously during the model formation process; and **given** the list of distinguishable objects; the following questions must be answered for each object using only the capabilities of an autonomous computing system:

    (a) Does the object appear in the digitized sensor data?

    (b) If so, how many times does it occur?

    (c) For each occurrence,

        i. Determine the location of the object in the sensor data,

       ii. Determine the 3-D location (translation parameters) of that object with respect to a known coordinate system, and

      iii. Determine the 3-D orientation (rotation parameters) with respect to known coordinate system.

3. (Optional) If there are regions in the sensor data that do not correspond to any objects in the list, model and store these regions in a way that they can be recognized if they occur in subsequently processed images. If an object is present that is not known to the system, the system should attempt to learn whatever it can about the unknown object from the given view.

The problem of successfully completing these tasks using real world sensor data while obeying the given constraints is the model-based rigid 3-D object recognition problem. This problem is not completely addressed in the object recognition systems discussed in the literature. More constrained problems that are limited to particular surface types or applications are normally addressed. If the stated rigid 3-D object recognition problem could be solved successfully by an automated system, that system would be quite useful in a wide variety of applications, ranging from automatic inspection and assembly to autonomous vehicle navigation. The problem is stated so that it may be feasible to use computers to solve the problem, and it is clearly solvable by people.

Item (3) above can be interpreted as a partial model-building task to be performed on data that cannot be explained in terms of known objects. It is not recognition because something is present in the data that the system "knows" nothing about. The vision system is being asked to learn from experience in a flexible manner.

How does one decide if a given algorithm solves the problem, and how can different algorithms be compared to see if one is better than another? The performance of object recognition systems could be measured using the number and type of errors made by a system in performing the assigned problem tasks on standardized sets of digitized sensor data that challenge the capabilities mentioned in the problem definition. The following list enumerates some possible types of errors that can be made by such systems:

1. Miss error: An object is clearly visible in the sensor data, but is not detected.

2. False alarm error: The presence of an object is indicated even though there is no evidence in the sensor data.

3. Location error: An object occurrence is correctly identified, but the location of the object is wrong. Location error is a vector quantity.

4. Orientation error: The object occurrence and position are determined correctly, but the orientation is wrong. Orientation error is also a vector quantity.

In the comparison of different object recognition systems, the term "successful" can be made quantitative by establishing a performance index that quantitatively combines the number, the type, and the magnitude of the various errors. If a system consists of many different components, its high-level performance depends upon the performance of each lower-level component. If each component of the system can achieve sufficiently low error rates in the tasks they perform, the entire system can achieve good performance. In particular, if low error image segmentations can be achieved using only general information about surfaces, then the high-level matching algorithms of object recognition systems would be much easier to analyze, develop, and test.

2.2 Mathematical Recognition Problem

It is often beneficial to define a problem in a stricter mathematical form to eliminate possible problem ambiguities. For example, how should a system respond if several distinct objects appear to be identical from a given viewpoint? Therefore, range image object recognition is now redefined in more precise mathematical terms as a *generalized inverse set mapping*. Intensity image object recognition is then briefly treated in the same formalism.

First, world modeling is addressed. The world is approximated as a set of N_{tot} rigid objects that can exist in different positions and orientations. The number of distinguishable objects is N_{obj}, and therefore, $N_{obj} \leq N_{tot}$. Two objects are not distinguishable if an average person cannot tell them apart using only shape cues. The i-th distinguishable object is denoted as A_i. The number of occurrences, or instances, of that object is denoted as N_i. This means that, in general, N_{tot} is the sum of the N_i's for all N_{obj} objects. People can recognize an enormous number of 3-D objects depending on personal experience ($N_{obj} > 50,000$ is probably a conservative estimate). The number of objects to be recognized by an object recognition system depends on the application and system training.

For small collections of objects, it is possible to explicitly represent each object as a separate geometric entity. But as the number of objects grows large, geometric features are likely to be repeated among the objects, and it becomes important to use these common features in an efficient way both for data storage during model formation and data retrieval during recognition. Also, it is sometimes difficult to decide what is an object and what is an assembly of objects. To resolve this difficulty, each object could possess its own coordinate system and a hierarchy of sub-objects located relative to that system. For the purposes of this simple discussion though, each object is considered as a separate geometric entity, and only sim-

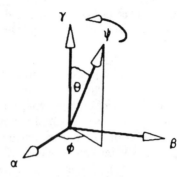

Figure 2.1: Rigid Objects in 3-D Space have 6 Degrees of Freedom

ple objects with no sub-parts and with only one instance are considered. Therefore, $N_{obj} = N_{tot}$ in this simplified situation. The general case of multiple instances of objects with sub-parts is not conceptually different than the simplified case, but it presents notation problems and important implementation difficulties for higher level recognition processing. The origin of each object coordinate system is defined at the center of mass of the object with three orthogonal axes aligned with the principal axes of the object. These parameters can be precisely determined for any given solid object or solid object model.

Each object occupies space, and at most one object can occupy any given point in space. Therefore, it is necessary to describe the spatial relationships between each object and the rest of the world. One way to describe spatial relationships is through the use of coordinate systems and transformations. For reference purposes, a world coordinate system is placed at some convenient location. Objects are positioned in space relative to this coordinate system using translation and rotation parameters. The translation parameters of an object are denoted as the vector $\vec{\alpha}$, and the independent rotation parameters are denoted as the vector $\vec{\theta}$ regardless of whether they represent Euler angles, roll/pitch/yaw angles, angle/axis coordinates, quaternions, or whatever format is preferred. The number of parameters for each vector depends on the dimension of the range image recognition problem. For example, a 2-D problem can be defined that requires only three parameters. For the 3-D case, the six parameters (or degrees of freedom) are written as follows:

$$\vec{\alpha} = (\alpha, \beta, \gamma) \quad \text{and} \quad \vec{\theta} = (\theta, \phi, \psi). \tag{2.1}$$

where $\vec{\alpha}$ is the translation vector and $\vec{\theta}$ is the rotation vector. See Figure 2.1 for the graphical meaning of these parameters. The *world model* W is defined as a set of ordered triples (object, translation, rotation):

$$W = \left\{ (A_i, \vec{\alpha}_i, \vec{\theta}_i) \right\}_{i=0}^{N_{obj}}. \tag{2.2}$$

The object A_0 is considered to be the sensor object with position $\vec{\alpha}_0$ and orientation $\vec{\theta}_0$. If a time-varying world model with deformable objects is required, all objects and their parameters can be functions of time. For the current purposes of single-view rigid object recognition, only static parameter values are of interest. The set of all objects, the *object list*, is denoted as $O = \{A_i\}$. The set of translations is denoted $\Re^t$, and the set of rotations is denoted $\Re^r$. In the 3-D object recognition problem, $t = 3$ and $r = 3$. In the much simpler 2-D case, $t = 2$ and $r = 1$. $\Re$ is the set of real numbers.

A range imaging sensor creates a range image projection of a scene. This projection is modeled as a mathematical operator P that maps elements in the set $\Omega_{t,r} = O \times \Re^t \times \Re^r$ into elements in the set of all scalar functions of $t - 1$ variables, denoted Ψ_{t-1}:

$$P : \Omega_{t,r} \rightarrow \Psi_{t-1}. \tag{2.3}$$

These real-valued functions are called *range image functions*. This projection operator might be *orthographic* or *perspective* [Newmann and Sproull 1979] [Foley and van Dam 1982]. For range image projections, different types of perspective transformations are possible as discussed in Appendix D. Any given projection operator may be written as

$$f(\vec{x}) = h_{A,\vec{\alpha},\vec{\theta}}(\vec{x}) = P(A, \vec{\alpha}, \vec{\theta}) \tag{2.4}$$

where $\vec{x}$ is the vector of $t - 1$ spatial variables in the focal plane of the sensor. The location $\vec{\alpha}_0$ and the orientation $\vec{\theta}_0$ of the sensor object are implicitly assumed arguments of the projection operator P because only one sensor is needed in this formalism. The range image function is denoted $f(\cdot)$ when the identity of the object and its parameters are unknown. The symbol $h(\cdot)$ with subscripts refers to the range image function of a known object at a known location and orientation. This notation indicates that the set of range image functions associated with a single object is an *infinite family of functions*. Two of the rotation parameters in the $\vec{\theta}$ vector have a particularly profound effect on this family of functions: the 3-D shape of the range image function changes as the object rotates. Translation parameters have no effect on shape whatsoever under orthographic projection, and they have a small effect under the perspective projections unless the sensor is close to the object of interest, e.g., closer than 10 times the maximum object dimension.

Since objects do not occupy all space, a convention is needed for the value of the range image function for values of the spatial vector $\vec{x}$ that do not correspond to object surface points. If the point $(\vec{x}, f(\vec{x}))$ cannot lie on an object surface, the value of $-\infty$ is assigned to $f(\vec{x})$. It is assumed that the value of the range image function increases as objects move toward the sensor. Hence, the projection of a set of M objects is written as

$$f(\vec{x}) = \max_{1 \leq i \leq M} h_{A_i, \vec{\alpha}_i, \vec{\theta}_i}(\vec{x}) \tag{2.5}$$

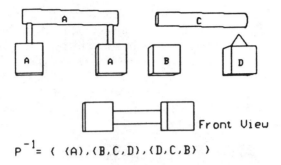

$$P^{-1} = (\ (A), (B, C, D), (D, C, B)\ )$$

Figure 2.2: Several Valid Interpretations of a Simple Scene

where the maximum operator provides for multiple object occlusion. The range image object recognition problem is now rephrased as follows: Given a range image function $f(\vec{x})$, which results from the range image projection of a 3-D world scene, determine the sets of possible objects with the corresponding sets of translation and rotation parameters that could be projected to obtain the given range image function. That is, determine the set of all interpretations

$$\omega_J = \left\{ (A_j, \vec{\alpha}_j, \vec{\theta}_j) \right\}_{j \in J} \tag{2.6}$$

such that each interpretation ω_J projects to the range image function $f(\vec{x}) = P(\omega_J)$ where J is an index set that depends on the possible valid interpretations of the range image.

These ideas are written more precisely using inverse set mappings. For each *single object* range image function, there is a corresponding inverse set mapping to yield all single objects that could have created the given object range image function. The inverse set mapping of P is denoted as the set P^{-1} where

$$P^{-1}(f(\vec{x})) = \left\{ (A, \vec{\alpha}, \vec{\theta}) \in \Omega_{t,r} : P(A, \vec{\alpha}, \vec{\theta}) = f(\vec{x}) \right\}. \tag{2.7}$$

An inverse set mapping takes sets from the power set of the range of the original mapping into sets in the power set of the domain:

$$P^{-1} : 2^{\Psi_{t-1}} \rightarrow 2^{\Omega_{t,r}}. \tag{2.8}$$

For static single image recognition purposes, the input sets in the power set $2^{\Psi_{t-1}}$ may be restricted to be singletons (single range images) without loss of generality. Therefore, $2^{\Psi_{t-1}}$ is replaced with Ψ_{t-1}. For multiple object range image functions, P^{-1} must be generalized due to possible combinations of objects as shown in Figure 2.2. Hence, given $f(\vec{x}) \in \Psi_{t-1}$, a generalized inverse set mapping $\mathbf{P}^{-1}$ is sought such that

$$\mathbf{P}^{-1}(f(\vec{x})) = \left\{ \omega_J \in 2^{\Omega_{t,r}} : \max_{j \in J} P(A_j, \vec{\alpha}_j, \vec{\theta}_j) = f(\vec{x}) \right\}. \tag{2.9}$$

Thus, the desired recognition mapping takes elements of the range image function space into the power set of the power set of $\Omega_{t,r}$:

$$\mathbf{P}^{-1} : \Psi_{t-1} \to 2^{2^{\Omega_{t,r}}}. \tag{2.10}$$

The range image object recognition problem can now be stated precisely and simply in terms of the generalized inverse set mapping: given the world model W with N_{obj} simple objects and given any realizable range image function $f(\vec{x})$, compute the generalized inverse projection set mapping $\mathbf{P}^{-1}(f(\vec{x}))$ to obtain all possible valid explanations ω_J (subsets of $\Omega_{t,r}$) of the function $f(\vec{x})$ in terms of the world model. There is only one valid scene interpretation in many cases, but a general-purpose vision system should be capable of generating the list of all valid scene interpretations if ambiguous single-view situations are encountered. The problem of determining the next best view from which sensor data should be acquired to eliminate ambiguity is a separate issue which must also be addressed for practical robotic vision systems [Kim et al. 1985] [Connolly 1985].

When is a scene interpretation valid? If an interpretation agrees perfectly with a human interpretation, then it is valid. If only small insignificant errors are made, an interpretation can be mostly valid without being perfectly valid. Therefore, the notion of validity should correspond to a measure of interpretation error. Given the above formalism, the interpretation error for a given implementation of the recognition mapping, a given image, and a given interpretation of that image could be expressed as follows. Let $e(\omega_J)$ denote the interpretation error for the interpretation ω_J where J is the interpretation index set that indexes objects in the world model. Let $\vec{\alpha}_j^a$ be the actual position of the j-th object in a scene, and let $\vec{\alpha}_j^e$ be the estimated position. Similarly, let $\vec{\theta}_j^a$ be the actual orientation of the object in a scene, and let $\vec{\theta}_j^e$ be the estimated orientation. Let $|A_j|$ be the number of pixels or the area occupied by the object A_j in the image. The following is an *example* of a possible recognition error function:

$$e(\omega_J) \quad = \sum_{\substack{j \in J \\ A_j \text{ in} \\ \text{image}}} |A_j| \left(w_t \|\vec{\alpha}_j^a - \vec{\alpha}_j^e\|_{\Re^t} + w_r \|\vec{\theta}_j^a - \vec{\theta}_j^e\|_{\Re^r} \right) \tag{2.11}$$

$$+ \sum_{\substack{j \in J \\ A_j \text{ not} \\ \text{in image}}} w_f |A_j| \quad + \sum_{\substack{j \notin J \\ A_j \text{ in} \\ \text{image}}} w_m |A_j|$$

where w_t, w_r, w_f, w_m are the weighting factors for translation errors, rotation errors, false alarm errors, and miss errors respectively. The rotation and translation norms in the expression are not intended to be the same.

There is no general theory regarding the computation of the recognition mapping. As a result, a wide variety of methods have appeared in the literature. It is proposed here that the generalized inverse set mapping can be computed most generally by recognizing the *individual surface regions* associated with the $h_{A,\vec{\alpha},\vec{\theta}}(\vec{x})$ *range image surface function families* of the individual objects. That is, it is proposed that the *object recognition* problem be solved by decomposing it into a *surface characterization* and *surface segmentation* problem combined with a *surface matching* algorithm constrained by possible object and surface structures. The pixel data in a range image is first characterized in terms of properties that are useful for grouping or segmentation. Once the image data has been segmented into individual surface regions, these surface descriptions can be matched against surface-based object model descriptions. Despite previous work done in surface characterization, surface segmentation, and computer vision systems research, more research and development is required to combine these concepts into a general purpose working solution. Little research has been done in 6 degree of freedom arbitrary smooth surface matching. A general surface matching metric is proposed later in Section 2.7.

The above formalism is easily augmented to state the object recognition problem for intensity images and other types of images. By applying an illumination-reflectance operator λ to the range image function f, an intensity image $I(\vec{x})$ is obtained that may be written as

$$I(\vec{x}) = \lambda(\vec{x}, \max_i\ P(A_i, \vec{\alpha}_i, \vec{\theta}_i)). \tag{2.12}$$

The function $\lambda(\cdot)$ requires the vector $\vec{x}$ and the range at that point $f(\vec{x})$ to determine the surface, the object, and the light source objects that are involved in reflecting light back toward the image sensor. The intensity image 3-D object recognition problem is much more difficult owing to the additional required inversion of the λ operator. Even if all possible object shapes are known and *a priori* knowledge of all possible surface reflectances and all possible illumination sources and their locations is given, the computational effort required to invert this $\lambda(\cdot)$ operator is prohibitive. Shape from shading [Ikeuchi and Horn 1981], shape from photometric stereo [Woodham 1981] [Coleman and Jain 1982], and shape from texture [Witkin 1981] techniques, for example, attempt to uniquely invert the λ operator to produce a range image function f.

Any type of image that is formed on a point-by-point basis and is dependent on the geometry of the scene can be considered in this formalism. People are able to understand images even when shading operators other than the natural illumination-reflectance operator are used to shade visible surfaces. For example, people can correctly interpret photographic negatives, radar images, scanning electron microscope images, or pseudo-colored images where the usual color and/or light-dark relationships are completely distorted. Other examples include range images where range is encoded as brightness. This suggests an insensitivity to the detailed nature of the λ operator and a dominance of surface geometry in visual perception.

This formalism provides a relatively unified framework in which range images, intensity images, and other images can be analyzed. When $\lambda(\cdot)$ is the simplest non-null operator, the *identity operator* $(f(\vec{x}) = \lambda(\vec{x}, f(\vec{x}))$, the model describes the range image understanding problem. When $\lambda(\cdot)$ is not the identity operator, another distinct image understanding problem is described. When $\lambda(\cdot)$ is the illumination-reflectance operator, the model yields a formulation for the intensity image understanding problem in terms of scene surfaces. From this point of view, the range image understanding problem is the unique, simplest problem in the set of digital surface interpretation problems for physical scenes. In addition, range image understanding appears to be a well-posed mathematics problem compared to the "ill-posed" intensity image understanding problem. Therefore, it may be argued that an analysis of range image understanding is a natural starting point for any type of two-dimensional image understanding research.

2.3 Recognition System Components

The specific tasks to be performed by an object recognition system are given above. It has also been suggested that one can measure how well these tasks are performed. But how are these tasks accomplished?

Recognition implies awareness of something already known. Thus, objects cannot be recognized unless they are already known to an object recognition system. Object knowledge can only be acquired during some type of model formation process. Although many different kinds of qualitative and quantitative object models, both view-independent and view-dependent, have been used for modeling real world objects for recognition purposes, at least some type of computer accessible representation is needed for storing and retrieving model information. It is concluded from these statements that an object recognition system requires (1) a model formation process, (2) a world model representation, and (3) methods for storing models into and retrieving information from the world model.

Once a library of objects is known to a system, how are objects detected in the digitized sensor data? To determine how recognition will take place, a method for matching the model data to the sensor data must be considered. A straightforward model-driven blind-search approach would entail transforming all possible combinations of all possible known object models in all possible distinguishable orientations and all possible distinguishable locations into a digital image format and then computing the minimum matching error metric between the sensed digital image and all images generated from model hypotheses. If intensity images were being used and light sources and surface reflectances were not pre-specified, then hypotheses about all possible light source locations and all possible surface

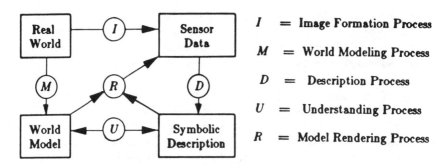

Figure 2.3: General Object Recognition System Structure

reflectance properties would have to be checked for each of the possible combinations above. In either case, the minimum matching error configuration of object models would correspond to the recognized scene. All tasks mentioned in the object recognition problem statement would be accomplished except for the characterization of unknown regions not corresponding to known objects. Of course, this type of approach would take an enormous amount of processing time even for the simplest scenes. A better algorithm is needed. In particular, if all pixels in an image can be effectively organized into a small number of pixel groups that will be meaningful to higher-level algorithms where each group of pixels is represented by a few parameters, it would be much easier to hypothesize matches with this set of pixel groups rather than doing pixel-by-pixel comparisons for every hypothesis in a high-level object or surface matching algorithm.

Since 3-D object models contain more 3-D object information than sensor data from a single view, one cannot transform sensor data into complete model data and perform global model matching in the model data format. However, matching with *partial* model data is possible. Given the incompleteness of single-viewpoint sensor derived models and the natural desire to reduce the large dimensionality of the input sensor data, it is usually advantageous to work in an intermediate domain that is computable from both the sensor data and the model data. This domain is called the *symbolic scene description domain*. A matching procedure can then be carried out on the entities in this intermediate domain, which are often called *features*. The best matching results should occur when a hypothetical object model configuration accurately represents the real world scene represented in the sensor data. A matching procedure and intermediate symbolic scene description mechanisms are necessary object recognition components for systems based on digital computers.

The interactions between the main components of a recognition system are diagrammed in Figure 2.3. The real world, the digitized sensor data domain, the world modeling domain, and the intermediate symbolic scene description are fundamental domains in any system. The mappings between these domains are listed. The image formation process (I) uses an imaging sensor to create intensity, range, or other types of images based purely on physical sensing principles. The description process (D) acts on the sensor data and extracts relevant, application-independent features. If this process only incorporates knowledge about (1) the image formation process and (2) rudimentary facts about the real world, such as the mathematical properties of surfaces, then there is hope that a system based on such a description process can be applied to new tasks by only changing the world model information. No *a priori* assumptions about objects should be incorporated in the description process for maximum flexibility. The description process (D) and the symbolic scene description domain are the central topics of subsequent chapters. Surface characterization and surface segmentation are examples of possible sub-processes of the data description process.

The modeling process (M) provides object models for real world objects. Object reconstruction from sensor data is one method for building models automatically. If an automated modeling system were used, the model formation process would include its own image formation and data description sub-processes that could possibly be shared with the recognition system. A fully automated model formation process is preferable, but is not required by the problem definition above, which addresses visual recognition, not world modeling. Hence, object models could also be constructed manually using computer-aided geometric design (CAGD) modeling programs. The understanding, or recognition, process (U) involves algorithms for matching between models and data descriptions. This process might include interacting data-driven and model-driven sub-processes where segmented sensor-data regions seek explanations in terms of models and hypothesized models seek verification from the data description. The rendering process (R) produces synthetic sensor data from either the object models or the symbolic scene description. A vision system must be able to communicate its understanding of a scene verbally *and visually* to any person operating the system. Rendering also can also provide an important feedback link because it allows an autonomous system to check on its own understanding of the sensor data by comparing synthetic images to the sensed images. Synthetically generated (rendered) range images are so similar to real range images that simple image differencing operations suffice for feedback computations to check hypothesized geometry against image geometry. Synthetically generated intensity images become more similar to real world images with each passing year. The concepts of rendering data descriptions and using feedback from the original data play important roles in Chapter 4. It is proposed that any object recognition system can be discussed within the general framework of this system model. Except for the addition of the rendering process, this description agrees with many of the ideas in Brooks [1982].

2.4   Capabilities of an Ideal System

What are the capabilities of an ideal system that handles the object recognition problem as defined? Some that might be realized by object recognition systems in the near future are summarized below:

1. It must be able to handle sensor data from arbitrary viewing directions without preference to horizontal, vertical, or other directions. This requires a view-independent modeling scheme that is compatible with recognition processing requirements.

2. It must handle arbitrarily complicated real world objects without preference to curved or planar surfaces or to convex or non-convex objects.

3. It must handle arbitrary combinations of a large number of objects in arbitrary orientations and locations without being sensitive to superfluous occlusions, i.e., if occlusion does not affect human understanding of a scene, then it should not affect an automated object recognition system either.

4. It must be able to handle a reasonable amount of random measurement noise and quantization noise in the sensor data without a significant degradation in system performance.

5. It should be able to analyze arbitrary scenes quickly and correctly.

6. It should not be difficult to modify the world model data to handle new objects and new situations.

7. It is desirable for the system to be able to express its confidence in its own understanding of the sensor data.

Although several range image object recognition systems in the literature have demonstrated impressive capabilities (the best known of these are perhaps the 3DPO system of Bolles and Horaud [1986] and the INRIA system of Faugeras and Hebert [1986]), no known existing computer vision systems have demonstrated all of these general purpose capabilities, and a substantial amount of research and development is still required to build such a system.

A general-purpose object recognition system has been described in detail to provide direction for the design of the various components of the system, specifically the data-driven description process. One major missing link in computer vision today is a general-purpose efficient, mathematically sound theory for recognizing non-convex objects with smooth curved surfaces. The best that can be done reliably today is to recognize primarily polyhedral or cylindrical objects and convex smooth surfaced objects. A specific goal that has not been achieved is a single system that can recognize polyhedra and quadrics as well as human faces, cars in a parking lot, and different types of trees.

2.5 Segmentation into Surface Primitives

The focus now shifts from general system-level concerns to the details of the data-driven description process. The input to a data-driven description process is a high-dimensionality image or digital surface: a large matrix of pixels where each pixel has an assigned value. The physical meaning of those values depends on the type of input image, whether it be range, intensity, or something else. It is assumed that the data satisfies the surface coherence property. The output description should satisfy several requirements:

1. Pixels should be grouped together into a relatively small set of symbolic primitives. The number of symbolic primitives should be much smaller than the number of pixels, but in general it will depend on the visual complexity of the input image.

2. The set of symbolic primitives should represent all pixels in the image, and all pixels should belong to one and only one symbolic primitive. Subpixel precision methods are not treated here because the discussions in this chapter and the rest of the text are equally valid for images that have been expanded and interpolated to whatever subpixel precision is desired.

3. All pixels within a group of pixels defined by a symbolic primitive should be consistent with each other with respect to a defining statement about that symbolic primitive.

The digital surface segmentation approach to data-description requires several internal, intermediate levels, where each level uses basic knowledge about surfaces since input images are digital surfaces. The first step is to characterize the input digital image or digital surface at every pixel using a small set of surface types. In order to do this, the local neighborhood of every pixel is examined and characterized by *local differences* in the form of partial derivative estimates and curvature functions. This first step reduces the dimensionality in the value assigned at each pixel: N-bit pixel values are transformed into 3-bit local surface type values. Chapter 3 goes into detail about the relationship between the fundamental shape descriptors of differential geometry and the surface curvature signs used to define surface type. Connected regions of identical surface type pixels provide the first level of grouping, a rough initial segmentation. Better initial segmentations are obtained as the resolution, or number of accurate bits in the pixel values, increases.

The second step takes the original image and the initial surface type segmentation and creates a refined segmentation based on *global similarities* in the pixel values. The shapes present in the digital surface data drive this second stage by selecting surface type shapes from a small but flexible set of approximating surface functions. Chapter 4 describes this process in detail. The refined surface primitives created by this second step generally group the pixels very effectively, but are constrained by the nature of the basic surface types isolated by the first step process and by the limitations of the small set of approximating surface functions.

To group pixels together from arbitrary smooth surface primitives, a third step is required to merge adjacent surfaces that belong to the same smooth surface. Chapter 5 describes one simple algorithm to achieve the required merging. The final output is a segmentation in terms of smooth surfaces, in which complicated smooth surfaces are described as composite patches of simpler smooth surfaces.

The implicit assumption is that most rigid object volumes of interest are bounded by relatively smooth surfaces. Although many object surfaces are physically textured, which may cause large variations in intensity, the actual variations in the range of textured surface points is quite small. By isolating the smooth surfaces in a range image of a scene, the scene surfaces are in a symbolic form that is suitable for matching to the object surface data available from the world model. The texture of the real surface is essentially treated as an additional random noise process superimposed on an underlying smooth surface with the presumed measurement and quantization errors. The understanding process (U) should use any texture statistics that are separate from measurement and quantization statistics as additional identifying features of the surface for recognition purposes. The list of interpretations corresponding to the generalized inverse set mapping could be trimmed based on the compatibility of model and data texture statistics. Texture is not pursued further except to note in Chapter 7 that textured and smooth surfaces have been segmented using smooth surface approximations.

2.6   Mathematical Segmentation Problem

The image segmentation problem has received a great deal of attention in the literature as discussed in Chapter 1. This problem admits a general analytical formulation in which a logical uniformity predicate is left unspecified. The logical uniformity predicate is the defining statement about the consistency or similarity properties of the pixels within a group or region of pixels. In this section, image segmentation is formulated in quantitative terms, and the logical uniformity predicate for the digital surface segmentation algorithm, the surface coherence predicate, is defined.

Separate spatial regions in an image correspond to different physical entities in a scene. When a set of different objects in a scene undergo an image projection, some of bounding surface primitives of each object may become partially visible or completely visible (unoccluded) connected regions in a digital image. Image understanding implies that these regions are isolated in the image and that relationships between the regions are established. This region isolation problem can be cast in the form of the general image segmentation problem using the surface coherence predicate.

The general segmentation problem is usually stated as follows [Horowitz and Pavlidis 1974] [Zucker 1976]: Given the set of all image pixels I and a logical uniformity predicate $P(\cdot)$, find a partition (or segmentation) S of the image I in terms of a set of regions R_i. Let N_R be the number of regions in the segmentation, and let $|R_i|$ be the number of pixels in the region R_i. The following segmentation conditions must hold for the set S:

$$\bigcup_{i=1}^{N_R} R_i = I \qquad \text{where } R_i \subseteq I \text{ for each } i$$

$$R_i \cap R_j = \phi = \text{Null Set} \qquad \text{for all } i \neq j \tag{2.13}$$

$$R_i \quad \text{is a 4-connected set of pixels}$$

$$\text{Uniformity Predicate } P(R_i) = \text{TRUE} \quad \text{for all } i$$

$$\text{If } R_i \text{ adjacent to } R_j \Longrightarrow P(R_i \cup R_j) = \text{FALSE.}$$

The result of the segmentation process is the list of regions

$$S = \{R_i\}_{i=1}^{N_R} \tag{2.14}$$

which is usually accompanied by an adjacent regions list denoted

$$S_A = \{(i_k, j_k)\}_{k=1}^{N_A} \tag{2.15}$$

where N_A is the number of adjacency relations and where the pair (i, j) indicates the adjacency of the ith region and the jth region:

$$(i, j) \in S_A \Longleftrightarrow R_i \text{ adjacent to } R_j. \tag{2.16}$$

The pair (S, S_A) is known as the region adjacency graph (RAG), where the regions are the nodes of the graph and the adjacency relationships are the arcs of the graph.

An important parameter of a segmentation algorithm is the smallest allowable region size, denoted $A_{\min}$:

$$A_{\min} = \min_{1 \leq i \leq N_R} |R_i|. \tag{2.17}$$

In general, the parameter $A_{\min} > 1$ should be specified to avoid degenerate, but otherwise valid segmentations in which every pixel is its own region and the uniformity predicate is trivially satisfied.

Although years of research have focused on the segmentation problem, few programs exist that correctly segment large classes of images, and no general purpose solutions exist. This has not been an insurmountable problem for many applications because vision system imaging environments can be constrained such that automated segmentation is achieved quickly and accurately. In less constrained imaging environments, high-level semantic knowledge about a scene is usually required in order to obtain accurate segmentations consisting of meaningful image regions.

The predicate $P(\cdot)$, left unspecified in the general segmentation definition, is given a general mathematical form below, called the surface coherence predicate. The surface coherence predicate is most meaningful for range images because sampled scene surfaces are directly represented in the digital surface data, but it can be applied to other types of images that exhibit the surface coherence property. Since many scene surfaces are relatively smooth, surfaces segmented in range images using the surface coherence predicate are likely to be meaningful surfaces.

In intensity images, it is common for scene surfaces that are relatively smooth to be textured, shadowed, marked, or painted in such a way that pixel intensity values corresponding to these surfaces do not yield a coherent digital surface in the intensity image. Rather, the gray levels of an intensity image may fluctuate wildly even though the image represents relatively smooth surfaces. Consider wood grain, brick, concrete, gravel, cork, burlap, carpet, or a matte surface with a complex shadow pattern. The surface coherence predicate is only appropriate for the large, but still very limited, class of intensity images in which texture, complex shadows, or surface markings do not dominate the image.

Assume that a piecewise-smooth digital image function $g(x, y)$ is defined on the image domain I. It is hypothesized that this image function results from a point-wise transformation $\lambda(\cdot)$ of the physical range image surface function $f(x, y)$ which is then scaled by a factor a and offset by another constant b. This image function is then corrupted by additive, zero-mean, finite-variance, stationary, random measurement noise $n(x, y)$ and finally quantized (truncated by the floor function $\lfloor \cdot \rfloor$) to form an integer measurement between 0 and $2^{N_{bits}} - 1$ where N_{bits} is the number of bits produced by the sensor digitizer:

$$g(x, y) = \lfloor a\lambda(x, y, f(x, y)) + b + n(x, y) \rfloor \qquad (2.18)$$

where as before (Equation 2.5)

$$f(x, y) = \max_i h_{A_i, \vec{\alpha}_i, \vec{\theta}_i}(x, y) \qquad (2.19)$$

for some set of objects $\{A_i\}$. When $f(x, y)$ is a diffuse matte surface and λ obeys the Lambertian diffuse reflection law, this equation is just another form of the image irradiance equation of Horn [1977]. If it is assumed that each object volume is bounded by a set of relatively smooth surfaces, then

$f(x, y)$ will consist of the range image projections of these surfaces subject to multiple object occlusion operation. Hence, the underlying geometric surface function $f(x, y)$ is assumed to be piecewise smooth. When digital image $g(x, y)$ includes texture as well measurement and quantization noise, let the zero-mean texture of the digital surface be incorporated in the noise process $\mathbf{n}(x, y)$ with the disadvantage that it is now a non-stationary process.

In order to pose the segmentation problem based on the surface coherence predicate, the characteristic function of an image region is introduced:

$$\chi(x, y, R_i) = \begin{cases} 1 & \text{if } (x, y) \in R_i \subseteq I \\ 0 & \text{otherwise.} \end{cases} \tag{2.20}$$

The piecewise smooth function $f(x, y)$ can then be written as

$$f(x, y) = \sum_{i=1}^{N_R} f_i(x, y) \chi(x, y, R_i) \tag{2.21}$$

where each $f_i(x, y)$ function describes a completely smooth surface primitive with no depth or orientation discontinuities over the region R_i. It is convenient to associate a piecewise-constant region label function $l_f(x, y)$ with the piecewise-smooth surface function $f(x, y)$ that associates an integer label i with each point (x, y):

$$l_f(x, y) = \sum_{i=1}^{N_R} i \, \chi(x, y, R_i). \tag{2.22}$$

If $\vec{a}_i$ is a parameter vector that completely determines the function $f_i(x, y)$, then the piecewise-smooth surface function $f(x, y)$ is completely determined by the parameter vector list $\{\vec{a}_i\}$ and the region label function $l_f(x, y)$. The generic goal of a data description process in computer vision is to extract a region label function and a list of parameter vectors given only $g(x, y)$ and knowledge of the λ operator.

The properties of the characteristic function and the assumption that the function $\lambda(\cdot)$ depends only locally upon each point $(x, y, f(x, y))$ in a digital image allows the following simplification:

$$\lambda(x, y, f(x, y)) = \lambda\left(x, y, \sum_{i=1}^{N_R} f_i(x, y) \chi(x, y, R_i)\right) \tag{2.23}$$

$$= \sum_{i=1}^{N_R} \lambda(x, y, f_i(x, y)) \chi(x, y, R_i).$$

This means that operating on a composite range image function with an illumination-reflection shading operator is equivalent to forming a composite intensity image by applying an illumination-reflection shading operator to each individual surface patch $f_i(x, y)$. The spatial arguments x and y are still included separately to allow for the possibility of shadowing or radiosity (mutual reflection) effects from other surfaces as in the rendering equation of [Kajiya 1986]. This yields a new statement of the original digital surface equation:

$$g(x, y) = \sum_{i=1}^{N_R} \lfloor a\lambda(x, y, f_i(x, y))\chi(x, y, R_i) + b + \mathbf{n}(x, y)\rfloor. \qquad (2.24)$$

If the composite functions $\lambda(x, y, f_i(x, y))$ are not piecewise smooth due to the action of λ, then difficulties will arise since assumptions have been violated. But if λ is sufficiently well-behaved (e.g. if only simple lighting and simple shadowing of matte surfaces is involved), then it is possible to refine or subdivide the region partition of $f(x, y)$ to create a new partition $\tilde{S} = \{\tilde{R}_i\}$ so that every composite function $\tilde{g}_i(x, y) = \lambda(x, y, f_i(x, y))$ is smooth over its corresponding support region $\tilde{R}_i$. In range imaging, nothing changes and $f_i = \tilde{g}_i$ since λ is the identity operator.

As described in Chapter 3, every smooth surface can be decomposed into constant-surface-curvature-sign surface primitives using the signs of the mean and Gaussian curvature. As argued in Chapter 4, the visible portions of these sign-of-curvature surface primitives are adequately approximated over digital image regions by low-order polynomial graph surfaces. Therefore, any smooth surface primitive $\tilde{g}_i$ defined over the region $\tilde{R}_i$ can be further partitioned or subdivided into a set of simple sign-of-curvature surface primitives $g_i(x, y)$ defined over regions R_i'. Moreover, each simple surface primitive $g_i(x, y)$ can be well approximated by a low-order polynomial graph surface $\hat{g}_i(x, y)$ of degree m. Hence, if $\tilde{S} = \{\tilde{R}_i\}$ is a segmentation of a piecewise-smooth image function into smooth surface functions $\tilde{g}_i$, then there exists a refinement S' of $\tilde{S}$ such that the sign-of-curvature surface primitives $g_i(x, y)$ over $R_i' \in S'$ are well represented by the approximating functions $\hat{g}_i(x, y)$. In the segmentation problem statement below, the regions R_i' are denoted simply as the regions R_i and the scale factor a and the offset value b of the digitization process are absorbed into the function definitions $g_i(x, y)$ for simpler expressions.

For images satisfying the surface coherence hypothesis, the digital surface segmentation/reconstruction problem is stated as follows:

- **Given** only the discrete, noisy, quantized pixel values of the digital surface $g(x, y)$ hypothesized to be of the form

$$g(x, y) = \sum_{i=1}^{N_R} \lfloor g_i(x, y)\chi(x, y, R_i) + \mathbf{n}(x, y)\rfloor. \qquad (2.25)$$

for some unknown set of sign-of-curvature surface primitives $G = \{g_i\}$ and some unknown set of regions $S = \{R_i\}$ that satisfy (1) the segmentation region conditions (2.13) and (2) the condition that $A_{\min}$ is greater than a minimum region size threshold T_R (e.g. $3 \le T_R \le 10$), **find** a set of approximate regions $\hat{S} = \{\hat{R}_i\}$ and a set of approximating functions $\hat{G} = \{\hat{g}_i(x, y)\}$ defined over the corresponding regions $\hat{R}_i$ such that the estimated number of regions and functions $\hat{N}_R = |\hat{G}| = |\hat{S}|$ is as small as is reasonably possible, the size of each region $|\hat{R}_i|$ is as large as is reasonably possible, and the approximation error metric ϵ given below is as small as is reasonably possible for the function $\hat{g}$ specified below. The function $\mathbf{n}(x, y)$ is assumed to be a zero-mean random field that provides the measurement and quantization errors for an otherwise ideal sensor. It may also provide surface texture for otherwise smooth surfaces. The approximation error ϵ is given by an error norm over the image I

$$\epsilon = \|g - \hat{g}\|_I \qquad (2.26)$$

where $\hat{g}$ takes the form

$$\hat{g}(x, y) = \sum_{i=1}^{\hat{N}_R} \hat{g}_i(x, y) \chi(x, y, \hat{R}_i). \qquad (2.27)$$

The precise meaning of the terminology "as is reasonably possible" is left undefined, but the qualitative meaning should be clear.

- If only the approximation error were required to be small and the A_{min} constraint were not specified, any algorithm could create a degenerate constant surface and a degenerate one-pixel region for every pixel in an image to yield zero approximation error. Similarly, if only the number of regions were required to be small, any algorithm could simply fit a single surface to the entire image minimizing the number of regions, maximizing the size of the regions, but also maximizing the approximation error. An ideal algorithm should segment an image the way a person would do it by balancing the opposing tendencies to minimize approximation error and region count. It is difficult to formulate a precise objective function for minimization that is effective and allows analytic solutions with existing optimization techniques. The digital surface segmentation approach does not use such an objective function, but does provide a function $\hat{g}$ for which both the approximation error and the number of regions are small and each region is as large as is reasonably possible.

- The surface coherence predicate is represented implicitly by the fact that all pixels (x, y) in region R_i have values $z(x, y)$ that lie sufficiently close to the smooth surface function values $g_i(x, y)$ given the variance of the noise process $\mathbf{n}(x, y)$. Moreover, if R_i and R_j are adjacent regions and if $(x, y) \in R_i$, then

$$|z(x, y) - g_i(x, y)| < |z(x, y) - g_j(x, y)| \qquad (2.28)$$

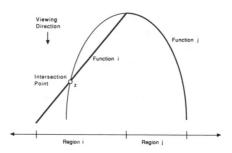

Figure 2.4: Possible Intersection of Adjacent Surface Regions

for almost every pixel in region R_i. The term "almost every" is used
because it is possible for the function g_j to intersect the function g_i
as shown in the example in Figure 2.4. The intersection set should
always correspond to a set of measure zero (i.e., a set with no area).

- The surface coherence predicate depends on the noise present in an
  image and may be written explicitly as

$$P_\epsilon(R_i) = \text{TRUE} \qquad \text{if } \|g - \hat{g}\|_{R_i} < \epsilon \qquad (2.29)$$

for some choice of the approximating function $\hat{g}$ and $P_\epsilon(R_i) = \text{FALSE}$
otherwise. The value of ϵ may be prespecified or it may be determined
from the image data as described in Chapter 4. The error norm is
only evaluated over the region R_i.

The problem in computing this decomposition is that *both the region set
and the approximating function set* are completely unknown given an arbitrary digital surface. Moreover, the number of regions and functions is not
given either. Nonetheless, reasonable decompositions are achieved by the
digital surface segmentation algorithm described in later chapters using a
combination of theoretical arguments and heuristics.

Not only is an image segmented by the surface coherence predicate that
all pixels in a region belong to a particular smooth surface, but an entire
image reconstruction $\hat{g}(x, y)$ is generated that looks quite like the original
image, and the 3-D shape of the individual surface regions are explicitly
approximated. This 3-D shape extraction aspect could be useful to a wide
variety of application systems based on range imaging sensors, whether it
be automated geometric modeling or automated object recognition.

Systems for segmenting digital surfaces following this general approach
have already been built based on planar approximating functions [Faugeras
1984] [Bhanu 1984] [Duda et al. 1979] [Herman 1985] [Haralick and Watson
1981] [Milgram and Bjorklund 1980] and quadric approximating surfaces of
volumes (often specifically cones or cylinders) [Nevatia and Binford 1977]

[Kuan and Drazovich 1984] [Smith and Kanade 1985] [Tomita and Kanade 1984] [Gennery 1979]. However, none of the systems discussed in the literature are able to handle arbitrary combinations of flat and curved surfaces on non-convex objects in a unified manner. The goal of this segmentation algorithm is to compute meaningful, accurate segmentations and noise-free image reconstructions of arbitrary digital surfaces without imposing limited models of particular smooth surfaces, such as quadrics and planes.

It is interesting to contrast the geometric image signal decomposition mentioned above with another commonly used type of signal decomposition. In 2-D Fourier analysis, the set of orthogonal basis functions is defined over the entire 2-D plane and is known prior to analysis. The decomposition problem is reduced to computing an integral or sum to obtain the basis function coefficients. A spatial surface function is effectively converted to a spatial-frequency function for frequency domain analysis. This conversion can be performed regardless of the spatial coherence of the original surface function. A region-based decomposition as described above can be obtained only if the coherent surface assumption is satisfied. However, rather than infinite support spatial-frequency basis functions, simple compact-support geometric shape functions are advocated. The capabilities of frequency-based signal processing techniques for arbitrary signals are limited when the information content of a spatial signal is explicit geometry. It appears that geometry-based signal processing may be more useful in such cases.

Frequency-based analysis allows simple compression of data if certain frequency bands can be ignored. However, an accurate description of surfaces in a scene requires low spatial frequencies for surface interiors and high spatial frequencies for surface boundaries, which limits the potential of this type of data compression. Moreover, spatial frequency information has been directly useful for interpretation only in very constrained circumstances. In geometry-based signal processing, coherent surface data is compressed into functional parameters and region descriptions, which appear to be directly useful for general purpose interpretation or model formation.

Before concluding this section, conventional error norms over the digital image I are listed explicitly. The image error $\epsilon = \|g - \hat{g}\|$ mentioned above usually takes the following discrete L_p form where $p = 1$ or $p = 2$:

$$\epsilon^p = \frac{1}{|I|} \sum_{(x,y) \in I} |g(x,y) - \hat{g}(x,y)|^p \qquad (2.30)$$

where $|I|$ is the number of pixels in the image I. If $p = 2$ is chosen, least squares fitting techniques are applicable. If the regions were estimated correctly so that there are no region segmentation errors ($R_i = \hat{R}_i$ for all i from 1 to $\hat{N}_R = N_R$), then the error norm is the weighted sum of errors for each region:

$$\epsilon^p = \frac{1}{|I|} \sum_{i=1}^{N_R} \epsilon_i^p |R_i| \qquad (\text{if } R_i = \hat{R}_i) \qquad (2.31)$$

where

$$\epsilon_i^p = \frac{1}{|R_i|} \sum_{(x,y) \in R_i} |g(x,y) - \hat{g}_i(x,y)|^p. \qquad (2.32)$$

This special case decomposition of the error norm in terms of the individual surface approximation functions is only correct if the estimated regions and the actual regions are identical. In general, the image error ϵ consists of contributions from both region segmentation errors and approximation errors.

2.7 Segmentation Errors

The ϵ value above measures the approximation error in the image description $\hat{g}(x,y)$. An example method for measuring image recognition error in terms of several different types of *recognition errors* was given in a previous section. Just as object recognition systems can commit high-level recognition errors, segmentation processes can commit several different types of low-level *segmentation errors* that may not influence the approximation error ϵ. In vision system evaluation, it is important to separate image understanding errors into those errors caused by high-level matching difficulties and those caused by low-level segmentation difficulties. Several image segmentation errors are listed below:

1. Boundary Error: Most of a region is correctly segmented, but the boundary of the region is not correctly positioned in the image. A region boundary must be substituted or modified to correct the error.

2. Region Merge Error: Two regions are merged even though a step or orientation discontinuity exists between the regions. A new region boundary must be inserted to correct the error.

3. Failure-to-Merge Error: Two regions that should have been merged are not merged and are separated by a meaningless boundary. A region boundary must be deleted to correct the error.

4. Same-Region-Label Error: Two non-adjacent regions are given the same label even though they should not be grouped together. A new region label is needed.

5. Different-Region-Label Error: Two non-adjacent regions are given different labels even though they should be grouped together. One label must be substituted for another to correct the error.

These errors require higher level knowledge for detection and correction. If such errors could be detected using low-level mechanisms, those mechanisms could theoretically be used to correct the segmentation errors. Levine and Nazif [1985] have developed a general-purpose low-level performance measurement scheme for image segmentation algorithms based on uniformity and contrast measures of regions and lines. But to measure relative performance of different segmentation algorithms, it is necessary to compute an error metric between two image segmentations.

The number of errors, the length of region boundaries, the areas of the involved regions, and the size of the differences in the regions involved in those errors might all be useful in establishing a segmentation error metric that could be used to compare different image segmentations. It seems possible that a generalization of the Levenshtein metric for two bit strings would be useful for a segmentation error metric: "What is the minimum number of region relabelings and insertions, deletions, and substitutions of region boundaries needed to derive one segmentation from the other?" Region boundary modifications might need to be weighted by the length of the region boundary for insertions and deletions and the magnitude of the boundary modification for substitutions. Little research has addressed these issues, so a simple example metric is suggested below.

The concept of distance between two regions is defined in Appendix E. This basic concept can be used to define a simple image segmentation error metric of the type that is needed for quantitative evaluations and comparisons of segmentations. Although this metric does not have all the desirable properties that one might want in quantifying the five types of errors listed above, it is a simple and interesting way to quantify the misclassified pixels in an image segmentation. Let $S = \{R_i\}$ be the "correct" segmentation of the digital image I with N_R regions and let $\hat{S} = \{\hat{R}_i\}$ be the automatically computed segmentation derived from the data with $\hat{N}_R$ regions. Let $N = \min(N_R, \hat{N}_R)$ be the number of correspondences between regions in the two segmentations. If $\hat{N}_R > N_R$ as is often the case, the implied correspondence between regions is computed by noting that R_i corresponds to $\hat{R}_i$ if $|R_i \cap \hat{R}_i| > |R_i \cap \hat{R}_j|$ for all indices $j \neq i$ that have not already been assigned. Correspondences are assigned sequentially in decreasing order of the region sizes in the segmentation with the fewest regions. The simple image segmentation error metric $e(S, \hat{S})$ for the image I is given by

$$e(S, \hat{S}) = \frac{1}{2|I|} \sum_{i=1}^{N} |R_i \triangle \hat{R}_i| \qquad (2.33)$$

where the symmetric difference operation between two sets is defined as $A \triangle B = (A - B) \cup (B - A)$. The error metric ranges from zero (if the both segmentations are identical) to one (if a completely wrong correspondence is established where all corresponding regions are disjoint). A completely wrong correspondence is impossible using the correspondence definition above. This error metric has the right properties as far as the boundary errors mentioned above are defined, but it seems to penalize the other four types of errors mentioned above too heavily.

2.8   Range Image Segmentation and Recognition

When range images are used as sensor input, the λ operator in the formalism above can be dropped because it is the identity operator. This implies that the surface primitives $g_i(x, y)$ are the sign-of-curvature surface primitives of the smooth surface primitives $f_i(x, y)$ that result from the decomposition of the range image function $f(x, y)$.

A proposed general-purpose approach for object recognition in range images based on the output from the digital surface segmentation algorithm is given below. This approach is speculative since no experimental results are given, but it provides a detailed example of how the segmentation output might be used.

The segmentation algorithm takes the digital surface function $g(x, y)$ and creates the intermediate "HK-sign map" image $\text{sgn}_{HK}(x, y)$ as described in Chapter 3 (H is mean curvature, K is Gaussian curvature). Each pixel in this intermediate image is given a sign-of-curvature surface type label: peak, pit, ridge, valley, saddle ridge, saddle valley, flat, or minimal. The HK-sign map is then used to find interior seed-region subsets $\hat{R}_i^0$ of the actual regions R_i. These seed regions are grown using a small set of approximating functions and an iterative, variable-order surface fitting algorithm to create refined region descriptions $\hat{R}_i$ and the approximate surface primitives $\hat{g}_i(x, y)$. Since a smooth surface primitive $f_i(x, y)$ may consist of several sign-of-curvature (HK-sign) surface primitives $g_i(x, y)$, it is necessary to perform a final merging operation on the approximated HK-sign surface primitives $\hat{g}_i(x, y)$ to create approximate composite smooth surface primitives $\hat{f}_i(x, y)$ that correspond to the underlying smooth surface primitives $f_i(x, y)$ in the range image of the scene.

Each approximated, smooth surface primitive $\hat{f}_i(x, y)$ should correspond to at least one surface on at least one object in the object list, or else it is a new surface shape that has never been encountered before and it needs to be learned. If the surface $\hat{f}_i(x, y)$ over its support region corresponds to a surface of the object A_j, then that object should be an element of the single surface inverse set mapping

$$(A_j, \vec{\alpha}_j, \vec{\theta}_j) \in P^{-1}(\hat{f}_i(x, y)) \tag{2.34}$$

for some translation $\vec{\alpha}_j$ and some rotation $\vec{\theta}_j$. If this is the only such triplet found in the search through the world model representation, then a valid surface correspondence between $\hat{f}_i$ and A_j is established. The object can be projected into the range image format and compared to the digital range image to check if the presence or absence of all other bounding surfaces of A_j can be explained. If so, then the object has been recognized in the image. But, given the data geometry $\hat{f}_i$ and the model geometry of A_j, how is the hypothesis of the correspondence between these two entities tested?

First, obviously false hypotheses are considered. Suppose that the digital surface segmentation yields smooth surface primitives $\hat{f}_i$ that can be classified into surfaces that are (1) definitely curved, (2) definitely flat, or (3) either flat or slightly curved. For surfaces that are either definitely flat or definitely curved, several hypotheses can be easily checked. For example, a spherical model surface cannot project to a flat data surface, and a simple polyhedral object model with sharp dihedral edges can never project to a spherical data surface. Therefore, curved-to-flat and flat-to-curved data-to-model hypotheses can be quickly dismissed without much computation. Assuming scale factors are known or can be computed, some definitely flat to definitely flat hypotheses can also be checked fairly quickly. Flat 3-D planar regions can be rotated into alignment and matched with subsequent 2-D bounding planar curve computations. For example, a small flat model surface bounded by a hexagon cannot project to a large flat data surface bounded by a quadrilateral, and such a test need only involve surface area. However, the converse is not true because a large flat model surface might project to a smaller flat data surface owing to occlusion.

The difficult problem is testing the general curved data surface to curved model surface hypothesis. For surfaces with significant curvature, basic surface types described in Chapter 3 (peak, pit, ridge, valley, saddle) must match. If the surface types don't match, the hypothesis can be rejected.

For surfaces with matching surface types and surfaces without significant curvature in at least one direction (where precise surface type can be difficult to determine), general surface shape matching must be addressed. Let $\vec{s}_j(u, v)$ be a 3-D parametric surface representation of an arbitrary curved surface bounding the object A_j. Let $\hat{f}_i(x, y)$ be the graph surface approximation of an underlying smooth surface primitive $f_i(x, y)$ extracted from range image data by the digital surface segmentation algorithm. The hypothesis is that the object A_j can be translated, rotated, and projected to create the range image function $f_i(x, y)$. Let $d_{ij}(\vec{\theta}, \vec{\alpha})$ be the L_p surface matching metric ($p = 1, 2$) for the given data surface $\hat{f}_i(x, y)$ defined over the region $\hat{R}_i$ and the model surface $\vec{s}_j(u, v)$ from the object A_j in the position $\vec{\alpha}$ and the orientation $\vec{\theta}$. Let $\mathbf{U}_{\vec{\theta}}$ be the 3x3 rotation matrix associated with the rotation parameter vector $\vec{\theta}$. The curved model surface to curved data surface matching metric can be expressed as the integral over the corresponding segmented region of the differences of the data surface provided by the segmentation algorithm and the *rotated, translated, reparameterized, projected* model surface provided by the world model:

$$d_{ij}^p(\vec{\theta}, \vec{\alpha}) = \frac{1}{|\hat{R}_i|} \int_{\hat{R}_i} |\hat{f}_i(x, y) - P(\mathbf{U}_{\vec{\theta}} \vec{s}_j(u(x, y), v(x, y)) + \vec{\alpha})|^p \, dx \, dy \quad (2.35)$$

where $P(\cdot)$ is again the range image projection operator that extracts the range value from the transformed model surface. This integral is referred to as the 3-D surface matching integral, which is a generalization of a similar 3-D curve matching integral. For every object, this surface matching metric should be minimized over all possible rotations and translations. Note that reparameterization is required for a direct comparison of data and model surfaces. If the minimized surface matching decision metric is small enough, then the model object A_j with its surface description $\vec{s}_j(u, v)$ corresponds to the data surface $\hat{f}_i$. This is a general statement of the hypothesis test for arbitrary model surface to arbitrary data surface correspondence.

Any approach to minimizing this integral will be an expensive computation, but it appears that the desired results might be computed relatively efficiently if sufficiently accurate range image processing can be done on sufficiently high-quality range images. First, a range image must be partitioned at least into elliptic ($K > 0$), hyperbolic ($K < 0$), and parabolic ($K = 0$) Gaussian curvature sign surface primitives. Further partitioning based on mean curvature simplifies some decisions. Therefore, the output of the digital surface segmentation algorithm is assumed to be available in this discussion.

Elliptic data surface primitives can be matched to elliptic model surface patches using the EGI approach as presented by Horn [1984], which is based on a uniqueness theorem about positive Gaussian curvature surfaces that is discussed in Chapter 3. The best rotation match might be computed by discrete orientation histogram matching, which yields the approximate best rotation matrix. Bhanu and Ho [1987] suggested that EGI histograms should be stored at multiple resolutions for more efficient, more accurate matching. The best translation vector can then be computed via relatively direct means once the appropriate rotation is known. The reparameterization problem can be addressed effectively by using ray tracing methods from computer graphics to evaluate $\vec{s}_j(u(x, y), v(x, y))$ at a dense sampling of appropriate (x, y) points, e.g. on the range image pixel grid, to yield a minimum matching metric for the hypothesized surface. Hence, the surface matching integral should be computable for all positive Gaussian curvature data surface patches.

Hyperbolic surfaces might be matched using the 4-vector orientation histogram concept of Liang [1987], which was described in the literature review of Chapter 1. Hyperbolic surfaces are always free of umbilic points implying that that such surface patches are uniquely determined by the mean and Gaussian curvature and the principal directions at each point. This information can be stored and matched similar to the EGI approach, preferably at multiple resolutions.

Parabolic (zero Gaussian curvature) surface primitives could probably be handled by special case logic for cylinders, cones, planes, and other parabolic surfaces. Many existing techniques for cylinders, cones, and polyhedra might be applied for those special cases. General parabolic surfaces are mapped via the Gauss map to space curve entities that lie on the Gaussian sphere. Therefore, space curve matching algorithms might be useful for matching parabolic data surfaces to parabolic model surfaces. However, it can be difficult to distinguish between small values and zero values of Gaussian curvature in the extracted data surface primitives. This may cause some problems in the matching algorithm, but the general approach seems to be feasible.

If a single unique feature point can be reliably isolated on the data surface and the model surface primitives (such as isolated curvature maxima points), then the translation is determined by the difference vector between the model and data feature points and the rotation can be determined by the surface normals and principal directions of the model and data surface primitives at the feature points. Reparametrization is again addressed via ray casting methods and the minimum matching metric would be computable. Although none of the above ideas have been implemented and tested yet, it appears that the surface matching integral can be computed such that, with an appropriately structured decision tree, it may be possible to test surface correspondence hypotheses in a theoretically sound manner for the vast majority of smooth surfaced objects using such an algorithm.

If there are N_R smooth surface regions in an image segmentation and N_S possible distinct smooth object surfaces in the world model, this could potentially require testing $N_R N_S$ correspondence hypotheses. But geometric surface correspondence hypothesis computations are just one part of the general matching computations that will be needed. Relational matching computations [Shapiro and Haralick 1981] must take place in conjunction with geometric matching computations. The adjacency relationships of model surfaces and data surfaces can play an important and powerful role in a general-purpose object recognition algorithm. A single adjacency constraint between two or three data surfaces can prune the search space of possible object matches dramatically [Bolles et al. 1983] [Grimson and Lozano-Perez 1984]. It appears that the feature-indexed methods of Knoll and Jain [1986] may also be applicable in reducing the number of detailed correspondence hypothesis tests.

The understanding process is envisioned to be a elaborate hypothesis testing algorithm where the hypotheses take the form of possible model surface to data surface correspondences, possible adjacency relationships, and possible special feature instances. If the surface segmentation and surface matching algorithms are robust enough, surfaces can be matched primarily by their shape, *not by their boundaries*, or by special feature points, as is done in most current approaches. Objects would even be recognizable if object feature points and edges were deliberately occluded. An ideal algorithm can make use of point and edge matching when possible, but should not rely on it completely. If these ideas are successful, there is real hope of successfully handling arbitrary surface shapes and occlusion with range imaging systems.

2.9   Summary

By examining object recognition requirements first, a system-level approach has been used for specifying the requirements of a particular vision system component, the data-driven description process. This process accepts a digital surface, such as a range image or intensity image, as input and produces a segmentation/reconstruction of that surface as output, which is a symbolic scene description in the terminology of this chapter. Such a process is necessary to object recognition efforts and should be considered within the appropriate context.

The term *digital surface segmentation* as used here implies that the following items have been computed: (1) a list of 2-D image regions where each region is described explicitly by continuous boundary curves, (2) a list of approximating smooth surface functions, one for each region, and (3) the approximation errors for each region as compared to the original digital surface data. The approximation errors are an indication of the confidence in a particular surface primitive relative to the median of the errors for the other surface primitives in the image. For human interpretation of segmentation results, the following items are also computed and displayed: (4) the reconstructed digital surface showing the algorithm's approximation of the image, and (5) a segmentation plot or region label image displaying the partitioned regions. This set of outputs is more than what is required from most intensity image segmentation algorithms.

This chapter has not speculated on how the output of the surface segmentation algorithm will be useful to object recognition in intensity images. As a worst case, the output will only be as useful as the output from an edge detection/edge linking/edge fitting algorithm if the region boundary curve functions are used as the output. If diffusely reflecting surfaces are known to be present in the scene, the smooth surface primitive information may be useful for shape from shading algorithms, as in [Bolle and Cooper 1984]. This subject area has many possibilities, but is left for future research.

Chapter 3

Surface Curvature Characteristics

3.1 Visible Invariance

Computing surface characteristics for pixel grouping purposes is the first step toward the final goals of object recognition and image understanding. The range image object recognition problem is being addressed with the aim of developing a general purpose approach that handles arbitrary surface shapes and arbitrary viewing directions. To handle the problem of arbitrary viewing directions, viewpoint invariant surface characteristics are needed that are general enough to describe both polyhedra and objects with arbitrary curved surfaces. This statement presumes the validity of *invariant features hypothesis* [Palmer 1983], which states that "shape perception is mediated by the detection of those geometrical properties of a figure that do not change when the figure is transformed in different ways." Viewpoint invariance is a desirable property for any surface characteristics derived from discrete image data or from model and data surface primitive representations.

A quantity is invariant with respect to a group of transformations if those transformations do not change its value. For example, the length of a 3-D line segment does not change under the group of pure rotation transformations, and is therefore said to be rotationally invariant, but the length of a 3-D line segment projected into a 2-D image plane does change under rotation and is not invariant. Opaque, rigid, physical objects do not, in general, possess explicit surface or edge features that are visible from any viewing angle. There are almost always degenerate viewing angles in which visible object features are radically different. For example, consider an object as simple as a cylinder. A flat planar surface with a circular boundary is visible when looking down the axis of a cylinder. In contrast, a curved surface with a rectangular projected boundary is visible when looking perpendicular to the axis direction. Figure 3.1 shows the two views under consideration. There are no explicit invariant features even in this simple case. (For example, the minimum projected silhouette area

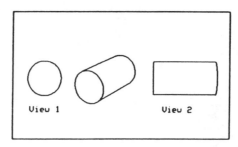

Figure 3.1: Two Views of a Cylinder with No Common Features

is not considered as an explicit feature.) The roundness of the cylinder manifests itself in both views, but in different ways. In the first view, an explicit circular range discontinuity boundary surrounding a flat region is visible while, in the second view, a constant, negative mean curvature, zero Gaussian curvature surface bounded by a projected rectangular range discontinuity boundary is visible. (Curvature definitions are given later in this chapter.) The computer vision literature often uses the term "invariant" to mean "invariant if visible." The term "visible-invariant" is suggested to be more specific.

A visible-invariant surface characteristic is a quantitative feature of visible surfaces that does not change under the set of viewing transformations that do not affect the visibility of that region. Hence, the set of transformations that leaves all portions of a particular surface patch visible depends on the shape of that surface patch. Since it would not be worthwhile to specify separate sets of transformations for each surface of interest, surface characteristics that are invariant to all rotation and translation transformations (the Euclidean rigid motion group) are sought. It is equally as important that surface characteristics are invariant to changes in the parameterization of a surface. When a visible, smooth, curved surface is sampled on a rectangular image grid from two different viewpoints, the effective grid parameterizations of the surface in the two corresponding range images are different. Hence, numerical visible-invariant surface quantities must also be invariant to changes in surface parameterization. The key point of these statements is that a general-purpose vision system should use visible-invariant features, but must also be aware that salient object features may not be visible even when an object is present and visible in the field of view. In comparison, some systems based on generalized cylinders seem to assume that roughly parallel curves or lines delineating the outline of a generalized cylinder will always be visible, e.g. [Brooks 1981]. General purpose systems must be able to handle degenerate alignment cases.

The visible-invariant surface characteristics chosen for this work are the *mean curvature (H)* and the *Gaussian curvature (K)*, which are referred to collectively as *surface curvature*. When a surface patch is visible, its surface curvature is invariant not only to *translations and rotations* of the object surfaces, but also to *changes in surface parameterization* (see Appendix A) under the orthographic range image projection. In addition, mean curvature is an *extrinsic* surface property whereas Gaussian curvature is *intrinsic*. These terms are discussed later, but are mentioned here to introduce their complementary nature. Differential geometry emphasizes that these are reasonable surface features to consider.

Since one seldom obtains perfect sensor data from the real world, it is desirable to compute a rich characterization of the surface that preserves surface structure information and is insensitive to noise. Noise insensitivity might be achieved by separately computing redundant information about a surface and then combining that information. For example, a rich geometric, low-level representation might consist of surface curvature characteristics as well as (1) surface critical points (local maxima, minima and saddle points), (2) large metric determinant points (range discontinuities), (3) principal directions, and (4) other miscellaneous surface properties to characterize a digital surface in more detail. These other characteristics provide complementary information that can be computed for a small additional cost once surface curvature is already being computed. This chapter shows the experimental results of computing surface curvature and other surface characteristics with discrete, noisy 8-bit range images to give the reader an idea of how well such quantities can be computed with real data. But the main theme, to be continued in Chapter 4, is that, given the surface characterization of a range image, it is possible to segment that range image into meaningful surface primitives based on the computed surface characteristics and the original range image. Range images are so explicit that it is not necessary to incorporate application-specific high-level information, such as a particular world model, in order to analyze and segment range images into meaningful surfaces.

3.2 Differential Geometry Review

In the previous chapter, it was noted that range image object recognition might be decomposed into a surface recognition problem, which is in turn relies on surface characterization and surface segmentation based on those characteristics. In this chapter, it was established that visible-invariant surface characteristics should be invariant to rotations and translations and surface parameterization changes so that they will be useful for 3-D object recognition using range images.

Before proceeding, the term "characteristic" should be defined. A *characteristic* of a mathematical entity, such as a surface function, is defined to be any well-defined feature that can be used to distinguish between different mathematical entities of the same type. One may consider ideal characteristics that *uniquely* determine a corresponding entity, or characteristics that are many-to-one (although the former are more desirable). A simple example of a characteristic that uniquely determines a function is a detailed description of the function itself. Another simple example of a many-to-one characteristic is roundness. A circle and an ellipse are both round closed curves. This *round* characteristic distinguishes them from rectangles, triangles, and other polygons, but it does not distinguish between circles and ellipses. In this chapter, the aim is to find a good mathematical characterization of range image function surfaces and apply it to digital range images. Differential geometry is used to motivate and justify the choice of surface characteristics, and for this reason, the basic concepts of differential geometry are reviewed, including curves, which are discussed in Chapter 6. This chapter attempts to compress the relevant mathematics into about ten pages and then stress a qualitative understanding of this mathematics. The knowledgeable reader can skip this tutorial material and resume reading at Section 3.4.

3.2.1   Space Curves

Before surfaces are treated, the corresponding theory for curves is reviewed to provide a better qualitative understanding of and a conceptual foundation for the more complicated surface concepts. It is well known that *curvature, torsion,* and *speed* uniquely determine the shape of 3-D space curves [Faux and Pratt 1979] [Hsiung 1981] [Lipschutz 1969] [O'Neill 1966]. General space curves are represented parametrically as a function of an interval of the real line. A curve C is written as follows:

$$C = \{\vec{x}(s) : a \le s \le b\}. \tag{3.1}$$

where $\vec{x}(s)$ is a vector function of a scalar argument s, which is *not* assumed to be arc length. Only *smooth* curves are considered where the components of the $\vec{x}$ vector have continuous second derivatives. The *tangent* unit-vector function $\vec{t}(s)$ is defined as

$$\vec{t}(s) = \frac{d\vec{x}(s)/ds}{\|d\vec{x}(s)/ds\|}. \tag{3.2}$$

The *normal* unit-vector function $\vec{n}(s)$ is defined as

$$\vec{n}(s) = \frac{d\vec{t}(s)/ds}{\|d\vec{t}(s)/ds\|}. \tag{3.3}$$

The *binormal* unit-vector function $\vec{b}(s)$ is defined as follows to complete a right-handed coordinate system:

$$\vec{b}(s) = \vec{t}(s) \times \vec{n}(s). \tag{3.4}$$

This coordinate system is shown in Figure 3.2. The *speed* $\nu(s)$ of a para-

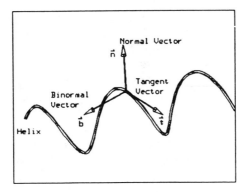

Figure 3.2: Tangent-Normal-Binormal Coordinate System on a Curve

metric curve C is defined as

$$\nu(s) = \|d\vec{x}(s)/ds\|. \tag{3.5}$$

The *curvature* of a parametric curve C can be defined as

$$\kappa(s) = \frac{\vec{n}(s) \cdot d\vec{t}(s)/ds}{\nu(s)}. \tag{3.6}$$

The *torsion* of a parametric curve C can be defined as

$$\tau(s) = -\frac{\vec{n}(s) \cdot d\vec{b}(s)/ds}{\nu(s)}. \tag{3.7}$$

These definitions provide a complete differential geometric description of a space curve. Given any parametric smooth curve C described by $\vec{x}(s)$ with respect to some coordinate system, these functions can be directly computed: $\vec{t}(s)$, $\vec{n}(s)$, $\vec{b}(s)$, $\kappa(s)$, $\tau(s)$, $\nu(s)$. The basic questions that are usually asked are the following: (1) How do these function descriptions change when a change in coordinate system occurs? (2) What function information corresponds to shape? translation? rotation? (3) Given the functions related to shape, do they uniquely determine the shape of the curve?

These questions were all answered by classical mathematics in the last century. From the definitions above, it is possible to formulate the Frenet-Serret equations. These equations are written here as a matrix ordinary differential equation:

$$\frac{d}{ds}\begin{bmatrix} \vec{t}(s) \\ \vec{n}(s) \\ \vec{b}(s) \end{bmatrix} = \begin{bmatrix} 0 & \kappa(s)\nu(s) & 0 \\ -\kappa(s)\nu(s) & 0 & \tau(s)\nu(s) \\ 0 & -\tau(s)\nu(s) & 0 \end{bmatrix} \begin{bmatrix} \vec{t}(s) \\ \vec{n}(s) \\ \vec{b}(s) \end{bmatrix}. \tag{3.8}$$

This state equation determines how the tangent-normal-binormal coordinate frame evolves as a function of the parameter s given an initial coordinate frame. The speed, curvature, and torsion functions of the skew-symmetric state transition matrix completely determine the evolution of the coordinate frame once initial conditions are given. If this first-order linear space-varying matrix ordinary differential equation were integrated over the entire length of the curve, one would only obtain what the coordinate frame does along the curve, not the curve itself. It is then necessary to integrate the tangent function given the starting point to obtain a complete description of the original curve. The general space curve reconstruction formula is

$$\vec{x}(s) = \int_0^s \vec{t}(s)\nu(s)ds + \vec{x}(0) \qquad \vec{x}(s) \in \Re^3 \qquad (3.9)$$

Thus, the curve C can be decomposed into different functional components with different invariance properties: $\vec{x}(0)$ is the starting point vector of three numbers that determine the starting point of the curve. $\vec{t}(0)$ is the initial tangent unit vector, which can be completely determined by two numbers. $\vec{n}(0)$ is the initial normal vector, which can be completely determined by one additional number. $\vec{b}(0)$ is the initial binormal vector, which is completely determined by the specification of the initial tangent and normal vectors. $\nu(s)$ is a normalization function that accounts for the 1-D intrinsic length geometry of the curve. If s is arc length along the curve, the speed is always one and thus may be dropped from all equations. $\kappa(s)$ is the scalar curvature function that determines the instantaneous radius of curvature at each point on the curve. $\tau(s)$ is the scalar torsion function that determines the instantaneous bending of the curve out of the tangent-normal plane.

For a general 3-D space curve, the explicit parameterization $\vec{x}(s)$ is specified by complete knowledge of three scalar functions. When the curve is expressed as the solution of an ordinary differential equation, it is necessary to know three scalar functions *plus* the initial conditions: three scalar translation *values* and three scalar rotation *values*. The component *functions* of $\vec{x}(s)$ change under rotation and translation whereas only the constant component *values* of $\vec{x}(0)$ and $\vec{t}(0), \vec{n}(0), \vec{b}(0)$ change in the differential geometric description. The speed, curvature, and torsion functions are invariant to rotation and translation coordinate transformations.

Moreover, there is a fundamental existence and uniqueness theorem for 3-D space curves that is proven as a direct consequence of the fundamental theorem of ordinary differential equations.

Existence: Let $\nu(s) > 0$, $\kappa(s) > 0$, and $\tau(s)$ be arbitrary continuous real functions on the interval $a \le s \le b$. Then there exists a unique space curve C, up to a translation and rotation, such that $\kappa(s)$ is the curvature function, $\tau(s)$ is the torsion function, and $\nu(s)$ is the speed function.

Uniqueness: If two curves C and C^* possess curvature functions $\kappa(s)$ and $\kappa^*(s)$, torsion functions $\tau(s)$ and $\tau^*(s)$, and speed functions $\nu(s)$ and $\nu^*(s)$ respectively such that

$$\nu(s) = \nu^*(s) > 0, \quad \kappa(s) = \kappa^*(s) > 0, \quad \tau(s) = \tau^*(s), \quad (3.10)$$

then there is an appropriate translation and rotation such that C and C^* coincide exactly implying they have the same shape.

This tells us that arbitrary 3-D smooth curve shape is completely captured by three scalar functions: curvature, torsion, and speed. For the special case of curves (not surfaces), it is possible to normalize any given parameterization so that the speed is always unity. This is equivalent to requiring that the s parameter be the arc length along the curve. In this case, curvature and torsion alone specify curve shape, but one has the extra piece of knowledge that the curve is parameterized by arc length.

3.2.2 Plane Curves

Before moving on to surfaces, which are 2-D manifolds embedded in 3-D space, the case of planar curves, which are 1-D manifolds in 2-D space, is examined due to the nature of its simplifications as compared to general space curves, which are 1-D manifolds in 3-D space. Not surprisingly, most non-moment-based 2-D shape description research makes use of the ideas covered here, which helps to motivate the proposed method of 3-D shape description. In addition, the contrast between the 2-D and 3-D shape recognition problems and 2-D and 3-D shape characteristics will be enhanced. The sign-of-curvature paradigm, developed in this chapter and in Chapter 4, is applicable to planar curves, surfaces, and higher dimensional geometric entities. In Chapter 6, the curvature of 2-D region boundaries (edges), which are planar curves, is used to characterize planar curve shape so that the region boundary can be segmented into linear and curved intervals.

Planar curves have zero torsion at all points on the curve. When this is true, there is no reason to consider the binormal vector in the state equation. The tangent-normal coordinate frame state equation simplifies as follows:

$$\frac{d}{ds} \begin{bmatrix} \vec{t} \\ \vec{n} \end{bmatrix} = \begin{bmatrix} 0 & \kappa(s)\nu(s) \\ -\kappa(s)\nu(s) & 0 \end{bmatrix} \begin{bmatrix} \vec{t} \\ \vec{n} \end{bmatrix}. \quad (3.11)$$

The general planar 2-D curve reconstruction formula can still be written the same as in the 3-D case. However, the 2-D case formula simplifies to the following special form for unit-speed curves $\vec{x}(s) = (x(s), y(s))$ where s is arc length:

$$x(s) = x(0) + \int_0^s \cos\left(\phi(0) + \int_0^\eta \kappa(\xi)d\xi\right) d\eta \quad (3.12)$$

$$y(s) = y(0) + \int_0^s \sin\left(\phi(0) + \int_0^\eta \kappa(\xi)d\xi\right) d\eta$$

where $\phi(0)$ is the initial tangent angle and $(x(0), y(0))$ is the starting point of the curve. For unit-speed curves only, curvature may be computed as

$$\kappa(s) = \frac{d}{ds} \tan^{-1}\left(\frac{dy/ds}{dx/ds}\right). \tag{3.13}$$

It is seen that arbitrary smooth planar curve shape is captured by two scalar functions: the speed function $\nu(s)$ and the curvature function $\kappa(s)$. Surface shape is captured by two almost exactly analogous 2x2 matrix functions: the *metric* and the *shape operator*, which generalize speed and curvature respectively. Many 2-D shape recognition techniques use (1) the curvature function, (2) the integral of the curvature function (usually known as the tangent angle function), or (3) the curve itself as specified by the integrals for $(x(s), y(s))$. Previous research in *partial* 2-D shape recognition has used either the tangent angle function, e.g. [Turney et al.1985], or the curvature function, e.g. [Grogan and Mitchell 1983].

3.2.3   Surfaces

Curvature, torsion, and speed uniquely determine the shape of curves. These characteristics are the ideal type of characteristic for a mathematical entity. They are invariant to coordinate transformations and they have a one-to-one relationship with curve shapes. Surface characteristics with similar properties are now discussed.

The parametric form of a general surface S with respect to a known coordinate system may be written as follows:

$$S = \left\{ \vec{x} \in \Re^3 : \begin{bmatrix} x \\ y \\ z \end{bmatrix} = \begin{bmatrix} d(u,v) \\ e(u,v) \\ f(u,v) \end{bmatrix}, (u,v) \in D \subseteq \Re^2 \right\} \tag{3.14}$$

This general parametric representation is referred to as $\vec{x}(u,v)$ where the x-component of the $\vec{x}$ function is $d(u,v)$, the y-component $e(u,v)$, and the z-component $f(u,v)$. In Section 3.4, the graph surface (Monge patch surface) form, where $x = d(u,v) = u$ and $y = e(u,v) = v$, is used to represent range image surface functions represented in digital range images. Surfaces can also be represented implicitly as the zero set of a function, the set of all (x, y, z) such that $F(x, y, z) = 0$, but this method of surface representation is not discussed here. Only *smooth* parametric surfaces are considered in this analysis in which all three parametric functions possess continuous second partial derivatives.

There are two basic mathematical entities that are considered in the differential geometry of smooth surfaces. In the classical mathematics of partial derivatives, they are known as the first and second fundamental forms of a surface [Hsiung 1981] [Lipschutz 1969]. Modern mathematics uses differential forms and favors an equivalent formulation of these quantities in terms of the metric tensor and the Weingarten mapping (the "shape" operator) [O'Neill 1966]. Complete knowledge of either of these forms at every surface point uniquely characterizes and quantifies general smooth surface shape. In general, the modern approach is preferred, especially by mathematicians, because it is a simpler formalism to work with once all the necessary terminology is established, but the classical approach is taken here since more people are familiar with partial derivatives than differential forms. The classical surface review begins by defining the fundamental forms of a surface in terms of a general surface parameterization $\vec{x}(u, v)$.

The first fundamental form I of a surface $\vec{x}(u, v)$ is given by

$$
\begin{aligned}
I(u, v, du, dv) &= d\vec{x} \cdot d\vec{x} = E du^2 + 2F du dv + G dv^2 \qquad (3.15) \\
&= [du \ \ dv] \begin{bmatrix} g_{11} & g_{12} \\ g_{21} & g_{22} \end{bmatrix} \begin{bmatrix} du \\ dv \end{bmatrix} \\
&= d\vec{u}^T [\mathbf{g}] d\vec{u}
\end{aligned}
$$

where the $[\mathbf{g}]$ matrix elements are defined as

$$
g_{11} = E = \vec{x}_u \cdot \vec{x}_u \qquad g_{22} = G = \vec{x}_v \cdot \vec{x}_v \qquad (3.16)
$$

$$
g_{12} = g_{21} = F = \vec{x}_u \cdot \vec{x}_v \qquad (3.17)
$$

and where the subscripts denote the partial derivatives

$$
\vec{x}_u(u, v) = \frac{\partial \vec{x}}{\partial u} \qquad \vec{x}_v(u, v) = \frac{\partial \vec{x}}{\partial v}. \qquad (3.18)
$$

$\vec{x}_u$ and $\vec{x}_v$ are referred to as the *u-tangent vector* and the *v-tangent vector* functions respectively, and they may or may not be orthogonal to each other. These two tangent vectors are shown in Figure 3.3 and are said to lie in and form a basis for the tangent plane $T(u, v)$ of the surface at the point $\vec{x}(u, v)$. The $[\mathbf{g}]$ matrix is known as the first fundamental form matrix or as the *metric* (or metric tensor) of the surface. Since the vector dot product is commutative, this $[\mathbf{g}]$ matrix is symmetric and only has three independent components. The E,F,G notation of Gauss is used along with the matrix element subscript notation because both are useful in different circumstances, and both occur often in the differential geometry literature.

The first fundamental form $I(u, v, du, dv)$ measures the small amount of movement $\|d\vec{x}\|^2$ on the surface at a point (u, v) for a given small vector movement in the parameter plane (du, dv) as shown in Figure 3.3. This function is invariant to surface parameterization changes and to translations and rotations of the surface. The first fundamental form depends only on the surface itself, and not on how the surface is embedded in 3-D space. Such properties are therefore referred to as *intrinsic* properties of

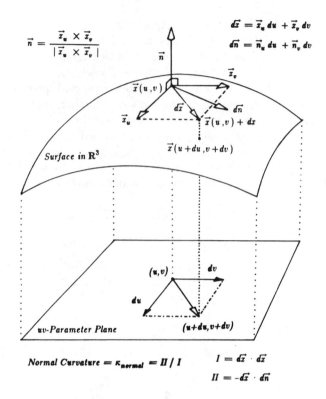

Figure 3.3: Local Coordinate Frame at Surface Point

a surface. In fact, the functions E,F,G determine all intrinsic properties
of a surface. The *metric* 2x2 matrix function plays the same role as the
scalar *speed* function does for curves. The intrinsic geometry of a curve is
one-dimensional whereas that of a surface is two-dimensional.

In contrast, the second fundamental form of a surface is dependent on
the embedding of the surface in 3-D space and is therefore known as an
extrinsic property of the surface. The second fundamental form II is given
by

$$
\begin{aligned}
II(u,v,du,dv) &= -d\vec{x} \cdot d\vec{n} = L\,du^2 + 2M\,du\,dv + N\,dv^2 \quad (3.19) \\
&= [du \quad dv] \begin{bmatrix} b_{11} & b_{12} \\ b_{21} & b_{22} \end{bmatrix} \begin{bmatrix} du \\ dv \end{bmatrix} \\
&= d\vec{u}^T [b] d\vec{u}
\end{aligned}
$$

where the [b] matrix elements may be defined as

$$
b_{11} = L = \vec{x}_{uu} \cdot \vec{n} \qquad b_{22} = N = \vec{x}_{vv} \cdot \vec{n} \qquad (3.20)
$$

$$
b_{12} = b_{21} = M = \vec{x}_{uv} \cdot \vec{n} \qquad (3.21)
$$

where

$$\vec{n}(u,v) = \frac{\vec{x}_u \times \vec{x}_v}{\|\vec{x}_u \times \vec{x}_v\|} = \text{Unit Normal Vector} \qquad (3.22)$$

and where the double subscripts denote the second partial derivatives

$$\vec{x}_{uu}(u,v) = \frac{\partial^2 \vec{x}}{\partial u^2} \qquad \vec{x}_{vv}(u,v) = \frac{\partial^2 \vec{x}}{\partial v^2} \qquad (3.23)$$

$$\vec{x}_{uv}(u,v) = \frac{\partial^2 \vec{x}}{\partial u \partial v} = \vec{x}_{vu}(u,v). \qquad (3.24)$$

The [b] matrix is the second fundamental form matrix and is also symmetric if the surface is well-behaved and the mixed partial derivatives are equal. The Gauss-like L,M,N notation is introduced again as above. These definitions allow us to discuss the "state" equation for surfaces.

The second fundamental form measures the correlation between the change in the normal vector $d\vec{n}$ and the change in the surface position $d\vec{x}$ at a surface point (u,v) as a function of a small movement (du, dv) in the parameter space. This is also indicated in Figure 3.3. The differential normal vector $d\vec{n}$ always lies in the tangent plane $T(u,v)$. The ratio of $II(u,v,du,dv)/I(u,v,du,dv)$ is known as the the normal curvature function κ_{normal}. Normal curvature at a surface point varies as a function of the *direction* of the differential vector (du, dv) in the parameter space. If $d\vec{n}$ and $d\vec{x}$ are aligned for a particular direction of (du, dv), that direction is called a *principal direction* of the surface at that surface point. The extrema of the normal curvature function at a given point occur in these directions and are known as the *principal curvatures*.

The Gauss-Weingarten equations for 3-D surfaces play the same role as the previously discussed Frenet-Serret equations for 3-D curves. The Gauss-Weingarten equations are written here as a matrix partial differential equation where the differential operator is a type of gradient operator that acts on the normal, u-tangent, v-tangent coordinate frame field:

$$\begin{bmatrix} \vec{x}_{uu} \\ \vec{x}_{uv} \\ \vec{x}_{vu} \\ \vec{x}_{vv} \\ \vec{n}_u \\ \vec{n}_v \end{bmatrix} = \begin{bmatrix} \frac{\partial}{\partial u} \\ \frac{\partial}{\partial v} \end{bmatrix} \begin{bmatrix} \vec{x}_u(u,v) \\ \vec{x}_v(u,v) \\ \vec{n}(u,v) \end{bmatrix} = \begin{bmatrix} \Gamma_{11}^1 & \Gamma_{11}^2 & b_{11} \\ \Gamma_{12}^1 & \Gamma_{12}^2 & b_{12} \\ \Gamma_{21}^1 & \Gamma_{21}^2 & b_{21} \\ \Gamma_{22}^1 & \Gamma_{22}^2 & b_{22} \\ -\beta_1^1 & -\beta_1^2 & 0 \\ -\beta_2^1 & -\beta_2^2 & 0 \end{bmatrix} \begin{bmatrix} \vec{x}_u(u,v) \\ \vec{x}_v(u,v) \\ \vec{n}(u,v) \end{bmatrix}.$$

$$(3.25)$$

The "transition" matrix in this state equation contains sixteen coefficient functions not yet defined. The *Christoffel Symbols of the Second Kind* Γ_{ij}^k (or connection coefficients) depend only on the metric functions $g_{ij}(u,v)$ and are defined as follows:

$$\Gamma_{ij}^k(u,v) = \frac{1}{2} \sum_{m=1}^{2} g^{km} \left(\frac{\partial g_{jm}}{\partial u^i} + \frac{\partial g_{mi}}{\partial u^j} - \frac{\partial g_{ij}}{\partial u^m} \right) \qquad (3.26)$$

where $u^1 = u$ and $u^2 = v$ and where g^{km} is the matrix inverse of g_{km}, which is the tensor notation for the metric [g] already defined. The Christoffel symbols are symmetric $\Gamma_{ij}^k = \Gamma_{ji}^k$ in i and j because the metric tensor is symmetric.

The last two row equations of this matrix equation are referred to as the Weingarten equations for 3-D surfaces whereas the top three row equations are know as Gauss' equations. The Weingarten equations' coefficients β_j^i depend on both the first and second fundamental form matrices:

$$\beta_j^i = \sum_{k=1}^{2} b_{jk} g^{ki} \quad \text{or} \quad [\beta] = [\mathbf{g}^{-1}][\mathbf{b}]. \tag{3.27}$$

The $[\beta]$ matrix is referred to as the shape operator matrix [O'Neill 1966] or the *Weingarten mapping* matrix. The Weingarten mapping maps tangent vectors to other tangent vectors in the tangent plane $T(u, v)$ associated with each point $\vec{x}(u, v)$. For example, $\vec{n}_u(u, v)$ is specified as a linear combination of the u- and v-tangent vectors. One can view the $[\beta]$ matrix as the entity that determines surface shape by relating the intrinsic geometry of the surface to the Euclidean geometry of 3-D space. It is the generalization of the *curvature* of plane curves.

It has been shown that all of the sixteen non-zero state matrix coefficient functions depend on only six scalar functions of two variables:

$$g_{11}(u,v) \quad g_{12}(u,v) \quad g_{22}(u,v) \quad b_{11}(u,v) \quad b_{12}(u,v) \quad b_{22}(u,v) \tag{3.28}$$

For brevity, these function are also referred to as the E,F,G,L,M,N functions. Assuming the first-order linear homogeneous space-varying partial differential matrix equation can be solved for the $\vec{x}_u, \vec{x}_v, \vec{n}$ coordinate frame, one can also solve for the parametric surface function in the neighborhood of a point (u_0, v_0) using the following 3-D surface reconstruction formula:

$$\vec{x}(u, v) = \int_{u_0}^{u} \vec{x}_u(\xi, v)d\xi + \int_{v_0}^{v} \vec{x}_v(u_0, \eta)d\eta \tag{3.29}$$

Just as for curves, there is a *fundamental existence and uniqueness theorem* for 3-D surfaces (credited to the mathematician O. Bonnet 1876):

Existence: Let $g_{11}(u, v), g_{12}(u, v), g_{22}(u, v)$ be continuous functions with continuous second partial derivatives. Let $b_{11}(u, v), b_{12}(u, v), b_{22}(u, v)$ be continuous functions with continuous first partial derivatives. Assume all six functions are defined in an open set D containing the point (u_0, v_0). If all six functions satisfy the following set of compatibility equations (3.31,3.32,3.33) and sign restrictions (3.30), then there exists a unique surface patch defined in the neighborhood of (u_0, v_0) such that g_{ij} and b_{ij} are the first and second fundamental form matrices respectively. Uniqueness is determined up to a translation and rotation. The sign restrictions are

$$g_{11} > 0 \qquad g_{22} > 0 \qquad \det[\mathbf{g}] = (g_{11}g_{22} - (g_{12})^2) > 0. \qquad (3.30)$$

The compatibility equations are as follows:

$$(b_{11})_v - (b_{12})_u = b_{11}\Gamma_{12}^1 + b_{12}(\Gamma_{12}^2 - \Gamma_{11}^1) - b_{22}\Gamma_{11}^2 \qquad (3.31)$$

$$(b_{12})_v - (b_{22})_u = b_{11}\Gamma_{22}^1 + b_{12}(\Gamma_{22}^2 - \Gamma_{21}^1) - b_{22}\Gamma_{21}^2 \qquad (3.32)$$

$$\det[\mathbf{b}] = b_{11}b_{22} - (b_{12})^2 = g_{12}\left((\Gamma_{22}^2)_u - (\Gamma_{12}^2)_v\right) + \qquad (3.33)$$

$$g_{12}\left(\Gamma_{22}^1\Gamma_{11}^2 - \Gamma_{12}^1\Gamma_{12}^2\right) + g_{11}\left((\Gamma_{22}^1)_u - (\Gamma_{12}^1)_v\right) +$$

$$g_{11}\left(\Gamma_{22}^1\Gamma_{11}^1 + \Gamma_{22}^2\Gamma_{12}^1 - \Gamma_{12}^1\Gamma_{12}^1 - \Gamma_{12}^2\Gamma_{22}^1\right)$$

The first two compatibility equations are known as the Mainardi-Codazzi equations. The third compatibility equation is a statement that the determinant of the second fundamental form matrix is a function of only the metric and is therefore an intrinsic property of the surface. This equation may be written in several different forms. It is known as the Gauss equation because it proves the *Theorema Egregium* of Gauss, which states that Gaussian curvature is a function of only E,F,G and their derivatives.

Uniqueness: If two surfaces S and S^* possess fundamental form matrices g_{ij} and b_{ij} and g_{ij}^* and b_{ij}^* respectively such that the following matrix equalities hold at every point of the two surfaces

$$g_{ij} = g_{ij}^* \qquad b_{ij} = b_{ij}^*, \qquad (3.34)$$

then there exists an appropriate translation and rotation such that S and S^* coincide exactly implying they have the same shape.

This tells us that arbitrary smooth surface shape is captured by six scalar functions: $g_{11}, g_{12}, g_{22}, b_{11}, b_{12}, b_{22}$ (the E,F,G,L,M,N functions).

It is difficult to interpret what each of these functions are individually telling us about surface shape however. There are several combinations of these functions that yield more easily interpretable surface shape characteristics. Particularly, there are two curvature functions, mean curvature (H) and Gaussian curvature (K), that combine the information in the six E,F,G,L,M,N functions in two different ways. These two curvature functions do not, in general, contain all the "3-D shape information" contained in the six E,F,G,L,M,N functions, but they do contain a substantial amount of useful information, which is described subsequently.

Under certain sets of constraints, the two curvature functions individually contain essentially all 3-D shape information. For compact, *convex* surfaces (where $LN > M^2$ at every point), there is a *single scalar function* (the Gaussian curvature function $K(u,v)$) that uniquely specifies surface shape [Chern 1957] [Hsiung 1981] [Minkowski 1897] [Horn 1984]. This is the Gaussian Curvature Uniqueness Theorem for convex surfaces. It can be shown that if simply-connected bounded regions of positive Gaussian curvature are isolated, then surface shape is uniquely determined within those regions if the Gaussian curvature function of the surface is known. Conditions are discussed later where the mean curvature function uniquely determines graph surface shape. It is called the Mean Curvature Uniqueness Theorem for graph surfaces. In addition, if a surface patch is completely free of umbilic points, mean and Gaussian curvature functions combined with the principal direction functions provide a unique description of the surface patch shape [Liang 1987].

3.3   Surface Curvature

It is established that general 3-D smooth surfaces are uniquely characterized by six scalar functions that completely determine surface shape and intrinsic surface geometry. These six functions are the independent elements of two 2 x 2 symmetric matrix functions of the surface. Two curvature functions that combine the information from the six E,F,G,L,M,N functions are now examined.

The shape operator (Weingarten mapping) matrix $[\beta]$ was defined in the previous section as the matrix product $[\mathbf{g}^{-1}][\mathbf{b}]$. Hence, the $[\beta]$ matrix combines the first and second fundamental form matrices into one matrix. This matrix is a linear operator that maps vectors in the tangent plane to other vectors in the tangent plane at each point on a surface. The metric $[\mathbf{g}]$ is the generalization of the speed of a planar curve whereas the shape operator $[\beta]$ is a generalization of the curvature of a planar curve. The *Gaussian curvature* function K of a surface can be defined from the first and second fundamental form matrices as the determinant of the shape operator matrix function as follows:

$$K = \det[\beta] = \det\left(\begin{bmatrix} g_{11} & g_{12} \\ g_{21} & g_{22} \end{bmatrix}^{-1}\right) \det\left(\begin{bmatrix} b_{11} & b_{12} \\ b_{21} & b_{22} \end{bmatrix}\right). \qquad (3.35)$$

The *mean curvature* function of a surface can be defined similarly as half the trace of the shape operator matrix function as follows:

$$H = \frac{1}{2}\text{tr}[\beta] = \frac{1}{2}\text{tr}\left(\begin{bmatrix} g_{11} & g_{12} \\ g_{21} & g_{22} \end{bmatrix}^{-1} \begin{bmatrix} b_{11} & b_{12} \\ b_{21} & b_{22} \end{bmatrix}\right). \qquad (3.36)$$

Hence, these two surface curvature functions are obtained by mapping the two fundamental form matrix functions into a single scalar function. The surface curvature functions (H and K) are the "natural" algebraic invariants of the shape operator. The natural algebraic invariants of a matrix are the coefficients of the characteristic polynomial of the matrix. Since a 2x2 matrix only has two natural algebraic invariants (the trace and determinant), these two surface curvature functions arise naturally in the analysis of surface curvature.

There are other ways of looking at surface curvature based on the curves that lie in the surface. At each point on a surface, there is a direction of maximum normal curvature and a direction of minimum normal curvature for all space curves that (1) lie in the surface, (2) pass through that point, and (3) have curve normals that align with the surface normal at that point. If κ_1 denotes the maximum principal curvature (the maximum of the normal curvature function) and κ_2 denotes the minimum principal curvature (the minimum of the normal curvature function), then one can compute the Gaussian and mean curvature in terms of these principal curvatures:

$$K = \kappa_1 \kappa_2 \qquad H = \frac{(\kappa_1 + \kappa_2)}{2}. \tag{3.37}$$

The principal curvatures κ_1 and κ_2 are the two roots of the quadratic equation:

$$\kappa^2 - 2H\kappa + K = 0. \tag{3.38}$$

Hence, if K and H are known at each point in a range image, it is straightforward to analytically determine the two principal curvatures:

$$\kappa_{1,2} = H \pm \sqrt{H^2 - K} \tag{3.39}$$

If $H^2 = K$ at a surface point, the point is known as an *umbilic* point to denote that the principal curvatures are equal and every direction is a principal direction. In other terms, the normal curvature function at an umbilic point is constant. A surface must be either locally flat or spherical in the neighborhood of an umbilic point.

The principal curvatures κ_1 and κ_2 are a perfectly valid pair of surface curvature descriptors, which are analytically equivalent to the mean and Gaussian curvature pair. The principal curvatures are the two eigenvalues of the 2x2 matrix shape operator and the extrema of the normal curvature function. They specify the curvature of surface curves in the directions of maximal and minimal normal curvature at each point. The two curvatures $\{H, K\}$ are compared to the principal curvatures $\{\kappa_1, \kappa_2\}$:

1. Principal curvature values should be associated with the corresponding principal directions for meaningful interpretation whereas mean and Gaussian curvature values are direction-free quantities. Hence, extra overhead is required with principal curvatures if the extra information in the principal directions is stored. The principal direction information is very important, and quite useful in its own right, but this comparison is between two scalar curvature values considered alone.

(a) Surface Types from Principal Curvature Signs

	$\kappa_1 < 0$	$\kappa_1 = 0$	$\kappa_1 > 0$
$\kappa_2 < 0$	peak	ridge	saddle
$\kappa_2 = 0$	ridge	flat	valley
$\kappa_2 > 0$	saddle	valley	pit

(b) Surface Types from Mean and Gaussian Curvature Signs

	$K < 0$	$K = 0$	$K > 0$
$H < 0$	peak	ridge	saddle ridge
$H = 0$	(none)	flat	minimal
$H > 0$	pit	valley	saddle valley

Figure 3.4: Surface Types Determined By Surface Curvature Signs

2. If only the signs of the principal curvatures are used to determine basic surface types, six surface types result: peak, pit, ridge, valley, flat, and saddle as shown in Figure 3.4(a). The signs of mean and Gaussian curvature yield *eight* basic surface types, as shown in Figure 3.4(b), because saddle surfaces can be resolved into saddle ridge, saddle valley, and minimal surfaces. Figure 3.5 shows the shapes of the eight surfaces. Note K cannot be strictly positive if H is zero.

3. Gaussian curvature exhibits isometric invariance properties that are not exhibited by either of the principal curvatures. In other terms, Gaussian curvature is an intrinsic property of a surface. Both principal curvatures and the mean curvature are extrinsic properties of a surface. Isometric invariance and intrinsic and extrinsic properties are discussed below in more detail.

4. The mean curvature is the average of the principal curvatures. Therefore, it is slightly less sensitive to noise in numerical computations than the principal curvatures. Gaussian curvature is more sensitive to noise.

5. The Gaussian curvature function of a convex surface uniquely determines the surface according to the Gaussian Curvature Uniqueness Theorem. A single principal curvature function does not permit a comparable theorem because of its directional nature.

6. As discussed in the Mean Curvature Uniqueness Theorem section later in this chapter, the mean curvature function of a graph surface taken together with the boundary curve of a graph surface uniquely determines the graph surface from which it was computed. Range

images are sampled graph surfaces. A single principal curvature function does not permit a comparable theorem because of its directional nature.

7. A few more numerical computations are required to compute principal curvatures as compared to mean and Gaussian curvature. Moreover, it is extremely simple to compute the sign of the mean and Gaussian curvature whereas principal curvature sign computations are more involved when given only partial derivatives.

The combination of surface curvature with principal directions is a richer description than surface curvature alone, but our interest here is in what can be concluded directly from only two scalar values at each point on a surface. To summarize, the pair $\{\kappa_1, \kappa_2\}$ contain the same surface curvature information as the pair $\{H, K\}$, but in a different form. There can be advantages and disadvantages working with either pair depending on the application. Brady et al.[1985] favored the principal curvatures and principal directions to form a line of curvature mesh surface description. Medioni and Nevatia [1984] worked with another pair of surface curvatures: $\{\kappa_1, K\}$. The same surface curvature information is maintained. For visible-invariant pixel labeling purposes, the sign of the mean and Gaussian curvatures can be computed most easily yielding the finest classification of surface types in image data.

The mathematical properties of the Gaussian curvature K and the mean curvature H are now discussed in more detail to stress the importance of these quantities to surface characterization and to give a better, more complete understanding of their qualities.

1. Gaussian and mean curvature are invariant to arbitrary transformations of the (u, v)-parameters of a surface as long as the Jacobian of the (u, v)-transformation is always non-zero (see theorem and proof in Appendix A). In contrast, the six E,F,G,L,M,N functions all *vary* with (u, v)-transformations. This means that the E,F,G,L,M,N functions depend directly on the choice of the u, v coordinate system even though they uniquely characterize the 3-D shape of the surface. Therefore, it is not desirable to use these six functions as shape characteristics because of their dependence on parameterization. Different views of the same surface yield different image parameterizations of the range image functions.

2. Gaussian and mean curvature are invariant to arbitrary rotations and translations of a surface because of the invariance of the E,F,G,L,M,N functions to rotations and translations (see theorem and proof in Appendix A). This is clear from the definition of these functions and the properties of dot products and cross products. Rotational and translational invariance necessary for viewpoint independent surface shape characteristics.

3. Gaussian curvature is an *isometric invariant* of a surface. An isometric invariant is a surface property that depends only on the E,F,G functions (and possibly their derivatives). Consider that any surface S with Gaussian curvature K may be mapped to any other surface S^* with Gaussian Curvature K^*. If the mapping is a distance-preserving isometric bijection, then $K = K^*$ at corresponding points on the two surfaces. An isometric mapping of surfaces is a continuous mapping where corresponding arcs on the surfaces have the same length.

4. Isometric invariants are also known as intrinsic surface properties. Therefore, Gaussian Curvature is an intrinsic surface quantity. Intrinsic properties have interesting properties for shape description. For example, the Gaussian curvature function K of a surface does not "care" how the surface is embedded in a higher dimensional space. In contrast, the mean curvature function H does care about the embedding; it is an extrinsic surface quantity and is not an isometric invariant. The surface defined by a sheet of paper is readily used to demonstrate these ideas: If the paper lies flat on a desk top, $K = 0$ and $H = 0$ at each point on the sheet of paper. If the paper is bent making sure that no kinks occur, it is still true that $K = 0$, but $H \neq 0$. When the paper bends, the way in which the surface is embedded in 3-D space changes, but the intrinsic properties of the surface do not change. The within-surface distances between points on the paper remain the same, and the interior angles of a triangle still sum to π radians. Gaussian curvature is intrinsic whereas mean curvature is extrinsic. If the paper were deformed as if it were made of rubber, then Gaussian curvature would change as well as mean curvature. Surface area is another type of intrinsic surface property.

5. Another way of looking at intrinsic properties is that they do not change sign when the direction of the normal vector of the surface is reversed. Outward-pointing normals are usually chosen for surfaces of objects. If the surface is just an orientable surface patch floating in space, the surface normal could be chosen to point in either direction. Gaussian curvature maintains its sign when the direction of the normal vector is flipped whereas mean curvature flips its sign. This is because the first fundamental form does not depend on the surface normal vector whereas the second fundamental form does.

6. Gaussian Curvature indicates *intrinsic surface shape* at individual surface points. When $K(u, v) > 0$ at the surface point $\vec{x}(u, v)$, then the surface is elliptic (*locally shaped like an ellipsoid*) in the neighborhood of that point. When $K(u, v) < 0$, the surface is hyperbolic (*locally saddle-shaped*). When $K(u, v) = 0$, the surface is parabolic: locally flat, cone-shaped, ridge-shaped, or valley-shaped. Mean curvature helps to describe surface shape at individual surface points

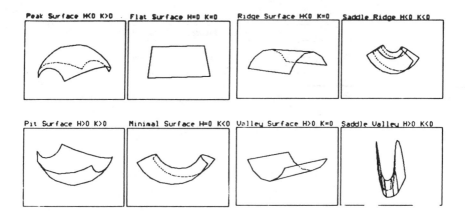

Figure 3.5: The Eight Visible-Invariant HK-Sign Surface Types

when considered together with the Gaussian curvature. Figure 3.5 shows drawings of the eight basic surface shapes. If $H < 0$ and $K = 0$, the surface is locally ridge shaped. If $H > 0$ and $K = 0$, the surface is locally valley shaped. If $H = 0$ and $K = 0$, the surface is locally flat or planar. If $H < 0$ and $K > 0$, the surface is locally ellipsoidal and peaked, i.e., the surface bulges in the direction of the surface normal. If $H > 0$ and $K > 0$, the surface is locally ellipsoidal and cupped, i.e., the surface bulges in the direction opposite that of the surface normal. If $K > 0$, one can never have $H = 0$. When $K < 0$, $H \neq 0$ indicates if the saddle surface is predominantly valley shaped ($H > 0$) or ridge shaped ($H < 0$). When $H = 0$ at every point on a surface, then that surface is referred to as a *minimal* surface. Minimal surfaces have many interesting mathematical properties [Osserman 1969] and are often studied in texts on partial differential equations. The eight surface types above are the only possible local surface types for smooth surfaces.

Note that each of the fundamental visible-invariant surface types is necessarily a simply shaped surface that can be well approximated by low-order polynomial surface functions. The key property of the sign of surface curvature characteristic is that arbitrary surfaces can be partitioned into a disjoint union of relatively simple surfaces no matter how complicated they might appear. This is the *smooth surface decomposition* concept. It is proposed that these basic HK-sign surface types form a set of symbolic primitives upon which a theory of image segmentation can be built. Meaningful smooth surfaces of finite area in a range scene may consist either of a single HK-sign surface primitive or a set of HK-sign surface primitives. This implies that adjacent smoothly joining HK-sign surface primitives may need

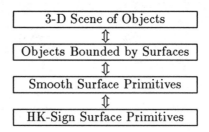

Figure 3.6: Segmentation Hierarchy of Geometric Entities

to be merged together to yield the perceived smooth surfaces of a scene as discussed in Chapter 5. Hence, there is a segmentation hierarchy for range image interpretation formed by the HK-sign surface primitives at the lowest level, the smooth surface primitives consisting of HK-sign surface primitives, the objects bounded by smooth surfaces, and the scene consisting of those objects at the highest level. This hierarchy of geometric entities is shown in Figure 3.6.

7. Gaussian and mean curvature are *local* surface properties. This allows surface curvature to be used in situations where *occlusion* is a problem because K and H do not depend on global properties of a surface.

8. As a final note of comparison between H and K, a spherical surface of radius a has constant mean curvature $H = \pm 1/a$ at every point on the surface where the sign depends on the direction of the outward or inward pointing normal. The spherical surface also has constant Gaussian curvature $K = 1/a^2$ at every point *independent* of the direction of the normal vector. This also points out the dimensions of the curvature quantities and indicates how these quantities will change under 3-D scale transformations.

There are many other interesting properties of Gaussian and mean curvature, but the above list highlights most of the relevant ones for our purposes.

If the sign of the surface curvature is reliably and accurately computed from high-resolution digital surfaces, these facts could be used directly by a surface matching algorithm to quickly reject false hypotheses. When two surfaces have exactly the same shape, they can be made to coincide via a rotation and a translation and are therefore said to be *congruent*. Congruence implies that an isometry exists between the two surfaces *and* that the shape operators of the two surfaces are equivalent. If the two surfaces are congruent, then there exists a matching between the mean and Gaussian curvature values at every point on the two surfaces. This implies that there is a matching between regions of constant sign of the mean and Gaussian curvatures on the two surfaces. Therefore, if there does not exist

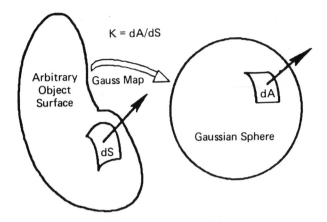

Figure 3.7: Gaussian Curvature is the Gauss Mapping Derivative

a matching between regions of constant sign of the mean and Gaussian curvatures of the two surfaces, then the two surfaces cannot be congruent and therefore cannot have the same 3-D shape. Since a combined mean and Gaussian curvature sign image has only eight levels, it may be possible to easily discard surfaces that do not have similar shape. Quick dismissal of false hypotheses is important for efficient matching algorithms.

Gaussian curvature and/or mean curvature can be defined and/or computed in several different ways:

1. **Gauss Map Derivative Definition for Convex Surfaces:** To give this definition, it is necessary to describe the Gauss map, which is shown pictorially in Figure 3.7. The Gauss mapping maps a point on a surface to a point on the unit sphere using information about the surface normal at the point. The unit surface normals at the surface points within the area ΔS on the surface are arranged in the unit sphere so that the tail of each normal vector is located at the sphere's center and the tip of the normal vector lies on the unit sphere's surface while preserving the direction of the normal vector. The solid angle on the unit sphere subtended by these corresponding normal vectors is denoted ΔA. The Gaussian curvature can be defined using the limit of the ratio of these two quantities if the surface is convex

$$ K = \lim_{\Delta S \to 0} \frac{\Delta A}{\Delta S}. \qquad (3.40) $$

This definition can be extended to handle non-convex surfaces, but solid angle computations must account for folds in the Gauss map where multiple distinct surface points map to the same surface normal.

2. **Parallel Transport Definition** [Misner et al.1973] [Abelson and diSessa 1980]: Suppose you start at a point P on a surface holding a vector that always points in the same direction, similar to a gyroscope. That direction is marked permanently on the surface at the starting point. You go for a walk while holding the vector by leaving the point P and later returning to it without crossing your path so that the path has enclosed an area ΔS. When arriving back at P, you compare the direction of your current vector with the reference direction, which was marked when you left the point, to obtain the angle $\Delta \alpha$. The Gaussian curvature of the surface at the point P is defined as

$$K = \lim_{\Delta S \to 0} \frac{\Delta \alpha}{\Delta S}. \tag{3.41}$$

The *sign* of K is given correctly here. This equation again shows a fundamental relationship between angles, area, and curvature on a surface.

3. **Gauss Map Jacobian Definition:** This definition is closely related to the area derivative definition, but in this case, K can be defined in terms of the surface normal and the u- and v-tangent vectors as

$$K = \frac{\|\vec{n}_u \times \vec{n}_v\|}{\|\vec{x}_u \times \vec{x}_v\|} \quad \text{where} \quad \vec{n} = \frac{\vec{x}_u \times \vec{x}_v}{\|\vec{x}_u \times \vec{x}_v\|}. \tag{3.42}$$

4. **Fundamental Form Matrix Coefficients Definitions:** Let $g = \det[\mathbf{g}]$ and $b = \det[\mathbf{b}]$. These definitions of K and H are an explicit statement of the first matrix definitions given earlier

$$K = \frac{b}{g} = \frac{b_{11}b_{22} - (b_{12})^2}{g_{11}g_{22} - (g_{12})^2} = \frac{LN - M^2}{EG - F^2} \tag{3.43}$$

$$H = \frac{g_{11}b_{22} + g_{22}b_{11} - 2g_{12}b_{12}}{2(g_{11}g_{22} - (g_{12})^2)} = \frac{EN + GL - 2FM}{2(EG - F^2)}. \tag{3.44}$$

5. **Partial Derivative Expressions:** K and H can be expressed directly in terms of partial derivatives of the parameterization if desired. The triple-vector product notation $[\ \vec{a}\ \vec{b}\ \vec{c}\ ] = \vec{a} \cdot (\vec{b} \times \vec{c})$ is used to simplify the expressions

$$K = \frac{[\vec{x}_{uu}\vec{x}_u\vec{x}_v][\vec{x}_{vv}\vec{x}_u\vec{x}_v] - [\vec{x}_{uv}\vec{x}_u\vec{x}_v]^2}{\|\vec{x}_u \times \vec{x}_v\|^4} \tag{3.45}$$

$$H = \frac{\vec{x}_v \cdot \vec{x}_v[\vec{x}_{uu}\vec{x}_u\vec{x}_v] + \vec{x}_u \cdot \vec{x}_u[\vec{x}_{vv}\vec{x}_u\vec{x}_v] - 2\vec{x}_u \cdot \vec{x}_v[\vec{x}_{uv}\vec{x}_u\vec{x}_v]}{2\|\vec{x}_u \times \vec{x}_v\|^3}.$$
$$\tag{3.46}$$

A few of the many different ways of looking at the mean and Gaussian curvature of a surface have been summarized. This list was intended to further stress the properties of these functions as shape descriptors and indicate how they are computed given a general surface parameterization. These two curvature functions are both *nonlinear* combinations of the six E,F,G,L,M,N functions.

The most important invariance properties of surface curvature for view-independent range image object recognition are the following: (1) invariance under changes in (u,v)-parameterization and (2) invariance under 3-D translations and 3-D rotations. The proofs are given in Appendix A. In addition, mean curvature H significantly complements Gaussian curvature K and vice versa in determining surface shape because H is extrinsic whereas K is intrinsic. Only *eight* basic local surface types are possible as discussed above, and these types are determined solely from the signs of the mean and Gaussian curvature. When K and H are considered together, they provide a good generalization of the curvature function of space curves. There are other functions of the E,F,G,L,M,N functions that are also useful, such as principal curvatures, but it has been shown that the emphasis on K and H is reasonable. Of course, it is easy to compute principal curvatures if mean and Gaussian curvature are already known and vice versa. It has not been proved that K and H are the optimal surface characteristics with respect to any criterion, but substantial justification has been given for their use as surface characteristics.

3.4 Graph Surface Curvature from Derivatives

Arbitrary 3-D surface shape is well characterized by two scalar functions, Gaussian curvature and mean curvature, which are independent of parameterization and invariant to rotations and translations. Given a range image with only discretely sampled, quantized data, how can one compute meaningful surface curvatures? To compute surface curvature from digital range images, estimates of the first and second partial derivatives of the range image function are needed. In this section, expressions for K and H are simplified for graph surfaces (Monge patches) because all range images and intensity images are sampled graph surfaces.

First, note that the parameterization for a graph surface takes a very simple form: $\vec{x}(u,v) = [u \ v \ f(u,v)]^T$. The T superscript indicates transpose so that $\vec{x}$ is column vector by convention. This yields the following formulas for the surface partial derivatives and the surface normal:

$$\vec{x}_u = [1 \ 0 \ f_u]^T$$

$$\vec{x}_v = [0 \ 1 \ f_v]^T$$

$$\vec{x}_{uu} = [0 \ 0 \ f_{uu}]^T \qquad (3.47)$$

$$\vec{x}_{vv} = [0 \ 0 \ f_{vv}]^T$$

$$\vec{x}_{uv} = [0 \ 0 \ f_{uv}]^T$$

$$\vec{n} = \frac{1}{\sqrt{1 + f_u^2 + f_v^2}}[-f_u \ -f_v \ 1]^T. \tag{3.48}$$

These vectors are combined using the dot product definitions given earlier to form the six fundamental form coefficients:

$$E = g_{11} = 1 + f_u^2 \qquad F = g_{12} = f_u f_v \qquad G = g_{22} = 1 + f_v^2 \tag{3.49}$$

$$L = b_{11} = \frac{f_{uu}}{\sqrt{1 + f_u^2 + f_v^2}}$$

$$M = b_{12} = \frac{f_{uv}}{\sqrt{1 + f_u^2 + f_v^2}} \tag{3.50}$$

$$N = b_{22} = \frac{f_{vv}}{\sqrt{1 + f_u^2 + f_v^2}}.$$

Hence, the five partial derivatives $f_u, f_v, f_{uu}, f_{uv}, f_{vv}$ are all that is needed to compute the six fundamental form coefficient functions for a graph surface.

Next, recall that Gaussian curvature is the ratio of the determinants of the two fundamental form matrices. This ratio is written directly in terms of the graph surface function derivatives as follows:

$$K = \frac{f_{uu}f_{vv} - f_{uv}^2}{(1 + f_u^2 + f_v^2)^2} = \frac{\det(\nabla\nabla^T f)}{(1 + \|\nabla f\|^2)^2} \tag{3.51}$$

where ∇ is the 2-D (u, v) gradient operator, and $\nabla\nabla^T$ is the Hessian matrix operator. Hence, if given a graph surface function $f(u, v)$ that possesses first and second partial derivatives, the Gaussian curvature can be computed directly.

Mean curvature is half the trace of the shape operator. It can also be written directly in terms of the graph surface function derivatives as follows:

$$H = \frac{1}{2}\frac{(1 + f_v^2)f_{uu} + (1 + f_u^2)f_{vv} - 2f_u f_v f_{uv}}{(1 + f_u^2 + f_v^2)^{3/2}} \tag{3.52}$$

$$= \frac{1}{2}\nabla \cdot \left(\frac{\nabla f}{\sqrt{1 + \|\nabla f\|^2}}\right).$$

where $(\nabla \cdot)$ is the divergence operator of vector calculus. Again, if given a graph surface function $f(u, v)$ that possesses first and second partial derivatives, the mean curvature can be computed directly.

3.4.1 Mean Curvature Uniqueness Theorem

It is important to note that the graph surface expression for H above (where H is known but f is not) is a non-homogeneous second-order elliptic quasilinear partial differential equation, which is known as the equation of prescribed mean curvature. If D is a subset of $\Re^2$ and H is an arbitrary function of two variables with continuous first partial derivatives defined over D, it is not possible to say whether or not a solution to the differential equation above even exists. By imposing certain restrictions, it is sometimes possible to prove the existence and the uniqueness of solutions.

Guisti [1978] proved that under certain extremal conditions, H alone *without Dirichlet boundary conditions* can *uniquely* determine f up to an additive constant (translations in the range z). Also, Gilbarg and Trudinger [1983] show that, under a set of certain other conditions (which include the restriction that the *boundary curve's* curvature must be greater than or equal to the absolute value of the sum of the principal curvatures of the surface at the boundary of the domain), there exists a unique solution f to the Dirichlet boundary value problem defined by H plus the function f restricted to the boundary of the region D.

There is a separate uniqueness theorem [Gilbarg and Trudinger 1983] that does not address existence which states that if (1) H is continuously differentiable, (2) f_1 and f_2 are both solutions to the partial differential equation above in D, and (3) $f_1 = f_2$ on the boundary of the domain D, then $f_1 = f_2$ throughout that domain. In this sense, a smooth surface function $f(u, v)$ defined over a compact domain D with a simple closed contour boundary ∂D is essentially equivalent to that surface's mean curvature function H taken together with the boundary curve of the surface f restricted to ∂D. Hence, H plus f on ∂D constitute an ideal type of graph surface characteristic. All "information" present in the original smooth range image function is maintained in the characteristic data. Given $f(u, v)$, one can compute $H(u, v)$, and, in theory, the Dirichlet problem can be solved to reproduce $f(u, v)$.

It must be stressed that this uniqueness property of the mean curvature function is only valid for graph surfaces. But since all range images and all intensity images are sampled graph surfaces, this is an important property for digital surface characterization. This mean curvature uniqueness theorem and the uniqueness theorem for positive Gaussian surfaces mentioned earlier indicate that the mean and Gaussian curvature substantially constrain visible graph surface shapes. Mean and Gaussian curvature together with the principal direction functions uniquely determine the shape of negative Gaussian curvature surfaces.

Since any digital image may be approximated arbitrarily well by a sufficiently smooth function that possesses first and second partial derivatives, the next problem to be addressed is computing estimates of these partial derivatives given the sampled data.

3.5   Estimating Derivatives of Digital Surfaces

Direct numerical differentiation is generally discouraged on all but the cleanest signal data because it tends to amplify noise and obscure signal content. Better derivative estimates have been obtained by combining data smoothing techniques with the differencing operations needed to estimate a derivative. The basic approach in the currently implemented method is the following: (1) given discrete sample data, determine a continuous differentiable function that best fits the data with respect to some criterion, and (2) compute the derivatives of the continuous function analytically and evaluate them at the corresponding discrete points. Ideally, it might be desirable to fit all data with one smooth surface, such as a smoothing spline. These methods are computationally expensive, have their own problems in derivative estimation near discontinuities, and should only be used if simpler, more efficient methods do not work well enough. For our purposes, a local least squares surface fit is computed within the $N \times N$ window around each pixel of the digital surface using separable convolutions, and the experimental results show that this approach is adequate. This method is based on a local least squares surface model using discrete orthogonal polynomials, which has been discussed in [Anderson and Houseman 1942] [Prewitt 1970] [Beaudet 1978] [Haralick and Watson 1981] [Bolle and Cooper 1984] [Haralick 1984]. For this reason, only the final results of the analysis that are required to implement the local quadratic surface approach are stated here.

Each data point in a given $N \times N$ window is associated with a position (u, v) from the set $U \times U$, where for convenience N is assumed odd:

$$U = \{-(N-1)/2, \ldots, -1, 0, 1, \ldots, (N-1)/2\}. \qquad (3.53)$$

The following discrete orthogonal polynomials provide local biquadratic surface fitting capability:

$$\phi_0(u) = 1, \quad \phi_1(u) = u, \quad \phi_2(u) = \left(u^2 - M(M+1)/3\right) \qquad (3.54)$$

where $M = (N-1)/2$. The biquadratic is the minimal degree polynomial surface type needed to estimated first and second partial derivatives. A corresponding set of $b_i(u)$ functions are the normalized versions of the orthogonal polynomials $\phi_i(u)$ given by $b_i(u) = \phi_i(u)/P_i(M)$ where the $P_i(M)$ are normalizing constants (polynomials in M), which are defined as $P_i(M) = \sum_u \phi_i^2(u)$. The three normalization constants are given by

$$P_0(M) = N \qquad P_1(M) = \frac{2}{3}M^3 + M^2 + \frac{1}{3}M \qquad (3.55)$$

$$P_2(M) = \frac{8}{45}M^5 + \frac{4}{9}M^4 + \frac{2}{9}M^3 - \frac{1}{9}M^2 - \frac{1}{15}M.$$

The normalized $b_i(u)$ basis functions and the $\phi_i(u)$ basis functions satisfy the orthogonality relationship

$$\sum_{u \in U} \phi_i(u) b_j(u) = \delta_{ij} \qquad (3.56)$$

where $\delta_{ij} = 1$ if $i = j$ and $\delta_{ij} = 0$ otherwise (the Kronecker delta). There is nothing unique about the way these functions are defined with respect to the normalization constants. The normalization constants of the $b_i(u)$ functions could just as well have been grouped with the $\phi_i(u)$ functions, or the square root of the normalization constants could have been grouped with both functions so that there would be no distinction between them. The latter is perhaps the most common practice, but in image processing, it is convenient to have rational normalization constants with no square roots so that integer arithmetic can be used after appropriate scaling of quantities by the denominator.

The recipe for computing derivatives at a sample point using odd size data windows is simple since the $b_i(u)$ vectors may be precomputed for any given window size, and convolved with the image data to provide derivative estimates. A surface function estimate $\hat{f}(u, v)$ is obtained in the form

$$\hat{f}(u, v) = \sum_{i+j \leq 2} a_{ij} \phi_i(u) \phi_j(v) \qquad (3.57)$$

that minimizes the total square error term

$$\epsilon^2 = \sum_{(u,v) \in U^2} (f(u, v) - \hat{f}(u, v))^2. \qquad (3.58)$$

The solution for the unknown coefficients is given by

$$a_{ij} = \sum_{(u,v) \in U^2} f(u, v) b_i(u) b_j(v). \qquad (3.59)$$

The first and second partial derivative estimates are then given by

$$f_u = a_{10} \quad f_v = a_{01} \quad f_{uv} = a_{11} \quad f_{uu} = 2a_{20} \quad f_{vv} = 2a_{02}. \qquad (3.60)$$

The total fit error is computed after the a_{ij} coefficients are determined:

$$\epsilon^2 = \sum_{(u,v) \in U^2} f^2(u, v) - \sum_{i,j} P_i(M) P_j(M) a_{ij}^2. \qquad (3.61)$$

Since the discrete orthogonal quadratic polynomials over the 2-D window are separable in u and v as shown in the above equations, partial derivative estimates can be computed for an entire range image using a separable convolution operator. This is much more efficient than non-separable convolution operations on a general purpose computer. These derivative estimates can then be plugged into the equations for the Gaussian curvature and the mean curvature. This describes all the mathematical details necessary to compute curvature functions $K(u, v)$ and $H(u, v)$ given samples from a continuous range image function $f(u, v)$.

The disadvantages of this local surface fit method are the following:

1. A different quadratic surface is fitted to the neighborhood of each point. No compatibility constraints are imposed on these surfaces so that the net continuous surface interpretation is meaningful. To correct this, one needs to make *a priori* assumptions about the digital surface data, such as a surface smoothness assumption. Making assumptions of this type is contrary to the data-driven goal of using as few *a priori* assumptions as possible. It may be possible to achieve better partial derivative estimates without making more restrictive assumptions via more computationally intensive methods, but the experience of many researchers indicates that this approach, also known as *Haralick's local facet model* approach, is one of the best image derivative estimation methods for the amount of computation required.

2. Intuition is contradicted when all columns (or rows) in a least squares derivative window operator are weighted equally. If one requests a 9x9 window least squares estimate of the first derivative of a range image at a particular pixel, the data that runs four pixels away has the same impact on the final estimate as does the data that runs directly through the pixel where the derivative is being estimated. This situation can be modified using weighted least squares techniques. The question then arises: What is the best assignment of weights? One might well argue that Gaussian or binomial weights should be used. Empirical evidence showed that the results differ only for large window sizes. Rather than explicitly changing the weights in the large windows used for surface curvature estimates, a binomial weight pre-smoothing filter is used before equally-weighted derivative window operators are applied. As described below, such a step can save computation in this surface characterization algorithm as well as providing a better weighting scheme.

There are other approaches to computing intrinsic differential geometric properties, such as Gaussian curvature. One interesting method that does not require partial derivative estimation is discussed in Appendix B. It requires more computation, it is only useful for intrinsic characteristics, and the experimental results were not as good as the local surface fit method. Despite the disadvantages listed above and the existence of other methods, good quality results have been consistently obtained here and elsewhere using the local surface fit (local facet model) approach.

It was found that relatively large $N \times N$ window sizes were needed to compute reliable estimates of surface curvature. Since it is necessary to compute five different derivative estimates, the image could be smoothed first with a small $L \times L$ window operator (L odd) where the smoothed values could be stored with higher precision. This intermediate smoothed image could then be convolved with small $M \times M$ derivative estimation window operators (M odd) where $L + M = N + 1$ to achieve the same results as the $N \times N$ windows. Assuming window separability and linear time requirements, the $N \times N$ windows require time proportional to $5N$ whereas the $L \times L$ smoothing and $M \times M$ derivative windows require time proportional to $N + 4M + 1 < 5N$. For example, one 7x7 binomial weight (approximately Gaussian) smoother and five 7x7 equally-weighted least squares derivative estimation operators save about 30% of the computations required for the equivalent 13x13 windows. These window operators are listed explicitly below.

Since all operators are separable, window masks can be computed as the outer product of two column vectors. The binomial smoothing window may be written as $[S] = \vec{s}\,\vec{s}^T$ where the column vector $\vec{s}$ is given by

$$\vec{s} = \frac{1}{64} \begin{bmatrix} 1 & 6 & 15 & 20 & 15 & 6 & 1 \end{bmatrix}^T \tag{3.62}$$

For a 7x7 binomial smoothing window, it is clear that an extra 12 bits ($12 = 2\log_2(64)$) of fractional information should be maintained in the intermediate smoothed image result. For an $L \times L$ binomial smoother, $2L - 2$ bits of fractional information must be maintained. The equally-weighted least squares derivative estimation window operators are given by

$$\begin{array}{ll} [D_u] = \vec{d_0}\,\vec{d_1}^T & [D_v] = \vec{d_1}\,\vec{d_0}^T \\ [D_{uu}] = \vec{d_0}\,\vec{d_2}^T & [D_{vv}] = \vec{d_2}\,\vec{d_0}^T \quad [D_{uv}] = \vec{d_1}\,\vec{d_1}^T \end{array} \tag{3.63}$$

where the column vectors $\vec{d_0}, \vec{d_1}, \vec{d_2}$ for a 7x7 window are given by

$$\vec{d_0} = \frac{1}{7} \begin{bmatrix} 1 & 1 & 1 & 1 & 1 & 1 & 1 \end{bmatrix}^T \tag{3.64}$$

$$\vec{d_1} = \frac{1}{28} \begin{bmatrix} -3 & -2 & -1 & 0 & 1 & 2 & 3 \end{bmatrix}^T \tag{3.65}$$

$$\vec{d_2} = \frac{1}{84} \begin{bmatrix} 5 & 0 & -3 & -4 & -3 & 0 & 5 \end{bmatrix}^T . \tag{3.66}$$

The partial derivative estimate images are computed via the appropriate 2-D image convolutions (denoted $*$):

$$f_u = D_u * S * f \qquad f_v = D_v * S * f \tag{3.67}$$

$$f_{uu} = D_{uu} * S * f \qquad f_{vv} = D_{vv} * S * f \qquad f_{uv} = D_{uv} * S * f. \tag{3.68}$$

The mean curvature and Gaussian curvature images are pixel-wise combinations of these derivative images. A toleranced signum function

$$\operatorname{sgn}_\epsilon(x) = \begin{cases} +1 & \text{if } x > \epsilon \\ 0 & \text{if } |x| \le \epsilon \\ -1 & \text{if } x < \epsilon \end{cases} \tag{3.69}$$

is used to compute the individual surface curvature sign images $\operatorname{sgn}_\epsilon(H)$ and $\operatorname{sgn}_\epsilon(K)$ using a selected zero threshold ϵ. These images are then used to determine the surface type label image or HK-sign map:

$$\operatorname{sgn}_{HK} = 1 + 3(1 + \operatorname{sgn}_\epsilon(H)) + (1 - \operatorname{sgn}_\epsilon(K)). \tag{3.70}$$

With this definition, the values of the surface type labels will run from 1 to 9, excluding 4.

3.6   Other Surface Characteristics

Many other surface characteristics besides surface curvature can be easily computed given the partial derivative estimates at each pixel of a digital surface. The use of view-dependent surface critical points for surface characterization was discussed by Nackman [1984]. He noted that critical points and ridge and valley lines surround slope districts in only four canonical ways. The critical points of a function $f(u, v)$ are those points (u, v) where $f_u(u, v) = 0$ *and* $f_v(u, v) = 0$. Since one must estimate f_u and f_v functions to compute K and H anyway, it is a simple mathematical step to additionally determine the critical points of the given range image by detecting the zero-crossings of the first partial derivatives. For surfaces, there are seven kinds of non-degenerate critical points where $f_u = f_v = 0$ and $K \ne 0 \ne H$:

1. Peak Critical Points: $H < 0$ and $K > 0$,

2. Ridge Critical Points: $H < 0$ and $K = 0$,

3. Saddle Ridge Critical Points: $H < 0$ and $K < 0$,

4. Minimal Critical Points: $H = 0$ and $K < 0$,

5. Saddle Valley Critical Points: $H > 0$ and $K < 0$,

6. Valley Critical Points: $H > 0$ and $K = 0$,

7. Pit Critical Points: $H > 0$ and $K > 0$.

In addition, there is one kind of degenerate critical point where $f_u = f_v = 0$ and $K = H = 0$: planar critical points. Hence, if the zero-crossings of the first partial derivatives are computed in addition to Gaussian and mean curvature, then a richer structural description of the digital range image surface is obtained even though critical points are view-dependent quantities.

The proposed critical point characterization is a generalization of the 1-D function characterization techniques. Computing critical points is the generalization of computing the zeros of the first derivative of a function of one variable. Computing the sign of Gaussian and mean curvature is a generalization of computing the sign of the second derivative to see if the function is concave up or down or if it is flat.

It is also convenient to compute four other quantities that may be of potential interest in surface characterization and range image segmentation. The first of these quantities is the square root of the determinant of the first fundamental form matrix:

$$\sqrt{g} = \sqrt{EG - F^2} = \sqrt{1 + f_u^2 + f_v^2}. \tag{3.71}$$

This *metric determinant* quantity can be summed over range image regions to obtain the approximate surface area of the region. This summation corresponds to the continuous formulation

$$\text{Surface Area} = \int \sqrt{1 + f_u^2 + f_v^2} \, du \, dv. \tag{3.72}$$

It can also be considered as an edge magnitude map since it is approximately equal to the square root of the sum of the squares of the first partial derivatives. This type of image is very similar to the output of edge detection algorithms. It can be thresholded to create a simple binary edge image, or a fast, local, non-directional, non-maxima suppression operator has been applied in experiments to create desirable one-pixel wide edges. In range images, these edges correspond to range discontinuities, which generally correspond to the occluding contour of an object. The existence of a range discontinuity and a surface region boundary along a curve in an image will reinforce the interpretation of that curve as an occluding object boundary for segmentation purposes.

A second extrinsic quantity that is easy to compute pointwise given the derivatives already computed is the so-called *quadratic variation*:

$$Q = f_{uu}^2 + 2f_{uv}^2 + f_{vv}^2. \tag{3.73}$$

When this function is integrated (summed) over a range image region, the integral (sum) is a measure of the *flatness* or *smoothness* of that region. This image function and the metric determinant image could be computed in parallel with the Gaussian and mean curvature using the computed derivative information and could be used to quickly provide surface area and flatness (smoothness) measures of the surface regions segmented later in the processing. The quadratic variation is the smoothness measure used

in the definition of thin-plate smoothing splines used in other computer
vision work even though Blake [1984] has pointed out that the surfaces
based on this measure are not viewpoint independent. It is interesting to
see what this measure looks like when computed locally from digital surface
data.

A third (intrinsic) quantity is the *coordinate angle function* Θ, which is
defined as

$$\Theta = \cos^{-1}(F/\sqrt{EG}) = \cos^{-1}\left(\frac{f_u f_v}{\sqrt{1 + f_u^2 + f_v^2 + f_u^2 f_v^2}}\right). \qquad (3.74)$$

This function measures the non-orthogonality of the u,v parameterization
at each point: $\Theta = \pi/2$ when the u- and v-tangent vectors are orthogonal,
and Θ ranges between 0 and π when they are not orthogonal. Also $\cos\Theta =$
0 implies that at least one of the first partial derivatives is zero in the graph
surface formulation. The zeros of this function form ridge and valley lines
that are useful in critical point configuration graphs [Nackman 1984].

The last quantities discussed in this section are the *principal directions*
of the surface at each point. The principal direction vectors of a surface,
along with either H and K or the principal curvatures, completely determine the shape operator (Weingarten mapping) of that surface. The lines
of curvature of digital surface can be computed by linking together principal directions at each point on a surface [Brady et al.1985]. Moreover, the
principal directions with surface curvatures uniquely determine the shape
of umbilic-free surfaces, as pointed out by Liang [1987]. The unnormalized
principal direction vectors *in the u-v plane* for the principal curvatures κ_1
and κ_2 are given by

$$\vec{\Phi}_1 = \left[\begin{array}{c} u_1 \\ v_1 \end{array}\right] = \left[\begin{array}{c} GM - FN \\ \frac{1}{2}(EN - GL) + g\sqrt{H^2 - K} \end{array}\right] \qquad (3.75)$$

$$\vec{\Phi}_2 = \left[\begin{array}{c} u_2 \\ v_2 \end{array}\right] = \left[\begin{array}{c} \frac{1}{2}(EN - GL) + g\sqrt{H^2 - K} \\ FL - EM \end{array}\right] \qquad (3.76)$$

where $g = EG - F^2$. Note that these directions are in general not orthogonal in the (u,v) parameter plane even though the 3-D principal direction
vectors in the tangent planes of surface points are orthogonal. These angles
are not currently used as surface descriptors in the surface segmentation
algorithm because it is not clear that they are useful unless a lines of curvature surface description approach, such as [Brady et al.1985], is taken. If
the lines of curvature of a surface can be isolated and used as u-v parameter curves, then the first and second fundamental forms are diagonal and
only four functions E,G,L,N are required to uniquely specify the shape of
the surface (F=M=0). In this special case, the 2x2 Weingarten mapping
matrix has the principal curvatures on the diagonal and zeros elsewhere.
There are definite advantages to working with such a parameterization, and
line of curvature approaches are useful for arbitrary smooth surfaces.

3.7 Summary

The proposed digital surface characterization process is summarized below. This process is critical to the segmentation process described in the next chapter, and it may be directly useful for some applications.

Input: A digital surface of sensed values $f(i,j)$ where $0 \le i \le (N_u - 1)$ and $0 \le j \le (N_v - 1)$ and $0 \le f \le 2^{N_{bits}} - 1$ where N_{bits} is the number of bits used for sensor data quantization.

Process: 1. Compute $f_u, f_v, f_{uv}, f_{uu}, f_{vv}$ images using separable window convolution techniques based on the local biquadratic surface model described above.

2. Compute K, H, $\sqrt{g}$, $\cos \Theta$, Q, and ϵ images using the analytical formulas given above,

3. Compute the zeros of f_u, f_v, $\cos \Theta$, K, and H.

Output: 1. Two three-level images $\mathrm{sgn}(K)$ and $\mathrm{sgn}(H)$, where $\mathrm{sgn}(\cdot)$ is the toleranced signum function that yields 1 if the argument is positive, 0 if the argument is approximately zero, and -1 if the argument is negative. These two functions can be combined into one eight-level function, known as the HK-sign map, via a linear combination of the signum functions as described earlier.

2. Three non-negative images $|H|$, $|K|$, and $\sqrt{H^2 - K}$ that describe the magnitude of the mean and Gaussian curvatures and the scaled magnitude of the difference of the principal curvatures respectively $((\kappa_1 - \kappa_2)^2/4 = H^2 - K)$.

3. A binary image $c(i,j)$ that is 1 when (i,j) is a critical point and 0 when it is not. Peak, pit, saddle ridge, saddle valley, and minimal critical points of smooth surfaces are always isolated critical points. Ridge and valley critical points can form planar curves. Planar critical points can form planar areas. Each resulting critical point, curve, or area is labeled with its appropriate classification.

4. Three non-negative images $\sqrt{g}$, Q, and ϵ are relevant to edge detection and useful for computing region features, such as surface area and flatness/smoothness. Fit error indicates the reliability of the partial derivative estimates, and therefore it also indicates the reliability of HK-sign and all other characteristics.

5. The binary images denoting the zeros of K, H, and $\cos \Theta$.

Note that a large amount of surface structure information about a N_{bits} digitized image can be "compressed" into eight levels (*only three bits*) when the signs of the Gaussian and mean curvature are used to create the HK-Sign map. This second-order sign information substantially constrains the

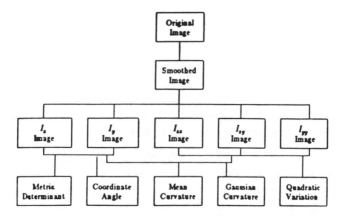

Figure 3.8: Surface Characterization Algorithm Structure

possibilities of visible surfaces and possesses visible invariance properties.
Also, the sign of a second-order quantity computed from digital sensor
data is more reliable than the magnitude because second derivatives are
so difficult to estimate accurately from noisy digital data. In addition, a
classified list of critical points, that also substantially constrains the surface,
can be computed. This list normally contains a very small number of points
compared to the total number of pixels in the range image and is useful
for view-dependent critical point configuration graph surface descriptions.
The other images provide additional, useful, overlapping information about
a digital surface.

Range discontinuities (step edges) and orientation discontinuities (roof
edges) have been computed by applying a simple non-directional, non-
maxima suppression algorithm to the images that may be interpreted as
edge magnitude images: $\sqrt{g}, |H|, \sqrt{H^2 - K}$, and $|\kappa_1|$. More robust edge de-
tection/linking algorithms, such as the Eichel edge linker/detector [Eichel
1985], have also been used with success to extract edges from these types
of images. Because the main theme is surface-based methods, more details
are not presented. It is noted that such images are useful for edge detection
purposes, and edge detection algorithms can quickly provide complementary information to surface-based algorithms.

3.8 Experimental Surface Characterization Results

A range image processing program was written to do the surface characterization computations in the C programming language on a VAX/UNIX
system. This program is an integral part of the digital surface segmentation algorithm presented in Chapter 4. The potentially parallel computational structure of this program is shown in Figure 3.8. All five derivative

images could be computed simultaneously after initial smoothing. Subsequently, all surface characteristics could be computed simultaneously after the derivative estimation stage. On a sequential machine, note that *all five* derivative images can be computed for the *cost of four* derivative images if the separable derivative operations are arranged correctly and separate memory is used for a scratchpad image and each output image. This is a 20% cost savings in the derivative computation stage.

The software accepts a square range image (with 8-bits of range) as input and generates the following images as output:

1. Smoothed Image: $f_{smooth}(u, v)$

2. Edge Magnitude Image: $\sqrt{g(u, v)}$

3. Local Flatness Measure Image: $Q(u, v)$

4. Local Quadratic Surface Fit Error Image: $\epsilon(u, v)$

5. Zeros of Mean Curvature: (u, v) such that $H(u, v) = 0$

6. Zeros of Gaussian Curvature: (u, v) such that $K(u, v) = 0$

7. Zeros of Coordinate-Angle Cosine Function: (u, v) such that $\cos(\Theta(u, v)) = 0$

8. Coordinate-Angle Cosine Function: $\cos \Theta(u, v)$

9. Sign Regions of Mean Curvature: $\text{sgn}(H(u, v))$

10. Sign Regions of Gaussian Curvature: $\text{sgn}(K(u, v))$

11. Magnitude of Principal Curvature Difference: $\sqrt{H^2(u, v) - K(u, v)}$

12. Maximum Principal Direction Angle: $\vec{\Phi}_1(u, v) = [u_1 \ v_1]^T$

13. Magnitude of Gaussian Curvature: $|K(u, v)|$

14. Magnitude of Mean Curvature: $|H(u, v)|$

15. Non-degenerate Critical Points Image: (u, v) such that $f_u(u, v) = f_v(u, v) = 0 \neq Q(u, v)$

16. Critical Points Image: $f_u(u, v) = f_v(u, v) = 0$

This output data characterizes the input range image in a way that appears to be useful for segmentation of sensor data and possibly for recognition of objects. A range image can be decomposed into the basic eight types of surface regions by using a combination of the $\text{sgn}(H)$ and $\text{sgn}(K)$ images, known as the HK-Sign map. Step edges and surface area can be obtained from the $\sqrt{g}$ image. It is possible to detect roof edges and ramp edges using the $|H|$ and $\sqrt{H^2 - K}$ images. Critical point configurations describe surfaces as in Nackman [1984]. Data-driven processing can yield rich, interrelated surface, edge, and point information.

The following points should be made about the experimental results:

1. All original range images were quantized to eight bits of range. Quantization noise alone caused many problems in the first computational tests on analytically computed surfaces, such as spheres. This was due to the fact that quantization noise is not independent and identically distributed, but rather it is correlated in a spatially dependent manner. The local least squares techniques used to determine the window operators are not designed to correctly handle such noise. In an attempt to alleviate this problem, the original image is smoothed using a binomial window smoothing operator that is two pixels larger than the quoted window operators used to do the derivative estimation, and the results are stored in a manner that maintains the fractional part of the smoothed value. This smoothing also tends to compensate for random noise in the two or three least significant bits of range data as well as partially decorrelate the quantization noise.

2. The output curvature images are also smoothed using the same type of smoothing operator that was used on the input to even out the variations in the surface curvature values. However, a smaller window size was used $(L - 4)$.

3. The surface curvature sign images are obtained using a zero threshold. That is, $\text{sgn}(K) = 0$ if $|K| < \epsilon_K$ Also, $\text{sgn}(H) = 0$ if $|H| < \epsilon_H$. The two thresholds were set to $\epsilon_K = 0.01 K_{max}$ and $\epsilon_H = 0.01 H_{max}$ for synthetic range images with no noise, where K_{max} and H_{max} are the maximum absolute values attained by the surface curvatures in the image. Noisy images required larger thresholds to obtain good HK-sign images. For the experimental results shown in Chapter 7, the two zero curvature thresholds were fixed to $\epsilon_H = 0.015$ and $\epsilon_K = 0.06$.

These items are important for interpreting the results displayed at the end of the chapter. Different smoothing schemes will create different surface curvature results. Different thresholds create different surface curvature sign images. Experiments with a smoothing algorithm that inhibits smoothing operations over range discontinuities, similar to Terzopoulos [1983] and Grimson and Pavlidis [1985] techniques, were also performed, and several different noise estimation alternatives were examined. No methods were found to be consistently better than those described above for the computation of surface curvature. As more than eight bits of range resolution become available from newer sensors, the pre-smoothing step will be proportionately less important than what it is for the current 8-bit data.

Experimental results for different object range images are shown in Figures 3.10 through 3.25. Each range image is discussed briefly below.

f_{smooth}	$\sqrt{g}$	Q	ϵ
zeros(H)	zeros(K)	zeros($\cos\Theta$)	$\cos\Theta$
sgn(H)	sgn(K)	$\sqrt{H^2 - K}$	Φ_1
$|H|$	$|K|$	$\nabla f = 0\,(Q \neq 0)$	$\nabla f = 0$

Figure 3.9: Surface Characterization Results Format

The results are shown in a sixteen (16) subimage format. The contents of each subimage are noted in Figure 3.9. Zeros of X images are white if the quantity X is zero and black if X is non-zero. Surface curvature sign images are coded as follows: *white = positive, gray = zero, black = negative.* Other images are scaled so that the image *minimum is black* and the image *maximum is white.* The exception to this rule is the range image itself: *white* is used for pixels *closest* to the observer (range is a minimum) whereas *black* is used for pixels *farthest* from the observer (range is a maximum). This convention is sometimes reversed by other authors. The author's experience is that, although possible, it is generally more difficult to visually interpret such reversed range images. It is analogous to the difference between black and white photographs and negatives, and most people prefer to look at positive photographic images over negatives. Convolutional window effects near the edges of the sixteen subimages are not relevant to the results. For several range images, a surface plot of the range image is also provided.

The range images shown here were obtained in two different ways. Synthetic range images of arbitrary 3-D object models from arbitrary views are generated using a combination of the SDRC/Geomod solid modeler [Geomod 1983] developed by Structural Dynamics Research Corporation to create object models, and the author's depth-buffer graphics software to create Cartesian orthographic range images (see Appendix D). Real range images were obtained from the Environmental Research Institute of Michigan (ERIM), which were acquired using an ERIM imaging laser radar [Svetkoff et al.1984]. The range image points in these images are obtained using equal angle-increment sampling. This equal-angle-increment sampling causes flat surfaces in the real world to be mapped into slightly warped surfaces in range images (see Appendix D).

The results for each object are considered individually. The first object is a coffee cup. Two gray scale images of two range images of this object are shown in Figure 3.10 along with a surface plot of the one on the right. The two range images were obtained from the ERIM imaging laser radar. The quality of these range images is almost comparable to that of synthetic range images. The surface characterizations of these range images are shown in Figure 3.11. A 7x7 derivative window operator was used. It has been found that the *zeros of the mean curvature* form a good line drawing of the object shape, which is similar to a Laplacian zero-crossings image. This is quite reasonable because the Laplacian, typically used to obtain edges [Marr 1982], is a second-order linear elliptic differential operator, whereas mean curvature is a second-order quasi-linear elliptic differential operator. The square root of the metric determinant, the quadratic variation, and the local quadratic surface fit error provide an interesting sequence of edge-detector-like images. Clusters of local maxima and saddle ridge critical points are found at the closer and farther rims of the cup respectively whereas local minima critical points are found on the inside of the cup and inside the handle. Despite the noise present in this real image, very few spurious critical points are found. The magnitude of the principal curvature difference image shows that the surface's principal curvatures differ most on the cup's rim.

A second range image from the ERIM imaging laser radar is shown in Figure 3.12 along with a surface plot. A histogram of this image shows that all 8-bit range values are confined to the 32 to 128 range with most values in the 96 to 128 range. This image represents a portion of a computer terminal keyboard. Two surface characterizations are shown in Figure 3.13. The top characterization was computed using a 3x3 derivative window operator, and the bottom was computed using a 5x5 window. It is easy to see the effect of the increase in window size. The concave shape of the top surface of the keyboard keys is detected by the small white regions in the mean curvature sign image. Again, the zeros of the mean curvature image yields a good line drawing of the keyboard. There are a large number of critical points on this surface as expected. The critical points are fairly well clustered into groups for the 5x5 window operator.

Two views of a road scene were selected from a range image sequence acquired by the ERIM imaging laser radar. Figure 3.14 shows the original range images with phase wraparound lines at thirty-two feet and sixty-four feet, the corrected range images with the first wraparound transition removed, and a surface plot of the corrected image on the right. A special purpose program removed the wraparound transitions automatically. This was easy in this case because of the smooth, almost flat shape of the road. The sixty-four foot line was not removed because the data beyond that range is excessively noisy. Figure 3.15 shows the surface characterization results for a 9x9 derivative window operator. The zeros of the mean curvature effectively isolate the ditches on the side of the road. The mean curvature sign image points out that the surface corresponding to the road itself is not flat in this image as expected from the angular sampling. The zeros of the cosine of the coordinate-angle occur whenever either of the first partial derivatives is zero. Because of the equal angle increment sampling, the flat road samples are warped yielding a line right up the center of the $\cos \Theta$ zeros image. Because the data beyond the sixty-four foot line was left in the image unwrapped, the maximum curvature points and the critical points all occur in this region, but have no physical meaning.

Figure 3.16 is a surface plot of the range image of a tilted torus (a polyhedral approximation of a torus). The surface characterization results for two different synthetic range views of the torus are shown in Figure 3.17. In the other view, the torus is tilted only five degrees. Note how well the surface critical points were detected. The structure of the ridge and valley lines in the zeros of the cosine of the coordinate-angle image gives important view-dependent information about the surface in terms of slope districts. Some irregularities in the curvature magnitude images occur because the object model from which the range image was generated is a polyhedral model. Note that the mean-curvature sign-image is almost exactly correct. The Gaussian curvature sign image shows that, to within the specified threshold, many parts of the surface are approximately flat.

A free-form undulating surface was created by "stretching a skin" over a series of curves using SDRC/Geomod. The range image for this surface is shown in Figure 3.18. The surface characterization results for two different views using 5x5 window derivative operator are shown in Figure 3.19. The critical points that are also maximum Gaussian curvature points tend to line up along the joining curve in the center of the range image when looking straight down on the surface. These points move predictably in the second view. These range images have no substantial range discontinuities; therefore, detailed slope magnitude variations are seen in the scaled edge map (square root of g) image. Note the slight changes in the surface curvature sign images between the two views.

To give an idea of how window size and noise level affect the results of the surface characterization algorithm, a synthetic image of a cube with three holes in it is used. Pseudo-random pseudo-Gaussian noise (rounded to the nearest integer) was added to the original image to create four different synthetic noisy images as shown in Figure 3.20. The surface characterization results for these four images are shown in Figures 3.21 through 3.25, which correspond respectively to additive Gaussian noise standard deviations (σ 's) of 2.3, 9.2, 16.0, and 22.9 gray levels (range levels) added to an original image with a dynamic range of 256 levels. The resulting noisy images were rescaled to fit into the 8-bit range. These images were then processed with 5x5, 7x7, 9x9, 11x11, and 13x13 derivative window operators. The following five figures have been selected to demonstrate the noise performance:

- Figure 3.21: 5x5 operator applied to the $\sigma = 2.3$ noisy image.

- Figure 3.22: 7x7 operator applied to the $\sigma = 9.2$ noisy image.

- Figure 3.23: 9x9 operator applied to the $\sigma = 16.0$ noisy image.

- Figure 3.24: 11x11 operator applied to the $\sigma = 22.9$ noisy image.

- Figure 3.25: 13x13 operator applied to the $\sigma = 22.9$ noisy image.

Note how well the sign of the mean curvature represents the important surface variations of the cube even in the presence of significant noise. The mean curvature images are surprisingly consistent and qualitatively meaningful in all five figures even though second derivatives of very noisy data are involved in its computation. The Gaussian curvature images are more susceptible to noise as expected, but the closest vertex of the cube is consistently marked as a high curvature spot. The degradation in the zeros of the cosine of the coordinate-angle is also interesting to observe. The critical point images are consistent despite the noise and demonstrate the necessity of a large window size to suppress spurious critical points in the presence of noise. Note that fewer spurious critical points result in the 11x11 operator, $\sigma = 22.9$ results shown in Figure 3.24, than in the 5x5 operator, $\sigma = 2.3$ results shown in Figure 3.21. The conclusion is that even though second derivative information is being used, the surface descriptors are still useful in the presence of noise if large enough window sizes are used. Moreover, the surface characteristics appear to degrade slowly as the noise level increases. In practical applications, it is unlikely that the noise would ever exceed the $\sigma = 9.2$ level.

The experimental results indicate the performance of this differential geometry based surface characterization approach for digital surfaces in the presence of noise. However, these results are still in a low level form and are not directly suitable for use by higher level processes. This is remedied by the pixel grouping and refined image segmentation processes addressed in the next chapter. The sgn(H) and sgn(K) images shown in this chapter can be combined as described above to create the HK-sign map, which does provide a rough initial segmentation of a digital surface. Combined HK-sign map images (visible-invariant pixel labelings) were not shown in this chapter because they are shown in Chapter 7 along with final segmentation results. The HK-sign map segmentations are rather noisy for the 8-bit images shown here, but as higher range resolution sensors become available, the initial HK-sign map segmentation will improve.

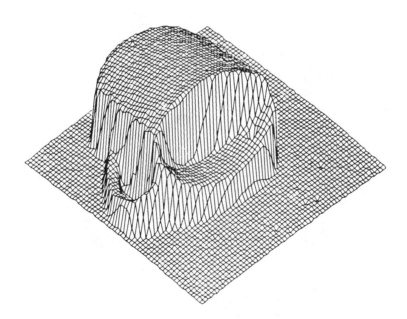

Figure 3.10: Coffee Cup Range Images and Surface Plot
(128x128 ERIM Range Images)

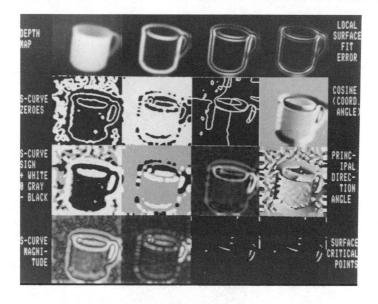

Figure 3.11: Surface Charaterizations of Two Views of Coffee Cup
(7x7 Derivative Window Operator, Zero Threshold=4%)

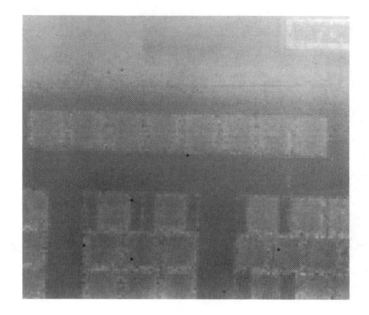

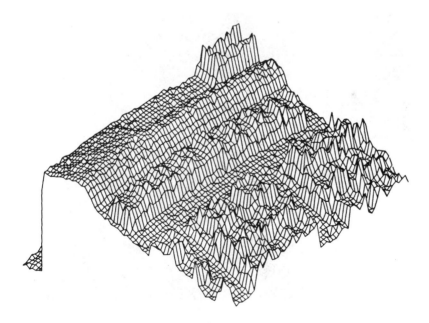

Figure 3.12: Keyboard Range Image and Surface Plot
(128x128 ERIM Range Image)

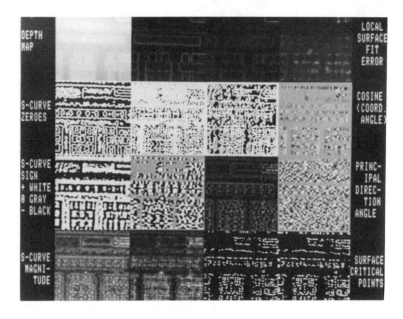

Figure 3.13: Surface Characterizations of Keyboard
(Top: 3x3 Window Operator Results, Bottom: 5x5 Window Results)

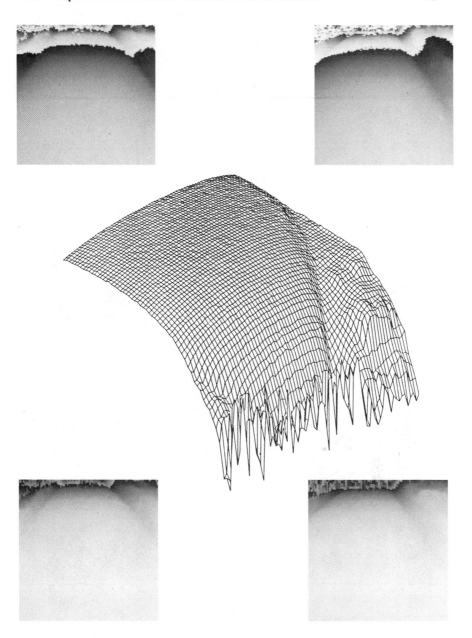

Figure 3.14: Original and Unwrapped Range Images of Road Scenes
(128x128 ERIM Range Images)

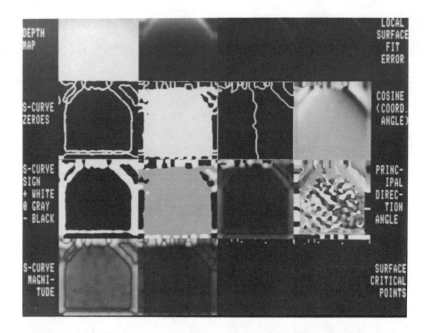

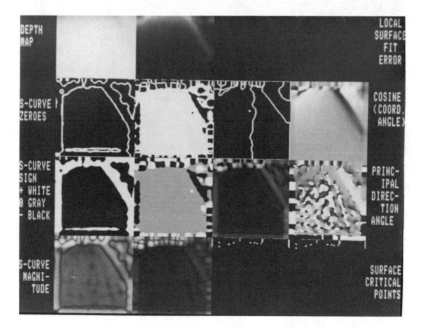

Figure 3.15: Surface Characterizations of Road Scenes
(9x9 Derivative Window Operator, Zero Threshold=2%)

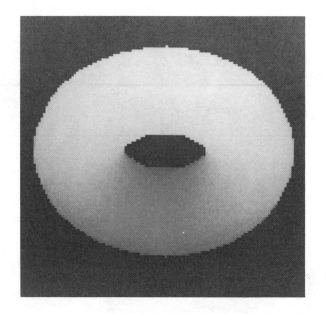

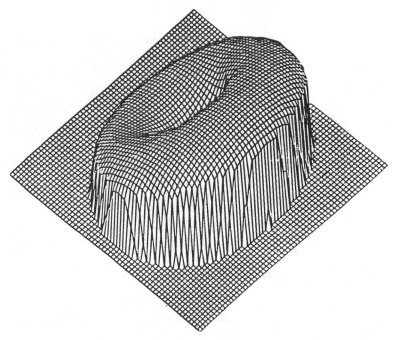

Figure 3.16: Range Image and Surface Plot of Tilted Torus
(128x128 Synthetic Range Image)

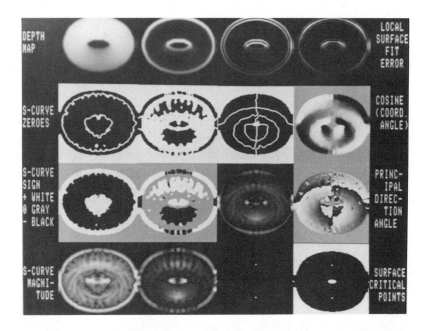

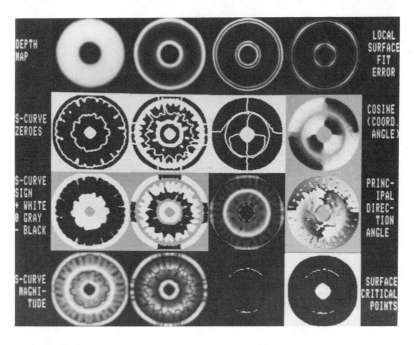

Figure 3.17: Surface Characterizations of Two Views of Torus
(5x5 Derivative Window Operator, Zero Threshold=1%)

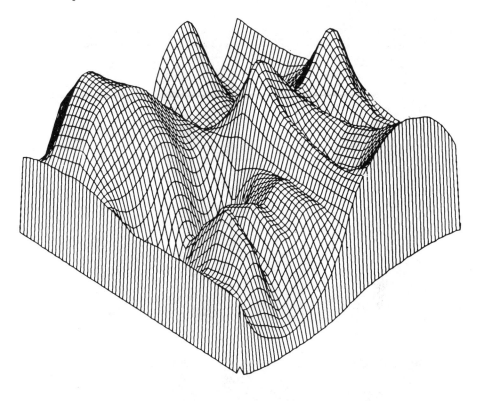

Figure 3.18: Surface Plot of Undulating Surface Range Image
(128x128 Synthetic Range Image)

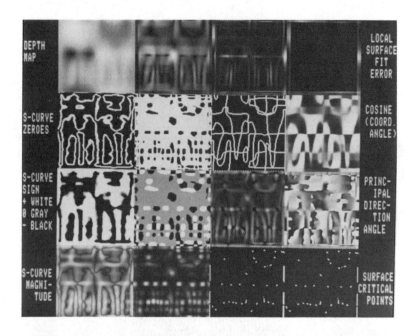

Figure 3.19: Characterizations of Two Views of Undulating Surface
(5x5 Derivative Window Operator, Zero Threshold=1%)

Figure 3.20: Block with Different Noise Levels (2.3,9.2,16,22.9)
(128x128 Synthetic Range Images)

Figure 3.21: Results for 5x5 Operator with σ=2.3
(Zero Threshold=6%)

Figure 3.22: Results for 7x7 Operator with $\sigma=9.2$
(Zero Threshold=12%)

Figure 3.23: Results for 9x9 Operator with $\sigma=16.0$
(Zero Threshold=14%)

Figure 3.24: Results for 11x11 Operator with σ=22.9
(Zero Threshold=14%)

Figure 3.25: Results for 13x13 Operator with σ=22.9
(Zero Threshold=14%)

Chapter 4

From Surface Labels to Surface Primitives

An analytical framework for object recognition and image segmentation was formulated in Chapter 2. It was proposed that objects can be recognized in range images in a general manner through surface characterization, surface segmentation, and surface matching. Although surface matching is inherently model-dependent, it was proposed that surface characterization and surface segmentation do not require knowledge of objects, only basic knowledge of surfaces. It was shown in Chapter 3 that differential geometric concepts for visible-invariant descriptions of continuous surfaces are applicable to digital surfaces even in the presence of quantization and measurement noise. That is, each point on a continuous or digital surface can be characterized by the spatial properties of other points on the surface in small neighborhoods surrounding the given point. The key difference is that, the neighborhood of a point consists of an uncountably infinite number of points in the continuous surface case whereas a small finite number of points form the neighborhood of a digital surface point.

As the name implies, the *differential* geometry of surfaces analyzes the *local differences* of surface points. Although *global similarities* in surface structure are also analyzed within the context of differential geometry, most existing theorems address only global topological similarities, such as the one-hole equivalence of a doughnut and a coffee cup with a handle. However, there are global shape similarity theorems for the surfaces of convex objects. The appropriate mathematics has already been successfully incorporated in Extended Gaussian Image (EGI) shape matching schemes, e.g. [Horn 1984]. Classical mathematics does not give much guidance for computational matching methods if local geometric descriptors are used to identify the shape of arbitrary *non-convex* objects from arbitrary viewpoint range image projections. Although special feature recognition approaches offer important advantages for applied computer vision systems, e.g. [Bolles and Horaud 1986], a successful surface matching algorithm for arbitrary surfaces would provide considerably more general object recognition capabilities. The aim is to use local difference information to help describe global similarities in surface points (digital surface pixels) for arbitrary surfaces without making domain-specific assumptions.

If the pixels of a digital surface can be correctly grouped into smooth surface regions that directly correspond to the surfaces of objects in a scene, this grouping process would provide a fundamental service to higher level model formation and recognition processes. In this chapter, a process for converting the local difference information in the HK-sign map into global similarity information is presented. The specific form of the desired global similarity information was set forth in Chapter 2. The goal is to convert the original digital surface into a set of graph surface approximation functions $\{\hat{g}_i(x, y)\}$ and an associated set of region descriptions $\{\hat{R}_i\}$ as guided by the surface characterization results.

4.1 Problems with HK-Sign Maps

It has been established that mean and Gaussian curvature possess many desirable properties for characterizing the 3-D shape of smooth surfaces, especially graph surfaces, and methods for computing mean and Gaussian curvature from digital surfaces through least squares derivative estimates have been examined. Experimental surface characterization results have been presented showing that meaningful differential geometric quantities can be computed even in the presence of noise by using an appropriate pre-smoothing operator on range images. However, it is still unclear at this point that a more precise data-driven range image segmentation can be achieved using this computed information unless higher resolution range imaging sensors are used. Three important observations are made about the results obtained thus far using the surface curvature characteristics approach:

Smoothing: Smoothing is needed to filter out local fluctuations in the data due to quantization and measurement noise so as to obtain reasonable differential geometric quantities from a digital surface. But as a result of linear low-pass filter smoothing, sharp discontinuities in range and orientation are blurred. The HK-sign surface labels, as currently computed, actually only reflect the geometry of the smoothed surface and not the original surface data. The final data-driven description, however, should be as precise as possible about the original image and should not contain misleading information about the original digital surface shape. Hence, the raw visible-invariant pixel labeling results obtained via smoothing, derivative estimation, and surface curvature computation must be refined into a more precise form. It is not clear at this point how this should be done, but it is a fundamental problem that must be addressed. Research by several investigators, e.g. [Terzopoulos 1983,1985] [Grimson and Pavlidis 1985], has explored the idea that the unwanted effects of smoothing can be

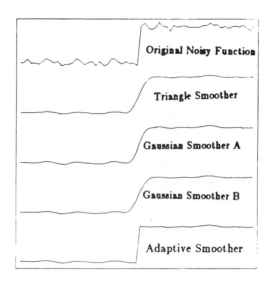

Figure 4.1: A Comparison of Different Smoothing Operators

eliminated, or at least significantly attenuated, by using adaptive smoothing and derivative estimation operators. That is, window operators may change shape and size depending upon local data variations. Figure 4.1 shows an example of a very simple adaptive smoothing filter that maintains the sharpness of the underlying step function by incorporating an estimate of the standard deviation of the the noise as compared to three different linear smoothing filters. If a discontinuity larger than three times the standard deviation of the noise is encountered, the smoothing window is truncated. Such an operator has been used as a separable filter on image rows and columns to form a two dimensional adaptive smoothing filter with interesting, but not completely satisfying results. The data takes on different step shapes in the linear fixed-window-size smoothing cases, but it is not distorted near the discontinuity by the adaptive smoother. Such operators are successful when the measurement noise is not too large and the discontinuities to be detected are sufficiently larger.

Sharp range and orientation discontinuities can be preserved and enhanced in the presence of noise in the surface segmentation algorithm despite the use of fixed window-size, fixed window-shape smoothing operators to compute sign-of-curvature features. This is accomplished by isolating smooth-surface primitive seed regions on both sides of a discontinuity and subsequently growing the seed regions outward. Pixels on either side of the discontinuity tend to become part of their respective, distinct surfaces. Figure 4.2 shows the basic concepts for a step edge, including smoothing, differentiation, sign of curvature, seed regions, and iterative fitting. This process is explained in detail in this chapter.

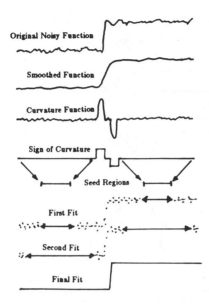

Figure 4.2: Basic Concepts of Digital Surface Segmentation Algorithm

Unwanted Connections Caused by Noise: In the presence of noise, HK-sign surface labels of one surface region tend to connect, in the sense of four-connectedness, with equivalent labels of neighboring, but distinct surface regions. This fact was observed in experimental results with real and synthetic image data and was not anticipated by the theory for smooth curved surfaces. It is not possible, in general, to simply isolate a four-connected region of pixels of a particular HK-sign type and identify that region as a single surface of the appropriate type. Even if it were possible to detect the unwanted connections and break them, the resulting connected regions are still found wanting because of their irregular shape, which does not accurately reflect the boundary of the underlying surface. But the goal is to use the HK-sign information to provide a decomposition of digital surfaces into simple, basic surface primitives. It is proposed that connected regions be isolated and contracted until a small, maximally interior, highly reliable, single surface seed region is isolated. This seed region is then grown via variable order surface fitting until it reaches its natural limits as defined by variations in the surface data. It will be shown that the HK-sign map can provide useful surface primitive regions in conjunction with a seed region extraction algorithm and with an iterative region growing algorithm based on variable order surface fitting.

Global Surface Properties Lacking: In order to perform model formation or surface matching between a range image description and a world model, it is advantageous to have an explicit, concise representation of a surface that possesses the global surface properties. A parametric equation for a surface is an example of an explicit concise representation. For example, ten coefficients or surface control points might accurately represent thousands of image pixels.

Assuming that the original surface is sufficiently smooth, the mean curvature function of a surface in addition to a boundary curve for that surface can be used to reconstruct the original surface, in theory, by solving an elliptic quasilinear partial differential equation. Even though this is true in continuous mathematics, the differential equation can seldom be solved in closed form and numerical methods are required. Thus, significant computation may be necessary to "invert" mean curvature to obtain a description of the original graph surface even if the continuous mean curvature function were known exactly. But as the experimental results in Chapter 3 indicated, the estimates of the mean curvature function are good, but still noisy. Although surface curvature is important for describing and processing surfaces in continuous or discrete form, it is doubtful that accurate surface reconstructions could be computed efficiently by numerically solving partial differential equations.

Much better alternatives exist for describing global shape properties of digital surfaces. As a trivial example, if mean and Gaussian curvature are both zero on a given surface patch, implying that the surface is planar, one would like to know the planar equation for that surface. A rich, concise, data description must be able to provide such information. If all pixels corresponding to a given planar surface can be correctly grouped together, one could perform a minimum error fit of a plane to those pixels of the digital surface to obtain a good estimate of the planar equation of that surface. This would certainly be easier, more efficient, and more accurate than attempting to solve the minimal-surface partial differential equation numerically using the boundary pixels of the planar surface. This surface fitting approach is fine for planes, but how can the shape of general, smooth, curved surfaces be described more directly and more precisely than through noisy estimates of the mean curvature and the surface boundary or the Gaussian curvature? The original digital surface itself provides the shape information in a non-symbolic, high-dimensionality signal form.

Surface curvature is not the most convenient "handle" for many global surface shape properties, but it is not clear what is. Past researchers have employed either polyhedral or quadric surface models to describe global surface properties, but have not successfully dealt with more complicated surfaces. Quadrics, though useful, unnecessarily impose symmetry requirements on the image data, requirements that will not be satisfied by arbitrary surfaces. It will be shown that an effective, data-driven description of global properties can be computed using a small set of approximating functions and still allow flat surfaces to be flat and curved surfaces to be curved without imposing high-level spherical, conical, or cylindrical models as past research has done. For the purposes of grouping pixels into smooth surface regions using surface fitting techniques, first, second, third, and fourth order bivariate polynomials are used to quickly provide approximate parametric descriptions of graph surface regions.

The three items above summarize the shortcomings of the HK-sign visible-invariant pixel label surface characterization as a general purpose description and briefly introduce the digital surface segmentation approach. The seemingly paradoxical motivation to compute a digital surface description for object recognition purposes without knowing anything about specific objects or even object classes prohibits the use of specific model-based techniques to counteract the above difficulties. If suitable surfaces can be fitted to any possible HK-sign region, such surface fits would provide general global surface information in an explicit, concise, symbolic form. As shall be shown, the undesired effects of smoothing and unwanted connections between regions are also both addressed using a variable order surface fitting approach to region growing.

4.2 Segmentation Algorithm Philosophy

Four underlying concepts form the basis of the segmentation algorithm: simple to complex hypothesis testing, initial guess plus iterative refinement, stimulus bound image analysis, and emerging commitment.

4.2.1 Simple to Complex Hypothesis Testing

A key idea behind the segmentation algorithm, which is independent of the chosen set of approximating functions, is that one should start with the simplest hypotheses about the form of the data and then gradually and automatically increase the complexity of the hypothesized form as needed. This idea gives rise to *variable order* surface fitting, which has not been used in previous segmentation algorithms. The HK-Sign map allows us to find large groups of identically labeled pixels. A small subset of those pixels, called a *seed region*, is chosen using a simple binary region contraction method that attempts to insure that every pixel in the small interior seed region is correctly labeled.

The simplest hypothesis for any surface fitting approach is that the data points in the seed region lie in a plane. The hypothesis is then tested to see if it is true. If true, the seed region is grown based on the planar surface fit. If the simple hypothesis is false, the algorithm responds by testing the next more complicated hypothesis, e.g. a biquadratic surface. If that hypothesis is true, the region is grown based on that form. If false, the next hypothesis is tested. This process continues until either (1) all pre-selected hypotheses have been shown to be false or (2) the region growing based on the surface fitting has converged in the sense that the same image region is obtained twice. Since all smooth surfaces can be partitioned into simple surfaces based on surface curvature sign, false hypotheses occur only if the isolated seed region surface-type labels are incorrect due to noise or an insufficient number of pixels in a region, or if the underlying surface bends much faster than the highest order approximating surface. The consequences of such false hypotheses are benign: bad seed regions are rejected immediately when the surface fit error is poor, and large quickly bending surfaces are broken into two or more surface regions that will join smoothly and will need to be remerged using the methods in Chapter 5.

4.2.2   Initial Guess Plus Iterative Refinement

Like many region growing schemes, the approach of this algorithm might be summarized as "make an initial guess and then iteratively refine the solution." This idea is at least as old as Newton's method for finding the zeros of a complicated function. Unlike other region growing schemes, the initial guess at the underlying surface segmentation is based on the visible-invariant differential geometric principles of Chapter 3. The iterative refinement process itself is based on function approximation and region growing. Once a surface has been fitted to the k-th group of connected pixels, the $(k + 1)$-th group of pixels is obtained by finding all new connected pixels that are compatible with the fitted surface of the previous group.

Although no proof is offered here, the segmentation algorithm exhibits the usual relationship between the quality of the initial guess and the number of iterations required. If the initial guess is very good, only a few iterations are required. Many iterations may be required if the initial guess is not so good. For bad initial guesses, it may happen that no number of iterations would yield convergence to a solution. The quality of the initial guess is related to the quality of the image data, and the performance of the segmentation algorithm tends to degrade gracefully with increasing noise levels.

4.2.3   Stimulus Bound Image Analysis

Variable-order surface fitting may be thought of as a hypothesis testing algorithm where the hypotheses can be automatically changed by the input data, and each surface fit is bound by (must conform to) the input image data. Therefore, the use of the adjective *stimulus bound* [Rock 1983] is suggested for the type of hypothesis testing done by the digital surface segmentation algorithm where the *stimulus* is the original sensed data values. In a stimulus bound process, all interpretive processing of the data is *bound* to the original stimulus in each stage of processing to reduce the probability of data interpretation errors. In the surface segmentation algorithm, each simple surface function hypothesis is tested against the original data via surface fitting followed by two tests: (1) an RMS fit error test (similar to a chi-square test), and (2) a regions test (similar to a non-parametric statistics runs test). Hence, each iteration and the final interpretation are bound by the original stimulus.

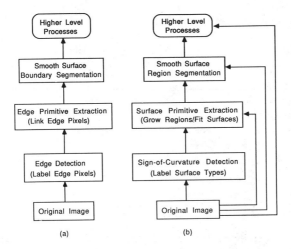

Figure 4.3: Conventional Edge Approach vs. Stimulus Bound Approach

It is generally acknowledged that vision algorithms should function at several different levels using associated vision modules to process signal and symbol information at different levels. It is often occurs that each level's vision module accepts input only from the previous, lower level and provides output only to the subsequent, higher level. Figure 4.3(a) shows a typical example of such a process. This assumption may be rooted in human visual models where retinal information is not directly available to the higher level cerebral processes. However, human vision is a fundamentally dynamic perceptual process in which subsequent, highly-correlated "video frames" are always immediately available to the visual system after any given instant in time. Therefore, it may be inappropriate to apply dynamic human visual model principles to static computational vision problems.

The *stimulus bound* philosophy states that the output from all lower level vision modules should be available to high-level vision modules. In particular, the original image from the sensor must be available to every vision module in a vision system as shown in Figure 4.3(b). In the digital surface segmentation algorithm, every pixel in every region is checked to see how close the sensed value at a given pixel is to the approximating surface function for the given region. The global grouping of pixels relies only on *simple differencing* between pixel values and the interpreted surface primitives as described in more detail in later sections. Without checking symbolic interpretations against the original data, a vertical chain of interpretive vision modules is only as robust as the weakest module. In other words, high level managers that never check the facts directly are easily mislead by subordinate entities. Many edge-based intensity image vision schemes have failed in practice because precise, correctly linked edges could not be extracted from real images and adequately verified.

In edge-based approaches, it is difficult to measure edge error directly against the original image data because an explicit edge description is not present in the original data. Surface-based algorithms may potentially have an advantage over edge-based algorithms because it is possible to check final image interpretations against the original data *at every image pixel* via simple image differencing. The final interpretation includes a reconstructed image that can be subtracted from the original image to create an *interpretation error image*, which can be used to evaluate the quality of the image interpretation globally and locally. This is only possible when an image interpretation includes segmentation and reconstruction information as described in the problem definition in Chapter 2.

4.2.4 Emerging Commitment

The digital surface segmentation algorithm is primarily data-driven in that only generic knowledge of surfaces, curvature, noise, and approximation are used. Of course, data-driven and model-driven elements must cooperate in any algorithm that attempts to interpret a digital image in terms of specific model information. An important feature of any image interpretation approach is the temporal process of commitment to its final interpretation. A special-purpose model-driven program can make a commitment to its set of possible interpretations when the program is written or compiled [Goad 1983] thus avoiding computations that might otherwise be required. A data-driven program may postpone commitment to a final interpretation in order to be more generally applicable, but it should reduce the amount of information that must be manipulated by later, higher level processes by generating intermediate symbolic primitives. Similar to the least commitment principle of Marr [1982], this segmentation approach follows a *principle of emerging commitment* that is *gradual* and *locally reversible*, but is not random. One must make steps toward image interpretation, yet it is impossible to always avoid errors that necessitate steps or labels being undone. An algorithm should make a series of small steps towards the goal, where each step need not produce perfect results, can easily be undone, but yet still produce useful information for the next step. Simulated annealing algorithms [Barnard 1986] [Geman and Geman 1984] also follow a principle of emerging commitment, but the digital surface segmentation algorithm described here is deterministically directed in its search process and provides a more structured output.

4.3 Segmentation Algorithm Description

It is assumed that (1) an original range image and (2) the eight level HK-sign map are given as input to the segmentation algorithm. All other surface characterization results are currently ignored by the segmentation algorithm to emphasize the importance of the fundamental surface type

labeling and the stimulus bound concept. In practice, it is advantageous
to incorporate other surface characteristics, especially edges, but the main
goal is to demonstrate the capabilities of a purely surface-based approach.
The other results in Chapter 3 should be viewed as a statement of the
quality of the differential geometric characterizations and an indication of
potentially useful features that can complement the current segmentation
approach.

The surface type label image (HK-sign map) has a reduced number
of levels for each pixel compared to the original image, but retains the
same spatial resolution. Hence, the label image is still a "signal" quantity
even though it measures local neighborhood surface type rather than range
or intensity as in the original image. But lower-dimensionality, symbolic
information is needed. A standard binary image connected-component algorithm (Appendix F) isolates four-connected regions of pixels of a fundamental surface type. As mentioned above, a given region may be undesirably connected to a distinct, adjacent region of the same type. Naive
attempts to fit surfaces to connected regions may work occasionally, but
fail most of the time, especially in the presence of noise. It is possible
to break these unwanted connections using a standard binary image 3x3
contraction (erosion) algorithm (Appendix F), but even then the HK-sign
regions may still not correspond directly to meaningful surfaces because of
preliminary smoothing distortions. A more elaborate strategy is called for.

In the digital surface segmentation algorithm, connected regions of pixels of a given surface type are extracted from the HK-sign map as ranked
by decreasing size. Each extracted region is then contracted (eroded) until
a sufficiently small number of pixels (greater than a fixed minimum value)
is obtained in the largest connected subregion of the extracted region. This
small region serves as the seed region to the iterative region growing algorithm. This algorithm is based on fitting variable order surfaces to the
original image data in the seed region and subsequent growth regions. The
region growing process is controlled directly by (1) the surface fit error
obtained at each iteration, (2) a pre-determined allowable error tolerance,
and (3) a regions test, which is a generalization of the one-dimensional
runs test of nonparametric statistics. The iteration continues until the
termination criteria are met at which point the computed surface region
description is rejected or accepted. Rejection decisions cause the associated
seed region to be marked off in a writable copy of the HK-sign map so that
subsequent attempts to use those pixels as a seed region will be prohibited.
Acceptance decisions similarly cause the accepted surface region pixels to
be marked off in the HK-Sign map. Accepted surfaces are also used to
update the following data structures ranked in order of importance to the
final segmentation:

1. Surface Coefficient List: $\{\vec{a}_i\}$,

2. Best-Fit Region Label Image: $l_{BF}(x, y)$,

3. Error Image: $e(x, y)$,

4. Best-Fit Reconstructed Image: $\hat{g}_{BF}(x, y)$,

5. First-Within-Tolerance Region Label Image: $l_{FW}(x, y)$,

6. First-Within-Tolerance Reconstructed Image: $\hat{g}_{FW}(x, y)$,

7. Best-Fit So Far Surface List: BFS list.

For each accepted surface primitive, the region growing stage of the segmentation algorithm outputs geometric reconstruction information and segmentation information:

1. The coefficients of the low-order polynomial graph surface equations $\vec{a}_i$ and the fit errors (mean absolute error, root-mean-square (RMS) error ϵ_i, and the maximum error), and

2. Three different region descriptions in the form of the region label images $l_{BF}(x, y)$ and $l_{FW}(x, y)$, and the BFS list.

Each of the three region descriptions may be considered as a single valid segmentation output on its own, but better results were usually obtained if these three output descriptions were combined via a heuristic region combination algorithm described in Chapter 5 that computes a single region description for each surface primitive. The final stage, also described in Chapter 5, merges surface primitives that join smoothly at their common boundary. A dataflow diagram for the entire process is shown in Figure 4.4. For easy reference, Figure 1.2 is duplicated here as Figure 4.5 to describe the sequential control flow of the algorithm (see also Appendix G). Section numbers are included with each step in the algorithm.

Unmarked connected components of the HK-Sign map are considered sequentially as ranked by region size until the average error in the error image falls below the prespecified error tolerance. If all unmarked connected components of the fundamental surface types above a given threshold size, e.g. 30 pixels, have been tested by the algorithm and the image error threshold has not been met, the algorithm automatically coalesces all unmarked pixels into a "last chance" binary image and reanalyzes all connected regions in the last chance binary image using the same approach outlined above. The last chance image pixels are essentially regarded as another fundamental surface type that is processed separately from the eight fundamental surface types. The maximum allowable surface fit error for surface region acceptance is relaxed (doubled) during this last chance stage in an attempt to recover useful information about the remaining pixels represented in the last chance image that are, by definition, noisier than average or previously misgrouped. Eventually, the algorithm stops either when the average image error is less than the pre-specified threshold or when all regions above the minimum region size threshold (30) in the last

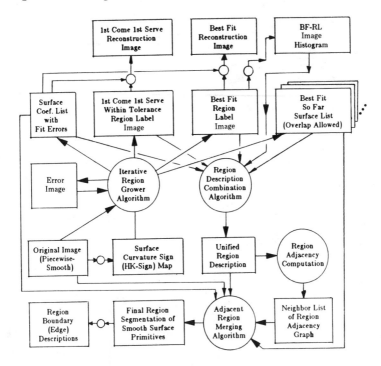

Figure 4.4: Dataflow Diagram for Segmentation Algorithm

hance image have been completely processed. At algorithm termination, the best-fit reconstructed image is very similar to the original image if it possessed the surface coherence property, and a list of surface regions has been generated that qualify as a segmentation of the digital surface into approximate HK-sign surface primitives. Since complicated smooth surfaces, such as the visible surface of a torus, may be segmented into several regions due to the limitations of the approximating functions and the nature of the HK-sign surface primitives. Adjacent surface regions that join smoothly at the boundary separating the regions are then merged to create the final segmentation in terms of smooth surface primitive regions.

The digital surface segmentation algorithm is a combination of simple component algorithms and simple data structures. Although it is referred to as a single algorithm, many relatively subtle variations on the same theme are possible. For example, despite a genuine intention to avoid the incorporation of *ad hoc* thresholds, it was necessary to include many thresholds in the region growing algorithm to achieve the desired performance. The standard results shown in Chapter 7 were created by a true blackbox algorithm in which all internal thresholds were held fixed for all twenty-two test images shown. Methods for adaptive thresholds that depend on

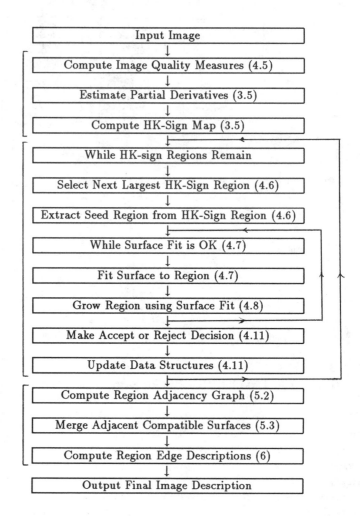

Figure 4.5: Sequential Control of Segmentation Algorithm

estimates of the image noise variance are also feasible and are discussed in Section 4.5. Several results are shown in Chapter 7. As another example, the standard results used only approximate surface continuity compatibility, or C^0 compatibility, to test new pixels during region growth. In Section 4.8.1, methods for insuring approximate surface derivative compatibility, or C^1 compatibility, and approximate surface normal compatibility, or G^1 compatibility (for first order geometric continuity), are discussed. Several results of applying this compatibility constraint are also shown in Chapter 7. Although not specifically discussed, it is also possible to require second derivative continuity or curvature continuity via similar means if the digital surface data is of high enough quality. None of the real range images discussed in Chapter 7 would be useful for testing this sort of higher order compatibility because they are too noisy. Also, Chen [1988] has recently demonstrated a method based on the QR decomposition method [Golub and VanLoan 1983] for testing the least square error compatibility of each new pixel as it is added. Hence, there is a whole realm of compatibility tests based on an underlying geometric or statistical theory that can be performed on new pixels during region growing. As a final example of algorithm variations, the allowable error tolerance function in Section 4.8 may take different functional forms as well as different thresholds. These forms and thresholds can affect the aggressiveness of region growth, the number of required iterations, and the quality of the segmented regions as well as the theoretical convergence properties. Several other algorithm variations were experimented with. The conclusion is that the algorithm is relatively stable with respect to small perturbations of component algorithms and their thresholds.

Each part of the region growing segmentation algorithm is described in detail in this chapter. The material is divided into main sections on seed region extraction, variable order surface fitting, region growing, termination criteria and convergence, and surface acceptance and rejection decisions with data structure updates. The subjects are presented sequentially, but several digressions are necessary to describe the many interconnections shown in the dataflow diagram in Figure 4.4. The combination of the three region descriptions and surface merging at smooth surface joins are treated as separate higher level vision modules and are the subjects of Chapter 5. Before entering the detailed component algorithm descriptions, two preliminary discussions on approximating functions and maximum allowable error tolerance specification must first be presented.

4.4 Approximating Function Selection

As discussed in Chapter 2, an image segmentation should consist of a set of approximating functions and a set of disjoint 2-D regions, one for each meaningful surface primitive in the original image. As indicated in Chapter 3, the eight fundamental surface shapes of the HK-sign surface primitives are relatively simple and should be much easier to approximate than arbitrary surface shapes. Arbitrarily complicated smooth surfaces can be decomposed into a disjoint union of these simple surface primitives. Hence, if these surface primitives can be approximated well, a composite surface description for arbitrary surfaces can be obtained.

For dimensionality reduction, the approximating functions should be representable by a relatively small amount of data. For generality, the approximating surfaces must be well-defined over arbitrary connected regions. Most surfaces in computer aided geometric design must be defined over quadrilateral domains. As stated above, surface primitives are used in an iterative region growing process. The approximating functions of the digital surface segmentation must be useful for extrapolation into neighboring areas of a surface in order for the region growing method to be successful. The ability to interpolate between pixels is also useful. If the iterative surface fitting approach to region growing is to be useful in real world applications, the approximating functions must be computable in a relatively short amount of time on suitable hardware given the data to be fitted. The approximating functions should also be easily differentiable so that directional derivatives, surface normals, and the differential geometric shape descriptors from Chapter 3 can be computed from them without significant computational expense. Finally, the set of approximating functions should be totally ordered, not partially ordered, so that each approximant is capable of describing lower order approximants exactly, but cannot approximate higher order functions. For digital surface description purposes, general 3-D surface representation capability is not needed because digital surfaces are discrete representations of graph surfaces.

Low-order bivariate polynomials $z = f(x, y)$ satisfy all of the above requirements, but what about other types of surface functions? Rational polynomial surface functions were investigated since they are often able to provide a better fit to data than non-rational polynomials using the same number of coefficients. However, the rational polynomial fitting algorithms require substantially more computation than non-rational approaches. Since rational polynomials of fixed degree do not form a linear vector space, many of nice theoretical properties of non-rational polynomials are lost. Moreover, special care must be taken to avoid denominator zeros during surface extrapolation.

Tensor-product spline surface functions are another possible choice for approximating surface functions, but arbitrary connected domain and extrapolation requirements present difficulties for these surface types since splines are not intended for extrapolation purposes. Quadrics and superquadrics provide only algebraic surface forms instead of the explicit linear parametric forms that are desirable for surface fitting in the presence of noise. Other types of surface functions found in the computer aided geometric design literature [Boehm et al.1984] and other mathematics literature, such as triangular surface patches, Gordon surfaces, Coon's patch surfaces, smoothing splines, Hardy's multiquadrics, and Shepard's method interpolants, all present different types of problems because they are intended for distinctly different purposes from what is needed here. Therefore, low order least squares-fitted bivariate polynomials have been chosen to satisfy the above requirements (see Appendix C). It has been found that these polynomials work quite well for perceptual organization tasks with a comparatively small computational and source code requirements. With all factors considered, they are the ideal choice for establishing the feasibility, the general characteristics, and the performance potential of the data-driven digital surface segmentation algorithm. If a better set of approximating functions were to be made available with an appropriate surface fitting algorithm, the entire approach with its theoretical and heuristic arguments would still carry through with little or no change. To maintain generality in the algorithm statement, it is assumed only that there exists a set of approximating functions F, that contains $|F|$ discrete function types that can be ordered in terms of the "shape potential" of each type of surface function relative to the set of fundamental HK-sign surface primitives.

First-order (planar), second-order (biquadratic), third-order (bicubic), and fourth-order (biquartic) bivariate polynomials are proposed as a useful set of approximating functions for HK-sign surface primitives. Bivariate polynomials of order five and higher are avoided for fitting purposes owing to potential oscillatory and numerical difficulties. Therefore, $|F| = 4$ and the set of approximating functions F can be written in the form of a single equation:

$$\hat{g}(m, \vec{a}, x, y) = \sum_{i+j \leq m} a_{ij} x^i y^j \qquad (m \leq 4) \qquad (4.1)$$

$$= a_{00} + a_{10}x + a_{01}y + a_{11}xy + a_{20}x^2 + a_{02}y^2 + a_{21}x^2y + a_{12}xy^2 +$$

$$a_{30}x^3 + a_{03}y^3 + a_{31}x^3y + a_{22}x^2y^2 + a_{13}xy^3 + a_{40}x^4 + a_{04}y^4.$$

The parameter space for F is $\Re^{15}$. Planar surfaces ($m = 1$) are obtained by restricting the parameter space to a three-dimensional subspace. Biquadratic surfaces ($m = 2$) are restricted to a six-dimensional subspace whereas bicubic surfaces ($m = 3$) are restricted to a ten-dimensional subspace. Any least squares solver for the matrix equation $[\Phi]\vec{a} = \vec{b}$ can be used to compute the parameter vector $\vec{a}$ and the RMS fit error ϵ directly from the digital surface data in a region (Appendix C). Moreover, a least squares approach based on the QR decomposition allows surface fits to be updated incrementally during the region growing process as new data points become available or as higher order approximations are needed [Golub and VanLoan 1983] [Chen 1988].

As with any set of approximating functions, there are some problems with low-order bivariate polynomial surfaces. Many common HK-sign surface primitives exist that cannot be exactly represented by bivariate polynomials. Hemispheres and cylinder halves provide two examples of shapes that fall into this category. It is claimed that, for perceptual grouping purposes, a fourth-order polynomial can approximate a semicircle or ellipse closely enough that the casual observer cannot distinguish between them, especially without a reference figure at hand. For example, consider Figure 4.6(a), which compares an ellipse and a least squares fitted, fourth order polynomial where 128 data points were used. The shape approximation is not bad. The average absolute error is 3.89 and the RMS error is

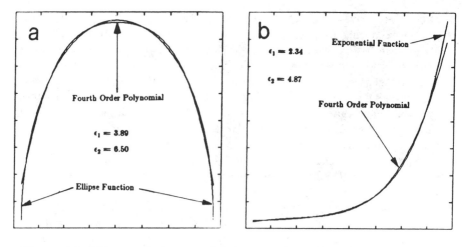

Figure 4.6: Ellipse and Exponential Compared to 4th Order Polynomials

6.50 on a scale from 0 to 255, or 2.5% of the dynamic range of the geometric signal. Consider also Figure 4.6(b), which compares an exponential function and a least squares fitted, fourth order polynomial where 128 data points have again been used. The average absolute error is 2.34 and the RMS error is 4.87 on a scale from 0 to 255, or 1.9% of the dynamic range. Although exponentially shaped surfaces are not commonly encountered in the real world, the infinite series formula for the exponential is seen to be approximated quite well by only five terms, including the constant term, on a finite interval. A second order approximation could not do nearly as well.

The main concern is that the fit is good enough for perceptual organization tasks in image segmentation, not for creation of computer aided geometric design quality surfaces. Every application will have different types of relevant surfaces. In other words, if strong evidence is given that a peak surface primitive exists in a digital surface, the proposed bivariate polynomials can be used to group all the pixels of that peak surface into a coherent surface region, even if the underlying surface is a hemisphere. This statement regarding the hemisphere was verified via experimental results and is considered in more detail later in this chapter. This type of approximate surface region description should provide few problems for higher level processes. For example, if an application specific algorithm were searching for spheres in a range image, the existence of a round region that is well-approximated by a polynomial with approximately constant surface curvature would provide extremely strong evidence that a sphere is present. The surface matching algorithm is expected to use the exact object's surface model, the approximate surface region description, *and the original data* in that region to verify that the surface is indeed a hemisphere. In other words, since the hemisphere has already been isolated, it is not difficult to fit the segmented pixels with a spherical surface and match that to the object model. However, special purpose algorithms are usually selected in practice to meet processing speed requirements.

4.4.1 Quadrics

Quadrics are general second order algebraic surfaces specified implicitly as the zero set of a function $f(x, y, z) = 0$:

$$f(x, y, z) = \sum_{0 \le i+j+k \le 2} q_{ijk} x^i y^j z^k = 0. \tag{4.2}$$

The general quadric cannot be written as $z = f(x, y)$ although the degenerate special case biquadratic polynomial surface can. If the world model and all relevant real-world surfaces consist only of quadric surfaces, including planes, then it is logical to use an approximating function set with only two function types: a plane and a quadric. One might argue that a quadric surface function should be included as one of the approximating functions since quadrics are common in geometric modeling systems and in manufactured parts produced on certain types of machine tools. There are several reasons not to include quadrics in this data-driven system. Although a quadric approximating function would handle problems with hemispheres or half cylinders, quadric approximations to an exponential surface would not be nearly as good as the biquartic. Quadric approximations impose symmetry requirements on surface primitives, a requirement that cannot be expected to be satisfied in a general-purpose data-driven image segmentation system, or even a general-purpose computer aided design system [Sarraga and Waters 1985]. In this sense, the biquartic polynomial approximant is more powerful for grouping purposes than the quadric approximant because the biquartic can come close to describing visible portions of quadric surfaces, but quadrics cannot come nearly as close to describing other types of non-quadric surfaces that are also well approximated by the biquartic. Moreover, the simplest least squares quadric fitting approaches, as in [Hall et al.1982] [Faugeras et al.1985], yield a minimum least squares error but do not minimize the error between the data points and the quadric surface as is done in polynomial surface fitting. Such fitting approaches are very sensitive to noise. Other approaches are possible, but generally require more computation.

If the quadric were included, what position would it occupy in the total ordering of the bivariate approximating functions. Should it come before or after the bicubic, or after the biquartic? If included before or after the bicubic, the quadric approximant would break the total ordering and require a Y-shaped partial ordering of approximating functions. There do not seem to be any general-purpose answers to these questions. Although quadrics can be introduced into an application system if needed, it is claimed that quadric surfaces do not belong in a data-driven digital surface segmentation theory. The use of quadric surfaces should be delayed until later phases of processing. Quadrics seem most appropriate for higher level application-specific matching algorithms for utilizing and recognizing certain types of symmetry in the image data. For example, if the selected world modeler uses only planes and quadrics as do many solid modelers, then quadrics will play a key role in the model-dependent surface matching algorithm.

4.5   Noise Estimation and Threshold Specification

Digital surfaces exhibit the property of "surface coherence" when sets of neighboring pixels are spatially consistent with each other in the sense that those pixels can be interpreted as noisy, quantized sampled points of a smooth surface. In order for the surface segmentation algorithm to group pixels based on underlying smooth surface primitives, it is necessary to know *a priori* how well the surface primitives should fit the data. The surface curvature zero thresholds, mentioned in Chapter 3, are also related to surface coherence and noise. This type of information should be derived from the image data in data-driven algorithm so that the algorithm can adapt to the noise conditions. This section describes two related simple quantities for estimating the average noise in an image if the additive noise process is relatively stationary across the image. The topics of noise and signal quality estimation are also discussed.

Sensor noise is a pervasive phenomenon. All sensors that operate above the temperature of absolute zero are at least subject to random thermal noise, which is modeled accurately as a white Gaussian noise process. Optical sensors, such as video cameras and imaging laser radars, detect quantized photons and are therefore subject to shot noise, which is accurately modeled as a Poisson noise process. Quantization noise is also involved whenever analog signals are digitized and is modeled using a uniform probability distribution. Therefore, algorithms that process real sensor data must be able to cope with sensor noise in various forms. Theoretical approaches are often developed in computer vision that are useless in practical applications because signal quantities cannot be computed accurately enough.

In communications theory, pure signals are transmitted over noisy channels to receivers that produce estimates of the pure transmitted signals. The additive noise model is commonly used to analyze this situation. Noise is modeled as a random process that can be measured when there is no signal. When a signal is sent, the random noise is modeled as simply being added to the signal. The job of the receiver is to reproduce the best possible version of the pure signal even though the received signal was corrupted by noise. The signal-to-noise ratio (SNR) measures the ratio of the signal power in the absence of noise to the noise power in the absence of the sig-

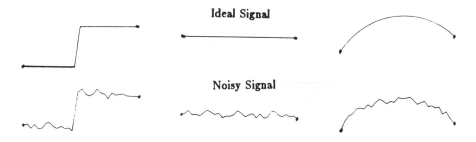

Figure 4.7: Depth Profiles for Step, Table Top, and Curved Surface

nal. This single scalar quantity is used to measure the quality of received signals. Digital signal processing and digital image processing problems, especially edge detection, are typically formulated in similar signal and noise terms.

In Chapter 2, the digital surface segmentation problem was stated in terms of a signal plus additive noise model. What happens to signal quality concepts like the signal-to-noise ratio when the information in the signal is fundamentally geometric? It is still possible to compute power spectral densities in the 2-D spatial frequency spectrum and to compute noise power in bandwidths of interest, but geometric concepts are lost in this approach. One can clearly imagine a very high quality digital surface without noise (very high range resolution samples of a smooth surface with no added noise), but it is difficult to define or measure noise in the absence of a surface "signal" when range images are concerned. The reason is that flat surfaces orthogonal to the viewing axis appear in a Cartesian orthographic range image as a constant plus measurement noise. Hence in this case, the "no signal" state is equivalent to a "flat surface" state, which is a perfectly valid scene surface signal. It is perhaps more difficult to meaningfully define the "power" in a surface shape, and shape is the information contained in a range image signal. A specific instance of this problem is now considered.

Suppose range images are digitized for part of a step, part of a table top, and part of a curved surface, such as a globe. Figure 4.7 shows ideal and noisy examples of the range variations in these images as a function of position along a scanline. Standard edge detection models measure the signal strength of the step image as the height of the step. But how does one define signal strength for the table top and globe surfaces? How is the quality of a range image of a flat table top defined? It is futile to employ measures similar to the signal-to-noise ratio because the signal, as normally defined, is zero for a flat surface. Yet, if two 8-bit range images of a flat table top are given where both image A and image B have a mean value of 127, but image A has a standard deviation of 2 range levels about the mean and image B has a standard deviation of 40 range levels about the

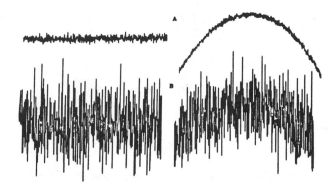

Figure 4.8: Different Noise Levels for Table Top and Curved Surface

mean, most people would say that image A is a higher quality range image than image B. It is assumed the orthographic range image is taken looking directly down on the table, as in the example range profiles in Figure 4.8. Similarly, if a curved surface is substituted for the table top, one could still easily decide which range image was of higher quality by looking at the local fluctuations in the noise from pixel to pixel. Therefore, any quality measure of a range image of a smooth surface should be independent of the shape of that smooth surface. The image quality measure should indicate properties of the noise and not properties of the smooth surface. This in turn implies that quality measures of a range image are not interested in range discontinuities or orientation discontinuities between surface regions, but rather in how smooth or how noisy are the smooth surfaces in the image. A process that measures the quality of the step range image will then ignore the magnitude of the step and focus on the smoothness or roughness of the flat surface data on both sides of the step. In other words, the image quality of a range image is related only to the average variance of the image noise process, not to any contrast properties of the signal. This is quite different than edge detection models of image signal quality that divide step edge height by noise variance estimates to get a signal-to-noise ratio.

Surface coherence is a concept that combines the smoothness of the smooth surfaces in a scene with the notion of the spatial extent of a surface. The key question is the following: How much visible surface area is required before the visible surface may be said to be "coherent," or spatially consistent, and processed as such? If a distinct scene surface only occupies one pixel in a range image, it makes no difference how smooth or how textured or how noisy that surface is, it will only cause an ideal range imaging sensor to register a single value for the range at that location, which could be quite different than neighboring values. Unfortunately, noise spikes, or statistical outliers, may occur in real images making it almost impossible to distinguish between a noise spike and a very small surface that occupies one pixel. However, even when statistical outliers do occur, it is extremely unlikely that four or more outliers would occur in adjacent pixels and all lie in the same plane. Therefore, the surface coherence concept might be formulated in terms of regions as small as four pixels if the data were of very high quality and fixed size window operators did not have to be used. But when convolution window operators are used for smoothing and derivative estimation, as in the surface characterization algorithm, it is difficult for the surface properties of very small surfaces to remain intact in the HK-sign map. Therefore, in order to be certain that the data-driven digital surface segmentation algorithm will produce meaningful results, a statement about the size of surfaces in the original image is needed. Ideally, an intelligent low-level algorithm might process an image and say, "The smallest meaningful region of interest is represented by a surface region approximately 7x7 pixels, and all smooth surface regions are corrupted by zero-mean additive Gaussian noise with a standard deviation of approximately 1 range level in the 8-bit dynamic range of the range image." Such an image would be an example of a range image exhibiting surface coherence, but unfortunately, it would be difficult for a low-level process that is devoid of concepts about meaningful surfaces to issue such a statement. However, it is possible for a low-level process to yield useful information about image quality and surface coherence. For the digital surface segmentation approach, a preliminary measure of the overall "smooth surface fittability" of the data is needed. Preferably, this measure could be computed quickly without actually fitting global surfaces and measuring fit errors.

This qualitative discussion above is now made more quantitative. In Chapter 2, the digital surface $g(x, y)$ is assumed to have the following form:

$$g(x, y) = \sum_{i=1}^{N_R} \lfloor g_i(x, y)\chi(x, y, R_i) + \mathbf{n}(x, y)\rfloor. \tag{4.3}$$

where $A_{\min} = \min |R_i|$ is the smallest region size present in the digital surface and the variance of the zero-mean noise process is given by $\text{var}(\mathbf{n}(x, y)) = E(\mathbf{n}^2(x, y)) = \sigma_n^2(x, y)$ where $E(\cdot)$ is the statistical expectation operator which averages over all images in a statistical ensemble. If the digital surface segmentation were already computed, the value of $\epsilon = \|g(x, y) - \hat{g}(x, y)\|$ might serve as a good estimate of the noise, but it is necessary to have an estimate of ϵ in order to compute the digital surface segmentation.

If the additive noise process $\mathbf{n}(x, y)$ is stationary over the image I, then $\sigma_n^2(x, y) = \sigma_I^2$ for every pixel (x, y) in the image. If the noise process is also ergodic, then spatial averages equal ensemble averages as the number of spatial samples goes to infinity. Nonrigorously, this implies roughly that

$$\sigma_I^2 \approx \frac{1}{|I|} \sum_{(x,y)\in I} \sigma_g^2(x, y) \tag{4.4}$$

where $\sigma_g^2(x, y)$ is a local estimate of the noise variance of the sample digital surface $g(x, y)$. The numerical value of σ_I would be the expected value of the RMS fit error of any least squares surface fits done to the digital surface data over a valid region if no quantization error were present. For any particular pixel, the variance of the quantization error is $\sigma_q^2(x, y) = 1/12$ for a uniform probability distribution over the unit interval. Therefore, even in the presence of quantization noise, the RMS fit error of least squares fits should not be much greater than σ_I.

The unsolved problem then is to obtain the individual noise estimates $\sigma_g^2(x, y)$ at each pixel. The following simple method, based on the RMS error of local planar surface fits, has been implemented and tested, and was found to be a useful indication of image noise variance, image quality, and surface coherence. It does not account for everything that is implied by the notion of surface coherence in that the necessary spatial extent of surfaces is not considered. One practical bonus of this approach is that the existing surface characterization software used for the results in Chapter 3 can compute the proposed image quality measures, which keeps the overall system implementation that much simpler. Better methods of measuring image noise variance, image quality, smooth surface fittability, or surface coherence are no doubt possible, but good results were obtained with the following method:

1. Perform a least squares planar fit $z = ax + by + c$ to every 3x3 neighborhood in an image using the separable convolution window operators described in Chapter 3 to get the slope of each plane $\sqrt{a^2 + b^2}$. In the notation of Chapter 3, the smoothing vector is $\vec{d_0} = (1/3)[1\ 1\ 1]^T$ and the first order difference vector is $\vec{d_1} = (1/2)[-1\ 0\ 1]^T$. The a coefficients at each pixel are obtained by convolving the window $\vec{d_0}\vec{d_1}^T$ with $g(x, y)$, the b coefficients are obtained by convolving $\vec{d_1}\vec{d_0}^T$ with $g(x, y)$, and the c coefficients are obtained using $\vec{d_0}\vec{d_0}^T$.

2. If the slope of the planar surface at a pixel is greater than a threshold slope (8), discard the pixel since it is probably at or near to a step discontinuity where planar fits are always bad.

3. Similarly, if the slope of the planar surface is exactly zero, the neighborhood of the pixel is likely to be synthetic data, saturated, or completely dark, and it should be discarded because it is not representative of smooth surfaces in a digital image.

4. If the pixel has not been discarded, compute the (order 1) planar RMS fit error for the 3x3 window $\epsilon_{1,3}(x, y)$ at the pixel (x, y) as described in Chapter 3, and accumulate the average mean-square error and the average RMS error. Increment the number of pixels processed.

Image Quality Measures for Test Image Database				
Image Name	ρ_1	Type	Source	Comments
Coffee Cup A	0.71	Range	ERIM	Very Good Quality
Coffee Cup B	0.84	Range	ERIM	Very Good Quality
Keyboard A	1.17	Range	ERIM	Good Quality
Keyboard B	1.35	Range	ERIM	Good Quality
Polyhedron	1.38	Range	ERIM	Good Quality
Ring on Polyhedron	1.61	Range	ERIM	Fair Quality
Curved Surface A	1.68	Range	ERIM	Fair Quality
Curved Surface B	2.15	Range	ERIM	Fair Quality
Road Scene A	0.72	Range	ERIM	Good Quality,No Detail
Road Scene B	0.79	Range	ERIM	Good Quality,No Detail
Auto Part	0.43	Range	INRIA	From (x,y,z) List
Block A	1.82	Range	Synthetic	Low Noise Added
Block B	5.93	Range	Synthetic	High Noise Added
Two Cylinders	1.79	Range	Synthetic	Low Noise Added
Complex Object	1.83	Range	Synthetic	Low Noise Added
Light Bulb	3.45	Range	Synthetic	Medium Noise Added
Torus	2.59	Range	Synthetic	Medium Noise Added
Circular Waves	1.54	Range	Synthetic	No Noise Added
Space Shuttle	2.29	Intensity	Camera	Poor Quality
Road Image	1.95	Intensity	Camera	Fair Quality
USC Girl	2.63	Intensity	Camera	Poor Quality
U-Mass House	2.96	Intensity	Camera	Good Quality,Detailed

Figure 4.9: Image Quality Measures for Noisy Images

5. After all pixels have been processed, compute two image quality measures ρ_1 and ρ_2 denoted ρ_p for $p = 1, 2$:

$$\rho_p = \left(\frac{1}{|I'|} \sum_{(x,y) \in I'} \epsilon_{1,3}^p(x, y) \right)^{1/p} \tag{4.5}$$

where $I' = I - I_{edge}$ where I_{edge} is the set of image pixels where the planar slope exceeds the given threshold.

This processing scheme assumes (1) that smooth surfaces generally do not curve much within a 3x3 window, and if they do, the surface slope is also large, and (2) there are relatively few orientation discontinuity pixels compared to the number of visible surface interior pixels in the image. Tests were also done with 5x5 windows and higher-order surfaces in both window sizes, but the 3x3 planar fit measure produced the most meaningful results in that the numbers were most highly correlated with the author's subjective notions of image quality. Also, two separate measures of image quality are computed because the ρ_1 measure averages out an occasional high variance pixel without much slope much better than the ρ_2 measure. However, the ρ_2^2 measure will be a better estimate of the stationary image noise variance σ_f^2 assuming that $\epsilon_{1,3}(x, y)$ is a good estimate of $\sigma_g(x, y)$.

Figure 4.9 shows the value of the ρ_1 quality measure for the images discussed in Chapter 7. There is a good qualitative agreement between the magnitude of the quality measure and humanly perceived visual quality of the images. More detailed images tend to have measures with higher values since the planar fits are worse on fine detail in the image data. Figure 4.10 displays the planar fit error image $\epsilon_{1,3}(x,y)$ for the coffee cup image and the block with three holes image. The intensity at each pixel in these images is the magnitude of the planar fit error, but the images are contrast stretched so absolute magnitudes are not meaningful. All step-edge regions are blackened by the chosen slope threshold since they are not of interest to the image quality measure. Figure 4.11 displays the planar fit error images for the Curved Surface A range image and the space shuttle intensity image. The quality measure ρ_1 is the average of the non-zero pixels in these images.

The quality measures allowed us to tie algorithm thresholds involved in the surface characterization and surface segmentation algorithms to the amount of noise in the image in an empirical manner. For example, let ρ_{cc} denote the image quality measure for the coffee cup image. The zero-curvature thresholds ϵ_H and ϵ_K for the surface characterization algorithm and the maximum allowable surface fit error threshold $\epsilon_{\max}$ for the surface segmentation algorithm are manually adjusted so that good segmentation results are achieved. Then, when an unknown image is presented to the system, the quality measures are computed. No variable information is used since the internal slope threshold (8) for the quality measure is fixed. If $\rho < \rho_{cc}$, then the empirically determined thresholds for the coffee cup should be lowered depending on the magnitude of the difference until good segmentation results are obtained. If $\rho > \rho_{cc}$, then the thresholds are similarly increased. A simple linear fit of manually optimized error thresholds for the region growing algorithm based on surface fitting yielded a relationship of $\epsilon_{\max} = 1.1 + 1.1\rho_1$. For the other measure, the relationship $\epsilon_{\max} = 2.5\rho_2$ was used in some of the experimental results of Chapter 7. This technique provides at least some basis for automated adaptive threshold selection for the surface segmentation algorithm. As noted in Chapter 7, it was possible to achieve good results over a large set of images using the same fixed set of thresholds for each image as long as the quality measure was below some threshold ($\rho_1 < 3$). Image segmentation is degraded significantly if the maximum allowable fit error threshold is smaller than suggested by the above equations. In contrast, image segmentation is not affected much as the threshold is increased over the suggested value unless the threshold was made unreasonably large.

The quality measures ρ_1, ρ_2 are proposed as simple measures of surface coherence for digital surfaces. When a quality measure is small ($\rho_1 \leq 1$ for 8-bit images), the 3x3 planar surfaces tend to fit the digital surface neighborhoods well and the segmentation algorithm is likely to do very well. Most synthetic images without added noise fall into this category and are not shown in the experimental results of Chapter 7 since they are usually easy to segment correctly. When the quality measure is in an

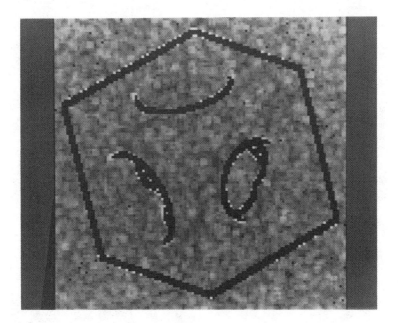

Figure 4.10: Planar Fit Error Images for Coffee Cup and Block

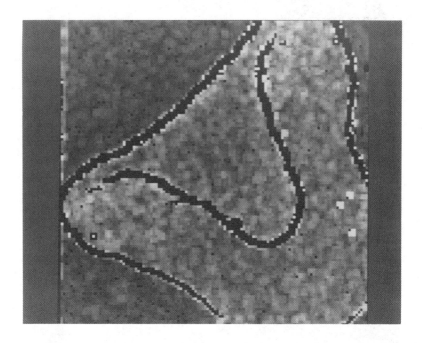

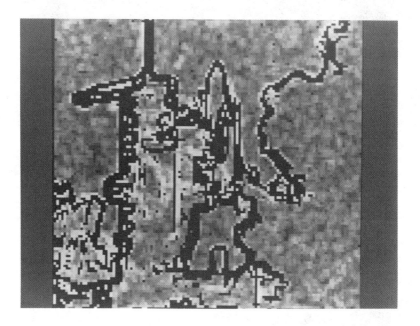

Figure 4.11: Planar Fit Error Images for Curved Surface A and Shuttle

intermediate range ($1 < \rho_1 \leq 3$) as is the case for most of the images listed in Figure 4.9, the segmentation algorithm generally does well, but may not yield all meaningful surfaces as separate distinct regions. When the quality measure is in a higher range ($3 < \rho_1 \leq 10$), the segmentation algorithm will yield some meaningful surfaces, but performance may vary widely from image to image depending on how large the noisy smooth surface regions are. One problem with $\rho_{1,2}$ is that it does not yield any information about the spatial extent of coherent surfaces in the image owing to its local nature. Despite this difficulty, it has been a useful tool for the wide variety of images discussed in Chapter 7.

4.6 Seed Region Extraction

Error threshold and approximating function selection have been discussed to set the stage for the actual algorithm description. The approximating function set $\hat{g}_i(x, y)$ and the error threshold ϵ_{max} shall appear as predetermined, but variable, elements in this description.

Given the original image and the HK-sign map, the algorithm begins by considering the HK-sign map. Most of the problems with the HK-sign map mentioned earlier are avoided by adopting the following strategy. The largest connected region of any fundamental HK-sign surface type in the image is isolated using an approach described below. If the isolated connected component region is contracted (eroded) repetitively using a 3x3 region contraction operator (Appendix F), the region will eventually disappear as long as the entire image is not of a single surface type. If the image is a single surface type, that case presents no problems as will be evident. After each contraction, or erosion, there exists a largest four-connected subregion of the original region. If the number of pixels in the largest connected subregion is recorded as a function of the number of contractions, a *contraction profile* for the original region is created. Figure 4.12 shows scaled contraction profiles for several different regions. Note that they all have similar shape, but that some go to zero faster than others. Given a threshold for the minimum number of seed region pixels, there will be a minimum number of pixels in the contraction profile that is greater than or equal to the given threshold. The largest connected subregion with the minimum number of pixels greater than or equal to this minimum seed region size threshold is assigned to be a *seed region*, or kernel region.

The minimum seed region size threshold must be greater than or equal to the minimum number of points required for the simplest surface fit. If the threshold is equal to the minimum number of points, then the surface fit can respond strongly to noise in the data. Therefore, the threshold should be somewhat greater than the minimum required number of pixels. Since three pixels are required to determine a plane and six pixels are required to determine a biquadratic, at least eight pixels in a region are required for

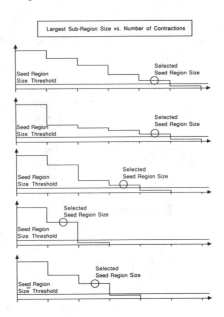

Figure 4.12: Contraction Profiles for Five Different Regions

the seed region. This provides a fair number of pixels for the planar fit, but also allows an increase in surface fit order if required. If it were possible to know the minimum spatial extent of meaningful surfaces in an image before processing, it would be advantageous to increase this threshold as much as possible, thereby increasing the speed of the sequential algorithm since not as many contractions would be needed.

Since the fundamental purpose of the contraction profile computation is to find a small enough isolated interior region that (1) is not inadvertently connected to any adjacent regions, and (2) is far enough inside the boundaries of the actual surface primitive to have escaped the undesired side effects of smoothing and differentiation at surface boundaries, there is an upper limit on the number of necessary contractions. This limit is based on the window size of the smoothing and derivative operators used in the computation of surface curvature for the HK-sign map. The combination of 11x11 smoothing and 9x9 derivative window operators is equivalent to 19x19 weighted least squares derivative window operators. In a 19x19 convolution, a given pixel is affected by the input data 9 pixels away from it on any side. Therefore, a limit of 10 contraction iterations is used since 10 contractions reduce a 20x20 binary block to nothing implying that there are no effects of the 19x19 window operators after the 10 contractions.

The simple method of finding the largest region of any HK-surface type using a generic connected component analysis program with a surface type label image is to (1) isolate the four-connected regions of each of the eight types separately treating each label as a separate binary image, (2) count the number of pixels in each region for each of the eight types and sort, and (3) choose the region with the maximum number of pixels from the maximum counts for each of the eight types. The problem with this approach is that the generic connected component analysis algorithm is a two pass algorithm and requires a significant amount of computation, or 16 passes, two for each surface type. This first step may take a long time for every time that a new seed region is to be computed. The best approach to the problem requires a special purpose connected component algorithm that only makes two passes over the surface type label image, but requires about eight times more memory so that it can keep track of all pixel labels of all eight types. From a software engineering point of view, it may be preferable to use a generic connected component algorithm if it can be done efficiently enough. Therefore, the following approach was employed that used generic image processing and sorting operations and required much less computation than the simple approach above:

1. Compute the surface type label image histogram. This is done with a very simple one pass algorithm.

2. Sort the eight non-zero pixel counts in the histogram that correspond to the eight fundamental surface types.

3. Compute the connected components of the surface type with the largest histogram pixel count as determined from the sorted histogram and isolate the largest region in the connected component list.

4. While the number of pixels in the sorted histogram for the next surface type is greater than the size of the largest region found so far, compute the connected components of the next surface type and isolate the largest region of that type and compare with the largest region found so far. Update the largest region found so far if necessary. Eventually, a surface type is reached where the total number of pixels in the histogram count is less than the largest connected region found so far. It is possible, but not probable, that all eight surface types will need to be checked via connected component analysis.

5. When the while loop terminates, return the largest connected region encountered so far as the largest connected region of any surface type.

This approach takes advantage of the very simple fact that the number of pixels in the largest connected component region of that type can never be larger than the number of pixels of that type in the image. At best, one histogram computation and one connected component analysis computation are required, saving seven expensive connected component analysis computations. At worst, the histogram computation does not help to save connected component analysis computations. On average, the histogram computation eliminated about five connected component algorithm executions out of the possible eight, which is a 62.5% reduction over the simple method first suggested with no real increase in memory requirements.

Methods have been described for (1) quickly selecting the largest connected region of any surface type and for (2) contracting that region to obtain a seed region subject to the minimum seed region size threshold. This ranking technique allows us to process the largest, most coherent, and hopefully, the most important and meaningful surfaces in an image first.

The "large to small" surface type region processing method has been a very useful approach for obtaining good seed regions, but it is not without weaknesses. At the risk of getting ahead of the detailed algorithm description, consider the following example. It might prove worthwhile to combine the size measure of a surface type region with the average error in the error image $e(x, y)$ over that region into one ranking measure. As described in more detail in the surface acceptance section, the error image records the error at each pixel for the best-fit surface that has been encountered so far. In addition, surface primitives are allowed to tentatively approximate other connected regions in the image that are adjacent to the grown seed region as well as other regions that not adjacent. For surface type regions that have not been tentatively approximated by other surface primitives, the average error in the error image will be a constant and the region size will be the sole determining factor in selecting the next region no matter what combination of region error and size is used. However, after several surface regions have been accepted in the sequential segmentation algorithm, it is possible that a larger region may be well approximated already and a smaller region has not been approximated at all. In this case, it seems that the smaller region should be processed next. But it is not clear how region size and surface approximation error can be meaningfully combined just as it was not clear in Chapter 2 in the segmentation problem definition. This topic is left for future research.

As a final note, one-pixel-wide lines of a single surface type in the HK-sign map have caused unnecessary computations on strange shaped regions owing to the connectivity caused by such lines. Although such lines are uncommon in the original HK-sign map, they tend to develop in the writable copy of the map during the updating procedures listed in the surface acceptance and rejection section. It is a simple matter to filter out these one-pixel-wide lines occasionally during the segmentation algorithm execution. It was found that this single pass filter broke many unwanted connections and saved a significant amount of computation without affecting the final results.

4.7 Iterative Variable Order Surface Fitting

Each isolated seed region is given as the input to the iterative region growing algorithm based on variable order surface fitting. The basic concepts of this algorithm are the following. First, it must be decided how well smooth surfaces should fit the data. The image noise estimation procedure discussed above provides an indication of the RMS fit error to be expected for least squares smooth surface fitting. This number guides the choice of the maximum RMS error threshold ϵ_{max} for the iterative surface fitting algorithm. The number ϵ_{max} is also used for the overall average image error threshold used to terminate the entire algorithm.

A plane is always fitted first to the small seed region using an equally weighted least squares approach described in Appendix C. If the seed region belongs to a surface that is not too highly curved, a plane will fit quite well to the original digital surface. This idea is basic to mathematics. If a small enough interval on the real line is considered, any smooth real-valued function of a single variable can be approximated well by a straight line on that interval. Linear approximations are often used to help analyze many nonlinear phenomena locally when more direct general methods are not available. If the plane fits the seed region within the maximum allowable error threshold for the RMS error, then the seed is allowed to grow. If not, the seed is fitted with the next higher order surface (the biquadratic in the current implementation) and the algorithm proceeds similarly. When the seed is allowed to grow, the functional description of the surface over the seed region is tested to determine what new pixels are compatible with the seed region. For example, if the value at a pixel is close enough to the surface fit of the seed region, that pixel is compatible with the seed region.

This process may be stated mathematically as follows. Let I be the rectangular image region over which the hypothetical piecewise smooth function $z = \sum g_i(x, y)\chi(x, y, R_i)$ is defined. Let $\hat{R}_i^0$ be the seed region provided by the seed region extraction algorithm that corresponds to the actual region R_i. This seed region is hypothesized to be a subset of the actual HK-sign surface primitive region R_i that will be determined as the seed region is grown:

$$\hat{R}_i^0 \subseteq R_i \subseteq I. \tag{4.6}$$

The HK-sign map provides subsets of the desired segmentation regions (the HK-sign surface primitive regions) through the seed region extraction process. The required task is to convert the seed region $\hat{R}_i^0$ to a full region $\hat{R}_i$ that approximates the desired region R_i.

As discussed above, a specific finite set F of approximating surface function types must be chosen for use in surface fitting. These surface functions must be able to provide for extrapolation into areas outside the local surface fitting region, and they must provide good approximation capabilities within the fitting region. Let $|F| = 4$ be the number of different types of surface functions to be used. Let $\vec{a}_i^k \in \Re^{15}$ be the parameter vector associated with the functional fit to the range values in a given connected region $\hat{R}_i^k$ where the superscript k denotes the k-th iteration in the iterative surface fitting process. The particular function order for the k-th iteration on the i-th region is m_i^k where

$$m_i^k \in \{1, 2, \ldots, |F|\}. \tag{4.7}$$

The surface function of order m_i^k is denoted $z = \hat{g}(m_i^k, \vec{a}_i^k, x, y)$. The surface fitting process, denoted $\mathbf{L}_{\hat{g}}$, transforms the original digital image $g(x, y)$, a connected region description $\hat{R}_i^k$, and the fit order m_i^k into the parameter vector $\vec{a}_i^k$ and the fit error ϵ_i^k:

$$(\vec{a}_i^k, \epsilon_i^k) = \mathbf{L}_{\hat{g}}(m_i^k, \hat{R}_i^k, g). \tag{4.8}$$

The surface fitting process has the property that the fit error

$$\epsilon_i^k = \|\hat{g}(m_i^k, \vec{a}_i^k, x, y) - g(x, y)\|_{\hat{R}_i^k} \tag{4.9}$$

is the minimum value attainable for functions of the form specified by m_i^k over all parameter vectors $\vec{a}_i^k$. Equally-weighted least squares surface fitting minimizes the error metric

$$(\epsilon_i^k)^2 = \frac{1}{|\hat{R}_i^k|} \sum_{(x,y) \in \hat{R}_i^k} |\hat{g}(m_i^k, \vec{a}_i^k, x, y) - g(x, y)|^2 \tag{4.10}$$

where $|\hat{R}_i^k|$ is the number of pixels in the region $\hat{R}_i^k$, or the area of the region. Least squares bivariate polynomial surface fitting is relatively fast, and the shape potential of polynomial surfaces is adequate for HK-sign surface primitives. Bivariate polynomial surfaces of orders 1, 2, 3, 4 have provided good approximations to the fundamental surface types in experiments.

Given (1) a connected region $\hat{R}_i^k$ where $k = 0$ for the original seed region, (2) the original digital image $g(x, y)$, and (3) the simplest function type m_i^k such that the fit error test and the regions test are passed, the parameter vector $\vec{a}_i^k$ and the RMS error ϵ_i^k are computed for the k-th iteration on the i-th HK-surface primitive region from the image. The parameter vector and the fit error are passed to the region growing process.

4.7.1   Fit Error Test

The fit error test is a simple heuristic version of the χ^2 test in statistics. Assuming a valid estimate of the noise variance in the image, the mean square error of a surface fit should be the same number. But since the mean square error of the surface fit is a random variable itself, there are variations in mean square error for different surface fits that depend partially on the size of the regions being fitted. Hence, the maximum allowable fit error $\epsilon_{\max}$

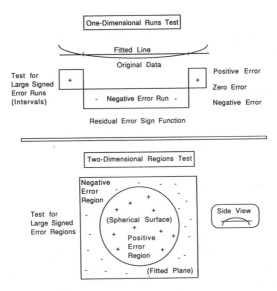

Figure 4.13: Runs Test and Regions Test for Noiseless Data Examples

must be somewhat greater the estimate of the standard deviation of the noise in the image. If the RMS fit error ϵ_i^k is less than the predetermined maximum allowable fit error threshold ϵ_{max} based on the image quality measures as described above, then the fit error test is passed and the region is allowed to continue growing. If not, then the order m_i^k is incremented by one, and the next higher order surface fit is computed. If all four fit orders were tried and the error was never less than the threshold, the seed region is rejected by marking off its pixels in the writable copy of the HK-sign map. Surface rejection decisions are discussed in a later section. The segmentation algorithm continues by looking for the next largest connected region of any surface type.

4.7.2 Regions Test

The fit error test decides if region growth for a particular fit order is allowed or not. However, it is possible for a lower order function to fit a higher order function within the maximum allowable fit error threshold over a region even though the lower order fit is not appropriate. Figure 4.13 displays a curve that is fitted well by a line, but the signs of the residuals of the fit form long runs. The analogous case for surfaces is also shown in which a plane approximates a part of a sphere. If it were possible to detect that a higher order function is present in the data before the error tolerance exceeded the error threshold, the region growth process could proceed more accurately in fewer iterations than is possible otherwise. Indeed, the presence of a

higher order function in the data can be detected without having to allow
the fit error to increase up to the given error threshold by analyzing the
distribution of the signs of the residual fit errors at each individual pixel
of the fit. First, the one-dimensional nonparametric runs test is described
and then certain aspects of this test are generalized for two-dimensional
purposes.

The nonparametric runs test is a general purpose tool to test for ran-
domness in a sequence of data points. The runs test is used in regression
analysis to test the pattern of sign changes in the residuals of a fit. Suppose
that a set of data points that lie directly on a line is given. Suppose also
that (1) low-variance, independent identically-distributed noise is added to
each data point in the sample to simulate sensor noise, (2) a line is fitted
to the noisy data points, and then (3) each noisy data point is marked with
a $(+)$ if it lies above the fitted line and a $(-)$ if it lies below the fitted line.
The sequence of $(+)$'s and $(-)$'s corresponding to the noisy data points
is examined. If the string $(-)(+)(+)(+)(-)$ occurs at some point in the
sequence, it is said that "a run of $(+)$'s of length 3" has occurred. Let n
be the total number of data points in the sequence, let n_1 be the number
of $(+)$'s, and let n_2 be the number of $(-)$'s. Thus, $n = n_1 + n_2$. Let r be
the total number of runs of residual signs in the sequence. This quantity
serves as the runs test statistic. Given a particular level of statistical significance, two functions may be derived $r_{\min}(n_1, n_2)$ and $r_{\max}(n_1, n_2)$ from
probabilistic arguments. If $r_{\min} < r < r_{\max}$, then it is likely that the noise
is random. Otherwise, one must reject the random noise hypothesis at the
given level of significance. For example, for 40 fitted data points with 20
$(+)$'s and 20 $(-)$'s, the number of runs is expected to be between 14 and
28 at the 0.025 level of significance [Daniel 1978]. There is an inverse relationship between the number of runs and the lengths of runs on average:
fewer runs imply longer runs, and more runs imply shorter runs.

When fitting surfaces over an arbitrary connected subset of a regularly
spaced rectangular pixel grid, the residual signs of a surface fit form 2-D
regions, not 1-D runs. One way to generalize the 1-D runs test to create a
2-D regions test is to perform horizontal and vertical runs tests on every
scan line and every column of the arbitrary shape fitted region. Such a
generalization decomposes a 2-D problem into two sets of 1-D problems.
Another method of generalization has been chosen that maintains a 2-D
"flavor," and is computationally much simpler given standard image processing tools, such as 3x3 contractions and connected component analyzers.

The first stage of the regions test algorithm is stated as follows. After
the approximant $\hat{g}(m_i^k, \vec{a}_i^k, x, y)$ has been computed for the region $\hat{R}_i^k$, form
two binary images $B^+(x, y)$ and $B^-(x, y)$ based on residual error signs.
Both binary images are initially zero (black) images at the beginning of
each regions test. The pixel (x, y) is set to one (white) in the B^+ image

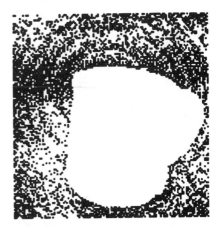

Figure 4.14: Residual Error Sign Binary Images for Surface Fit

only if the data value lies above the approximated value:

$$\text{If } (x,y) \in \hat{R}_i^k \text{ and } g(x,y) > \hat{g}(m_i^k, \vec{a}_i^k, x, y) \implies B^+(x,y) = 1. \quad (4.11)$$

Similarly, The pixel (x, y) is set to one (white) in the B^- image only if the data value lies below the approximated value:

$$\text{If } (x,y) \in \hat{R}_i^k \text{ and } g(x,y) < \hat{g}(m_i^k, \vec{a}_i^k, x, y) \implies B^-(x,y) = 1. \quad (4.12)$$

A connected region in the B^+ image is directly analogous to a run of $(+)$'s in the 1-D example just as a connected region in the B^- image is directly analogous to a run of $(-)$'s. Figure 4.14 shows examples of the binary images for the surface fitted to the data from the table that supports the coffee cup. Let $n = |\hat{R}_i^k|$, the number of pixels in the fit region. Let $n_1 = |B^+|$ be the number of white pixels in the binary image B^+, and let $n_2 = |B^-|$ be the number of white pixels in the binary image B^- so that $n = n_1 + n_2$. The framework thus far is a precise generalization of the runs test. But what should the test statistic be? The number of four-connected regions in the two binary images might be used, but attempts to use this test statistic were unsuccessful because relatively large connected regions may result even in the presence of random binary patterns of pixels.

What is really needed from a regions test in surface fitting? The 1-D runs test checks for too many runs and too few runs. The most runs are obtained when $(+)$ and $(-)$ residuals always alternate; every run is of length one and $n_1 \approx n_2$. The most four-connected regions in an image are obtained when both residual error sign images are perfect checkerboard patterns; every region has one pixel and $n_1 \approx n_2$. Although such error patterns are not random, regression analysts are not usually that interested in the "too many runs" (regions) case when the question of interest is the order of a low-order polynomial fit. Consider a linear fit to a section of a curve with no noise added as shown in Figure 4.13. There will be exactly three runs independent of the number of data points and independent of the fit error. The (+)'s and (−)'s cluster into long intervals. Consider a planar fit to a section of a spherical surface with no noise added. There will be exactly two regions independent of the number of data points and independent of the fit error. The white pixels in the residual error sign binary images will cluster into large regions. Based on this line of reasoning, it is proposed that a 2-D regions test for regression analysis should try to detect large homogeneous regions of white pixels in the residual error sign images. This test must decide if a higher order function in the approximating function set is needed.

The second stage of the regions test algorithm is as follows. Once the residual error sign images B^+ and B^- are formed, contract (erode) each binary image once. Then compute the size of the largest region in each eroded residual error sign image. Divide these two sizes by the total number of pixels in the fitted region to obtain two percentages. Choose the larger of the two percentages as the test statistic. If the test statistic exceeds a given threshold, e.g. 2%, then a higher order surface approximation function is needed. Otherwise, the residual error signs are said to be random. This test is written in mathematical notation as follows. Let $E(\cdot)$ be the 3x3 binary image erosion (contraction) operator that maps binary images to binary images (as described in Appendix F), and let $\Lambda(\cdot)$ be the largest connected component region operator that maps binary images to four-connected regions. The test statistic for the regions test is defined as

$$r(B^+, B^-) = \frac{1}{n} \max(|\Lambda(E(B^+))|, |\Lambda(E(B^-))|). \qquad (4.13)$$

In the iterative region growing algorithm based on variable order surface fitting, the regions test plays a fundamental role in increasing the fit order m_i^k when required. The regions test is phrased as a rule:

- **Regions Test Rule:** If $r(B^+, B^-) > r_t$ and $m_i^k < |F|$, then increment the fit order m_i^k by one for the next surface fit iteration; otherwise, do nothing.

For the standard fixed threshold results shown in Chapter 7, the threshold was $r_t = 0.02$. Some results are also shown for the adaptive threshold $r_t = 0.009 + 0.002\rho_2$. This rule says that when the fitted surface lies above (or below) a sufficiently large number of four-connected pixels, a higher order surface is needed. If the highest order surface is already being used, do not bother to perform the test because the results will be ignored for order incrementing purposes. The regions test is not absolutely necessary to obtain good results for all images in the database of test images if one can afford to spend time searching for just the right error threshold ϵ_{max}. However, when the regions test is used, many surface regions converge in fewer iterations, most curved surface segmentations improve, and a large range of maximum allowable surface fit error thresholds may be used providing the same segmentation results. Despite the additional computations required per region growing iteration for planar, biquadratic, and bicubic fits, the benefits far outweigh the costs.

The regions test is a heuristic test based on the runs test of nonparametric statistics. The thresholds mentioned above were determined empirically via experimental testing, not by theoretical means. Therefore, a specific level of statistical significance cannot claimed for this threshold as can be done in the 1-D runs test. Nonetheless, the regions test performs the necessary task extremely well with an algorithm based solely on 2-D concepts. Moreover, only the basic image processing operations of binary image contraction and connected component analysis are needed to do the test.

Although the regions test is not applied to fourth order surfaces during the fitting iterations, this test can be useful in evaluating the final fourth-order surface fit to a large set of data. If sufficiently large residual-sign regions are detected for a given fourth-order surface primitive region, then the surface primitive may not be capturing subtle curvature properties in the data even though the surface fit error is small. If the regions test fails on the final surface, it may be necessary to analyze the region more closely if detailed surface structure is required for particular applications.

4.8 Region Growing

After a surface is fitted to a region, the surface description is used to grow the region into a larger region where all pixels in the larger region are connected to the original region and are compatible in some sense with the approximating surface function for the original region. On the k-th iteration for the seed region corresponding to the actual HK-surface primitive region R_i, the region growing algorithm accepts the original digital surface $g(x, y)$, the approximating function $\hat{g}(m_i^k, \vec{a}_i^k, x, y)$ from the surface fitting algorithm, and the surface fit error ϵ_i^k from the fit to the seed region. The first step is to compute the absolute value difference image $\Delta g_i^k(x, y)$ given by

$$\Delta g_i^k(x, y) = |\hat{g}(m_i^k, \vec{a}_i^k, x, y) - g(x, y)| \qquad (4.14)$$

in which pixels have small values if the original digital surface data lies close to the approximating surface and have large values otherwise. This image is thresholded to form the (zeroth-order) compatible pixel binary image $C_i^k(x, y)$, which is defined as

$$C_i^k(x, y) = \begin{cases} 1 & \text{if } \Delta g_i^k(x, y) \le w(\epsilon_i^k) \\ 0 & \text{if } \Delta g_i^k(x, y) > w(\epsilon_i^k) \end{cases} \qquad (4.15)$$

where $w(\epsilon_i^k)$ is the error tolerance threshold that determines how close to the surface pixels must be so that they are considered compatible. Almost all pixels in the original region $\hat{R}_i^k$ are compatible with the approximating surface function $\hat{g}(m_i^k, \vec{a}_i^k, x, y)$ because the pixels in that region determined the surface fit. Thus, the compatible pixel image consists of pixels from the growing region and all other pixels in the image that are sufficiently close to the approximating surface. The next region $\hat{R}_i^k$ will be extracted from this thresholded difference image $C_i^k(x, y)$.

The compatible pixel image C_i^k has a complicated dependence on everything that has been discussed so far: (1) the region $\hat{R}_i^k$ and therefore also on the seed region extraction algorithm that created the first region $\hat{R}_i^0$ from which it was derived, (2) the function $\hat{g}$ and the order m_i^k and all the properties of that function type, (3) the parameter vector $\vec{a}_i^k$ and error ϵ_i^k, which are in turn dependent on the surface fitting algorithm and the original digital surface g and the current region $\hat{R}_i^k$, and (4) the error tolerance function $w(\epsilon) > \epsilon$.

Although not indicated in the equations above, the compatible pixel image also depends indirectly on all the surfaces and regions previously discovered in the image owing to the surface acceptance process discussed in a later section. This indirect dependence plays a key role in the region growing algorithm so this material must be introduced now.

For simple surfaces with precisely defined surface boundaries at sharp step and orientation discontinuities, the influence of previously accepted surface regions is negligible or non-existent, but for noisy digital surfaces without sharply defined boundaries, the influence can be substantial. When a surface region iteration terminates and the surface is accepted by successfully passing the test rules discussed subsequently, the magnitude of the residual error at each pixel of the grown surface region is stored in the error image $e(x, y) = |\hat{g}(x, y) - g(x, y)|$ to explicitly note the spatial distribution of the approximation errors. The surface region label i for each pixel of the accepted surface region is stored in the best-fit region label image $l_{BF}(x, y)$ to explicitly note the pixels that the approximating surface fits to within the specified threshold. During the thresholding operation that forms the compatible pixel image, each pixel must not only have an error less than $w(\epsilon_i^k)$, but it must also have an error less than the current best-fit error in the error image. If both conditions are not satisfied, then the pixel is not considered compatible with the growing surface region despite the fact that the allowable error tolerance requirement is met. The error image approach provides a "soft inhibition" capability for pixels already associated with a given surface primitive as opposed to strictly forbidding the reassignment of pixels to other surfaces once they have been assigned to one surface. That is, a previous surface primitive may approximate the value at a pixel well enough for that pixel to be associated with the previous surface primitive, but if the current surface primitive approximates the pixel value better, then the pixel can be relabeled with the current surface primitive label if the pixel meets connectivity requirements with other pixels as discussed later. This error image approach eliminates many problems associated with the order dependent properties of the sequential algorithm, which can be encountered without the error image data structures on some input images. Also, the results of this approach are also useful for determining smooth surface merges between surface primitives in the presence of noise.

The error image is an example of a region growth inhibiting data structure. Other region growth inhibiting data structures could be used during the construction of the compatible pixel image. For instance, surfaces should not grow over step edges or roof edges by the definition of a smooth surface. If reliable estimates of step edges (range discontinuities) and roof edges (orientation discontinuities) can be computed separately, the resulting edge pixels could be used as a mask of pixels that are incompatible for region growth. For example, if a binary edge image containing reliable, but partial segmentation information were obtained from another process, that binary edge image could be logically AND'ed with the binary compatible pixel image to possibly subdivide some of its regions if edge pixels were 0 and non-edge pixels were 1. The reason for doing this will be clear when the details for extracting the next region description $\hat{R}_i^{k+1}$ are described below. Since our main topic is surface-based segmentation, edge detection and combinations of edge-based and region-based approaches are not discussed here. However, this seems to be a feasible method for combining edge-based results with the surface-based region growing algorithm.

The compatible pixel image $C_i^k(x, y)$ generally consists of many different regions, not just the growing region. The largest connected region in the compatible pixel image that overlaps the given region $\hat{R}_i^k$ is chosen to be the next region $\hat{R}_i^{k+1}$. If $\Lambda(B)$ is the largest connected region in the binary image B as defined in the regions test section, let $\Lambda(B|R)$ be the largest connected region in the binary image B that overlaps the region R. This notation allows to define the next region as

$$\hat{R}_i^{k+1} = \Lambda\left(C_i^k | \hat{R}_i^k\right) = \Phi(\hat{R}_i^k) \tag{4.16}$$

where $\Phi(\cdot)$ represents all operations required to compute the next region $\hat{R}_i^{k+1}$ from the current region $\hat{R}_i^k$. The next region $\hat{R}_i^{k+1}$ must have the property that it is the largest connected region in the compatible pixel image satisfying

$$\hat{R}_i^k \cap \hat{R}_i^{k+1} \neq \phi = \text{Null Set.} \tag{4.17}$$

This constraint is required because it is possible to get larger connected regions in the compatible pixel image than the connected region corresponding to the growing region. The surface fitting algorithm is then applied to the next region

$$(\vec{a}_i^{k+1}, \epsilon_i^{k+1}) = \mathbf{L}_{\hat{g}}(m_i^{k+1}, \hat{R}_i^{k+1}, g) \tag{4.18}$$

to obtain a new parameter vector and a new surface fit error. This region is allowed to grow again if $\epsilon_i^{k+1} < \epsilon_{\max}$ and it maintains the same order m_i^k if the regions test is passed. The compatible pixel image is then recomputed $C_i^{k+1}(x, y)$, the largest connected overlapping region is extracted and so on until the termination criteria are met. The termination criteria are discussed in the next section.

When the surface fitting process yields an RMS fit error greater than the maximum allowable fit error threshold $\epsilon_i^k \geq \epsilon_{max}$, the algorithm immediately increments the surface order $m_i^k := m_i^k + 1$ to the next most general surface in the ordered finite set of approximating functions, and reattempts a surface fit of the higher order surface type if there are enough pixels in the connected region being fitted. If m_i^k reaches the maximum value $|F|$ and the surface still does not fit the data to within the maximum allowable error threshold ϵ_{max}, or if there are not enough pixels in the region to attempt a higher order fit, then the iterative surface fitting algorithm terminates and attempts to accept the surface region even though the ideal termination criteria have not been met. If $\epsilon_{max} < \epsilon_i^k < 1.5\epsilon_{max}$ and $m_i^k = |F|$, then the surface region is accepted because it is close enough to being acceptable. It was found experimentally that this extra 50% margin of acceptance allows the region growing iteration to yield useful results that might not otherwise be obtained. Although the software package allows the user to set the acceptability factor, the default setting of 1.5 was never changed.

4.8.1   Parallel vs. Sequential Region Growing

The parallel region growing approach is entirely equivalent to a sequential spiraling region growing approach *until the last iteration*. At the last iteration, the compatible pixel image is checked for compatible non-adjacent regions. This is an important feature of the segmentation algorithm as described later in the section on surface acceptance and rejection decisions. By performing the parallel region growth at each iteration and displaying the results, one can monitor the compatibility of other image regions during each iteration.

On a sequential machine, the parallel approach requires more computation, but the simplicity of the algorithm also has its advantages. It requires less than 10 lines of code in a loop over all pixels in the image because a generic connected component analysis operation and an image boolean operation do all the difficult work. Sequential methods must maintain the appropriate data structures to manage holes in the growing region since arbitrary shapes are allowed. On a parallel machine, the time required to compute the compatible pixel image depends on the number of pixels that can be processed by each independent processor. The separate connected component processing step is still required by the parallel approach, but this is common generic operation that has to be implemented anyway. Sequential spiraling algorithms can be parallelized somewhat, but the time savings, if any, would probably be negligible. For the 128x128 images processed in Chapter 7, the parallel approach required only a few seconds per region growth on a VAX/11-780.

4.8.2   Surface Normal Compatibility

The compatible pixel image can be post processed to zero out any pixels that do not possess "surface normal continuity" compatibility with the approximating surface. Let $g_x(x, y)$ and $g_y(x, y)$ denote the first partial derivative estimates of the local surface as computed from the image data at the pixel (x, y) via separable convolutions as described in Chapter 3. Let $\hat{g}_x(x, y)$ and $\hat{g}_y(x, y)$ denote the first partial derivatives of the approximating surface as computed from the polynomial coefficients at the pixel (x, y). Let $\vec{n}(x, y)$ be the unit normal vector as determined by the data, and let $\hat{\vec{n}}(x, y)$ be the unit normal vector as determined by the approximating polynomial surface:

$$\vec{n} = \frac{\left[\begin{array}{ccc} -g_x & -g_y & 1 \end{array} \right]^T}{\sqrt{1 + g_x^2 + g_y^2}} \qquad \hat{\vec{n}} = \frac{\left[\begin{array}{ccc} -\hat{g}_x & -\hat{g}_y & 1 \end{array} \right]^T}{\sqrt{1 + \hat{g}_x^2 + \hat{y}_v^2}} \qquad (4.19)$$

A pixel is compatible in the sense of surface normal continuity if the angle between the two unit normals is less than some threshold angle θ_t:

$$\cos^{-1}(\vec{n} \cdot \hat{\vec{n}}) \le \theta_t. \qquad (4.20)$$

For several surface normal compatibility experimental results shown in Chapter 7, the threshold angle is given by $\theta_t = 12 + 16\rho_2$ degrees, where the coefficients were determined empirically. The surface normal test may be rewritten in the following form to avoid square roots and to incorporate the derivative values directly:

$$\frac{(g_x - \hat{g}_x)^2 + (g_y - \hat{g}_y)^2 + (g_x \hat{g}_y - g_y \hat{g}_x)^2}{(1 + g_x^2 + g_y^2)(1 + \hat{g}_x^2 + \hat{g}_y^2)} \le \sin^2(\theta_t). \qquad (4.21)$$

Since the compatibility test for surface normal continuity involves many computations per pixel, it is only applied to those pixels that have passed the compatibility test for surface continuity. The standard segmentation results shown in Chapter 7 were obtained without the surface normal compatibility test. On images that have no small orientation discontinuities, the segmentation does not suffer any degradation by omitting this test and the algorithm runs much faster. However, a data-driven smooth-surface segmentation algorithm should always perform the test to insure that growing regions do not inadvertently grow over small or noisy orientation discontinuities. Chapter 7 show several examples where significant improvements in segmentation quality were obtained by including the surface normal compatibility test.

To relate the region growing pixel compatibility requirements to the mathematical and computer aided geometric design literature, the following alternative terminology is introduced. Without the surface normal compatibility requirement, it may be said that the segmentation algorithm requires approximate C^0 continuity of new pixels during region growth. With the surface normal compatibility requirement, it may be said that the algorithm requires approximate G^1 continuity, first-order geometric continuity. If the compatibility requirement were expressed as

$$(g_x - \hat{g}_x)^2 + (g_y - \hat{g}_y)^2 \leq t_1, \tag{4.22}$$

then the algorithm would be requiring only approximate C^1 continuity. If the second derivatives were also required to be approximately equal, the algorithm would be requiring approximate C^2 continuity. If the mean and Gaussian curvatures were required to be approximately equal, this would be termed approximate surface curvature continuity. Very high quality high-resolution image data is needed before such second-order continuity requirements can be imposed. Schmitt et al.[1986] addressed first order geometric continuity of surface patches fitted to range data.

4.8.3 Error Tolerance Thresholds

The error tolerance function $w(\cdot)$ is a function that increases the value of ϵ_i^k so that, if a pixel really lies on the smooth surface $\hat{g}(m_i^k, \vec{a}_i^k, x, y)$ and if ϵ_i^k is an estimate of the standard deviation of the measurement noise, then one is reasonably sure that almost all pixels that belong to the smooth surface are correctly grouped with that surface. The error tolerance threshold is used for requiring the continuity of the grown surface and is also helpful for rejecting statistical outliers in the image data thereby making the least squares fitting procedures much more robust than in more conventional applications. For example, a reasonable form of the error tolerance function $w(\cdot)$ is

$$w(\epsilon) = w_0\epsilon \quad \text{where} \quad w_0 = 2.8 \tag{4.23}$$

because approximately 99.5% of all samples of the smooth surface corrupted by additive normally-distributed measurement noise will lie within this error tolerance. In this simple error tolerance function, the factor w_0 controls the "aggressiveness" of each region growing iteration and therefore, partially controls the speed and accuracy of the iterative surface fitting process. If w_0 is too large, a surface primitive can grow right over an orientation discontinuity if it is not sharp enough. If w_0 is too small, each iteration may only include a few more pixels making the iteration process quite slow and possibly causing regions of the digital surface to be subdivided and labeled separately. Hence, a trade-off decision must be made regarding the two undesirable tendencies. A factor of 2.8 has been used to obtain good performance on the reasonable quality images in Chapter 7. Smaller factors that are larger than 2.3 usually achieve similar results, but take more region growing iterations to find the same surface region and are therefore much slower. For some extremely noisy images where $\rho_1 > 4$, this w_0 factor must be in the neighborhood of 2.1 so that the region growth is very careful and not aggressive.

Regardless of the factor w_0, the error tolerance function $w(\cdot)$ must take on the following hard limit modification or else no progress can be made when the fit is very good on data limited by quantization error:

$$w(\epsilon) = \max(1.1, w_0\epsilon). \tag{4.24}$$

This is *the standard error tolerance function* used for almost all experimental results shown in Chapter 7. Since the integer levels of the digital surface are necessarily quantized to one level during digitization, attempts to find compatible pixels with discrete levels that are less than one discrete level from the approximating surface are not very successful on average. The threshold 1.1 was chosen arbitrarily to satisfy the need for a threshold slightly greater than one, and it has worked quite well in all experiments.

Several tests were performed with a more aggressive variant of the error tolerance function listed above. This function is referred to as $w_A(\cdot)$, and it involves the max-norm (sup-norm) of the functional fit. Let the error ϵ_∞ represent the max-norm error between an approximant $\hat{g}(m_i^k, \vec{a}_i^k, x, y)$ and the data $g(x, y)$ over the region $\hat{R}_i^k$:

$$\epsilon_\infty = \max_{(x,y)\in\hat{R}_i^k} |\hat{g}(m_i^k, \vec{a}_i^k, x, y) - g(x, y)| \tag{4.25}$$

Since the ϵ in the other definitions above is a Euclidean error norm, it is written as ϵ_2 in the expression for the aggressive error tolerance function:

$$w_A(\epsilon_2, \epsilon_\infty) = \max(1.1, w_0\epsilon_2, \epsilon_\infty). \tag{4.26}$$

This error tolerance function provided faster algorithm performance in general because region growth was more aggressive. Moreover, this error tolerance function is able to guarantee ideal, unique, fixed-point convergence of the iterative algorithm because region growth is bounded above and monotonically increasing (see Section 4.10). Slightly better results were obtained for several specific cases, but much worse results were obtained in other cases. Linear, convex combinations of cautious and aggressive error tolerance functions were also tried so that seed regions experienced fast growth when the fit error was small relative to ϵ_{max}, and established regions slowed their growth as their surface fit errors increased. The use of other types of functions was also explored. Experimental tests showed that the final segmentation results could be sensitive to the choice of the error tolerance function. The standard error tolerance function mentioned above was the best choice for most images in the test image database presented in Chapter 7.

4.8.4 Another Variation on the Iteration

There is a slight variant of the Λ function that also insures ideal, unique fixed-point convergence of the region growing iteration (see Section 4.10) even when the standard error tolerance function is used. After the largest connected region overlapping the current region is found, the current region may not be completely contained in the new region if the standard error tolerance function is used. To guarantee convergence, the current region can be unioned (OR'ed) with the new region from the compatible pixel image to insure that this new unioned region properly contains the current region. Thus, region growth is monotonic and bounded by maintaining the inclusion of previous iteration's region. Although good results were obtained on several images using this monotonicity guarantee, experiments showed that this was not a good policy for many images in the test image database.

A region must be able to let go of pixels that do not fit well anymore after any given iteration. The key point is that testing an approximation residual error against the error tolerance function threshold is a very simple, computationally efficient method for determining the compatibility of new pixels with the other pixels in a region. Because it is so simple, it can make mistakes and allow pixels that don't belong to be a part of region. Therefore, the error tolerance function and the region iteration must allow these pixels to leave the region when it is clear that they don't belong. Hence, monotonic region growth does not jibe with the methods for forming the compatible pixel image. Chen [1988] shows a method for testing the effects on the least squares fit for each new pixel as it is added using QR decomposition and updating methods [Golub and VanLoan 1983]. If such a method were used during region growth, it could theoretically do a much better job of rejecting inappropriate pixels during region growth. These topics are discussed in more detail in the section on termination criteria and convergence.

4.9   Hemisphere Surface Example

To make the ideas above on region growing and variable order surface fitting clearer, consider the actions of the algorithm on a simple, hemispherical surface as a specific example of all the topics discussed so far. The surface characterization algorithm labels almost all the pixels on the spherical surface as type *peak* assuming the zero curvature thresholds are not too large (in which case the *flat* label may occur often). The spherical surface is necessarily either bounded by pixels of other fundamental surface types or by the edges of the image, or by both. These spherical surface pixels form a connected region of *peak* pixels in the HK-sign map that are identified at some point in the large-to-small seed region extraction process. When this peak region is chosen by the seed region extraction algorithm, it will first perform the contraction sequence on it to counteract smoothing effects and possible unwanted connections to other adjacent peak regions. A small seed region is isolated somewhere in the interior of the spherical surface.

It will be located at the center of the peak region if no region holes were caused by noise. Otherwise, it will be located at another interior position within the peak region.

The currently implemented algorithm uses only four types of surfaces: planar, biquadratic, bicubic, and biquartic polynomial surfaces. First, a plane is fitted to the small seed region. If the seed region is small enough, then (1) the fit is good, (2) the region is grown, and (3) the regions test and the fit error threshold test do not trigger an increase in the fit order in the first few iterations. Depending on the error tolerance function and the size of the hemispherical surface, two or three planar fit (order 1) region growing iterations are computed. If the noise level in the data is not large compared to the fit error threshold, the regions test eventually causes an increase in the fit order after sufficient growth. For example, this might take place after the third planar iteration. This biquadratic surface type will fit well at first, yielding the best-fit elliptic paraboloid. But as the surface grows, the highest order (biquartic) surface will eventually be invoked by another regions test. If the entire hemispherical surface is visible and large enough, even the fourth-order surface-fit error may eventually exceed the maximum allowable fit error threshold although not by much (it will remain within the 50% acceptance zone mentioned above). This surface is accepted as a surface primitive when the iteration terminates. Almost all pixels on the hemispherical surface will be identified as part of the surface primitive except for those close to the boundary. Most of those close to the boundary will be assigned to the biquartic surface during the surface acceptance process described later. In that process, the accepted surface primitive region is dilated and neighboring pixels that are closer in range value to the biquartic surface than any other surface are assigned to the biquartic surface. This example shows how visible quadric surface pixels can be effectively grouped together without a quadric approximant.

4.10 Termination Criteria and Convergence

Any iterative algorithm requires termination criteria so that the algorithm stops appropriately when the desired information has been obtained from the iteration. If the termination criteria for an iterative algorithm are improperly formulated, the iteration is capable of continuing forever unless it is interrupted by other means. Any iterative process can be made to terminate after a maximum finite number of steps, but from a mathematical point of view, it is clearly preferable to use algorithms that provably converge to a unique limit. However, such algorithms do not necessarily always yield the desired information one may want. A mathematical proof cannot force people to like the results of an algorithm. In computer vision, the quality of a vision algorithm's output is usually judged by a human observer who is naturally an expert in the visual interpretation of scenes. But when the quality of an algorithm's output is evaluated subjectively by the human mind, it is difficult to arrive at consistent mathematical models for optimizing algorithm performance. Ideally, vision algorithms should have a firm mathematical basis and should yield results acceptable to a human observer.

As pointed out earlier, ideal convergence is guaranteed if the region growing algorithm insures that

$$\hat{R}_i^k \subseteq \hat{R}_i^{k+1} \subseteq I. \tag{4.27}$$

This is called the *monotonicity requirement* for growing regions. Since the sequence of image regions is monotonically non-decreasing and bounded above by the entire image region I, the iteration must converge in a finite number of iterations. When $\hat{R}_i^k = \hat{R}_i^{k+1}$, the algorithm converges and yields the following information: $\hat{R}_i = \hat{R}_i^k$, $\vec{a}_i = \vec{a}_i^k$, $m_i = m_i^k$, $\epsilon_i = \epsilon_i^k$. Since any given seed region must stop growing eventually, it will yield either a correct, meaningful surface region or an incorrect, meaningless surface region, which could be the entire image. Experiments with monotonic growth versions of the region growing segmentation algorithm were performed, and it was found that, although these versions may appear more attractive mathematically, they do not always produce the best results that are obtainable with other versions of the algorithm that do not insure convergence via purely monotonic region growth. The fundamental problem with requiring that each subsequent region be a superset of the given iteration's region is that bad pixels (statistical outliers) picked up in one iteration can never be dropped in subsequent iterations. This implies that there is something wrong with either the simple pixel error compatibility requirement for new pixels or the monotonicity requirement. When the standard error tolerance function $w(\epsilon) = \max(1.1, w_0\epsilon)$ is used to determine new pixel compatibility and the monotonicity requirement is not used, bad pixels may enter a region on one iteration and leave on a later iteration depending on results of the surface fitting. Hence, the effect of a few bad pixels is not cumulative in this case. This is a necessary property for good segmentation performance if the standard error tolerance function is used.

Experimental tests have shown that the monotonicity requirement and the simple new pixel compatibility requirement using the standard error tolerance function are in general incompatible with each other. If monotonicity is required, the compatibility test can never make a mistake. If the standard error tolerance function is used for the compatibility requirement, monotonicity cannot be imposed without causing difficulties for some images. There are several promising directions for maintaining the monotonicity requirement and improving the new pixel compatibility test so that bad pixels never get the chance to become part of the growing region. Chen [1988] describes a QR updating method [Golub and VanLoan 1983] for testing the least squares compatibility of new pixels as they are added to a growing geometric entity. This requires more computation for each pixel compatibility check, but since it is doing a recursive least squares fit with each new pixel observation (essentially a square root Kalman filter), it is not necessary to perform a separate surface fitting procedure. In fact, surface fitting and region growing become a single operation. Although there are several technical problems related to order dependence and thresholds with this method also, a method of this type appears to be a promising direction for future improvements. Also, the rejection of statistical outliers (bad pixels) is directly addressed in the field of robust statistics based on influence functions [Hampel et al. 1986]. Iteratively re-weighted least squares and least median squares surface fitting algorithms might allow the surface fitting component of the segmentation algorithm to ignore any bad pixels included by the monotonicity requirement, or robust methods may allow the rejection of outliers during region growth. These methods can easily increase computational requirements by a factor of 5 and probably more. Other types of surface fitting algorithms, such as L_1 [Abdelmalek 1980] or L_∞ minimax [Powell 1981] algorithms, might also provide better results than the L_2 approach used here, but with more computation. One source of theoretical difficulties is the fact that a least squares L_2 algorithm provides the surface fits, but the L_∞ max-norm is used for new pixel compatibility tests. Therefore, an L_∞ surface fitting algorithm may be in order. No experimental results are available to validate any of the above ideas at this point in time, but they are the top candidates for further research.

The alternative hypothesis is now pursued by discarding the monotonicity requirement, and it is assumed that there is nothing wrong with the compatibility test using the standard error tolerance function. One might argue that no matter what mathematical technique is used, some mistakes are bound to be made in grouping new pixels with a growing region in the presence of noise. The standard error tolerance function and the compatibility test provide perhaps the simplest and fastest method for adding new pixels and for ungrouping mistakenly grouped pixels during the iteration. The termination criterion used is also particularly simple and guarantees convergence: stop the iteration if $|\hat{R}_i^{k+1}| - |\hat{R}_i^k| \leq \eta$ for a small value of η, such as 5 pixels. Although ideal, unique region convergence is obtained in the vast majority of observed cases if $\eta = 0$, the termination criterion only requires approximately equal size regions, not the same region. Therefore, the segmented region may not have any provable uniqueness properties, which would be desirable. Assuming this approach is "correct," what methods might be used to analyze its convergence properties, gain insight into possible improvements or inherent difficulties, and make theoretical statements about region uniqueness?

Iterative algorithms have naturally received a great deal of attention in the optimization and numerical analysis literature. Most analysis requires the assumption of continuous or differentiable functions. Two representative theoretical results are quoted from Dahlquist and Bjork [1974] and

Luenberger [1984]. This is intended to provide an interesting view of difficulties involved in attempting to analyze the convergence properties of the
region growing segmentation algorithm using existing mathematical theory.

First, the contraction mapping approach mentioned in [Dahlquist and
Bjork 1974] is briefly discussed to point out the concept of ideal fixed-point
convergence, which is normally sought. Suppose an initial vector (a seed
element) $\vec{x}_1$ from the real vector space $\Re^n$ is given. The iterative process
Φ that maps $\Re^n \to \Re^n$ is written as

$$\vec{x}_{k+1} = \Phi(\vec{x}_k). \tag{4.28}$$

Suppose that there exists a fixed point $\vec{x}_0$ such that

$$\vec{x}_0 = \Phi(\vec{x}_0), \tag{4.29}$$

and that *all first partial derivatives* of Φ exist in an n-ball $B_r(\vec{x}_0)$ of finite
radius r around the fixed point $\vec{x}_0$. The (i,j)-th element of Jacobian ma-
trix $\mathbf{J}_\Phi(\vec{x})$ is given by the partial derivative $\partial \Phi_i / \partial x_j$ where x_j is the j-th
component the $\vec{x}$ vector and Φ_i is the i-th component function of the Φ
vector function. The function $\Phi(\cdot)$ is a contraction mapping if the matrix
norm of $\mathbf{J}_\Phi(\vec{x})$ is less than one. If $\Phi(\cdot)$ is a contraction mapping on the set
$B_r(\vec{x}_0)$, then the iteration will converge to the unique fixed point $\vec{x}_0$ for
any choice of the initial point $\vec{x}_1 \in B_r(\vec{x}_0)$:

$$\vec{x}_0 = \lim_{k \to \infty} \vec{x}_{k+1} = \lim_{k \to \infty} \Phi(\vec{x}_k) = \Phi(\lim_{k \to \infty} \vec{x}_k) = \Phi(\vec{x}_0). \tag{4.30}$$

The fixed point theorem for complete metric spaces (metric spaces where
all Cauchy sequences converge) can be used to prove this theorem. A
necessary condition that the iteration converge is that the spectral radius
(maximum eigenvalue) of the Jacobian matrix evaluated at the fixed point
is less than one.

Luenberger [1984] proves the following, more general Global Convergence Theorem. Let X be an arbitrary metric space and let $\mathbf{A}$ be an
algorithm that maps points $\vec{x}$ in X to subsets of X. In this case, the
iterative operation is written as

$$\vec{x}_{k+1} \in \mathbf{A}(\vec{x}_k) \tag{4.31}$$

to allow the same starting point $\vec{x}_1$ to evolve into different states depending
upon other initial conditions. Let $\Gamma \subseteq X$ be a given set of valid solutions
to the iterative problem. It is shown in Luenberger [1984] that the limit of
any convergent subsequence of $\{\vec{x}_k\}$ is a solution if

1. All points in $\{\vec{x}_k\}$ are contained in a compact set $S \subseteq X$,

2. There is a continuous function $Z : X \to \Re$, known as a descent
   function, such that

(a) If $\vec{x} \notin \Gamma$, then $Z(y) < Z(x)$ for all $\vec{y} \in \mathbf{A}(\vec{x})$, and

(b) If $\vec{x} \in \Gamma$, then $Z(y) \leq Z(x)$ for all $\vec{y} \in \mathbf{A}(\vec{x})$.

3. The algorithmic mapping $\mathbf{A}$ is closed at all points outside the solution set Γ.

The required closed property of the point-to-set mapping $\mathbf{A}$ is the generalization of the continuity property of point-to-point mappings [Luenberger 1984].

Can these existing theoretical results be applied to the convergence analysis of the iterative region growing segmentation algorithm? Instead of vectors of real numbers most often used in optimization and numerical analysis, the segmentation algorithm works with four-connected regions in images. If I is the set of pixels in an image, then 2^I is the power set of the set of all pixels, which is the set of all subsets of pixels of the image. Many of the sets in the power set are not four-connected sets of pixels. Therefore, let C^I represent the set of all four-connected subsets of pixels in an image such that a single region is represented. Hence, $C^I \subseteq 2^I$ is the space of the region quantities for the iterative process that is comparable to the vector space $\Re^n$ or the metric space X. Every region R in the set C^I may be represented by a binary vector (a bit string) of length $|I|$, the number of pixels in the image I. The explicit constraint on all binary vectors $R \in C^I$ is that the number of four-connected component regions is exactly one. The iterative region growing algorithm may then be viewed as a mapping Φ of connected regions to connected regions:

$$\Phi : C^I \to C^I, \qquad \hat{R}_i^{k+1} = \Phi(\hat{R}_i^k). \tag{4.32}$$

This connected region space is a finite space although the size of the space $|C^I|$ is quite large.

The convergence question can now be phrased as follows: **Given** the original digital surface, denoted simply g, which is the noisy, sampled, quantized version of an underlying piecewise-smooth function as stated in Chapter 2

$$g(x,y) = \sum_{i=1}^{N_R} \lfloor g_i(x,y)\chi(x,y,R_i) + \mathbf{n}(x,y) \rfloor, \tag{4.33}$$

and **given** a seed region $\hat{R}_i^0$, which is a subset of the actual region R_i that corresponds to a relatively smooth surface in the real world scene represented by the digital surface, **show that**

$$\lim_{k \to \infty} \hat{R}_i^k = \hat{R}_i \approx R_i \tag{4.34}$$

where $\hat{R}_i^{k+1} = \Phi(\hat{R}_i^k)$. The approximate equality symbol $\hat{R}_i \approx R_i$ implies that the distance between the two region descriptions is small:

$$d(\hat{R}_i, R_i) = |\hat{R}_i \Delta R_i| < e(\rho(g(x,y))) \tag{4.35}$$

where $e(\rho(g(x,y)))$ is the maximum allowable amount of region estimation error given the image quality measure ρ of the digital surface $g(x,y)$, where ρ measures the amount of noise in the data. The pair (C^I, d) form a metric space, as proved in Appendix E, where Δ is the symmetric difference operation for sets, which is defined by

$$A\Delta B = (A - B) \cup (B - A). \tag{4.36}$$

If regions are represented as bit strings (binary vectors), the region distance metric above is identical to the *Hamming distance* between the bit strings: the number of bits that differ.

The question can now at least be posed in a framework similar to the framework required to apply existing theories. Does a unique "fixed point" region in the region space C^I exist such that $\hat{R}_i = \Phi(\hat{R}_i)$? Computing the Jacobian matrix for Φ is not defined since the concept of a derivative is not defined. Each element of the binary region vector only takes on two values: zero (pixel not in region) or one (pixel in region). Moreover, it would be difficult to write down the function Φ in closed form so that it could be analyzed even if derivatives could be defined. Therefore, the Jacobian matrix approach is not useful for this problem.

The Global Convergence Theorem appears to be potentially useful. Since the region space is a finite metric space (Appendix E), let the solution set Γ_i be the set of regions that are within some distance $e(\rho(g(x,y)))$ of the actual region as above. The descent function might be defined as the distance from any region to that set:

$$Z(\hat{R}_i^k) = \min_{R \in \Gamma_i} d(R, \hat{R}_i^k) \tag{4.37}$$

so that if each iteration can be shown to yield a region strictly closer to the solution set than the last region, then the descent function constraints would be satisfied. The only problem is that, even though this has always happened as the iterative process proceeds, it is difficult to mathematically demonstrate that this will always be true for any digital surface.

Although a good theory is worth a thousand computer runs, and although a finite metric space model has been established, it is unclear at this point in time that such a process can be effectively analyzed for unique convergence purposes. A counterproof of unique fixed-point convergence was experimentally observed once on a particular region in the USC girl intensity image. where at some point in the iterative process, two regions were obtained such that $R_1 = \Phi(R_2)$ and $R_2 = \Phi(R_1)$, which would go on *ad infinitum* unless detected and stopped. However, both regions were good approximations to the final desired region in which case it could be said that both regions were members of the solution set and that the iteration did converge to the solution set in the sense of the Global Convergence Theorem. For the digital surface segmentation algorithm, it has been found that reasonable results are obtained by terminating the region growing iteration when region growth slowed below the rate specified by η above. This simple test prevents oscillations and gets the region close enough to the desired solution that the surface acceptance processing can recover the desired region almost exactly.

In conclusion, unique fixed point $R = \Phi(R)$ convergence is not provable for the current version of the iterative region growing algorithm without the monotonicity requirement because a counterexample was observed. Moreover, the algorithm is sufficiently complicated that no insight was gained about how such a counterexample, which occurred on a noisy image region, can arise. Using the current termination criteria as stated, this algorithm (1) must converge, (2) converges in an average of seven iterations for the image database in Chapter 7, (3) has always converged in less than twenty-six iterations during the processing of thousands of seed regions, and (4) ordinarily yields good results. It may be possible to prove convergence to an approximate solution set in the sense of the Global Convergence Theorem [Luenberger 1984], but this has not yet been accomplished owing to the complexity of the algorithm. It was found that the quality of the segmentation output does exhibit a dependence on the maximum allowable fit error threshold $\epsilon_{\max}$, the error tolerance function $w(\epsilon)$, the zero curvature thresholds ϵ_H and $epsilon_K$ used to obtain the HK-sign map as well as the regions test threshold r_t and the surface normal compatibility threshold θ_t, if that compatibility test is used. A complete mathematical theory of the process should account for all these effects. There are many open problems in this area because the fundamental goal is to compute high-quality segmentations that are useful and meaningful, but the human mind is currently providing the evaluation function for these quality measures of usefulness and meaning. Mathematical theories and algorithms must be self-contained and still agree with human interpretations.

4.10.1 Termination Rules

The termination criteria for the iterative surface fitting algorithm are stated explicitly below in terms of the following quantities:

1. The current surface fit error: ϵ_i^k,

2. The maximum allowable error threshold: $\epsilon_{\max}$,

3. The current and previous region sizes: $|\hat{R}_i^k|$ and $|\hat{R}_i^{k-1}|$,

4. The current and previous fit orders: m_i^k and m_i^{k-1} .

These quantities are used at each iteration to decide whether to continue fitting and growing or to stop.

The termination criteria are expressed as a set of rules and the reasoning behind each criterion is summarized.

- **Rule 1:** If $\epsilon_i^k > \epsilon_{max}$ and $m_i^k \geq |F|$, then terminate the iteration.
  This rule is required due to the limitations of a finite set of approximating functions (fitting orders). The larger the set of fitting orders, the less likely it will be that this rule is needed, but any finite set of fitting orders requires this check for digital surfaces that bend and flex more than the most flexible function order. In the current implementation, $|F| = 4$. That is, four types of bivariate polynomial surface functions are used: planar, biquadratic, bicubic, and biquartic. Because the surface fitting algorithm responds to the fit error exceeding the error threshold by increasing the order of the surface fit, this criterion expresses the fact that the algorithm must quit when it runs out of fitting orders and the fit is still not good enough. If there are not enough pixels in the growth region to support the fitting of a higher order surface, then the algorithm must stop also. Hence, $|F|$ in Rule 1 is actually dependent on $|\hat{R}_i^k|$, the number of pixels in the growth region. For example, if the region size is less than 15, then $|F| = 3$. If the region size is less than 10, then $|F| = 2$.) But since most regions contain more than 15 pixels, this subtlety is seldom encountered with digital surfaces that exhibit the surface coherence property.

- **Rule 2:** If $|\hat{R}_i^k| - |\hat{R}_i^{k-1}| \leq \eta$, then terminate.
  This is a necessary, but not sufficient, condition for ideal unique mathematical region convergence. The two region descriptions are not checked for equivalence on a pixel by pixel basis; only the size needs to be checked in practice. While convergence to exact equality conditions where $\eta = 0$ is usually observed, it often takes much longer to achieve exact equality than to achieve good approximate equality. Moreover, it is difficult for the human observer to discriminate between approximately and exactly equal iteration results in describing a meaningful region in an image. Furthermore, the surface acceptance process will catch any nearby region pixels that should have been included. Therefore, only approximate equality is necessary for termination. That is, if the region size does not increase by at least $\eta = 5$ pixels during any iteration, or by 0.2% after the first five iterations, the two region sizes are assumed to be equal for termination criteria purposes. The "less than" condition prevents grow-shrink oscillations that are possible since the monotonicity requirement is not used.

- **Rule 3:** If $m_i^k \neq m_i^{k-1}$, do not terminate yet using Rule 2.
  At least two iterations are required for a given surface fit order m_i^k before the algorithm is allowed to stop due to Rule 2. This "meta"-rule is exercised only occasionally, but it was important to include it for those cases. If it is not included, the fitting potential of the higher order surface function may not be used effectively, and the algorithm

terminates before it should. In other words, pixel counts from one fitting order should not be compared directly with pixel counts of a higher fitting order.

These three rules state all the essential concepts involved in terminating the region growing iteration. A maximum limit on the number of possible iterations is imposed to prevent long iterations. In all tests done to this point, the maximum limit of 30 iterations has never been reached, and the average number of iterations for all regions in the images shown in Chapter 7 is approximately seven.

4.11 Surface Acceptance and Rejection Decisions

After the region growing iterations have terminated, one is left with the compatible pixel image $C_i(x, y)$ and the grown region description $\hat{R}_i$ along with the approximating function parameters $\vec{a}_i, m_i$ and the fit error ϵ_i. For grown regions that exceed the error threshold $\epsilon_{\max}$ slightly, an acceptance zone above the error threshold is defined such that any surface regions with fit errors in that zone are accepted. The acceptance zone used for all experiment results is $\epsilon_{\max} \leq \epsilon_i \leq 1.5\epsilon_{\max}$. Surface regions with fit errors beyond the acceptance zone are rejected.

When a grown surface region is rejected for any reason, the seed region responsible for the grown surface region is marked off in a writable copy of the HK-sign map as having been processed, which prohibits the use of the same seed region again. When a grown surface region is accepted, all pixels in the accepted region are similarly marked off in the HK-sign map so that they are not considered for subsequent seed regions. In this respect, surface rejection and surface acceptance are similar. However, the surface acceptance process is much more elaborate in that it updates several other data structures besides the writable copy of the HK-sign map: the surface coefficient list $\{\vec{a}_i\}$, the error image $e(x, y)$, the best-fit region label image $l_{BF}(x, y)$, the first-within-tolerance region label image $l_{FW}(x, y)$, and the best-fit so far surface list. In addition, two reconstructed images are maintained to allow visual interpretation of the results of the algorithm during execution and afterwards: the best-fit reconstruction image $\hat{g}_{BF}(x, y)$ and the first-within-tolerance reconstruction image $\hat{g}_{FW}(x, y)$.

To describe how these data structures interact with the rest of the algorithm, their purpose and initialization conditions are described first, followed by the surface acceptance update procedure.

1. The error image $e(x, y)$ is a floating point array the same size as the digital image $g(x, y)$. It is used to define the smallest fit error encountered so far at each pixel between the best-fit surface and the original digital surface subject to region connectivity constraints. The average of the contents of the $e(x, y)$ is computed after each surface

acceptance to check if the total image error is less than the threshold ϵ_{max} in which case the entire segmentation algorithm terminates and the methods in Chapters 5 and 6 are executed. The $e(x, y)$ is initialized by setting each pixel to a large value. The large value should be large enough to cause the algorithm to try to find a surface for almost every pixel, but it should also be small enough that a few pixels won't cause the average image error to be too high. The value 1024 is used by the program.

2. The best-fit region label image $l_{BF}(x, y)$ is an integer array the size of the input image $g(x, y)$ that keeps track of which surface regions correspond to which errors in the error image $e(x, y)$. When a surface pixel has less than the current error in the $e(x, y)$ at that pixel, the new error is assigned to the $e(x, y)$ and the identification number of that surface, its region label i, is assigned to corresponding pixel in the region label image $l_{BF}(x, y)$. Also, the best-fit reconstruction image $\hat{g}_{BF}(x, y)$ is assigned the value of the surface function $\hat{g}(m_i, \vec{a}_i, x, y)$ at the point. Thus, the $l_{BF}(x, y)$, the $e(x, y)$, and $\hat{g}_{BF}(x, y)$ form an important, closely related image triplet that influence and monitor the iterative process in a way that alleviates most difficulties caused by implicit order dependence of the sequential algorithm. The $l_{BF}(x, y)$ is initialized to a "no label" state by giving each pixel a marker denoting that no region owns that pixel. The reconstruction image $\hat{g}_{BF}(x, y)$ is initialized to 0, or black. For most cases, the best-fit region label, error, and reconstruction images contain all useful segmentation and approximation information, especially if the surface normal compatibility constraint is used. However, there are cases where the following first-within-tolerance region label image and the BFS surface list are also useful, especially cases where a smooth surface primitive consists of many HK-sign primitives.

3. The first-within-tolerance region label image $l_{FW}(x, y)$ keeps track of the first accepted surface region to fit the data at each pixel within the error tolerance threshold $w(\epsilon_i)$. Once a pixel in the $l_{FW}(x, y)$ region label image is assigned, it is never changed, but by definition the first accepted surface fit at the given pixel was reasonably good. This information complements the information in the best-fit region label image, especially when a smooth surface primitive consists of multiple HK-sign surface primitives. The first-within-tolerance reconstruction image $\hat{g}_{FW}(x, y)$ is also assigned the value of the surface function $\hat{g}(m_i, \vec{a}_i, x, y)$ at that point. The $l_{FW}(x, y)$ is initialized to the "no label" state in which each pixel contains a marker denoting that no region owns that pixel. The reconstruction image $\hat{g}_{FW}(x, y)$ is also initialized to 0, or black.

4. The best-fit so far surface list (BFS list) is a third data structure that allows for multiple surfaces to be defined at the same pixel. When regions grow, they are inhibited by the previously computed error of the best-fit surfaces via the error image $e(x, y)$ and are limited by the maximum error threshold ϵ_{max}. If the residual error at a pixel is less than the error tolerance threshold $w(\epsilon_i)$ and is less than the current error image $e(x, y)$ value then the pixel is assigned to the given surface. Because later surfaces can grow "under" the best-fit error of earlier surfaces if they fit better, it is possible for several different surface regions to have owned the same pixel at different stages in the algorithm. The best-fit so far surface list maintains a snapshot of each best-fit surface region when it was accepted. When surfaces grow substantially into one another, this information is strong evidence of a smooth surface merge. This surface merging evidence motivates the maintenance of this third type of surface description mechanism, which must be able to assign multiple surface labels to the same pixel. Since a region label image cannot be used, separate run-length-encoded region descriptions are written to an intermediate file. Since this list is built as the algorithm proceeds, no initialization is required.

The combination of the surface coefficient list, the two region label images, the BFS surface list, the error image, and the two reconstruction images provide an effective complete means for storing and monitoring the actions of the iterative region growing algorithm as it operates on different seed regions in an image. The most important information is contained in the best-fit error image $e(x, y)$, the best-fit region label image $\hat{g}_{BF}(x, y)$, and the surface coefficient list $\{\vec{a}_i\}$.

The surface acceptance module receives the compatible pixel image $C_i(x, y)$ and the converged growth region $\hat{R}_i$ as input. The compatible pixel image first undergoes an inexpensive 3x3 window refinement operation that (1) connects over single pixel holes in regions where statistical outliers are located and eliminates single isolated pixels, (2) fills in single pixel notches in regions, and finally (3) trims off single pixel protrusions. The filling and trimming operations increase the local smoothness of region boundaries for relatively little computational cost. The global smoothness of region boundaries is addressed in Chapter 6. The form of these operations is the following: for each pixel in the binary compatible pixel image, examine the 9-bit pattern of the pixel and its eight neighboring pixels. Modify the given pixel based on pre-decided allowable shapes for 3x3 neighborhoods in binary images. Such operations can be computed quickly with a lookup table of 512 9-bit entries. Examples of these operations are shown in Figure 4.15. These operations greatly enhance the humanly-perceived quality of the resulting region descriptions. Under the assumption of surface coherence, one pixel regions are not meaningful regions. They are usually associated with noise effects and can therefore be ignored.

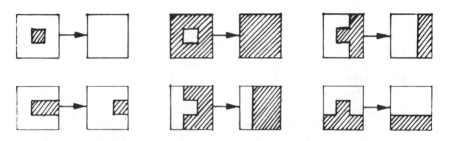

Figure 4.15: Example 3x3 Window Region Refinement Operations

The largest connected region of the refined compatible pixel image that overlaps the final version of the connected growth region is the final connected region of interest. This region is accepted unconditionally after the error tolerance check $\epsilon_i < 1.5\epsilon_{max}$ and an absolute minimum region size check $|\hat{R}_i^k| > 4$ pixels. When this region is accepted, the error image $e(x,y)$ is updated with the absolute value of the residual fit error at each pixel. The dynamic "regions may change" best-fit region label image $l_{BF}(x,y)$, the static "regions are fixed" first-within-tolerance region label image $l_{FW}(x,y)$, and their corresponding reconstruction images are updated with the surface region labels and surface range values at each pixel respectively. The best-fit so far surface region description is also written to the static BFS list file as mentioned above.

4.11.1   Neighboring Pixels

After the above operations, the updated surface region is dilated (expanded) N_D times to include all neighboring pixels of the region that are sufficiently close to the region of interest. The neighboring pixel values of the fitted surface are evaluated and compared to the original image values and are used to update the error image $e(x,y)$, the region label image $l_{BF}(x,y)$, and the reconstruction image $\hat{g}_{BF}(x,y)$ *under the condition* that the absolute value of the residual error at each pixel (1) is less than the best-fit error encountered so far, which is stored in the error image $e(x,y)$, (2) is within a very loose tolerance $5w(\epsilon_i)$, and (3) is connected to the original region by pixels satisfying the same properties. This step allows pixels that should be grouped with a grown surface region, but do not fit within the error tolerance $w(\epsilon_i^k)$, to be associated with that surface region as long as a better fitting surface does not come along subsequently and reassociate those pixels. This procedure remedies most of the shape limitations of the bivariate polynomial approximants and improves the quality of both the segmentation and the reconstruction image. None of these neighboring pixels are marked off in the HK-sign map since they do not fit within the error tolerance. They are not considered to be correctly associated with a surface unless no other grown surface fits better.

As discussed in the hemispherical surface example section above, the boundary region pixels at the steepest sloped area of the hemisphere may not fit the biquartic surface to within the specified tolerance. This extra expansion step allows the correct association of most pixels with the hemispherical boundary region despite the inability of a fourth order polynomial to bend exactly like a semicircle.

The value of N_D, the number of dilations, presents yet another requirement for a heuristically or analytically determined constant. For larger values of N_D, more computation is required and the probability of incorrectly assigning a pixel to a wrong surface is increased. The smaller the value of N_D, the greater the chance that a pixel belonging to a particular surface may be missed. For the current implementation of the algorithm, $N_D = 6$ has served quite well. The values 4 and 8 also worked well in experiments.

4.11.2 Non-Adjacent Regions

The remaining set of compatible pixels that resulted from the final region growing iteration may contain regions that logically belong to the same physical surface, but are not directly connected to the grown seed region in the compatible pixel image. These regions must be tested to decide if they logically belong to the same physical surface associated with the grown seed region or if they occurred due to a chance intersection of the fitted surface with the data in another area of the image. One very useful, but heuristic, rule has been formulated regarding the acceptance of compatible regions that are not four-connected to the grown seed region, but seem to be a logical part of the grown seed region because of the shape consistency with the fitted surface.

- Double Contraction Shape Stability Rule: If a non-connected, compatible pixel region does not vanish after two contractions (erosions) and has an RMS fit error to the surface function of the grown region that is less than $1.5\epsilon_{max}$, then accept that non-adjacent region unconditionally as part of the original grown region.

Double contraction shape stability is a heuristic criterion developed empirically by closely observing the performance of the region growing algorithm on hundreds of surfaces. If a region is contracted twice and still has more than enough points to fit a plane (four), that region is said to be double-contraction stable. Such a region must have at least 25 connected pixels and must have a smoothly shaped boundary and have few or no holes. This rule has performed remarkably well in that those regions that satisfy it have always been logically related to the grown region, but it is sometimes too strict to accept regions that should have been accepted since they were visible non-adjacent regions of the same surface. When surface normal compatibility is required, this heuristic shape test performed better than the standard results shown in Chapter 7.

If a non-adjacent region in the compatible pixel image is double contraction stable and the RMS fit error is small enough, then this region is given the exact same treatment as the seed-related growth region: the error image $e(x, y)$, the region label images, their associated reconstruction images, and the BFS surface list are updated unconditionally. The region is then dilated, and the neighboring pixels are used to conditionally update the error image $e(x, y)$, the best-fit region label image $l_{BF}(x, y)$, and the best-fit reconstruction image $\hat{g}_{BF}(x, y)$ as described above.

If a non-adjacent region of the compatible pixel image is double contraction stable and the RMS fit error is *not* small enough, then the region is dilated and used to conditionally update only the error image $e(x, y)$, the best-fit region label image $l_{BF}(x, y)$, and the best-fit reconstruction image $\hat{g}_{BF}(x, y)$. The first-within-tolerance region label image $l_{FW}(x, y)$ and the BFS list are not updated. This is a safe practice because the HK-sign map is not updated and the errors that go into the error image are generally larger than the maximum allowable fit error tolerance, and therefore, it is easy for subsequently processed surfaces to claim pixels already assigned during this phase if those surfaces fit the data well. Yet this step has established useful correspondences that could not be obtained otherwise.

If a non-adjacent region of the compatible pixel image is not double contraction stable, then the region is discarded. Regions of this type are fairly common owing to the nature of the parallel region growing process unless the computationally expensive surface normal compatibility requirement is imposed. For example, if a plane is fitted to a given region, that plane usually slices through the rest of the digital surface yielding many compatible pixels that are close to the plane, but they do not form large connected regions of a regular shape. The double contraction stability requirement is used to filter out these regions. It acts as a combination region-size and region-shape filter. When surface normal compatibility is required, most pixels in this category are not compatible and do not need to be processed.

As noted in the section on region growing, the parallel region growing algorithm is logically equivalent to sequential spiraling region growing algorithms *except for this final stage* in which compatible regions that are not adjacent may be assigned the same surface region label as the main surface grown from the seed. In the coffee cup image in Chapter 7, the flat background visible through the handle of the cup is correctly assigned to larger background surface without high-level knowledge, only the RMS surface fit error and the double contraction shape stability rule.

4.12 Summary

The segmentation algorithm's successes, documented in Chapter 7, result more from an effective combination of simple component algorithms than from the sophisticated capabilities of any single processing step. Moreover, the algorithm is relatively stable with respect to small changes in these simple component algorithms and small changes in internal thresholds.

The iterative region growing algorithm based on a variable order approximating surface function accepts (a) the HK-sign map and (b) the original image as input and produces as output (1) three separate surface region descriptions for each region as well as (2) the surface equation and the surface fit errors for each region. Two reconstruction images are also created that allow the user to visually evaluate the quality of the surface approximations. Segmentation into meaningful smooth surface primitives is not yet complete because it is necessary to integrate the three separate region descriptions into one consistent region description for each surface primitive. At that point, surface primitives that join smoothly at their shared boundaries should be merged together to create the final surface region description. These topics are discussed in Chapter 5.

Chapter 5

Description Combination and Region Merging

The iterative region growing algorithm isolates surface regions *sequentially* based on the original HK-sign map regions. As discussed in Chapter 4, three different region descriptions are recorded for each region so that the effects of the sequential processing might be accounted for in the final segmentation. The static first-within-tolerance region description and the dynamic best-fit region description computed by the algorithm provide a dual region decomposition that can be integrated by a higher level process that understands how the region descriptions were created. The first-within-tolerance region description is obtained by a "monotonic" computational process that employs strict approximation requirements and strict updating procedures. The best-fit region description is obtained via a more flexible "non-monotonic" computational process that controls only the connectivity of the growing region and does not control the connectivity of the previously discovered regions if they are affected by the liberal best-fit updating procedures. The best-fit so far surface list complements these two dual region descriptions by retaining a snapshot of the best-fit regions at the time of region definition.

There are many different ways that these three complementary region descriptions could be combined to create a final region description for each region. It is conceivable that different applications might require different integration algorithms depending on the end goal. Whatever methods might be used, these methods could be categorized as monotonic and non-monotonic in the sense used above. Monotonic algorithms move straight toward the goal and never modify past decisions, such as a decision to assign a given pixel to a particular region. They are simpler on average than algorithms that are not monotonic, but can also be more susceptible to error. Reasonable results have been obtained using a simple monotonic algorithm to integrate the three region descriptions. Although a monotonic integration algorithm may not in general produce the optimal results for every possible image, the simplicity of this heuristic region description combination algorithm merits consideration given the quality of the experimental results obtained with it.

After the presentation of the region description combination algorithm, region adjacency graph computations, which yield the list of adjacent regions eligible for smooth surface merging, are discussed briefly. Each adjacency relationship is tested for merging based on very approximate first order geometric (G^1) smooth surface join criteria. All appropriate regions are then merged to create the final smooth surface region description. Each region description consists of one or more polynomial surface patches associated with original surface regions. These composite surface patches are hypothesized to be meaningful scene surfaces for recognition and image understanding purposes.

5.1 Region Description Combination

None of the three region descriptions have always been satisfactory considered on their own. The best-fit region label image $l_{BF}(x,y)$ is the most important region description but is often fragmented near region boundaries where regions can lose their original connectivity properties as better fitting surfaces are encountered depending on the amount of noise in the image and the complexity of the smooth surfaces. Examples of this fragmentation are shown in Chapter 7. The first-within-tolerance region label image $l_{FW}(x,y)$ is not fragmented due to strict updating constraints, but regions often have ragged edges and gaps are created between adjacent regions due to the strict error requirements. The best-fit so far surface list (BFS list) generally contains overlapping region descriptions that need to be modified for the final segmentation output, which requires that each pixel belong to one and only one region.

A simple solution to the combination problem that has yielded good results is to union the three descriptions while disallowing any pixels already assigned to another region. Let $\hat{R}_i^{BF}$ be the region description obtained for the i-th surface primitive from the best-fit region label image $l_{BF}(x,y)$. Let $\hat{R}_i^{FW}$ be the region description obtained for the i-th surface primitive from the first-within-tolerance region label image $l_{FW}(x,y)$. Let $\hat{R}_i^{BFS}$ be the region description obtained for the i-th surface primitive from the best-fit surface list (BFS list). Then $\hat{R}_i^U$ is defined as the union of the three surface descriptions:

$$\hat{R}_i^U = \hat{R}_i^{BF} \cup \hat{R}_i^{FW} \cup \hat{R}_i^{BFS} \tag{5.1}$$

The final, combined region description is then obtained from the union description by masking off all regions defined thus far:

$$\hat{R}_i = \hat{R}_i^U - I_R \tag{5.2}$$

where

$$I_R = \bigcup_{j=1}^{i-1} \hat{R}_j \tag{5.3}$$

and where

$$A - B = A \cap \text{Not}(B) \tag{5.4}$$

is the standard set difference operation. The universal set for complementation is the set of all image pixels I.

The ordering of the regions affects the final descriptions of all regions because of the differencing operation in Equation (5.2). For lack of a better philosophy in this sequential approach, an ad hoc "bigger is better" assumption is used to order the regions for processing by the combination algorithm. Since the best-fit region label image $l_{BF}(x,y)$ possesses the best segmentation in terms of the surface fit error if region connectivity is not considered, the regions are processed according to the number of pixels in the best-fit region label image $l_{BF}(x,y)$. Hence, a histogram of the best-fit region label image $l_{BF}(x,y)$ is computed, sorted, and then used to order the region combination process. This ordering based on best-fit region size tends to suppress difficulties that have been encountered with the order dependence of the sequential processing of the iterative region growing algorithm.

The proposed method is simple and insures that no pixel is assigned to more than one region. It is a monotonic algorithm in that no pixel is ever reassigned to another region once it has been assigned to a given region. This method assumes that the largest (first) region is a correctly segmented region. Since the first region is chosen because it is the largest region represented in the best-fit region label image $l_{BF}(x,y)$, the first region is typically a well-defined, reliable, meaningful, high quality region without jagged boundaries. If the first region is of high quality, then the other regions that follow have also tended to be of high quality.

5.1.1   Final Region Surface Primitives

Once all the regions have been defined by the sequential, monotonic, region description combination algorithm, an intermediate list of polynomial surface primitives and regions is available for further processing. There is a correspondence between these bivariate polynomial surface primitives and the ideal theoretical HK-sign surface primitives, but it is not necessarily a one-to-one correspondence. All planar surface primitives correspond directly (one-to-one) to flat HK-sign surface primitives. Since biquadratic surfaces must have constant Gaussian curvature sign because the second derivatives are constants, biquadratic surface primitives correspond directly (one-to-one) to curved HK-sign surface primitives only if they are peaks, pits, ridges, or valleys. The one exception here is that saddle-shaped biquadratic surfaces can consist of combinations of both saddle ridges and saddle valleys depending on the exact shape of the surface. Although many fitted bicubic and biquartic surfaces do correspond to single HK-sign surface primitives in the same way the biquadratic surfaces do, the flexibility of the higher order surfaces allows them to bend, to grow into other adjacent, smoothly joined regions, and to describe more than just one of the basic HK-sign surface primitives in the data. This does not generally cause problems in terms of the final segmentation results, but causes the intermediate list of surface primitives to not coincide exactly with the HK-sign surface primitive list that one might compute analytically.

An attempt was made to constrain higher order surfaces so that the sign of the Gaussian curvature (K-sign) remained constant over an entire higher order surface. Such a constraint would yield a better correspondence between theoretical HK-sign surface primitives and the polynomial surface primitives produced by the algorithm. Since a biquadratic is always fitted to a region before higher order surfaces are fitted, the sign of the Gaussian curvature (K-sign) of the biquadratic was computed and assigned to higher order surfaces before any surface fitting was done. During the region growing procedure, any pixels with a different K-sign were not allowed to be compatible with the polynomial surface even though they would be compatible otherwise. This inhibited the growth of surfaces into areas that would have been occupied by the non-inhibited algorithm. This inhibition requires the extra computational expense of evaluating the Gaussian curvature at each compatible pixel based on the polynomial surface description, which is considerable for higher order surface polynomials. This effort to obtain better HK-surface primitives did not work as planned for most images. The problem was that once a zero curvature threshold was decided, there was always a region in some image with a little too much noise that caused the higher order surfaces to warp slightly to conform to the data, and thereby exceed the curvature threshold. These pixels, which did indeed belong to the surface and were considered part of that surface under the biquadratic surface fit, were now disregarded at this advanced stage in the region growing process as incompatible because of the K-sign constraint. They were left unclaimed by the surface to which they logically belonged, and later became one or more separate surface primitives. The desired effect was achieved in several images in that the growth of the higher order surfaces was inhibited into regions of different Gaussian curvature sign. But in other images the added constraints caused many regions that were previously correctly interpreted to subdivide into meaningless regions. This type of region growing constraint was abandoned for these reasons and another reason discussed below.

If an approximating polynomial surface is capable of growing from one HK-sign surface primitive into another adjacent HK-sign surface primitive, then these two surface primitives must be approximately smoothly joined because polynomial surfaces cannot kink or tear. Why should the algorithm bother to separate smoothly joined regions of different HK-sign types in one stage of the algorithm if the next stage will need to join them together anyway? Despite the theoretical appeal of a guaranteed one-to-one correspondence between all HK-sign surface primitives and the fitted bivariate polynomial surfaces, it was decided that high order surfaces should be allowed to grow without constant surface curvature sign constraints so that the algorithm did not make extra work for itself. The primary interest is in a final, meaningful, smooth surface segmentation, not in the theoretical, intermediate, mathematical decomposition of surfaces. When the surface normal compatibility requirement is not used, this non-restriction of higher order surfaces has caused a few relatively minor problems in detecting small angle orientation discontinuities in noisy images as shall be pointed out in the experimental results of Chapter 7. However, the surface normal compatibility constraint has worked well as long as regions on both sides of the orientation discontinuity are large enough.

5.2   Region Adjacency Graphs

A region adjacency graph is a set of disjoint regions accompanied by a set of adjacency relations between the regions in the set. The regions are the nodes of the graph, and the adjacency relationships are the undirected arcs of the graph. The region description combination algorithm produces a single region list, but an adjacency algorithm is needed to compute the adjacency relationships of the region list and store them in a neighbor list. Given the finalized region label image containing N regions that are in direct contact with each other (no pixels are left unlabeled and there are no gaps between regions), two methods to compute the eight or four connected neighbor list that require different amounts of computation and memory are described:

1. The neighbor list can be computed using only a single histogram array $h(i)$ of length N with N passes over the finalized region label image where the histogram array is initialized to zero before each pass. For the i-th pass, increment the j-th location of the histogram $h(j)$ whenever a pixel with the label i has an eight or four connected neighbor with the label $j \neq i$. At the end of the i-th pass, add the (i, j) relationship, and the count if needed, to the neighbor list if the $h(j)$ histogram count is non-zero. The histogram count indicates the strength of the adjacency, which is related to the digital arc length of the separating boundary.

2. The neighbor list can be computed more efficiently with more memory using a region label pair histogram array $h(i, j)$ of size $N \times N$ with 1 pass over the finalized region label image. As usual, initialize the array to zero. For each pixel with region label i that has an eight or four connected neighbor with a label $j \neq i$, increment the histogram

count $h(i,j)$ at the (i,j) location in the histogram. At the end of the single pass over the region label image, add the (i,j) relationship $(i < j)$ to the neighbor list if the sum $h(i,j) + h(j,i) > 0$. The sum of the histogram counts is twice the number of pixel adjacency relations.

The second method requires N times less computation and N times more memory the first process.

An alternative approach that requires substantially more memory (e.g. N bitmaps), but can bridge gaps of n pixels between regions without requiring a large window size for label comparisons is described. The main benefit of this approach is that it directly provides overlapping region descriptions that are necessary for the surface merging computations discussed in the next section. For example, the first-within-tolerance region label image $l_{FW}(x, y)$ contains gaps between regions such that the algorithm in the above paragraph would fail to find all adjacency relationships using only a 3x3 window. To find adjacencies with this method, each region should be stored as efficiently as possible. For the software implementation of the algorithm, a bitmap was used as a tradeoff between storage space and ease of use. Regions are dilated (expanded) an appropriate number of times depending on the size of the gaps that need to be bridged or the desired size of the overlap region created by intersecting dilated regions. Two dilations were used so that touching adjacent regions would have a four-pixel wide overlap for the surface merging computations to be discussed in the next section. Three-pixel wide gaps can also be bridged for adjacency checks in region label images with gaps. This would require 7x7 comparison windows using the method described above, a significant increase in computation.

The stored dilated regions (in bitmap or other condensed form) are checked for overlap (a non-null intersection) to decide if two regions are adjacent. If the min/max box for each region is stored along with each region description, many overlap checks are quickly dismissed with negligible computation. When an overlap check indicates overlap, the adjacency relationship is noted, and the overlap region, the two surface equations, and the fit errors are then given to the smooth surface merge decision module along with original image to decide if a smooth surface join, an orientation discontinuity, a step discontinuity, or some combination of the above exists between the adjacent regions.

Algorithms have been described for computing region adjacency graphs: two standard algorithms and a special purpose algorithm for providing the required information to the surface region merging algorithm described next.

5.3 Region Merging

Two surface primitive regions should be merged if and only if they are adjacent to each other and they join smoothly at the boundary curve sepa-

Figure 5.1: An Anomalous Break in Parameter Curve for Noisy Torus

rating the surface regions. Continuous, differentiable surface functions join *smoothly* along a boundary curve if the local surface description of both surfaces is the same at all points on the curve. In other words, the first and second fundamental forms, or equivalently the metric and the shape operator, of the two surfaces should be equal along the boundary curve. If these quantities are equal along the curve, then the following statements are also true: (1) both sets of surface normals along the curve are completely aligned, and (2) the line integral of the norm of the surface difference vector along the curve is zero due to equality of surfaces at boundary.

Unfortunately, there are no boundary conditions placed on the approximating functions since they are used for extrapolation during the region growing procedure. Hence, two grown surface primitives may belong to the same smooth surface, but may have different local surface behavior at the boundary between the surfaces because of the lack of explicit boundary conditions during the surface fitting process. As an example of undesirable local behavior of surface primitives, consider the break in a parameter curve from the best-fit reconstructed range image of a noisy torus as shown in Figure 5.1. The top function shows cross-sections of two polynomial surface approximants that should have joined smoothly given that the data joins smoothly. The bottom function represents the actual range values along that parameter curve. The fixed maximum allowable fit error threshold used in Chapter 7 was larger than it needed to be for this image $\epsilon_{max} = 4.2$. This allowed the polynomial surfaces to wander farther from the data than they should have for the given noise level. This break could perhaps be attenuated via the use of a weighted least squares fit where large weights are associated with the pixels near the boundary of the surface region, but this may undesirably change the surface fit on the interior of the region. The surface normal compatibility requirement attenuates this phenomenon significantly, but does completely eliminate it. No matter what approximations are made to obtain surface equations near the boundary, it is certain that ideal equality of surface parameters at the boundary curve will never be obtained reliably given noisy discrete

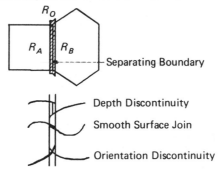

Figure 5.2: Adjacent Region Boundary Terminology

image data. Hence, notions of approximate equality and the accompanying thresholds appear to be necessary once again.

Assuming thresholds are necessary anyway, surface regions are not re-fitted to obtain better boundary pixel descriptions. Instead, an attempt is made to judge the smoothness of the join between two surfaces based on (1) the equally weighted least squares approximations obtained during the region growing process, (2) a small region containing the boundary of interest, and (2) the original data.

It is now assumed that surface equation A for region A, surface equation B for region B, the overlapping intersection region of the dilated region descriptions R_O, and the pixel values of the original image in the overlapping region are all given. A decision must be made regarding the boundary between surfaces A and B. The smooth surface join question is the primary issue since the two regions will either be merged or not merged. A secondary, but important, issue is to answer the step discontinuity, orientation discontinuity or combination discontinuity question. Figure 5.2 shows a top view of two adjacent regions and the corresponding overlap region R_O as well as side views of the three possible continuity states across the boundary. A set of heuristic rules have been developed to make the region merging decision based on several different quantities related to the geometry of the two surfaces. The quantities of interest are presented below along with the corresponding rules.

5.3.1 Region Merging Decision Rules

The region merging decision rules are formulated to determine if two approximating surfaces join smoothly at their separating boundary. The boundary is represented by the boundary region, the overlapping region contained in the dilated region descriptions of both surfaces. This region may be as many as four pixels wide. Let us consider this boundary region as the compact support for two approximating surface functions. If the two surfaces do not intersect at all over the support region and the mean separation distance between the two surfaces is sufficiently large, one may conclude that the two surfaces do not join smoothly along the boundary curve and that a pure step discontinuity exists at the boundary. If the two surfaces do intersect or if the mean separation distance is small, then there is not a pure step discontinuity and there is a possibility that the surfaces join smoothly. Surface normal information is then used to evaluate the compatibility of the two surface orientations over the support region. If the orientations of the surfaces are compatible and no step discontinuity exists, a smooth surface join is detected. Two quantities are used: (1) the average of the angular separations of the normal vectors at each point, and (2) the angular separation of the average normal vectors of the two surfaces over the support region. If both of these quantities have the same approximate numerical value and at least one of them is less than a specified threshold, then the two surfaces have roughly the same orientation in space over the support region. In accordance with the stimulus bound philosophy, the angular threshold depends on the surface fit errors to the original data over the support region. If both surface fits are good, the angular threshold is small. If either or both surface fits are poor, the angular threshold is large. This simple adaptive threshold scheme has been effective in providing meaningful smooth surface joins in a variety of noise levels over a wide variety of images.

The logic of the decision making process can be stated briefly. A boundary is either a pure step discontinuity or it is not. If it is not a step discontinuity, the boundary is then either a smooth surface join or it is not. If it is neither a step discontinuity or a smooth surface join, then it may be an orientation discontinuity or some combination of all three states. For surface merging decisions, no further distinction is needed.

The first decision parameter is the easiest to compute, the most exact, and perhaps the most meaningful. Let R_O be the overlapping region obtained by intersecting the dilated region descriptions for surface regions A and B. Let $z_A(x, y)$ be the surface value at the pixel (x, y) considered as part of surface A and let $z_B(x, y)$ be the surface value at the pixel (x, y) considered as part of surface B. The extrapolating properties of the bivariate polynomials are used to define surface values not within a region. The average error, or *mean separation*, is defined as

$$e_0^{AB} = \frac{1}{|R_O|} \sum_{(x,y) \in R_O} (z_A(x, y) - z_B(x, y)). \tag{5.5}$$

The mean separation is a *signed quantity*. It may positive or negative, depending on whether or not surface A is mostly over surface B or mostly under surface B. The average absolute error, referred to as the *mean separation distance*, is defined as

$$e_1^{AB} = \frac{1}{|R_O|} \sum_{(x,y)\in R_O} |z_A(x,y) - z_B(x,y)|. \tag{5.6}$$

The mean separation distance is always non-negative and is not the same as signed mean separation quantity. In general, it is always true that

$$|e_0^{AB}| \le e_1^{AB}. \tag{5.7}$$

Let the first decision parameter be d_1, which is defined as

$$d_1 = \frac{e_1^{AB} - |e_0^{AB}|}{e_1^{AB}} \ge 0. \tag{5.8}$$

If surface A is above surface B at every point in R_O, then d_1 is exactly zero because $e_0^{AB} = e_1^{AB}$. But if one pixel of surface B goes above surface A, these quantities cease to be equal and the decision parameter becomes positive.. Similarly, if surface A is below surface B at every point in R_O, then d_1 is still exactly zero because $e_0^{AB} = -e_1^{AB}$. If one pixel of surface A goes above surface B, then these quantities cease to be equal again. Hence, $d_1 = 0$ for a pure step discontinuity independent of the magnitude of the mean separation distance. It increases as the surfaces intersect one another and is bounded by the value 1.0, which is obtained only when $e_0^{AB} = 0$. This can occur when the two surfaces clearly intersect at the boundary, and the mean separation on one side of the surface intersection exactly cancels the mean separation on the other side of the intersection. Hence, d_1 is a useful descriptive parameter of a boundary curve between two regions.

- **Rule 1:** If $d_1 = 0$, then surfaces A and B do not intersect each other and a step discontinuity exists at the boundary between surface A and B. If $e_1^{AB} > 2.5$ discrete image levels (for example), a sufficiently high contrast step-edge exists and the boundary is classified as a step discontinuity. If not, the boundary is a very low contrast step edge, and it may actually be a smooth surface join. In this case, a decision is not made until other rules are applied.

The threshold 2.5 performed well over a wide set of images. In practice, this threshold might be set using application-specific assumptions about step discontinuities. Also, d_1 was not required to be exactly zero for a step discontinuity. As long as the decision parameter was smaller than a threshold of 2%, this was small enough to imply the existence of a step discontinuity. For object recognition algorithms, it is possible to tell which region is occluding and which region is occluded using the sign of the mean separation.

The alignment of surface normals of the two surfaces forms the basis for the two second decision parameters d_{20} and d_{21}. These parameters are designed to be useful for arbitrary curved or planar surface joins. Let $\vec{n}_A(x,y)$ $(\vec{n}_B(x,y))$ be the unit surface normal at the pixel (x,y) computed from the bivariate surface polynomial for surface A (B). The first of the two decision parameters based on normal vectors is computed on a pointwise basis as the arc cosine of the average dot product between surface normals at each point:

$$d_{20} = \cos^{-1} \left(\frac{1}{|R_O|} \sum_{(x,y) \in R_O} (\vec{n}_A(x,y) \cdot \vec{n}_B(x,y)) \right). \tag{5.9}$$

This quantity averages the angular difference of the surface normals at each point. If the orientation of the two surfaces is approximately the same over the support region around the boundary, then d_{20} will be small. It is noted that yet another parameter could be based on the mean absolute value of the surface normals inner product.

The second of the two surface normal decision parameters is computed by averaging the normal vectors over each surface and then computing the arc cosine of the dot product of the average normals:

$$d_{21} = \cos^{-1} \left(\frac{\vec{n}_A \cdot \vec{n}_B}{\|\vec{n}_A\|\|\vec{n}_B\|} \right) \tag{5.10}$$

where

$$\vec{n}_A = \frac{1}{|R_O|} \sum_{(x,y) \in R_O} \vec{n}_A(x,y) \qquad \vec{n}_B = \frac{1}{|R_O|} \sum_{(x,y) \in R_O} \vec{n}_B(x,y). \tag{5.11}$$

Hence, this quantity averages the normal vectors for the two surfaces separately over the support region, and then renormalizes the average surface normals to find the angular separation of the average normals. If the orientation of the two surfaces is approximately the same over the support region around the boundary, then d_{21} will also be small. If both d_{21} and d_{20} are small simultaneously, then the surfaces are constrained to have approximately the same orientation. These two parameters are used together in the following rule:

- **Rule 2:** If Rule 1 does not apply and $e_1^{AB} \leq 15$ discrete levels (for example) and either d_{20} or d_{21} is less than or equal to 25 degrees and $|d_{20} - d_{21}| < 25$ degrees, then the two surfaces A and B are merged.

The thresholds are suggested examples of the numbers used for the results in Chapter 7. These particular thresholds are quite loose implying that regions might be mistakenly merged, but few merges should be missed. These thresholds assume that the surface normal compatibility requirement was not imposed during region growth.

If A and B are both planar surfaces, then $d_{21} = d_{20}$. In this special case, these two decision parameters should not be computed and the planar equation should be used to determine the normal vectors instead of Equations (5.11). Also for intersecting planes, the 25 degree threshold can be made as small as necessary before a merge is allowed. For example, this would be useful in a polyhedral domain. Two planar surfaces also allow the formation of a perfectly defined dihedral edge in 3-D space. For the current software implementation, no surfaces are given special treatment, and the same angular thresholds are used regardless of surface type. The thresholds of 15 discrete levels and 25 degrees were chosen for their good performance over the entire test image database. In practice, application-specific knowledge should be used to assign these thresholds. For orientation discontinuities, $\vec{n}_A$ and $\vec{n}_B$ can be used to label straight or curved edges as predominantly convex or concave. Such labels are useful in matching [Sugihara 1979].

The second rule is a good rule as long as the local approximations for surface A and surface B fit the data well in the overlapping region R_O. However, if the surfaces do not fit well, it is necessary to be considerably more tolerant of differences in surface normal direction to achieve the correct merges. Toward the goal of detecting the goodness of the fit over the support region, the average absolute errors for both surfaces are computed:

$$e_1^A = \frac{1}{|R_O|} \sum_{(x,y) \in R_O} |z_A(x,y) - g(x,y)| \qquad (5.12)$$

$$e_1^B = \frac{1}{|R_O|} \sum_{(x,y) \in R_O} |z_B(x,y) - g(x,y)| \qquad (5.13)$$

where $g(x,y)$ is the discrete level from the original image. If either or both of these two values are greater than a certain large percentage of the mean separation distance, the surface fit is not considered adequate to finalize a definite decision that the surfaces do not join smoothly. Therefore, the following rule, which is based on the original image data, was also included:

- **Rule 3:** If Rules 1 and 2 do not apply and both surface A and surface B are not planar and $e_1^{AB} < 1.3 \max(e_1^A, e_1^B)$, then re-apply Rule 2 using a doubled angular threshold of 50 degrees and a doubled step threshold of 30 levels.

For particularly noisy surfaces, it was necessary to include such a rule in order to get meaningful surface merges on complex surfaces. When there is not much noise present, the rule has no impact on merging decisions because it is not invoked. However, in noisy images there is a tradeoff in that certain orientation discontinuities that are not very prominent are merged across and are not present in the final segmentation results. These thresholds again assume that surface normal compatibility requirements were not imposed during region growth.

A fourth rule is needed to terminate the decision tree structure of the rules in this chapter:

- **Rule 4:** If Rules 1, 2, and 3 do not apply, then the boundary between the surfaces A and B is not a smooth surface merge and it is not a pure step discontinuity. It may be a pure orientation discontinuity, or it may be any combination of the three possible states of surface boundaries. Further processing is required to discriminate these possible states.

Since the boundary is not a smooth surface join, the segmentation output does not require further analysis of the edge. Rule 1 provides easily computed, reliable *negative* evidence about the existence of a smooth surface join whereas Rules 2 and 3 provide *positive* evidence. In object recognition systems, it may be advantageous to label each region boundary segment as an occluded step discontinuity, an occluding step discontinuity, a convex orientation discontinuity, a concave orientation discontinuity, or a smooth surface join. The decision parameters above provide sufficient information for such labeling.

It has been observed empirically that if two regions in the BFS list overlap by a significant amount, then this is the strongest positive evidence available that the two surfaces should be merged because each surface approximates the other well within the maximum allowable error tolerance over a large number of pixels. This condition is actually checked first before any of the above rules are applied.

- **Rule 0:** If $|\hat{R}_A^{BFS} \cap \hat{R}_B^{BFS}| > 0.35|R_O|$, then surfaces A and B should be merged and Rules 1, 2, 3, 4 need not be checked.

This rule is discussed last because it is not based on general-purpose 3-D surface shape arguments, but on the algorithm-specific nature of the region growing process.

These merging rules represent simple criteria for deciding if two surfaces should be merged or not using approximate G^1 (first order geometric) continuity concepts similar to the surface normal compatibility requirement. They are not intended as an optimal set of statistical decision rules, but rather a set of geometry-based rules that capture the basic ideas for testing the smoothness of joins of the polynomial approximation functions in the presence of noise. The segmentation approach is much less data-driven at this stage in the processing. Although the algorithm is still based on general properties of surfaces, the necessary thresholds are more related to the interests of perceiving entity than to the properties of the data. The advantages of the approach are that it provides a clear cut interface for the usage of application-specific information.

5.4 Final Region Segmentation Output

Three region descriptions are combined to create a unified set of surface primitive regions that is generally of better quality than any of the three region descriptions considered individually. Adjacency relationships are then computed from the unified list, and each pair of neighbors is tested for merging by applying the set of rules described above. If a smooth surface merge decision is affirmative, then the unified polynomial surface primitive region descriptions for the two regions are merged to create a new smooth surface primitive region. After this process has been done for every pair of neighbors, the final smooth-surface primitive region list is formed consisting of all non-merged and merged polynomial-surface primitive regions. This smooth-surface primitive region list is the final output of the segmentation algorithm. The surface equations and the unified region descriptions of the polynomial surface primitives are maintained to allow the correct surface equations of the merged smooth surface regions to be used with the appropriate pixels within the merged regions. If adjacency relationships of the final regions are required, the final output is rerun through a region adjacency algorithm creating the final smooth-surface primitive region neighbor list. If data-driven parametric descriptions of region edges are required to complement the data-driven parametric descriptions of the graph surface primitives, then the boundary pixels of each region can be fed to the sign-of-curvature edge fitting algorithm discussed in Chapter 6, which generates polynomial edge interval descriptions. If only a segmentation plot is required, this can be computed directly from the final region list without further computations. In the experimental results section, both parametric edge descriptions and segmentation plots are used to display the segmentation algorithm output. The smooth surface primitives are left in the crude form of composite polynomial surfaces. If better application surfaces are needed, the segmented pixels should be fitted directly with application surfaces.

Chapter 6

Region Edges

Edges play a dominant role in computer vision research, but have received little attention so far. Although independent edge detection and edge linking algorithms are not of direct concern to the digital surface segmentation algorithm, the topic of parametric edge description is of significant interest. Since the approximate shape of smooth graph surfaces in images is given parametrically by the approximating graph surface functions $z = \hat{g}_i(x, y)$, it would be convenient if the support region of the graph surface could also be formulated parametrically as $(x(s), y(s))$. However, the 2-D image regions associated with these approximants are specified in a *non-parametric*, digital form as a list of connected image pixels at this point in the algorithm. The boundary of an image region can be encoded very compactly as an 8-neighbor chain code, which is a general method for describing region boundaries in a discrete image, but it is not as desirable as a parametric curve representation.

A functional edge description offers the same advantages of the functional surface description: groups of pixels are represented concisely and mathematically for higher-level processes. For example, if the boundary of a planar region happens to form a quadrilateral, it is preferable to have a linear description of the linear edges for higher level processing rather than a chain code. There are many model-based methods, such as the Hough transform [Duda and Hart 1972], for isolating linear edges in edge maps, but a data-driven edge description algorithm that characterizes both straight and curved edges in a unified manner is desired. An edge segmentation algorithm is sought that will partition an arbitrary digital curve into meaningful intervals and generate an explicit representation for each interval.

In this chapter, the sign-of-curvature paradigm developed for surface description is used to describe the arbitrary digital edges that bound the arbitrary four-connected regions created by the digital surface segmentation algorithm. By adapting the sign-of-curvature approach for processing graph surface mappings $\Re^2 \rightarrow \Re^1$ so that it can process planar curve mappings $\Re^1 \to \Re^2$, two goals are accomplished: (1) a data-driven region boundary (edge) description algorithm is derived that complements the smooth surface primitive description obtained thus far, and (2) the general, dimension-independent nature of the sign-of-curvature surface algorithm for processing $\Re^n \to \Re^m$ mappings is presented in a simple context that provides an illuminating vantage point and several interesting contrasts.

The input to the edge description algorithm is an eight-connected set of pixels that form a one-pixel-wide path through the image. The approach does not require a closed edge path although closed paths arise naturally when boundaries of connected regions form edges. Hence, any edge detection/linking algorithm that yields eight-connected one-pixel-wide edges can provide input to this edge description algorithm. Before describing the edge algorithm in detail, a framework for discussing edges in different dimensions is established since the surface-based edge detection mechanism that provides input to the edge description algorithm is quite different from most existing edge detectors. Also, although higher dimensional segmentation algorithm will not be discussed, the following presentation hints at how the sign-of-curvature paradigm can be generalized to higher dimensions.

6.1 Edge Detection and Dimensionality

The concepts of edges, boundaries, discontinuities, and dimensionality are extremely important in computer vision, but are sometimes confused by conflicting terminology. Consider terms like "3-D images" and "3-D edge detectors" that imply totally different mathematical entities depending on the context in which they are used. For example, the term "3-D image" is used by some to refer to (1) a range image acquired by a range imaging sensor, such as an imaging laser radar, which measures range as a function of two spatial variables, and it is used by others to refer to (2) stacks of density images obtained from a volume imaging sensor, such as a CAT scanner, which measures density (attenuation) as a function of three spatial variables. The 3-D edge detector of Zucker and Hummel [1981] is a surface detector for volume images, not an edge detector for range images in the usual sense of the term. The following material is an attempt to provide a common framework for several computer vision terms.

An multidimensional n-D signal or *image* (not the usual mathematical term "image") represents a piecewise smooth mapping $\vec{f}(\vec{x})$ from $\Re^n \to \Re^m$ where $\vec{x} \in \Re^n$ and $\vec{f}(\cdot) \in \Re^m$. One usually encounters with n-D *scalar* images where $m = 1$, but n-D *m-vector* images are also encountered, as in multispectral image processing, where m is an integer larger than one. Specifically, a 1-D scalar image represents a mapping of the type $y = f(x)$, which is a graph function of one variable. A 1-D 2-vector image represents a mapping of the type $(x, y) = (f(s), g(s))$, which is a planar curve, the main topic of this chapter. A 2-D scalar image represents a mapping of the type $z = f(x, y)$, which is a graph surface as discussed in previous chapters. A 3-D scalar image represents a mapping of the type $w = f(x, y, z)$, which is a graph function defined over a volume.

Intensity images, range images and any image viewable on a video monitor are scalar 2-D images in this terminology. This does not contradict the "2.5-D image" term applied to range images since half of a dimension is not defined here, but it sets a guideline for not referring to range images as 3-D images. Range images are 2-D scalar images just like intensity images, only the *interpretation* of the pixel values is different. The term "digital surface" applies to any 2-D scalar image that exhibits surface coherence. The term *3-D image* is reserved for real three dimensional images, such as those obtained by stacking CAT scan data in biomedical imaging. Any sequence of 2-D images, such as the image sequences analyzed in dynamic scene analysis, may be considered as a 3-D image entity. Subsets of the domains of 1-D, 2-D, and 3-D images are intervals, regions, and volumes respectively. The size of these subsets are lengths, areas, and volumes respectively.

An order-0 discontinuity point in an n-D image, a *step-edge* point, is a point at which there exists a unit-norm direction vector $\vec{u} \in \Re^n$ ($\|\vec{u}\| = 1$) such that, for α strictly non-negative,

$$\lim_{\alpha \to 0} \vec{f}(\vec{x} + \alpha\vec{u}) \neq \vec{f}(\vec{x}). \tag{6.1}$$

An image without any points of this type is a C^0 image. It is assumed that simple order-0 discontinuities in an n-D image form connected $(n - 1)$-D geometric entities. More pathological arrangements of discontinuities are possible, but are not considered here. For a piecewise smooth 1-D scalar image function $y = f(x)$, order-0 discontinuity points form 0-D sets (points) that are the boundaries of the continuous pieces of the image. These discontinuity points represent the "0-D step edges" in the 1-D image. The same ideas hold for planar curves, which are 1-D 2-vector images. For a piecewise smooth 2-D scalar image function $z = f(x, y)$, order-0 discontinuity points form 1-D sets (curves) that are the boundaries of the continuous pieces of the image. These discontinuity points represent the "1-D step edges" in a 2-D image: range discontinuities in a 2-D range image and intensity discontinuities in a 2-D intensity image for example. For a piecewise smooth 3-D image function $w = f(x, y, z)$, order-0 discontinuity points form 2-D sets (surfaces) that are the boundaries of the continuous pieces of the image. In this case, the "2-D step edges" of a 3-D density image are the *surfaces of solid objects*.

Since the real world may be modeled as a time-varying 3-D density image $w = f(x, y, z, t)$ where objects are defined as 3-D volumes where w exceeds a threshold, range imaging sensor *hardware* determines the 2-D step edges in a 3-D density image to create a 2-D range image that represents the surface boundaries of 3-D object volumes in a scene using physical principles [Besl 1988]. A *software* algorithm must then detect the digital 1-D step edges in the digital 2-D image to find the 1-D edge boundaries of the surfaces in the range image. That is, range imaging sensors directly detect digital surfaces (boundaries of volumes), but digital edges (boundaries of surfaces) must be extracted computationally from a range image. Video cameras, on the other hand, detect light reflected from object surfaces (the 2-D step edges of a 3-D image) to create a 2-D intensity image, which has a completely different meaning than a range image. The implicit assumption, which is not always true, that intensity edges coincide with meaningful scene edges motivates the desire to detect the order-0 discontinuities in intensity images. This is the edge detection problem addressed so often in the literature. For range and intensity imaging both, digital surfaces are created by the sensor, but digital edges are *computed* from the digital surface and are not ordinarily sensed directly by hardware using physical principles. The meaning of an edge or a surface depends on the type of physical quantity being sensed by the sensor.

An order-1 discontinuity point in an n-D scalar image, a *roof-edge* point, is a point $\vec{x}$ at which there exists a unit-norm direction vector $\vec{u} \in \Re^n$ such that the directional derivative at the point $\vec{x}$, defined as

$$\lim_{\alpha \to 0} \frac{f(\vec{x} + \alpha\vec{u}) - f(\vec{x})}{\alpha} = \vec{\nabla}f(\vec{x}) \cdot \vec{u}, \qquad (6.2)$$

is *not* a well-defined quantity because the value depends on whether α approaches zero from the positive or negative side. An image without any points of this type is a C^1 image. It is assumed that simple order-1 discontinuities in an n-D image form connected $(n-1)$-D geometric entities. Again, more pathological arrangements of these discontinuities are not considered. For a piecewise smooth 1-D image function $y = f(x)$, order-1 discontinuity points form 0-D sets (points) that are the boundaries of the smooth *differentiable* pieces of the image. These discontinuity points represent the "0-D roof edges" in the 1-D image. The same ideas hold for planar curves, which are 1-D 2-vector images. For a piecewise smooth 2-D image function $z = f(x, y)$, order-1 discontinuity points form 1-D sets (curves) that are the boundaries of the differentiable pieces of the image. These discontinuity points represent the "1-D roof edges," or the orientation discontinuities, in a 2-D image. For a piecewise smooth 3-D image function $w = f(x, y, z)$, order-1 discontinuity points form 2-D sets (surfaces) that are the boundaries of the differentiable pieces of the image. In this case, the "2-D roof edges" of a 3-D density image are found in the interior of objects.

Higher order discontinuities in n-D images exist, but correspond to changes in image curvature, not image smoothness. Order-0 and order-1 discontinuities in n-D images form the boundaries of *smooth* image regions and are therefore the most prominent types of discontinuities in the perception of piecewise smooth images.

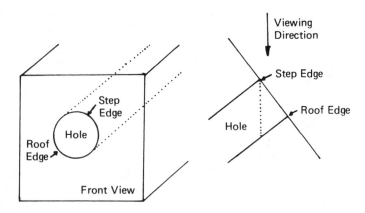

Figure 6.1: Circular Hole in Tilted Flat Surface Has Two Edge Types

If range image segmentation is to be accomplished using the edge detection paradigm, both step-edge range discontinuities and roof-edge orientation discontinuities must be detected and linked together (integrated) to
create a partition of smooth surface primitives. Although the edge detection approach is popular for range images (e.g. [Bolles et al. 1983] [Tomita
and Kanade 1984] [Herman 1985] [Smith and Kanade 1985]), it certainly
is not the only possible approach. For practical applications, an appropriate mix of edge-based and surface-based approaches will probably provide
the best results in the least amount of time for general-purpose processing.
The goal of this book is to demonstrate the advantages of surface-based
processing.

As an example of the differences between edge- and surface-based approaches, consider a circular hole drilled in a flat surface viewed obliquely
as shown in Figure 6.1. A circular edge would be visible in a range image
of the hole. One half-circle is a step edge whereas the other half-circle is
a roof edge. An edge-based method must first detect both types of edges
separately and then link them together to get the set of pixels that form
the circle. In contrast, the surface-based approach finds and fits the pixels
belonging to the flat surface, and a circular boundary is created around
the hole where the range image pixels do not fit well with the flat surface
description. Hence, edges are indirectly detected in the surface-based approach as boundaries of smooth surfaces. Roof edges and step edges do not
need to be discriminated, computed explicitly, or linked together.

The dimensionality of different types of images has been defined along
with the dimensionality of two types of edges that occur in each type of image. Order-0 and order-1 discontinuities (step and roof edges) were defined
as the key edge types for range image perception of scenes with smooth surfaces. Order-0 discontinuities are the primary type of edges given attention

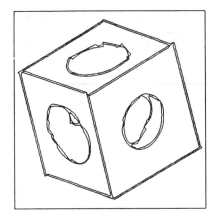

Figure 6.2: Edge Descriptions of Region Boundaries for Block

in intensity image processing work. Imaging sensors create 2-D images, but range imaging sensors explicitly detect the 2-D step edges (surfaces) of 3-D density images (objects in field of view). Explicit digital computation is normally required to detect 1-D edges in any type of digital 2-D image.

6.2 Edge Algorithm Description

The input to the edge description algorithm is the definition of a 2-D four-connected region associated with a smooth surface. The output is an approximate parametric function representation of the region boundary. As an example of the output for several regions, the set of all boundary descriptions for a view of the block with three holes is shown in Figure 6.2. Since all image pixels belong to one and only one region, region boundary pixels are not shared by separate regions. To simplify processing requirements, each region was processed independently and the centers of the region boundary pixels were used as the edge point locations. Two region boundaries, one for each adjacent region, are drawn explicitly for every physical edge. The internal processing steps of the edge algorithm parallel the steps of the surface characterization algorithm and the iterative region growing algorithm based on variable order surface fitting. Those two algorithms together produced the polynomial graph surface descriptions. In this chapter, the edge characterization algorithm and the iterative interval growing algorithm based on variable order curve fitting are used together to produce parametric descriptions of edges.

Each part of the edge description algorithm is described in detail subsequently to note the subtle differences of edge description as opposed to surface description. The material is divided into main sections on edge definition, edge characterization, seed interval extraction, edge curve fit-

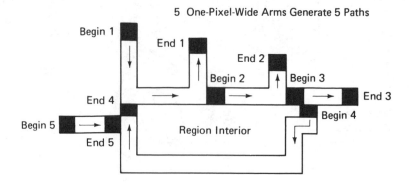

Figure 6.3: Regions with One-Pixel-Wide Arms Cause Multiple Paths

ting, interval growing, termination criteria, interval acceptance, and interval merging at smooth interval joins.

6.3   Edge Definition

Edges are defined directly from a 2-D four-connected region description in the following manner. If a region pixel is four-adjacent to a pixel that is not in the region, then that pixel is an edge pixel. This process creates a one-pixel-wide eight-connected edge map (binary image) representing the boundaries of the region. If there are no one-pixel-wide "arms" of the region, then the edge map contains only simply followable, non-branching, closed edge paths: one path for the outline of the region and one path for each hole in the region. Simply followable means that a simple 3x3 window searching algorithm can determine the next pixel in the binary edge image given the current pixel and the last pixel of an edge sequence. If one-pixel-wide region arms exist, as shown in Figure 6.3, then the edge map of pixel-center locations is still followable except that the one-pixel-wide edge path(s) are not closed. This difficulty can be remedied by an algorithm that uses the outer boundary points of an edge pixel as edge pixel location(s) rather than the pixel-center location. If necessary, one-pixel-wide region arms can also be eliminated using iterative applications of the 3x3 burr trimming operator discussed in Chapter 4 until the region description and the number of pixels in the region does not change. Therefore, it is assumed that the edge algorithm can obtain input in the form of a single, simply followable, one-pixel-wide, eight-connected chain of pixel locations, but it is not required that the pixel chain close on itself.

Since the edge input is assumed to be simply followable, a simple edge following algorithm using only 3x3 windows can be used to create two parameterization functions, or edge vectors, $x(s)$ and $y(s)$ that describe the curve exactly as a function of arc length. This representation is straightforward except for the diagonal vs. non-diagonal point spacing issue. In order to use discrete orthogonal polynomials for 1-D least squares derivative estimation similar to the methods used in Chapter 3, equally spaced points are needed (see also Appendix C). However, the northwest, northeast, southeast, and southwest neighbors of a pixel are $\sqrt{2}$ pixel spacings away from the central pixel of a 3x3 neighborhood whereas north, south, east, and west neighbors of a pixel are only one pixel spacing away. Hence, eight-connected edge pixels are not equally spaced as an edge is followed. Also, since edges are computed as boundaries of four-connected regions in the digital surface segmentation approach, it is desirable that a north neighbor move followed by a west neighbor move is basically equivalent to a northwest neighbor move. For these reasons, the diagonal pixel spacing is labeled as two pixel spacings even though this is not correct Euclidean geometry. For example, a northwest neighbor is considered two pixel units away from a given center pixel instead of $\sqrt{2}$. This assignment of two distance units to each diagonal pixel spacing allows for equally spaced data points to be used, which considerably simplifies edge vector processing. A more accurate technique that maintains equal spacing better is to replace horizontal and vertical moves by 5 discrete distance units and diagonal moves by 7 discrete distance units [Shahraray and Anderson 1985]. The diagonal distance is then 1.4, which is an error of only 1% as opposed to the error of 40% with the method described above. The edge description process is independent of the simplifying assumptions made here, and the results in Chapter 7 are surprisingly good given such crude simplifications.

An edge following algorithm can be stated as follows for a simply followable edge. Given a starting point, make it the current pixel and look for a 4-connected neighbor first. If a 4-connected neighbor is found, add the new pixel to the edge vectors describing the edge. If no 4-connected neighbors are found, look for an 8-connected neighbor that is not 4-connected. If an 8-connected neighbor is found, add two new (x,y) locations to the vectors describing the edge. The first of these is halfway between the current pixel and the eight-connected neighbor; the second is the eight connected neighbor. Hence, the length of an equivalent chain code, the number of edge pixels, and the arc length of the $(x(s), y(s))$ edge vector descriptions are not the same in general. Simple extra steps to maintain "equally" spaced edge pixels in the edge definition phase can save significant processing time in the edge characterization phase since derivative estimates based on least squares curve fits can be computed via simple inner-product computations [Anderson and Houseman 1942]. Figure 6.4 shows a set of simply followable edge pixels and the $x(s)$ and $y(s)$ edge vectors plotted as a function of arc length for the outside boundary of the block.

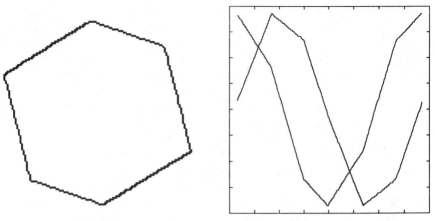

Figure 6.4: Original Edge Pixels and Periodic $x(s)$ and $y(s)$ Functions

6.4   Edge Characterization

Once the edge description vectors $x(s)$ and $y(s)$ have been formed, the data in these vectors is first smoothed to filter the quantization and edge detection noise. Then the derivatives dx/ds and dy/ds are computed using discrete orthogonal polynomials as described in Chapter 3. The tangent angle function vector is then formed as follows:

$$\phi(s) = \tan^{-1}\left(\frac{dy/ds}{dx/ds}\right). \tag{6.3}$$

Special processing is required to handle phase wrapping, but the final approximation to the tangent angle function represents a smooth differentiable function due to the initial smoothing of the data. There is no ambiguity involved in unwrapping the phase angle because the x and y coordinates can only vary by one pixel spacing for each increment of arc length. The curvature function for plane curves is computed directly as the derivative of the tangent angle function:

$$\kappa(s) = \frac{d\phi(s)}{ds}. \tag{6.4}$$

Curvature can also be computed directly from an equivalent formulation in terms of the first and second derivatives of x and y with respect to s [Faux and Pratt 1979,pg.28]. The toleranced sign-of-curvature function $\text{sgn}_\epsilon(\kappa(s))$ is then computed using a preset zero threshold ϵ:

$$\text{sgn}_\epsilon(\kappa(s)) = \left\{ \begin{array}{ll} \frac{\kappa(s)}{|\kappa(s)|} & \text{if } |\kappa(s)| > \epsilon \\ 0 & \text{if } |\kappa(s)| \leq \epsilon \end{array} \right. . \tag{6.5}$$

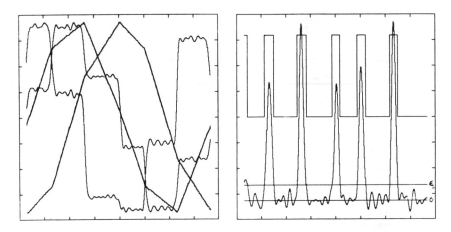

Figure 6.5: X and Y Derivatives and Curvature Function of Block

The sign-of-curvature function of this digital edge segmentation algorithm is exactly analogous to the HK-sign map of the digital surface segmentation algorithm. This function is then given to the iterative edge fitting algorithm along with the original unsmoothed edge vectors $(x(s), y(s))$.

Figure 6.5 shows the dx/ds and dy/ds derivatives of the block boundary overlaid on top of the edge parameterization vectors as well as the curvature function of the block boundary with overlays. The curvature function has the zero level and the ϵ level marked at the bottom of the plot. The sign-of-curvature function is also overlaid on top of the curvature plot. Each peak in the curvature function yields a square pulse in the sign-of-curvature function.

6.5 Approximating Function Selection

Just as approximating functions were needed for surface fitting, a finite set of approximating functions are needed for edge fitting. However, instead of eight HK-sign surface primitives, there are only three sign-of-curvature edge primitives: convex curves (positive curvature), concave curves (negative curvature), and a straight line (zero curvature). The shapes of the sign-of-curvature edge primitives are relatively simple, and arbitrarily complicated piecewise smooth curves can be decomposed into a disjoint union of such curve primitives. If these edge primitives are approximated well, then the entire edge can be approximated well.

The requirements of approximating functions for edge primitives are similar to the requirements of HK-sign surface approximants. A small, ordered, finite set of approximating functions is required that can

1. Approximate well any smooth curve of constant sign-of-curvature over an interval of finite length,

2. Extrapolate accurately to arbitrary points outside the interval used for fitting (this permits interval growing),

3. Interpolate to locations between edge pixels,

4. Allow use of a quick, computationally efficient curve fitting algorithm,

5. Be easily differentiated, and

6. Be represented by a comparatively small amount of data.

Low order univariate polynomials (up to fourth order) with vector coefficients were selected as the set of approximating functions for sign-of-curvature edge primitives. Therefore, the number of approximating functions $|F| = 4$ and the set of approximating functions F for edge primitives can be written as two scalar equations:

$$
\begin{aligned}
\hat{g}_x(s) &= a_0 + a_1 s + a_2 s^2 + a_3 s^3 + a_4 s^4 \\
\hat{g}_y(s) &= b_0 + b_1 s + b_2 s^2 + b_3 s^3 + b_4 s^4,
\end{aligned}
\tag{6.6}
$$

or as one 2-vector equation,

$$
\left[\begin{array}{c} \hat{g}_x(s) \\ \hat{g}_y(s) \end{array} \right] = \sum_{i=0}^{m} \left[\begin{array}{c} a_i \\ b_i \end{array} \right] s^i.
\tag{6.7}
$$

In the terminology defined above, an edge is a 1-D 2-vector image and is approximated by a polynomial in one variable with 2-vector coefficients. The goal of the edge description algorithm is to segment that 1-D edge image into meaningful intervals that are either curved or straight. A least squares edge fitting algorithm computes the parameter vectors $\vec{a}$ and $\vec{b}$ and the RMS fit error $\epsilon = \max(\xi, \eta)$ from the edge vectors in an interval very quickly since only inner products are required to do least squares fits. A key difference between edge fitting and surface fitting is that edge fitting amounts to performing convolutions since discrete orthogonal polynomials may be used for any interval of equally spaced data. Since surfaces do not always form rectangular or regular regions, the general least squares problem must be solved as discussed in Appendix C.

The problems with these polynomial approximants are the same as in the case of surfaces. But as also stated earlier, the main concern is that the functional fit is good enough for perceptual organization of edge pixels. If an application is interested in circles, the data-driven edge description output of this algorithm can be used to isolate curved intervals of approximately constant curvature to guide the testing of hypotheses about circles. Circle fitting is faster when circles are present in the data, but is ineffective when the data does not consist of circles. All of the other arguments of the previous section against quadric surfaces apply here against conic curves, the general second-degree algebraic curve form.

6.6 Error Tolerance Specification

Just as the surface segmentation algorithm required an error threshold for the RMS error that one was willing to tolerate for surface fits, the edge segmentation algorithm requires an error threshold for edge fitting. This threshold could also be tied back to an image quality measure mentioned previously since noisier images are going to have noisier edges. However, since the maximum difference in the x or y coordinates for a unit change in arc length is always one, good quality images with reasonable quality edges can be segmented well using a fixed threshold for the RMS curve fit error. All edge results in Chapter 7 were obtained with a fixed RMS error threshold of $\epsilon_{max} = 0.96$. Compare this well-behaved property for digital edges with digital surfaces where the maximum difference in z for a unit change in x or y is not bounded by the fact that the surface data is discrete.

6.7 Seed Interval Extraction

Given the original edge vectors $x(s)$ and $y(s)$ and the sign-of-curvature vector $\text{sgn}(\kappa(s))$, the algorithm begins by looking for the largest interval of any type $\{-1, 0, +1\}$ in the sign-of-curvature vector. Rather than contracting this interval with an erosion (contraction) algorithm as is necessary in the surface region case, this interval is simply shrunk by a factor of two about the center point of the interval if there are more than eight pixels in the interval; otherwise, the interval is not contracted. This new interval is the seed interval. Hence, the difficulties and the computational expense in finding and maintaining connected component descriptions of regions are not present in applying the sign-of-curvature paradigm to edges owing to the simplicity of intervals compared to regions. The edge segmentation algorithm requires much less time per digital edge pixel than the surface segmentation algorithm requires per digital surface pixel.

6.8 Iterative Variable Order Edge Fitting

Each isolated seed interval is given as the input to the iterative edge interval growing algorithm based on variable order edge fitting. The basic concepts of this algorithm are the following. First, it is decided how well smooth curves should fit the edge data. This is given by the maximum allowable RMS fit error threshold ϵ_{max}. A line is always fitted first to the seed interval using the standard equal weighting least squares approach based on discrete orthogonal polynomials as described in Chapter 3 and Appendix C. If the seed interval belongs to an edge that is not too highly curved and not too noisy, a line will fit quite well to the original edge vector data. If one considers a small enough interval on the real line, any smooth real-valued function of a single variable can be approximated well by a straight line. If the line fits the seed interval to within the maximum RMS fit error threshold, then the seed is allowed to grow. If not, the seed is fitted with the next higher-order curve (the quadratic in this implementation) and the algorithm proceeds similarly. When the seed is allowed to grow, the functional description of the curve over the seed interval is tested against all edge pixels in the edge vectors for the interval growing operation.

It is assumed that a specific finite set F of approximating curves is given and the maximum allowable RMS curve fit error is given ϵ_{max}. These edge functions provide extrapolation beyond the current edge fitting interval, and they provide good approximation capabilities to sign-of-curvature primitives over a finite interval. Let E be the set of all edge pixels on a given edge and let I_i be the unknown set of N_I underlying disjoint intervals that partition the set of edge pixels:

$$E = \bigcup_{i=1}^{N_I} I_i \quad \text{such that } I_i \cap I_j = \phi \ \forall i \neq j \tag{6.8}$$

Just as for surfaces, it is assumed that the data in digital edge vectors $x(s)$ and $y(s)$ is of the form

$$x(s) = \sum_{i=1}^{N_I} \lfloor x_i(s)\chi(s, I_i) + n_x(s)\rfloor \qquad y(s) = \sum_{i=1}^{N_I} \lfloor y_i(s)\chi(s, I_i) + n_y(s)\rfloor \tag{6.9}$$

where $n_x(s)$ and $n_y(s)$ are both zero-mean, finite-variance noise processes, where $\chi(s, I_i) = 1$ if $s \in I_i$ and zero otherwise, and where $x_i(s)$ and $y_i(s)$ are unknown sign-of-curvature functions. One difference here is that the underlying edge function is piecewise-smooth and *continuous* on E. The goal of the edge segmentation algorithm is to recover a set of $\hat{N}_I$ intervals $\{\hat{I}_i\}$ and approximating functions $\hat{x}_i(s)$ and $\hat{y}_i(s)$ from the set F such that (1) the continuous piecewise-smooth functions $\hat{x}(s)$ and $\hat{y}(s)$ given by

$$\hat{x}(s) = \sum_{i=1}^{\hat{N}_I} \hat{x}_i(s)\chi(s, \hat{I}_i) \qquad \hat{y}(s) = \sum_{i=1}^{\hat{N}_I} \hat{y}_i(s)\chi(s, \hat{I}_i) \tag{6.10}$$

approximate the edge vectors $x(s)$ and $y(s)$ as well as possible over the entire edge, (2) each interval $\hat{I}_i$ is as large as is possible, and the number of intervals $\hat{N}_I$ is as small as possible.

Assuming the polynomial form of the approximating function set F as given above, let $\vec{a}_i^k \in \Re^5$ and $\vec{b}_i^k \in \Re^5$ be the parameter vectors of the polynomial fits to the x and y coordinates of the edge respectively in the current i-th interval $\hat{I}_i^k$ for the k-th iteration. The seed interval corresponding to I_i is assumed to be $\hat{I}_i^0$. Let $|F| = 4$ be the number of different orders of edge functions to be used. The order of a particular function is referred to as $m_i^k \in \{1, 2, \ldots, |F|\}$. As described above, the approximation function of order m_i^k is denoted $\hat{x}_i^k(s) = \hat{g}(m_i^k, \vec{a}_i^k, s)$ and $\hat{y}_i^k(s) = \hat{g}(m_i^k, \vec{b}_i^k, s)$. The edge fitting process, denoted $\mathbf{L}_{\hat{g}}$, converts the original edge data $\{x(s), y(s)\}$, an interval definition $\hat{I}_i^k$, and the fit order m_i^k into the parameter vectors and the individual RMS fit errors:

$$(\vec{a}_i^k, \xi_i^k) = \mathbf{L}_{\hat{g}}(m_i^k, \hat{I}_i^k, x) \qquad (\vec{b}_i^k, \eta_i^k) = \mathbf{L}_{\hat{g}}(m_i^k, \hat{I}_i^k, y). \qquad (6.11)$$

The single fit error statistic is given by $\epsilon_i^k = \max(\xi_i^k, \eta_i^k)$ where the individual fit errors

$$\xi_i^k = \|\hat{g}(m_i^k, \vec{a}_i^k, s) - x(s)\|_{\hat{I}_i^k} \qquad (6.12)$$

$$\eta_i^k = \|\hat{g}(m_i^k, \vec{b}_i^k, s) - y(s)\|_{\hat{I}_i^k}$$

are the minimum values attainable for all functions of the form specified by m_i^k. Equally-weighted least squares curve fitting minimizes the fit errors

$$(\xi_i^k)^2 = \frac{1}{|\hat{I}_i^k|} \sum_{s \in \hat{I}_i^k} |\hat{g}(m_i^k, \vec{a}_i^k, s) - x(s)|^2 \qquad (6.13)$$

$$(\eta_i^k)^2 = \frac{1}{|\hat{I}_i^k|} \sum_{s \in \hat{I}_i^k} |\hat{g}(m_i^k, \vec{b}_i^k, s) - y(s)|^2$$

where $|\hat{I}_i^k|$ is the length of the interval $\hat{I}_i^k$. Least squares polynomial curve fitting of equally-spaced data points is accomplished very efficiently via inner products [Anderson and Houseman 1942] and the "shape potential" of polynomial curves is adequate for sign-of-curvature edge primitives.

If the edge fitting process yielded a fit error that is not below the maximum error threshold $\epsilon_i^k > \epsilon_{\max}$), then the algorithm increments the edge order m_i^k and performs the higher order curve fit if there are enough pixels in the connected interval being fitted. A non-parametric statistics runs test, analogous to the regions test for surfaces, is also performed at each iteration for linear, quadratic, and cubic fits to see if a higher order function is necessary. This involves computing two residual error sign functions for both the x and y function fits. The number of runs in each residual error sign function is computed, and the minimum number of runs, the smaller of the two, is used as the test statistic. Given the number of edge pixels in the fit and the test statistic, a one-sided runs test is performed to see if there are too few runs. If there are too few runs, a higher order function is needed and value of m_i^k is incremented for the next iteration.

To summarize, given (1) an interval $\hat{I}_i^k$ beginning with the seed interval where $k = 0$, (2) the original edge vectors $\{x(s), y(s)\}$, (3) the lowest function order $m_i^k \le |F|$ such that $\epsilon_i^k < \epsilon_{\max}$, the parameter vectors $\vec{a}_i^k$ and $\vec{b}_i^k$ and the maximum RMS fit error $\epsilon_i^k = \max(\xi_i^k, \eta_i^k)$ are computed. When the error is less than the predetermined maximum allowable error threshold $\epsilon_{\max}$ and the runs test is satisfied for both x and y component functions, then the interval is allowed to grow using the same order curve fitting; otherwise, the order of the curve fitting is incremented. If all possible fit orders were tried and the error was never less than the threshold, the best highest order fit is accepted as a good approximation to the pixels on that interval even though the ideal convergence condition may not have been met. If the highest order fit is not sufficiently good, intervals should theoretically be rejected by the edge segmentation algorithm to maintain parallels with the surface segmentation approach. Interval rejections have never occurred with the test image database of Chapter 7 using the 50% acceptability zone as was used for surfaces, and so it does not seem to be necessary to include such an acceptance/rejection test for edges. This property seems to result from the well-behaved property that $x(s)$ and $y(s)$ cannot change by more than one discrete level for any unit change in arc length. Hence, the maximum possible digital derivative of the edge data is one. Digital surfaces rarely exhibit such controlled variations.

6.9   Edge Interval Growing

The approach for the edge segmentation algorithm is the same as for the surface segmentation algorithm. After a polynomial curve is fitted to an interval, the original edge description is used to grow the interval into a larger interval where all pixels in the larger interval are connected to the original interval and compatible with the approximating edge function for the original edge.

For each edge pixel $s \in E$, the entire set of edge pixels, the two values

$$\hat{x}_i^k(s) = \hat{g}(m_i^k, \vec{a}_i^k, s) \qquad \hat{y}_i^k(s) = \hat{g}(m_i^k, \vec{b}_i^k, s) \qquad (6.14)$$

are computed and compared to $x(s)$ and $y(s)$ respectively to see if the edge pixel s is compatible with the approximating edge function. It is assumed that almost all pixels in the original interval are compatible with the approximating edge function because the pixels in the region were used to obtain the edge interval fit. If the maximum of the magnitudes of the differences between the computed edge pixel location and the original edge pixel location is less than the allowed tolerance $w(\epsilon_i^k)$, then the pixel $s \in E$ is set to one in the binary compatible pixel vector $C_i^k(s)$. Otherwise, it is incompatible and set to zero:

$$C_i^k(s) = \begin{cases} 1 & \text{if}\ \ \max(|\hat{x}_i^k - x(s)|, |\hat{y}_i^k(s) - y(s)|) \le w(\epsilon_i^k) \\ 0 & \text{otherwise.} \end{cases} \qquad (6.15)$$

The standard error tolerance function $w(\epsilon) > \epsilon$ that was used for surfaces in Chapter 4 is also used for edges.

Just as with surfaces, the compatible set of edge pixels depends indirectly on all edge intervals previously discovered in the edge vectors. For sharply defined edge interval boundaries, such as those at the vertices of the cube shown earlier, the influence of other already determined edge intervals is negligible or non-existent, but for noisy edges, the influence may be more important. When an edge interval iteration terminates and the edge interval and its approximation are accepted, the error at each pixel of the grown edge interval is stored in an edge error vector $e(s)$ to explicitly note the spatial distribution of the approximation errors, and the edge interval label i for each pixel of the accepted edge interval is stored in an interval label vector $l(s)$ to explicitly note the pixels that the approximating edge fits best. During the interval growing process that forms the compatible pixel vector, each pixel is also checked to insure that the pixel error is less than the best-fit error $e(s)$ encountered so far. If this condition is not satisfied, then the pixel is not considered to be compatible with the growing edge and is not marked as such.

The largest connected interval in the compatible pixel vector that overlaps the growing interval $\hat{I}_i^k$ is then extracted to create the next interval $\hat{I}_i^{k+1}$. This iterative process of interval definition via largest overlapping interval extraction is expressed using the function $\Lambda(\cdot|\cdot)$ as in Chapter 4:

$$\hat{I}_i^{k+1} = \Lambda(C_i^k|\hat{I}_i^k) = \Phi(\hat{I}_i^k) \tag{6.16}$$

where $\Phi(\cdot)$ represents all operations required to compute the interval $\hat{I}_i^{k+1}$ from the interval $\hat{I}_i^k$. The output interval $\hat{I}_i^{k+1}$ must have the property that it is the largest interval in the binary compatible pixel vector satisfying

$$\hat{I}_i^k \cap \hat{I}_i^{k+1} \neq \phi = \text{Null Set}. \tag{6.17}$$

Hence, the interval growing approach can be formulated in the same terms as the region growing approach.

Although this parallel method works and theoretically parallels the surface segmentation algorithm, the inherent simplicity of intervals as compared to regions or volumes makes the special case of 1-D edge segmentation much different than higher-dimensional segmentation cases. Sequential interval growing is so simple compared to sequential region or volume growing that it makes sense in practice to use a sequential approach during the iterative process. The parallel interval growth operation can still be performed after the last iteration if one is interested in detecting non-adjacent compatible intervals. In other words, the interval $I_i^k = [a, b] \subseteq E$ can be grown by simply testing if $a - 1$ and $b + 1$ are compatible with the approximating function. Update the values $a := a - 1$ and $b := b + 1$ and test for compatibility again. Repeat this procedure until *neither* endpoint can be moved. Then begin the next iteration via another curve fit. Fixed point (interval) convergence $I_i = \Phi(I_i)$ is guaranteed for this monotonic, bounded sequential edge interval growing algorithm if higher order surface fits were always available. The edge processing with $|F| = 4$ parametric polynomial curves generally yields such convergence, and if the fit error exceeds the maximum allowable fit error threshold, it has never been by more than a few percent, which is nowhere near the 50% acceptability zone. Owing to the unit slope constraint on the digital edge data, no problems were encountered with the monotonicity requirement for interval growing based on curve fitting. This was not true of the monotonicity requirement for region growing based on surface fitting.

The simple compatibility requirement can be generalized to require curve normal or slope C^1 compatibility similar to the surface normal compatibility requirement for growing surfaces. That is, the normal or the slope of the parametric polynomial curve should be within some angular tolerance of the edge normal or the edge slope respectively as estimated from the raw data in the original edge vectors. If the edge data is good enough, approximate second derivative C^2 continuity or curvature continuity might also be required for a finer edge segmentation. Also, recursive least squares techniques can be used without difficulties to combine the region growing and edge fitting processes into one recursive process as in Chen [1988]. Test statistics similar to ϵ_i^k and $w(\epsilon_i^k)$ are used. The computational advantages of QR updating are significant since the addition of a new edge pixel and the incrementing of the order of the curve fit can both be accomplished recursively [Golub and VanLoan 1983]. As mentioned previously, recursive QR updating is essentially the same as matrix square root Kalman filtering. Only the simple compatibility requirement was used for the experimental results shown in Chapter 7.

6.10 Termination Criteria

The termination criteria are very simple for the edge segmentation algorithm.

- **Rule 1:** If $\epsilon_i^k > \epsilon_{\max}$ and $m_i^k \geq |F|$, then terminate the iteration. This rule says that if the edge fit error increases above the predetermined threshold and if no more fit orders remain in the finite set, then terminate the iteration.

- **Rule 2:** If both of the end pixels of an interval did not move since the last iteration, then terminate the iteration. This says that the iteration should stop when interval growing stops, which implies .

Quick fixed-point (interval) convergence has been experienced with the edge segmentation algorithm for every edge interval ever tested (thousands of edge intervals). This phenomena is apparently due to (1) the maximum unity slope property of digital edge functions, and (2) the property that intervals only have two degrees of freedom, the start and stop end points.

Compare these digital edge properties to digital surface properties: (1) there are no such unity surface slope constraint, and (2) discrete image regions have huge number of degrees of freedom limited only by the size of the image.

6.11 Edge Interval Acceptance

All grown edge intervals are currently accepted. Other intervals in the binary compatible pixel edge are accepted if the intervals exceed a certain length threshold, and if the RMS edge fit errors are small enough. Whenever any interval is accepted, it is marked off in a writable copy of the sign-of-curvature function so that none of the interval pixels are capable of being involved in another seed region.

An error vector $e(s)$ and the interval label vector $l(s)$ are updated when an interval is accepted. These two vectors are used to monitor and control growth during the interval growing process in the same way as in the surface algorithm. Gaps between intervals are usually very small and easily handled by adding straight line connections if they occur. It is not necessary to maintain separate interval label descriptions as in the surface algorithm; interval fragmentation cannot occur because only two end points are needed to describe the interval.

6.12 Interval Merging and Interval Connections

Region boundaries or one-pixel-wide edge descriptions are digital edges, which are modeled as noisy quantized piecewise-smooth planar curves that consist of smooth-curve edge interval primitives bounded by order-1 curve tangent discontinuities. Smooth-curve edge interval primitives may consist of multiple sign-of-curvature edge interval primitives, which are approximated by up to fourth-order parametric polynomial curves. Such curves are easily converted to Bezier curve or B-spline representations if needed [Faux and Pratt 1979]. A set of interval merging rules similar to those in the surface algorithm can be defined to control the merging of adjacent smoothly joined sign-of-curvature edge interval primitives. The rules are based on the average differences in functional descriptions and average differences in edge tangents (or edge normals) within a small interval of overlap where two edge intervals join. The boundaries of the smooth edge-interval primitives are simply the breakpoints between the intervals that do not join smoothly. This algorithm is considerably simpler than the surface merging algorithm.

When displaying the results of the edge description/segmentation algorithm, segmented intervals must be connected with each other to obtain visually appealing edges. The end pixels of adjacent intervals are connected with straight lines in the simplest scheme. This is adequate for current purposes although the final results do appear undesirably jagged. The curve intervals should be intersected to obtain the breakpoints at curve tangent discontinuities. Smooth curve merges could be handled by (1) representing the curve primitives as B-splines, (2) concatenating the knot sequences of the two curves to be merged, (3) eliminating half the duplicated knots at the join and spreading the remaining duplicated knots out over the one or two pixel merging interval, thereby creating a single smooth B-spline description for the entire segmented smooth curve primitive. Although this provides a smooth curve, the new description is not necessarily unique for the given set of input pixels. Other constraints could be applied to provide uniqueness if desired, but since the entire curve description is approximate, this is a relatively unimportant topic.

6.13　Summary

The iterative edge interval growing algorithm based on variable order approximating curve functions accepts the sign-of-curvature function and the original edge vectors as input and produces parametric descriptions of the segmented edge intervals. A list of polynomial coefficients and fit errors for each edge interval primitive are created by the algorithm. Smooth edge-interval end points are also computed. This type of edge description method is primarily data-driven, handles arbitrary edge shapes, and can be used with any edge detector/linker that creates the appropriate type of digital edges: one-pixel-wide, 8-connected, simply followable edges. It is interesting, not only for its own merits as an edge description mechanism, but also because the same sign-of-curvature paradigm provides useful algorithms for segmenting planar curves and graph surfaces. Although not described here, it is not difficult to see that the sign-of-curvature paradigm can be extended to higher dimensions to describe and segment n-D m-vector multidimensional signals, digital versions of mappings from $\Re^n \to \Re^m$. For piecewise-smooth 3-D images, such as density images, there are 27 different sign-of-curvature volume-primitive types, and the fourth-order trivariate polynomial requires 35 coefficients. The first and second fundamental form matrices become 3x3 matrices. It will also be interesting to apply the sign-of-curvature paradigm to segment registered range and intensity images and dynamic scenes, but such an extension is beyond the scope of this text. For digital surfaces, a unified approach to edge and surface description and segmentation in images is important theoretically and practically in that improvements in one algorithm are immediately available to the other via the appropriate modifications.

Simple variants of this edge segmentation algorithm exist that are also useful. As mentioned above, sequential edge interval growing is preferred to parallel edge interval growing since intervals are so simple compared to regions. Sequential outward growth is equivalent to the parallel growth approach except at the last iteration. It is not absolutely necessary to maintain an error vector or an interval label vector if the sign-of-curvature vector is used to keep track of pixels that have been approximated and those that have not. The disadvantage is that several pixels near interval joins will be associated with the first-within-tolerance edge interval, which may not be the best-fit edge interval. As with the surface algorithm, the edge algorithm will also function without the runs test. Moreover, the edge algorithm functions better without the runs test than the surface algorithm does. The net effect of these other simplifications is some relatively minor jaggedness between edge intervals.

Chapter 7

Experimental Results

This chapter critiques and displays the results of the digital surface segmentation algorithm applied to a set of twenty-two test images containing real and noisy synthetic range images and real intensity images. These images were selected from a group of images used as a test image database for the experiments. All input images are 128x128 pixels with eight bits per pixel, except for one 256x256 8-bit intensity image of a house scene from the University of Massachusetts at Amherst. All real range images were acquired from an Environmental Research Institute of Michigan (ERIM) AM phase-difference imaging laser radar sensor except for the Renault Auto Part image, which was created by converting a range data xyz-file from the French INRIA range imaging sensor into a range image using a special purpose program written by the author. All results have been obtained using software written by the author in the C programming language on the UNIX 4.2 BSD operating system running on a VAX/11-780.

For each input image, the following standard set of images are displayed in the following order:

1. Original Image (Gray Scale),

2. Best-Fit Reconstructed Image (Gray Scale),

3. HK-Sign Map (Gray Scale),

4. Final Region Label Image (Gray Scale),

5. Final Segmentation Plot Overlaid on Original Image (Gray Scale),

6. HK-Sign Map Segmentation Plot (Binary),

7. Best-Fit Segmentation Plot (Binary),

8. Final Labeled Segmentation Plot (Binary), and

9. Edge Description Plot (Binary).

The eight-level HK-sign map demonstrates the intermediate surface characterization output and the input to the iterative region-growing algorithm. This format is different than in Chapter 3 in which separate sgn(H) and sgn(K) images were displayed. The best-fit reconstructed image shows the visual quality of the approximate surface representation. The best-fit segmentation plot shows the underlying segmentation in the best-fit region label image (buffer) corresponding to the best-fit reconstructed image. The final segmentation plots show the quality of the final segmentation output (obtained via the methods of Chapter 5) both alone and overlaid on the original image. The edge description plots show the parametric edge interpretations obtained by applying the sign-of-curvature method to edges as described in Chapter 6. This set of images graphically describes the primary information available from the algorithm. Other available results are included for several images, such as the best-fit segmentation plot results obtained when the surface normal compatibility requirement is imposed.

The original image is the only variable input to the "black box" digital surface segmentation algorithm for the *standard* results shown in this chapter. All internal parameters, input thresholds, and window sizes were constant for all standard results on all twenty-two images. A fixed set of thresholds does, of course, represent a compromise for some images and may be inappropriate for others, but seeing fixed threshold results over many images helps in evaluating the strengths and weaknesses of the algorithm. Noticeably better results were sometimes obtained using modified thresholds. Modified threshold results are noted in figure titles when included. If the surface normal compatibility constraint was used, then the automatically determined adaptive thresholds mentioned in the text were also used unless otherwise noted. This combination of algorithm features enhanced the performance of the algorithm on good quality images, but better results have also been obtained by overriding the automatically set thresholds.

Several of the fixed internal parameters and other inputs required by the algorithm are summarized below for the standard results.

1. Pre-Smoothing Window Size for Surface Characterization: (11x11),

2. Derivative Window Size for Surface Characterization: (9x9),

3. Curvature Smoothing Window Size: (7x7),

4. Zero Curvature Thresholds: 0.015 (Mean) and 0.006 (Gaussian),

5. Regions Test Threshold r_t: 0.02,

6. Error Threshold ϵ_{max}: 4.2 levels on 8-bit scale,

7. Error Tolerance Factor: 2.8,

8. Acceptability Zone Factor: 1.5.

This list summarizes several algorithm inputs that were fixed. Any other inputs, thresholds, or constants required by the algorithm that are not mentioned here were assigned to their default values mentioned previously in the text. When surface normal compatibility was required, the following adaptive thresholds were based on the L_2 image quality metric ρ_2:

1. Error Threshold ϵ_{max}: $2.5\rho_2$ levels,

2. Regions Test Threshold r_t: $0.009 + 0.002\rho_2$,

3. Surface Normal Compatibility Threshold θ_t: $12 + 16\rho_2$ degrees.

In addition, the pre-smoothing window size and derivative window sizes were all 7x7, and the curvature smoothing window size was 5x5 for the surface normal compatibility results.

7.1 Real Range Images

For all images, at least two pages of figures are presented at the end of the chapter in a separate results section. The first figure page contains the original and best-fit reconstruction images, the HK-sign map (surface type image), and the final region label image in one photograph, and the final segmentation plot overlaid on the original image in the second photograph of the figure. The second figure consists of a set of four plots: the initial segmentation in the HK-sign map, the best-fit region label image (buffer) segmentation, the final region segmentation, and the boundary edge descriptions.

7.1.1 Coffee Cup Range Images

The two coffee cup range images from an ERIM imaging laser radar are good quality images of a simple object. The original range images, their best-fit reconstruction images, and the final segmentation overlay are shown in Figures 7.1 and 7.5. The reconstructed range images show that the surface primitives interpreted by the algorithm accurately represent the image data. In Figures 7.2 and 7.6, four separate images are represented. Figures 7.2(a) and 7.6(a) show the initial segmentations obtained by computing the signs of the mean and Gaussian curvature at every pixel and drawing boundaries around connected regions of the same surface curvature sign. Figures 7.2(b) and 7.6(b) represent the segmentations in the best-fit region label image. After the region combination and region merging processes have operated on the region growing algorithm output, the final labeled region segmentations are obtained, which are shown in Figures 7.2(c) and 7.6(c). Figures 7.2(d) and 7.6(d) display the parametric edge descriptions of the edge intervals of the region boundaries in the final region segmentations.

Figures 7.6(b),(c),(d) show that the cup handle was divided into two separate surfaces, mainly the top side of the handle and the inside of the handle. When modified thresholds were used, the handle is segmented as one region as shown in the overlaid segmentation plot of Figure 7.5. In Figures 7.2(d) and 7.6(d), straight parallel edges on the side of the cup are identified as straight, and the curved edges are identified as curved in the context of the edge segmentation algorithm despite noisy image data near the edges.

Figure 7.3 displays plots of four different quantities as a function of the number of iterations in the region-growing process for the four surface primitives in the coffee cup A image. Automatically scaled plots are shown for (1) the RMS surface fit error, (2) the total number of compatible pixels, (3) the size of the growing region, and (4) the order of the fitting surface. Note how the RMS fit error always drops each time the fit order is incremented.

Figure 7.4 shows the entire segmentation information for the coffee cup A image as stored in the best-fit so far surface list. The four regions correspond to the background surface, the exterior cup body, the interior cup body, and the handle. The data includes the surface type of the seed region, the type of the final fitted polynomial, the coefficients of the bivariate polynomial, the three different fit errors, and a run-length encoded version of the region. The edge parameterizations of the region are not included here.

The final segmentations in both images delineate the outside cylindrical surface of the cup, the background table surface (which was recognized in two parts despite the topological separation of the small patch visible through the handle in Figure 7.6(c)), the inside cylindrical surface of the cup, and the cup handle surface, which is represented either as one symbolic primitive or two depending upon the input thresholds (compare segmentation plot of Figure 7.5 and Figure 7.6(c)).

Although the hole in the body of the cup in the first image is not big enough to merit its own surface region description in the standard results, it is visible in the error image. Figure 7.7 shows the thresholded error image overlaid on the original range image. This output image type is included only for this view of the coffee cup to show that such small features can be isolated even though they do not form a coherent surface region in the image. Note how well the hole in the coffee cup body is isolated. Other large errors in the image approximation occur only at occluding edges except for 6 sporadic noise points that occurred due to sensor characteristics. Figure 7.8 displays a reconstruction image obtained by applying the surface equations to the final region segmentation. Hence, this is slightly different than the best-fit reconstruction and the first-within-tolerance reconstruction images mentioned in Chapter 4.

This segmentation algorithm knows nothing about *cylinders*, much less anything about coffee cups, yet all surfaces are meaningful to people who understand the semantic content of the image. Except for the small hole in the side of the cup, this range image is the epitome of a coherent digital surface. Moreover, this image shows the ability of the algorithm to identity non-adjacent separated regions.

Note the straightness of the edges bounding the outside cylindrical surface region in the final segmentation output in Figure 7.6(d) as compared to the straightness in the original image. The edges in the original image are not very straight owing to noise effects from the range sensor at steeply sloped surfaces and occluding edges. The straightness of the net edge description is due primarily to the surface approximation method combined with region refinement techniques that use 3x3 window mappings as discussed in Chapter 4.

The quality measure ρ_1 is 0.84 for the image where the handle is visible and 0.71 for the other image where it is not. These values are higher than those for synthetic images without noise, and lower than those for the synthetic images with $\sigma = 2.3$ additive white pseudo-Gaussian noise. The ρ_2 measure for the cup with handle image is 1.02 and 0.89 for the hidden handle image. The average error in absolute residual error image for the entire image reconstruction, including edge pixels, is 1.46.

Figure 7.9 displays the notion of surface coherence. The original image and the reconstruction image are shown in gray scale in Figure 7.5 and appear to be very similar. If a random gray scale lookup table is used to transform the gray levels in these two images randomly, the two images in Figure 7.9 are obtained. These images may be thought of as contour plot images in which each range level is assigned a separate gray level. The noisy top image is the original image, and the clean bottom image is the noise-free reconstruction image. The original data does exhibit noticeable surface coherence in spite of the measurement noise. This surface coherence in the data allows the digital surface segmentation algorithm to produce a perfectly coherent reconstruction image.

Figures 7.10 and 7.11 show the results of digital surface segmentation with the surface normal compatibility constraint. Figure 7.10 shows the best-fit region label image segmentation after 3x3 cleanup window operators have been applied. This image shows that an extra small region near the base of the handle was created that was not found in Figure 7.6(b). The surface normal compatibility constraint has little effect on the coffee cup results.

Figure 7.11 shows the original range image and the reconstructed range image side by side above two shaded images: one created from the raw range data by using digital surface derivatives to estimate the surface normals and the other created from the smooth surface primitives extracted from the range image by the segmentation algorithm. The data description is almost a computer-aided design (CAD) surface representation of the visible surfaces of the coffee cup, but a close inspection shows that the surfaces describing the handle do not merge smoothly enough to create a plausible CAD representation. Moreover, the cylindrical coffee cup surfaces are slightly, but noticeably out of round.

7.1.2 Computer Keyboard Range Image

A similar set of experimental results are presented for two range images of a computer terminal keyboard in Figures 7.12, 7.13, 7.14, and 7.15. The original and reconstructed gray scale images in Figures 7.12 and 7.14 appear washed out due to the low contrast of this range image. The smooth surface shape of the keyboard body is fairly complicated as is evident by the intermingling of the keyboard surfaces in the best-fit region label image as shown in Figures 7.13(b) and 7.15(b), especially Figure 7.15(b). This fragmentation and overlapping of the surface primitive descriptions is strong evidence for a smooth surface merge as discussed in Chapter 5. Figures 7.13(c) and 7.15(c) show that the surfaces are correctly merged in the final region segmentation. Despite the low contrast of the original image, good standard results were obtained using the fixed set of thresholds.

Slightly different parts of the keyboard are visible in the two images. Two different versions of the same scene are included to show the small variations in the output that are possible with slight variations in the input. The ρ_1, ρ_2 quality measures for the Figure 7.12 keyboard image are (1.17,1.46) as compared to (1.35,1.68) for the Figure 7.14 image. For the reconstructed image in Figure 7.16, the average absolute error in the error image was 1.96. The noise in both images is very non-stationary because the noise level on the diffuse keyboard body is low whereas the noise level on the much shinier keys is high. The quality of range measurements from imaging laser radars is dependent on the surface reflectance properties.

Despite minor differences in the output for the two images, the overall consistency is reasonably good. The actual key surfaces are combined together into single regions due to the large fit error tolerance (4.2). Lower thresholds can be used to detect individual key surfaces, but the segmentation becomes much more ragged.

Figures 7.16 and 7.17 show the results of imposing the surface normal compatibility constraint in processing the keyboard B image. Figure 7.16 shows the best-fit reconstruction and Figure 7.17 shows the best-fit region label image segmentation. Modified thresholds were used for this image as compared to the automatically determined adaptive thresholds used for all other surface normal compatibility images included in this chapter. Several individual keys of the keyboard were isolated. The subtle but complicated surface shape of the keyboard body at the top of the image is segmented well using the surface normal constraint. This subtle surface shape is also visible in the HK-sign maps in Figures 7.12(a), 7.13(a), 7.14(a), and 7.15(a). For this range image, surface normal compatibility did make a big difference, but the thresholds had to be adjusted manually to obtain the best results.

7.1.3 Polyhedron

A range image of a step-shaped polyhedron resting on a table top is shown in Figure 7.18 along with the best-fit reconstructed image. The net refinement of the edges between the best-fit region label image segmentation and the final region segmentation is shown in Figure 7.19(b),(c). The three visible facets of the polyhedron are correctly segmented. Many approaches to image analysis in the literature are only able to handle simple scenes like this.

7.1.4 Ring on Polyhedron

A ring (a roll of masking tape) was placed on top of the step-shaped polyhedron for this ERIM range image. Note in Figure 7.20 how the steeply slanted surfaces of the outer ring surface in the image are very noisy compared to the other images shown here. Despite these noisy areas, the overall image segmentation is good. A region merge error occurred in the standard results. Region 6 on the polyhedron in Figure 7.21(c), which was Region 4 in Figure 7.19(c), has acquired a small part of Region 3, which was Region 2 in Figure 7.19(c). The standard fixed threshold algorithm is capable of distinguishing between these two surfaces when both were completely visible as shown in Figure 7.19(c). The image quality measures for the polyhedron without the ring were $\rho_1 = 1.38$, $\rho_2 = 1.71$ whereas the measures for the polyhedron with the ring were $\rho_1 = 1.61$, $\rho_2 = 2.05$ The occlusion by the ring created a boundary that caused Region 6 to grow into the portion of Region 3 apparently because of the extra noise in the image. Also, the small portion of the background visible through the ring did not receive the same label as the background surface for the standard fixed set of thresholds. Modified thresholds results have shown that the region can be recognized as part of the background.

The edge description results are overly jagged because curve fitting is done directly to edge vector data, which in this case does not represent the underlying smooth edges as well as one would like. This jaggedness can be avoided by fitting smoothed edge data rather than the raw edge data, but then the region boundaries may move inwards at corners in ways undesirable for maintaining a complete image segmentation. For consistency, curves are fitted to the raw edge data in the same way that surfaces are fitted to the image data. An adaptive maximum allowable RMS error could be defined using a noise estimation algorithm on the raw edge data before processing. Also, an edge tangency compatibility approach could be used similar to the surface normal compatibility.

Figure 7.22 shows a pair of surface coherence images similar to those shown in Figure 7.9. The original image and the reconstruction image are mapped through random gray scale lookup tables to obtain the top image and the bottom image respectively. It is difficult to see any structure in the noisy top image, but the digital surface segmentation algorithm has generated a perfectly coherent reconstruction image.

Figures 7.23 and 7.24 show results when the surface normal compatibility condition was required during region growing. Figure 7.23 shows the best-fit region label image segmentation after processing with 3x3 lookup table operators. The small part of Region 3 that was grouped with Region 6 in the standard results is correctly isolated owing to inclusion of surface normal checking. However, it was not correctly associated with Region 3 because the amount of noise in the data. Also, although it is not shown in the figure, the small piece of background surface visible between the ring and the steps was correctly associated with the rest of the background surface using the automatically determined adaptive thresholds used with the surface normal compatibility processing.

In the same format as Figure 7.11, Figure 7.24 shows the original range image and the reconstructed range image side by side above two shaded images: one created from the raw range data by using surface derivatives estimates to compute the surface normals and the other created from the smooth surface primitives extracted from the range image by the segmentation algorithm. The average absolute error between this reconstructed range image and the original range image is 3.31. This average includes all pixels including the bad data on the steep slopes of the ring.

7.1.5 Curved Surface A

The cobra head surface in the ERIM range image in Figure 7.25 is called Curved Surface A. Owing to the regular shape of this surface, the polynomial surface primitives were able to describe the data well as indicated by the similarity between Figure 7.26(b) and Figure 7.26(c). The image quality measures are $\rho_1 = 1.68$, $\rho_2 = 1.95$.

7.1.6 Curved Surface B

Curved Surface B in Figure 7.27 is significantly different than the Curved Surface A. This curved surface cannot be well approximated by a single bivariate polynomial, and the best-fit region label image became fragmented as shown in Figure 7.28(b). A variety of a surfaces grew and mixed with each other. The final segmentation in Figures 7.28(c) shows that the smoothly joining surface primitives did join together correctly during the region merging process described in Chapter 5. For this image, the final segmentation result could have been obtained more easily with an edge detector.

7.1.7 Road Scenes

The two range images in Figures 7.29 and 7.31 were selected at random from a sequence of range images taken from a vehicle with an ERIM imaging laser radar. The edges of the road are visible in Figures 7.30(b) and 7.32(b), which show the best-fit region label image segmentation. A line appears across the middle of the road for two reasons: (1) The limited bending capability of the fourth order surface, the extreme warping of the flat road surface beyond that point due to equal-angle increment sampling (see Appendix D), and the viewing angle of the surface combined to cause the growing surface to stop, and (2) there is a small bump in the road at that point as shown in the raw range data in Figure 7.34. The surfaces of the road and the road shoulders are completely merged together during the region merging process to create a final region segmentations that are worthless for the given application. In this case, the segmentation algorithm could be stopped prior to region combination and region merging by using application-specific assumptions about the geometry of the road. This has been done here by displaying the intermediate best-fit segmentation, not the final segmentation, in the overlaid plot images in Figures 7.29 and 7.31.

Better results were obtained when the surface normal compatibility constraint was obtained. Figure 7.33 shows the best-fit region label image segmentation for road scene B, which indicates that none of the road surfaces grew off the road as occurred in both standard results cases with fixed thresholds. The standard adaptive thresholds and the surface normal checking both contributed to the better results. The image quality measures of road scene B are $\rho_1 = 0.79$, $\rho_2 = 1.09$ and average reconstruction error was 0.96. This points out that the fixed threshold of $\epsilon_{max} = 4.2$ was much too large for these images. Figure 7.34 shows shaded images for both the original range image and the extracted surfaces. The bump in the road that caused the main road surface to stop growing is clearly visible in the shaded image, but cannot be seen at all in the range image presentations. The sides of the road are also much easier to see.

7.1.8 Renault Auto Part

The original data for the auto part from the INRIA range sensor is formatted as a list of (x, y, z) coordinates. Although the data is easily divided into scan lines, a different number of pixels occurred on each scan line, and the pixels were not always regularly spaced. This data was converted to a 64x64 range image, which was then expanded to a 128x128 range image, and smoothed to create the input image used for the standard results. Although the best-fit reconstruction image in Figure 7.35 and the best-fit region label segmentation images are tolerable, the final region segmentation is not meaningful due to the high fixed maximum fit-error threshold of 4.2. Moreover, the poor quality of the segmentation in Figure 7.36(c) shows what can go wrong with the simple region description combination algorithm of Chapter 5 if there are problems with its input. The image quality measures are $\rho_1 = 0.43$ and $\rho_2 = 0.63$ which imply that the image data is not very noisy and the fixed set of thresholds are inappropriate. By reducing the fit-error threshold to the more appropriate value 1.7, the modified threshold results shown in the overlaid plot image of Figure 7.35 were obtained.

Figures 7.37 and 7.38 shows the reconstruction image and the best-fit region label image segmentation obtained using surface normal compatibility and automatic adaptive thresholds. The average absolute residual error for the reconstructed image was 1.48. The segmentation consists of much smaller surface primitives than the best-fit segmentation in Figure 7.36(b), but this 2.5-D segmentation looks more similar to the 3-D segmentations produced by [Faugeras and Hebert 1986] [Bhanu 1984] [Henderson 1983].

7.2 Synthetic Range Images

Although synthetic images generally lack the realism of actual data, it has been found that synthetic range images with added noise are fairly realistic and adequately test algorithm capabilities. The range image synthesis problem is much simpler than the intensity image synthesis problem because it depends only upon geometry. The SDRC/Geomod solid modeler was used to create several different non-convex 3-D solid polyhedral object models. The author's depth-buffer display program converted the object models to range images given viewing conditions. The use of synthetic range images was very useful to this research effort and will be even more critical to object recognition research since arbitrary views of 3-D objects can be obtained more easily, more quickly, and more inexpensively using the depth-buffer approach than can be obtained by manipulating actual objects in front of a range imaging sensor.

7.2.1 Block with Three Holes

The block with three holes drilled through it provides an interesting non-convex combination of flat and cylindrical surfaces. Figures 7.39 and 7.43 show the block with two different levels of added noise: $\sigma = 2.3$ and 9.0 respectively. The corresponding ρ_1 image quality measures are 1.82 and 5.93. These images were also analyzed in Chapter 3. If the equation $\epsilon_{max} = 1.1 + 1.1\rho_1$ guides the selection of a maximum fit-error threshold, the ϵ_{max} thresholds of 3.1 and 7.6 should be used. It is usually not a serious problem to use a threshold slightly larger than the value predicted by the simple equation. The problem with the auto part segmentation is representative of what may happen when the threshold is too much larger. Because 3.1 is not too much less than the standard fixed 4.2 threshold, the results shown in Figure 7.40 were expected to be reasonable. However, 7.6 is significantly greater than the 4.2 threshold and poor results are expected since the algorithm cannot function properly with a fit-error threshold that is too large. When the maximum fit-error threshold is not large enough, higher order surfaces are invoked when they are not needed allowing the shape potential of the higher order surfaces to respond to the noise in the data rather than to the structure in the data. Figure 7.44 shows the failure of the algorithm on the noisier block. However, by increasing the ϵ_{max} threshold to 8.0, the results shown in the overlaid segmentation plot image in Figure 7.43 are obtained. These results are quite good considering the noise level in the image. A key point here is that the image quality measures can be used to predict the success or failure of the algorithm for a given threshold and suggest a more appropriate threshold.

Figures 7.42 and 7.43 show surface normal compatibility results for the low-noise block. Figure 7.42 shows the best-fit region label image segmentation which shows that the two cylindrical surfaces inside the right-hand hole are correctly segmented. These two surfaces were merged in the standard result images. Figure 7.43 displays shaded images for the original range image and the extracted surface primitives.

7.2.2 Two Joined Cylinders Embedded in Plane

Figure 7.45 shows two connected cylinders with different diameters embedded in a sloped plane. The sloped plane kinks and becomes flat in the upper left and lower right hand corners of the image as is indicated in Figure 7.46(b). The same noise level used with the less noisy block image is also used here ($\sigma = 2.3$). The ρ_1 image quality measure is 1.79, and good results are expected using the standard fixed set of thresholds. The results are good, but a few curious things have happened. Region 3 in Figure 7.46(c) really consists of two different surfaces: the round body of the smaller cylinder and the flat bottom of the larger cylinder. A second order surface was fitting the round body of the smaller cylinder, but included pixels in the bottom of the large cylinder. A fourth order surface was eventually invoked, and it fluted outward to fit the bottom even though the object model had two perpendicular surfaces here. The bottom of the small cylinder was such a small surface that it caused the fourth order surface to bend slightly to include it, too. Surface normal compatibility eliminates these problems.

The kinks in the sloped plane, which are visible in Figure 7.46(b), are not present in Figure 7.46(c) due to the large fixed dihedral angle threshold of 25 degrees for arbitrary surface joins. This threshold is to be determined by the application using the algorithm and is too large for this image. It has tended to be too large for plane-to-plane intersections, but it has worked well for curved surfaces. The planar equations for all three planar background areas are available from the iterative region growing algorithm if plane-to-plane intersections need to be computed. To summarize, the most important orientation discontinuities in the scene are detected, but some less important orientation discontinuities are missing due to region growing and region merging factors in the presence of noise. The region growing problems are fixed using surface normal compatibility and the region merging problems are fixed by computing exact plane to plane intersections and using a separate threshold.

7.2.3 Object with Protrusions over Sphere

Figure 7.47 shows a brick-shaped object with two protrusions suspended above a hemispherical background surface. One protrusion consists of a base cone joined with a cylinder whereas the other consists of a base cylinder joined with a sphere. The amount of noise that was used for the two cylinders and the block was added to this range image ($\sigma = 2.3$). The hemispherical background surface is well segmented in Figure 7.48(b), but it was merged with flat pieces of the background, as shown in Figure 7.48(c), owing to a small dihedral angle at the joining boundaries in the noisy image and the large angular thresholds.

Due to the flexibility of the higher order surfaces, the base cone surface of one protrusion grew together with the round body of the joined cylinder. Similarly, the cylindrical base of the other protrusion grew together with the joined sphere surface. The perceptual organization of the pixels in the segmentation output is reasonable, but small orientation discontinuities in noise were generally very difficult to isolate without invoking the surface normal compatibility requirement. Such orientation discontinuities were easily isolated in synthetic images without noise without the additional requirement.

7.2.4 Light Bulb

The light bulb in Figure 7.49 is an interesting surface because it demonstrates a smooth join between a positive Gaussian curvature surface, the spherical part of the bulb, and a negative Gaussian curvature surface, the stem of the bulb connecting the threaded base with the spherical part. Figure 7.50(b) shows that one fourth-order surface grew out to fit both positive and negative Gaussian curvature surface primitives. Another surface was required to approximate the threaded metal base of the light bulb. These two surfaces merge smoothly to yield a simple figure-ground segmentation. Even though it would have been trivial to obtain this segmentation by thresholding the original image, it is important to note that the flexibility of the surface approximants is adequate to handle such non-convex curved surfaces. Moreover, the boundary between the positive and negative Gaussian curvature regions of the bulb is easily recoverable from the polynomial surface. The added noise for this image had a standard deviation of $\sigma = 3.4$.

7.2.5   Torus

A torus is a fourth-order algebraic surface not easily approximated by planes, quadrics, or low-order bivariate polynomial graph surfaces. It also demonstrates a smooth join between a positive Gaussian curvature surface, the outside of the torus, and a negative Gaussian curvature surface, the inside of the torus. The torus in Figure 7.51 incorporates $\sigma = 3.4$ additive noise. The standard digital surface segmentation algorithm with fixed thresholds grew several surfaces to approximate the complicated shape as shown in Figure 7.52(b). The region merging algorithm noted the smooth joins of those surfaces and coalesced them to create the correct final region description shown in Figure 7.52(c).

7.2.6   Circular Waves

A surface that is more complicated and more difficult to approximate with planes, quadrics, and/or low-order polynomials is the circular waves surface shown in Figure 7.53. This surface is generated by the equation

$$z(x, y) = \sin^2(\omega\sqrt{x^2 + y^2}). \tag{7.1}$$

No noise was added to this image. Quantization noise is the only noise present, but it is substantial because the ρ_1 quality measure is 1.54. This surface consists of smooth joins of many different fundamental HK-surface types, all arranged in a circularly symmetric manner around the center of the image. The best-fit region image segmentation in Figure 7.54(b) shows that a large number of approximating surfaces were needed to approximate the complicated surface. This segmentation exhibits many interesting symmetries on the noiseless data, but is not perfectly symmetric. The region merging algorithm correctly merged almost all of the surface primitives, but three surfaces were obtained instead of one as might be expected. A narrow annulus, located at the first trough of the wave moving out from the center, did not merge with the rest of the surface regions, but it is circularly symmetric as shown in Figures 7.54(c),(d) and Figure 7.53(b). This seems to be due to the fact that the collection of region shapes inside the annulus is quite different than the region shapes outside the annulus causing the associated surface primitives not to meet smoothly enough.

7.3   Intensity Images

The entire digital surface segmentation algorithm is based only on the knowledge of surfaces. Since intensity images are also digital surfaces, the algorithm can be applied to intensity images for segmentation purposes. If the intensity image data exhibits surface coherence, the segmentation algorithm should work. And just as the only difference between range images and intensity images is in the meaning of the values at each pixel (depth vs. light intensity), the difference in the algorithm output lies in how the surface segmentation is interpreted. An intensity smooth surface primitive does not necessarily correspond to a 3-D smooth surface primitive of objects in a scene although it may. It may possess shape information in the sense that shape from shading algorithms extract shape from intensity images, but it does not explicitly represent shape in a scene. *Intensity image surface primitives have an entirely different meaning than range image surface primitives.* However, the algorithm appears to be useful for intensity image segmentation purposes as long as this fundamental difference is kept in mind. Even throwing away the surface information obtained by the segmentation algorithm, the algorithm does create edge images in which all edges are guaranteed to be closed. In this sense, the algorithm may be considered as yet another edge detector, but the image description is much richer because it allows one to reconstruct a reasonable version of the gray scale image from the image description.

7.3.1   Space Shuttle Intensity Image

The original shuttle image, the reconstructed image, and the overlaid segmentation plot image are shown in Figure 7.55. The reconstructed image lacks detail whenever the detail in the original image consists of only a few pixels (10 or less). For example, the windows on the cockpit of the shuttle only occupy about three pixels and are therefore missed in the image reconstruction. The surface-curvature sign segmentation in Figure 7.56(a) appears to be completely meaningless when compared to the shuttle image. This is unlike most range images where some semblance of image structure is perceivable. However, it provided enough information to the region growing algorithm to allow it to create the best-fit region label image segmentation shown in Figure 7.56(b). The final segmentation is displayed in Figures 7.56(c) and 7.55. The segmentation algorithm would be expected to perform well because the ρ_1 quality measure is only 2.29 and the ρ_2 quality measure is 2.71. And the segmentation turned out better than one might expect. The sky, the main body of the shuttle, the gantry, and many smoke clouds are isolated as intensity image smooth surface primitives. *The exact same fixed set of standard thresholds were used for the shuttle image and all intensity images as were used for all the range images.* This is a strong testimonial to the soundness of the digital surface approach when the same program with the same set of input thresholds and window sizes can segment the coffee cup images, the keyboard images, the block with holes image (low-noise), and the space shuttle intensity image without a single modification, even without adaptable thresholds.

Figures 7.57 and 7.58 show the results of imposing the surface normal compatibility constraint on the shuttle intensity image. The best-fit reconstruction image is shown in Figure 7.57, and the best-fit region label image is shown in Figure 7.58. The average absolute residual error was 4.32. The overall quality of the segmentation is similar to the standard results. The gantry region is not as detailed owing to the difficulty in obtaining good surface normal estimates on finely detailed regions. On the other hand, the bright flame region below the shuttle is now segmented as a single region compared to the fragmented standard results. It is not clear which segmentation is better in this case.

7.3.2 Road Image

Figure 7.59 shows an intensity image of a road scene from an Autonomous Land Vehicle sequence. Again, the surface-curvature sign segmentation appears almost structureless. The best-fit region label segmentation is somewhat fragmented in Figure 7.60(b). However, the reconstructed image is good, and the results in Figure 7.60(c) even appear to be useful for navigation. Anywhere in Region 1 appears to be valid road surface. The right edge of the road is particularly well-defined, and the sky, hills, and grass are also segmented. The ρ_1 image quality measure is 1.95, and the ρ_2 measure is 2.27.

Figures 7.61 and 7.62 show the best-fit reconstructed image and the best-fit region label image segmentation obtained using surface normal compatibility. A valid drivable road region has again been segmented in the image. This best-fit segmentation appears to be better than the standard threshold best-fit segmentation result.

7.3.3 USC Girl

Two standard images from the image processing literature were selected. The first of these is the USC girl image. A 128x128 (8-bit) version of the original 512x512 (5-bit) image was used as the input to the segmentation algorithm. Two shrinking stages were used where four pixels are averaged and replaced by a single pixel with the average value in order to get the 128x128 image. This input image, the standard algorithm reconstruction image, and the overlaid segmentation plot image are shown in Figure 7.63. The segmentation results in Figure 7.64 are not nearly as good as the space shuttle or road image results, but are still reasonable for such a complicated image. The facial features caused significant difficulties for the region growing algorithm. The ρ_1 image quality measure is poor (2.63), and a lot of small detail is needed for an adequate description of the image.

Figure 7.65 shows the best fit reconstruction image and Figure 7.66 shows the overlaid segmentation image for the results obtained using the aggressive error tolerance function discussed in Chapter 4. For this image, the results were much better than those obtained with the standard algorithm. This significant improvement with the larger error tolerance function is probably related to the fact that the original image was digitized to five bits. Even though smoothing during shrinking helped, the effect of the original quantization was still present in the 128x128 image as was determined by histogram analysis. Hence, the surface coherence properties were different for this image than any other images discussed in this chapter.

7.3.4 U-Mass House Scene

The second standard image from the literature is a U-Mass house scene shown in Figure 7.67 along with the best-fit reconstruction image for the standard results. A slightly different format was adopted for this set of results because of the complexity of the image. This image is 256x256 pixels (8-bits) obtained by a simple averaging of the original red, green, and blue components of a color image. As usual, the surface curvature sign segmentation in Figure 7.68(a) appears to be a jumbled mess of small regions except for some large pieces of the sky. The best-fit region label segmentation in Figure 7.68(b) provides enough image detail that one can distinguish the outline of the house and the pants of the person walking in front of the house. The final region segmentation, obtained from the region merging process, is easier to interpret though. The road surface is successfully merged into two large regions separated by the white line in the center of the road. Even the shadow of the person walking in front of the house is isolated. The garage door is segmented into a shadowed portion and an unshadowed portion. The lawn is represented by only three different large image regions.

One major unexpected difficulty, however, is that the roof of the house is not merged into a single region. Figure 7.69 shows the overlaid segmentation plot image for the standard thresholds and a different overlaid segmentation plot image obtained using a slight modification in thresholds. The house roof produced substantially different wrong results in both cases owing to the roof texture. The front lawn, the side of the house, and the sideyard tree are much less fragmented in the modified threshold results.

The modified threshold results in the four image format and the best-fit reconstruction image are shown in Figure 7.70. The algorithm stopped in both cases when it reached the maximum number of regions (currently limited to 254), which caused the large black (unfitted) regions in the reconstructed images. The trees in this image and the USC girl's hair show that the algorithm can successfully segment large regions of similar texture if they are mostly surrounded by non-textured regions.

Figures 7.71 and 7.72 show the best-fit reconstruction image and the best-fit region label image segmentation using surface normal compatibility on the 256x256 house scene image. This best-fit segmentation is superior in quality to the final smooth surface segmentation for the standard and modified threshold results. Hence, a definite improvement in segmentation quality was achieved via automatic threshold setting and surface normal compatibility. The surface normal compatibility constraint worked better here than for the 128x128 images since more pixels were available for the detailed image features. Note how well the bushes and the shutters are segmented compared to the other results. Also the roof of the house was segmented as one region and the roof of the garage was segmented as another region. Moreover, the maximum number of regions was the same, but the surface normal compatibility algorithm yielded fewer regions. Comparing these results to the other surface normal compatibility results shown above, it is concluded that the surface normal compatibility requirement should be used whenever enough pixels are present for the detailed features. It seems to do quite well in many cases with the main disadvantage being a suppression of detail relative to the standard algorithm in some cases.

7.4   Segmentation Results

The following pages contain all the figure material referred to in the previous sections.

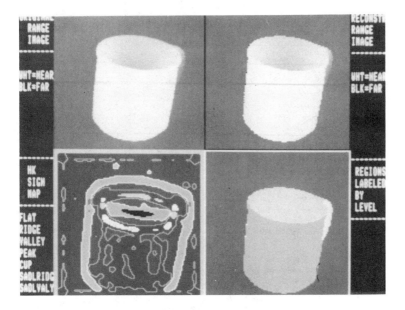

(a) Standard Results for Coffee Cup A

Figure 7.1: (b) Standard Results for Coffee Cup A

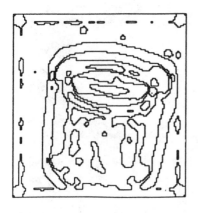

(a) Surface-Curvature-Sign Segmentation

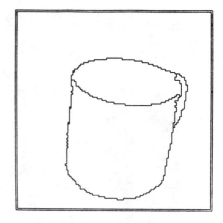

(b) Best-Fit Region Label Buffer Segmentation

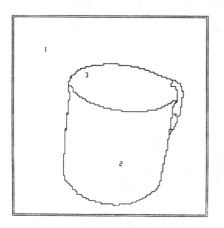

(c) Final Region Segmentation

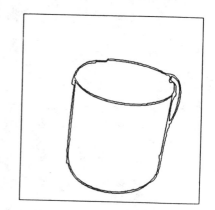

(d) Edge Descriptions of Final Regions

Figure 7.2: Standard Results for Coffee Cup A

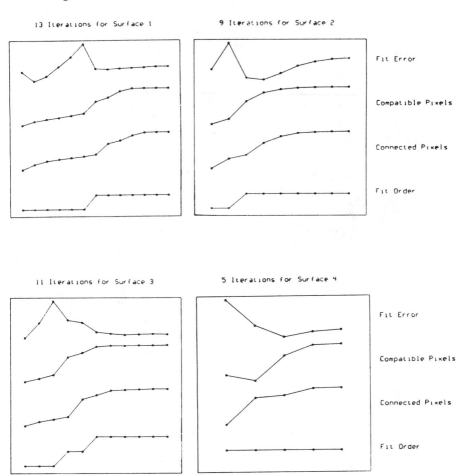

Figure 7.3: Iterative Quantities for Coffee Cup A

```
Surface Decomposition for '/c/pjb/dzo/rd/cofcup'

128 x 128 Image
●-------------( 10112 )( 21 22 )
1 0 <> Surface_# 1  of Type: Flat (SR=0)
1 : Biquadratic Surface
a= 42.11871856  b= 0.1324443081  c= 0.1324603535
d= 2.531914397e-05  e= -0.001066936789  f= -0.001336066869

17.1789 0.948533 0.697403 (e8,e2,e1), 0.836687


===Region_# 0 ===
10112 Pixels
1 1 Min(Col,Row)
126 126 Max(Col,Row)
  1,1  -126    2,1  -126    3,1  -126    4,1  -126    5,1  -126    6,1  -126
  7,1  -126    8,1  -126    9,1  -126   10,1  -126   11,1  -126   12,1  -126
 13,1  -126   14,1  -126   15,1  -126   16,1  -126   17,1  -126   18,1  -126
 19,1  -126   20,1  -126   21,1  -126   22,1  -126   23,1  -126   24,1  -126
 25,1  -126   26,1  -126   27,1  -126   28,1  -126   29,1  -126   30,1  -126
 31,1  -53   31,77 -126   32,1  -48   32,82 -126   33,1  -45   33,86 -126
 34,1  -42   34,90 -126   35,1  -41   35,93 -126   36,1  -40   36,96 -126
 37,1  -38   37,97 -126   38,1  -37   38,100-126   39,1  -37   39,105-126
 40,1  -36   40,107-126   41,1  -36   41,108-126   42,1  -35   42,109-126
 43,1  -35   43,110-126   44,1  -35   44,111-126   45,1  -35   45,111-126
 46,1  -36   46,112-126   47,1  -36   47,112-126   48,1  -36   48,112-126
 49,1  -36   49,112-126   50,1  -36   50,112-126   51,1  -36   51,112-126
 52,1  -36   52,112-126   53,1  -36   53,112-126   54,1  -36   54,112-126
 55,1  -36   55,112-126   56,1  -36   56,111-126   57,1  -35   57,111-126
 58,1  -35   58,111-126   59,1  -35   59,111-126   60,1  -35   60,110-126
 61,1  -35   61,110-126   62,1  -35   62,110-126   63,1  -35   63,109-126
 64,1  -35   64,108-126   65,1  -35   65,108-126   66,1  -34   66,108-126
 67,1  -34   67,108-126   68,1  -34   68,107-126   69,1  -34   69,107-126
 70,1  -34   70,106-126   71,1  -34   71,106-126   72,1  -34   72,105-126
 73,1  -34   73,104-126   74,1  -34   74,104-126   75,1  -34   75,103-126
 76,1  -33   76,103-126   77,1  -33   77,103-126   78,1  -33   78,103-126
 79,1  -33   79,103-126   80,1  -33   80,103-126   81,1  -33   81,103-126
 82,1  -33   82,103-126   83,1  -33   83,102-126   84,1  -33   84,102-126
 85,1  -33   85,102-126   86,1  -33   86,102-126   87,1  -33   87,102-126
 88,1  -33   88,102-126   89,1  -33   89,101-126   90,1  -32   90,101-126
 91,1  -32   91,101-126   92,1  -32   92,101-126   93,1  -32   93,100-126
 94,1  -32   94,100-126   95,1  -32   95,100-126   96,1  -32   96,100-126
 97,1  -32   97,99 -126   98,1  -32   98,99 -126   99,1  -32   99,99 -126
100,1  -32  100,99 -126  101,1  -32  101,99 -126  102,1  -33  102,99 -126
103,1  -33  103,99 -126  104,1  -33  104,98 -126  105,1  -35  105,98 -126
106,1  -35  106,98 -126  107,1  -37  107,98 -126  108,1  -38  108,97 -126
109,1  -38  109,96 -126  110,1  -39  110,95 -126  111,1  -40  111,94 -126
112,1  -41  112,93 -126  113,1  -41  113,91 -126  114,1  -44  114,90 -126
115,1  -45  115,88 -126  116,1  -47  116,87 -126  117,1  -48  117,85 -126
118,1  -51  118,83 -126  119,1  -55  119,80 -126  120,1  -57  120,75 -126
121,1  -126 122,1  -126  123,1  -126  124,1  -126  125,1  -126  126,1  -126

●-------------( 3550 )( 71 94 )
2 1 <> Surface_# 2  of Type: Ridge (SR=0)
1 : Biquadratic Surface
a= 63.99488353  b= 4.094335504  c= -0.1058567425
d= -0.006149136159  e= -0.0259604799  f= -0.001810010176

32.0241 1.40682 0.922395 (e8,e2,e1), 1.06979


===Region_# 0 ===
3550 Pixels
34 49 Min(Col,Row)
104 116 Max(Col,Row)
 49,38 -39   50,38 -41   51,38 -41   52,38 -43   53,38 -45   54,39 -46
 55,39 -49   56,39 -51   57,39 -53   57,102-104  58,39 -57   58,99 -103
 59,40 -60   59,97 -103  60,39 -66   60,92 -103  61,38 -69   61,72 -76
 61,82 -103  62,37 -103  63,37 -103  64,38 -102  65,38 -103  66,37 -103
 67,37 -102  68,37 -102  69,37 -102  70,38 -102  71,37 -102  72,36 -102
 73,36 -102  74,36 -100  75,36 -100  76,36 -101  77,35 -101  78,35 -101
 79,35 -100  80,35 -100  82,35 -100  83,36 -100  84,36 -100
 85,36 -99   86,36 -99   87,36 -99   88,37 -99   89,37 -99   90,36 -98
 91,35 -98   92,35 -97   93,35 -97   94,35 -98   95,36 -98   96,35 -97
 97,35 -97   98,34 -97   99,34 -97  100,34 -97  101,34 -97  102,35 -95
102,97 -97  103,36 -94  104,36 -94  105,37 -94  106,39 -92  107,40 -92
108,40 -94  109,41 -94  110,41 -93  111,44 -92  112,48 -91  113,49 -89
114,51 -86  115,55 -83  116,60 -79

●-------------( 1392 )( 48 38 )
3 1 <> Surface_# 3  of Type: Ridge (SR=0)
2 : Biquartic Surface
a= 157.4399722  b= -19.62574422  c= 27.27931146
d= -0.2204406377  e= 0.4470255448  f= -0.6037057168
g= -0.000968308332  h= 0.005012401199  i= -0.003749576079
j= 0.004865094677  k= 1.975843894e-05  l= -2.502699807e-05
m= -1.068317868e-05  n= 9.477578463e-06  o= -1.624752069e-05

5.37639 1.1303 0.882234 (e8,e2,e1), 1.02928


===Region_# 0 ===
1392 Pixels
40 32 Min(Col,Row)
107 59 Max(Col,Row)
 32,54 -73   33,50 -79   34,47 -84   35,44 -87   36,43 -90   37,42 -92
 38,42 -95   39,40 -97   40,41 -99   41,41 -101  42,42 -42   42,46 -101
 43,47 -102  44,46 -103  45,46 -103  46,46 -104  47,45 -104  48,45 -106
 49,46 -106  50,47 -102  50,106-107  51,46 -102  51,106-107  52,47 -100
 53,49 -100  54,51 -99   55,53 -99   56,56 -99   57,59 -97   58,64 -95
 59,68 -91

●-------------( 101 )( 106 63 )
4 0 <> Surface_# 4  of Type: Flat (SR=0)
1 : Biquadratic Surface
a= 11184.29226  b= -181.2193238  c= -42.24864178
d= 0.3289854366  e= 0.7434851996  f= 0.04904402549

12.4756 2.96491 2.27134 (e8,e2,e1), 2.82357


===Region_# 0 ===
101 Pixels
104 43 Min(Col,Row)
111 72 Max(Col,Row)
 43,107-108  44,104-109  45,107-110  46,108-110  47,108-110  48,108-111
 49,108-111  50,109-111  51,109-111  52,109-110  53,108-110  54,108-110
 55,108-110  56,107-110  57,106-110  58,106-109  59,106-109  60,106-109
 61,105-109  62,105-109  63,105-108  64,105-107  65,105-107  66,105-107
 67,105-107  68,104-106  69,104-106  70,104-105  71,104-105  72,104-104
```

Figure 7.4: Surface Primitive Information for Coffee Cup A

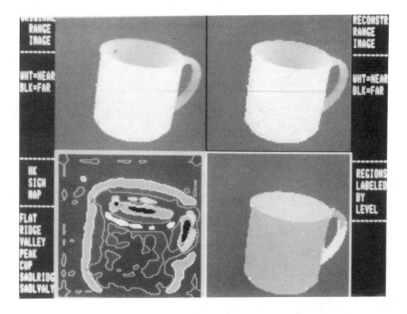

(a) Standard Results for Coffee Cup B

Figure 7.5: (b) Modified Threshold Results for Coffee Cup B

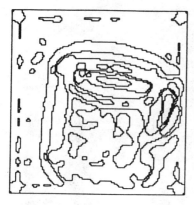

(a) Surface-Curvature-Sign Segmentation

(b) Best-Fit Region Label Buffer Segmentation

(c) Final Region Segmentation

(d) Edge Descriptions of Final Regions

Figure 7.6: Standard Results for Coffee Cup B

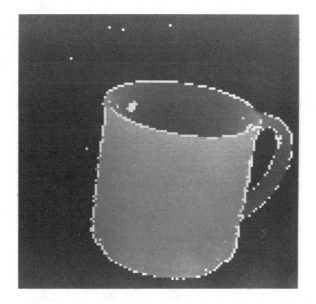

Figure 7.7: Thresholded Error Image Overlaid on Original Image

Figure 7.8: Final Best Fit Reconstruction Image for Coffee Cup B

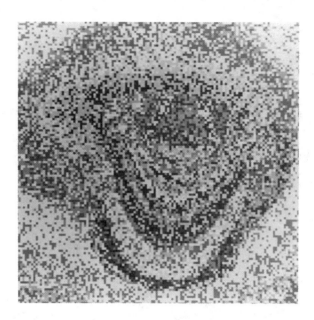

(a) Coffee Cup B Image Mapped Through Random Lookup Table

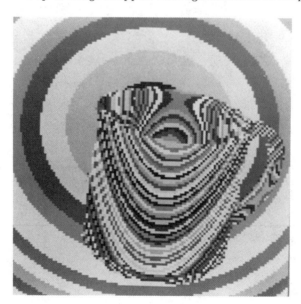

Figure 7.9: (b) Final Reconstruction Image with Random Gray Levels

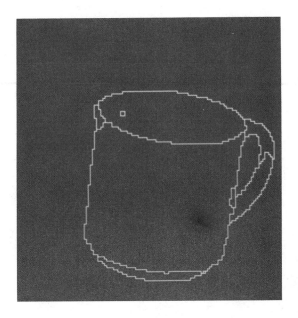

Figure 7.10: Best-Fit Segmentation using Surface Normal Compatibility

Figure 7.11: Shaded Images for Raw Data & Reconstructed Surfaces

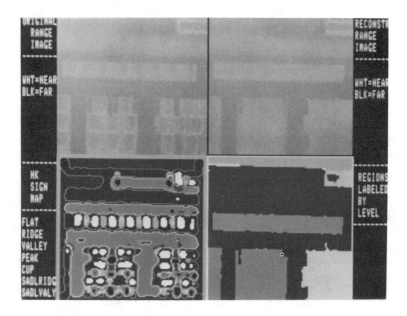

(a) Standard Results for Keyboard A

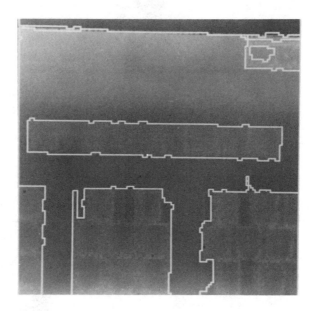

Figure 7.12: (b) Standard Results for Keyboard A

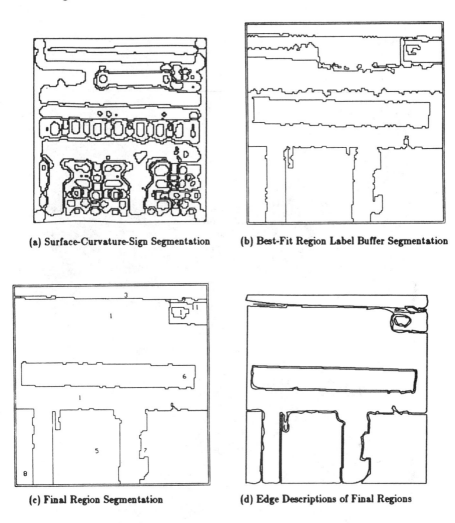

(a) Surface-Curvature-Sign Segmentation   (b) Best-Fit Region Label Buffer Segmentation

(c) Final Region Segmentation   (d) Edge Descriptions of Final Regions

Figure 7.13: Standard Results for Keyboard A

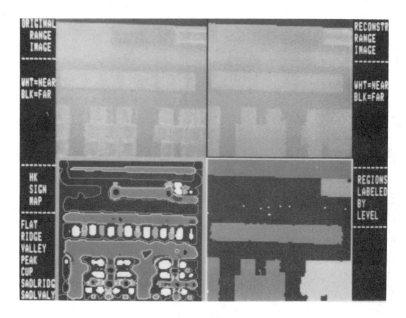

(a) Standard Results for Keyboard B

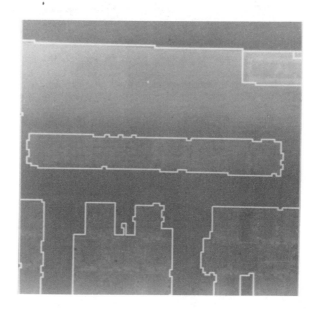

Figure 7.14: (b) Standard Results for Keyboard B

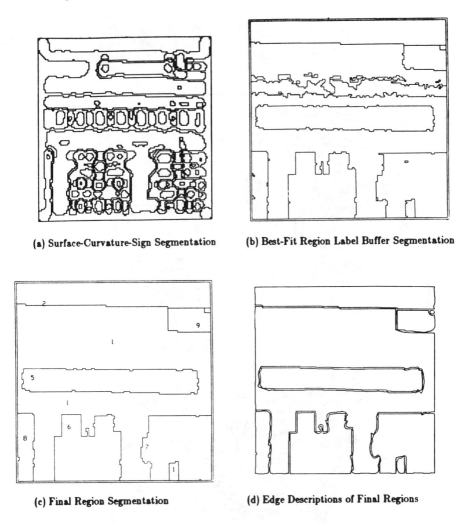

(a) Surface-Curvature-Sign Segmentation   **(b) Best-Fit Region Label Buffer Segmentation**

(c) Final Region Segmentation   **(d) Edge Descriptions of Final Regions**

Figure 7.15: Standard Results for Keyboard B

Figure 7.16: Reconstructed Image using Surface Normal Compatibility

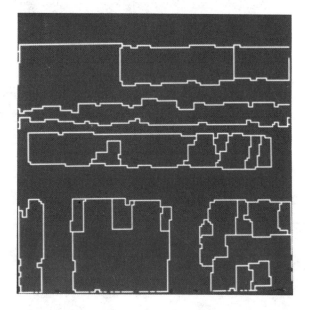

Figure 7.17: Best-Fit Segmentation using Surface Normal Compatibility

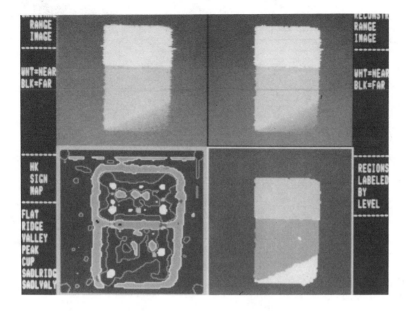

(a) Standard Results for Polyhedron

Figure 7.18: (b) Standard Results for Polyhedron

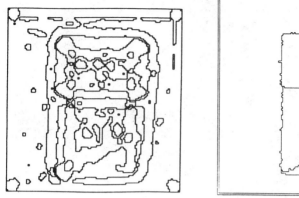

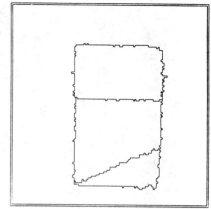

(a) Surface-Curvature-Sign Segmentation   (b) Best-Fit Region Label Buffer Segmentation

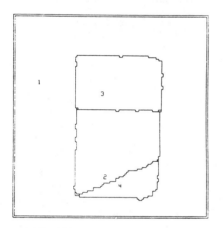

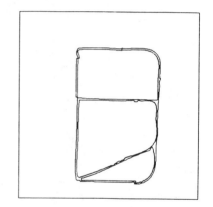

(c) Final Region Segmentation   (d) Edge Descriptions of Final Regions

Figure 7.19: Standard Results for Polyhedron

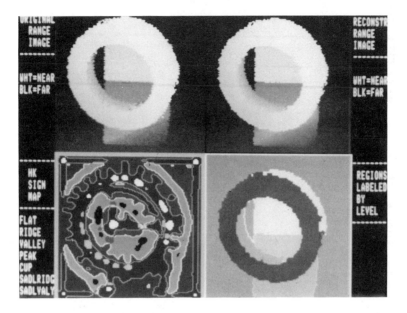

(a) Standard Results for Ring on Polyhedron

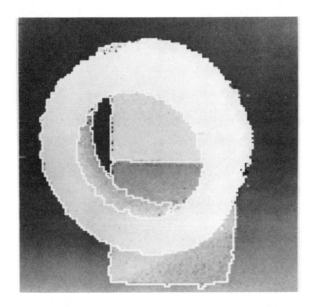

Figure 7.20: (b) Standard Results for Ring on Polyhedron

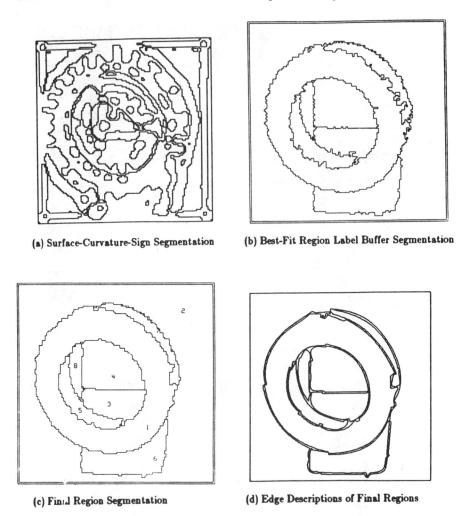

(a) Surface-Curvature-Sign Segmentation   (b) Best-Fit Region Label Buffer Segmentation

(c) Finid Region Segmentation   (d) Edge Descriptions of Final Regions

Figure 7.21: Standard Results for Ring on Polyhedron

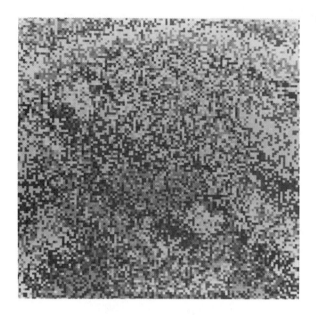

(a) Ring on Polyhedron Image Mapped Through Random Lookup Table

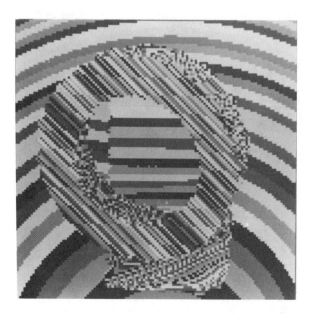

Figure 7.22: (b) Final Reconstruction Image with Random Gray Levels

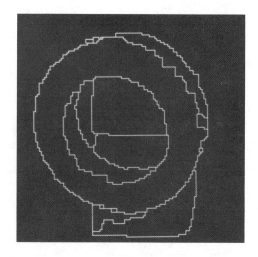

Figure 7.23: Best-Fit Segmentation using Surface Normal Compatibility

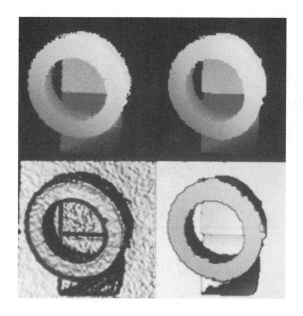

Figure 7.24: Shaded Images for Raw Data & Reconstructed Surfaces

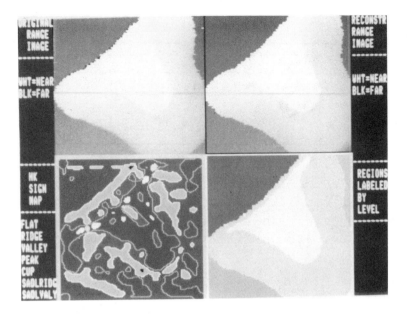

(a) Standard Results for Curved Surface A

Figure 7.25: (b) Standard Results for Curved Surface A

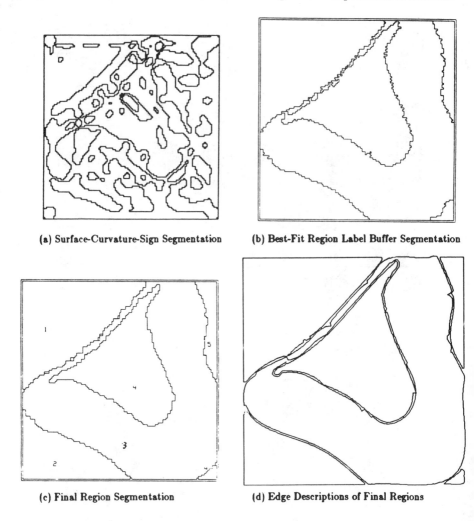

(a) Surface-Curvature-Sign Segmentation   (b) Best-Fit Region Label Buffer Segmentation

(c) Final Region Segmentation   (d) Edge Descriptions of Final Regions

Figure 7.26: Standard Results for Curved Surface A

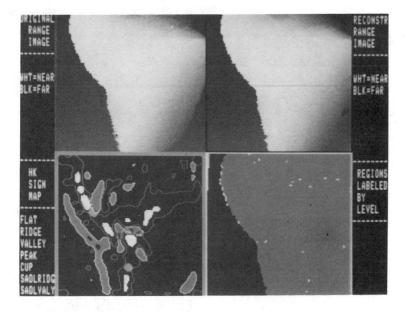

(a) Standard Results for Curved Surface B

Figure 7.27: (b) Standard Results for Curved Surface B

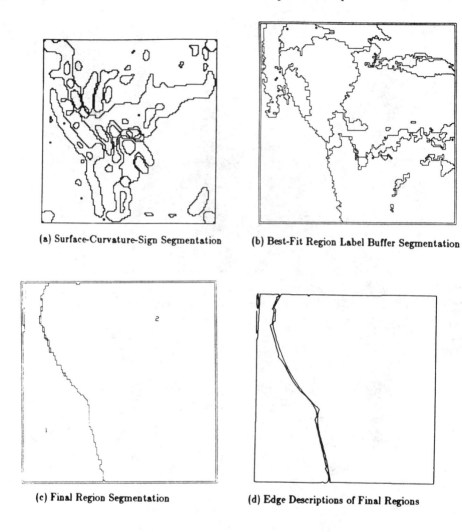

(a) Surface-Curvature-Sign Segmentation   (b) Best-Fit Region Label Buffer Segmentation

(c) Final Region Segmentation   (d) Edge Descriptions of Final Regions

Figure 7.28: Standard Results for Curved Surface B

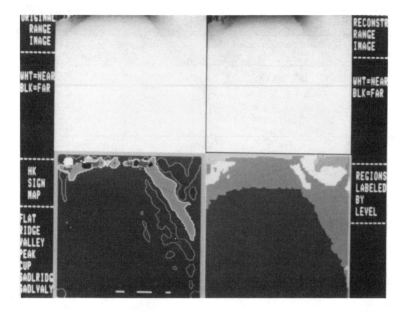

(a) Standard Results for Road Scene A

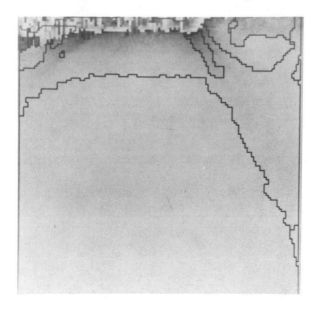

Figure 7.29: (b) Standard Results for Road Scene A

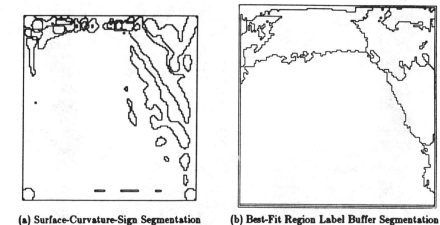

(a) Surface-Curvature-Sign Segmentation   (b) Best-Fit Region Label Buffer Segmentation

(c) Final Region Segmentation

The final region segmentation indicates that
the range image represents one smooth surface.

Figure 7.30: Standard Results for Road Scene A

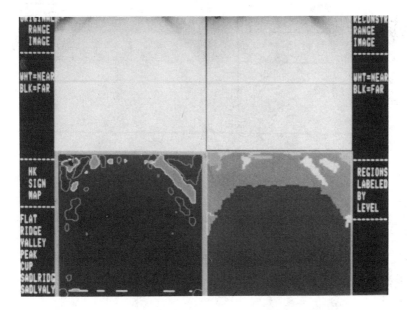

(a) Standard Results for Road Scene B

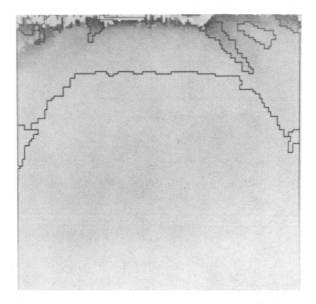

Figure 7.31: (b) Standard Results for Road Scene B

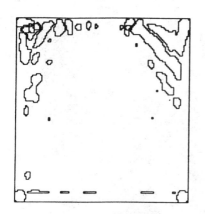

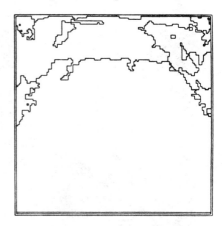

(a) Surface-Curvature-Sign Segmentation   **(b) Best-Fit Region Label Buffer Segmentation**

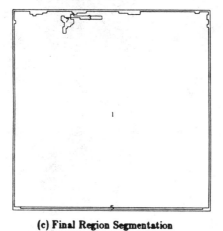

(c) Final Region Segmentation

Figure 7.32: Standard Results for Road Scene B

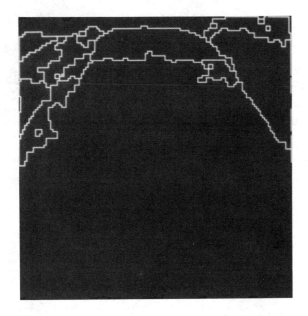

Figure 7.33: Best-Fit Segmentation using Surface Normal Compatibility

Figure 7.34: Shaded Images for Raw Data & Reconstructed Surfaces

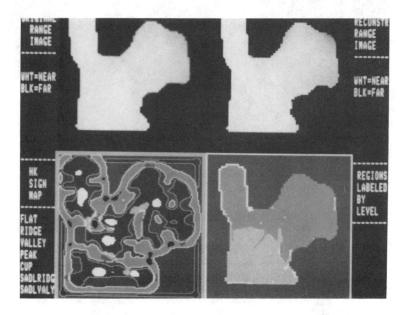

(a) Standard Results for Auto Part

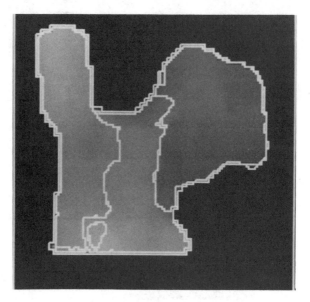

Figure 7.35: (b) Modified Threshold Results for Auto Part

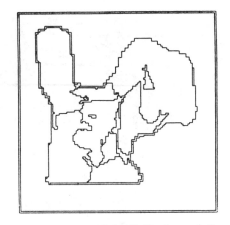

(a) Surface-Curvature-Sign Segmentation   (b) Best-Fit Region Label Buffer Segmentation

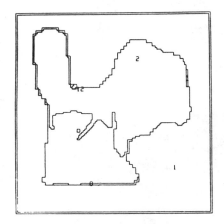

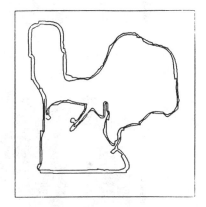

(c) Final Region Segmentation   (d) Edge Descriptions of Final Regions

Figure 7.36: Standard Results for Auto Part

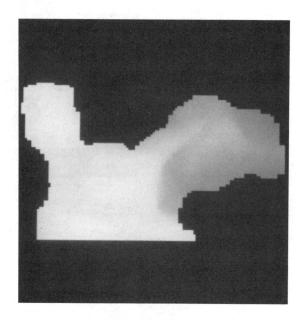

Figure 7.37: Reconstructed Image using Surface Normal Compatibility

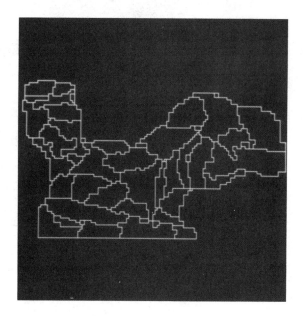

Figure 7.38: Best-Fit Segmentation using Surface Normal Compatibility

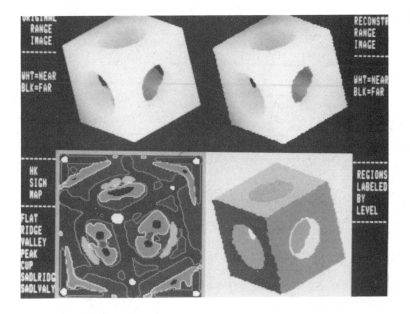

(a) Standard Results for Block with Holes (Low-Noise)

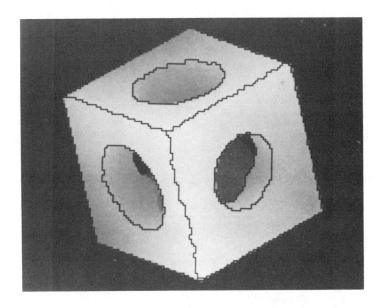

Figure 7.39: (b) Standard Results for Block (Low-Noise)

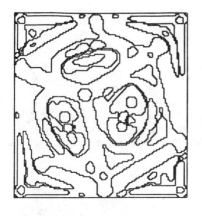

(a) Surface-Curvature-Sign Segmentation

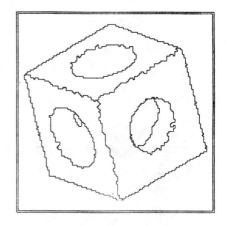

(b) Best-Fit Region Label Buffer Segmentation

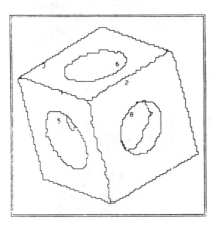

(c) Final Region Segmentation

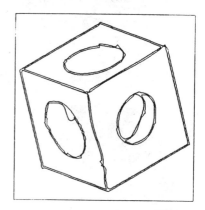

(d) Edge Descriptions of Final Regions

Figure 7.40: Standard Results for Block (Low-Noise)

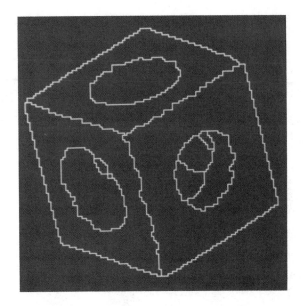

Figure 7.41: Best-Fit Segmentation using Surface Normal Compatibility

Figure 7.42: Shaded Images for Raw Data & Reconstructed Surfaces

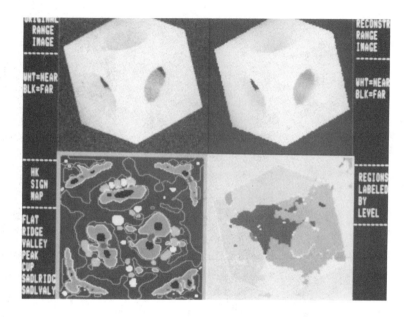

(a) Standard Results for Block (High-Noise)

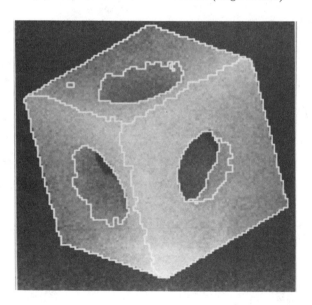

Figure 7.43: (b) Modified Threshold Results for Block (High-Noise)

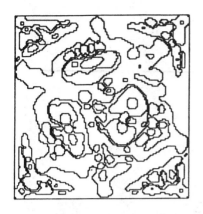

(a) Surface-Curvature-Sign Segmentation

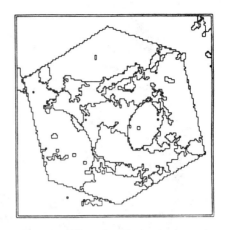

(b) Best-Fit Region Label Buffer Segmentation

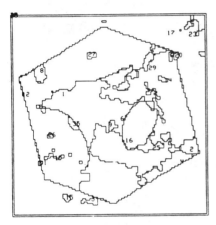

(c) Final Region Segmentation

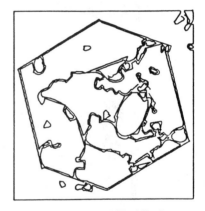

(d) Edge Descriptions of Final Regions

This is an example of segmentation algorithm
failure when the error tolerance threshold is
set below the image noise level.

Figure 7.44: Standard Results for Block (High-Noise)

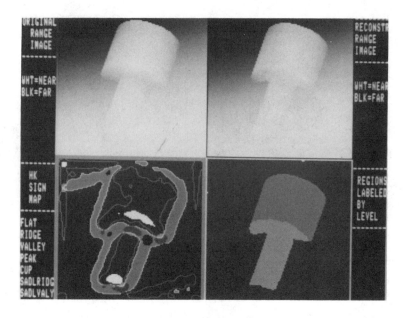

(a) Standard Results for Two Cylinders

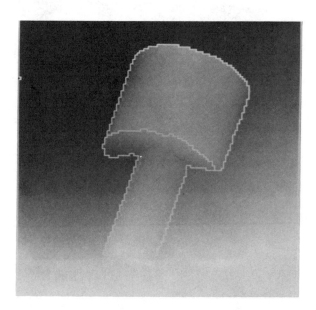

Figure 7.45: (b) Standard Results for Two Cylinders

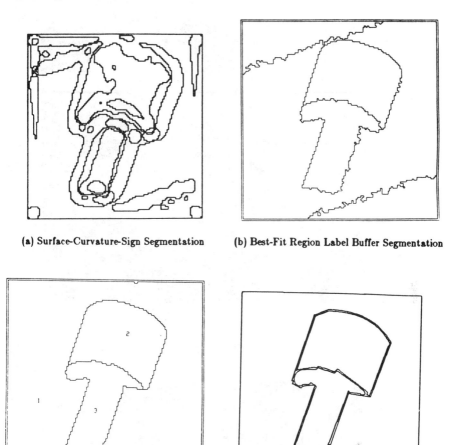

(a) Surface-Curvature-Sign Segmentation   (b) Best-Fit Region Label Buffer Segmentation

(c) Final Region Segmentation   (d) Edge Descriptions of Final Regions

Figure 7.46: Standard Results for Two Cylinders

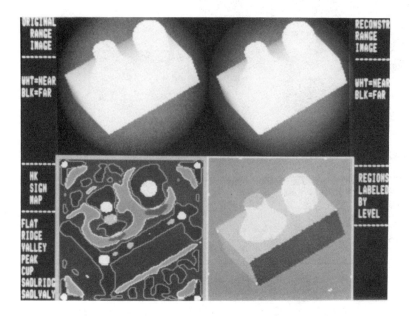

(a) Standard Results for Object with Protrusions

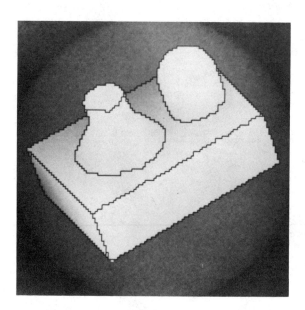

Figure 7.47: (b) Standard Results for Object with Protrusions

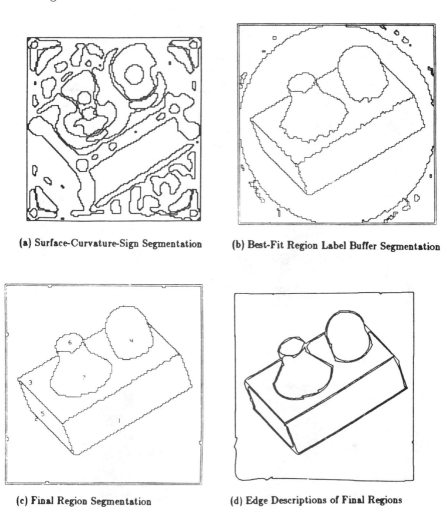

(a) Surface-Curvature-Sign Segmentation

(b) Best-Fit Region Label Buffer Segmentation

(c) Final Region Segmentation

(d) Edge Descriptions of Final Regions

Figure 7.48: Standard Results for Object with Protrusions

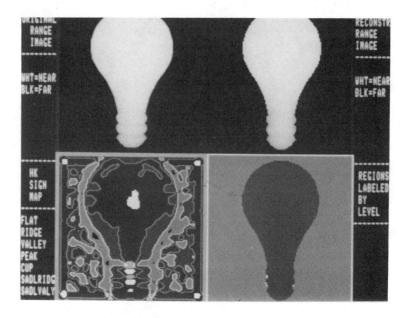

(a) Standard Results for Light Bulb

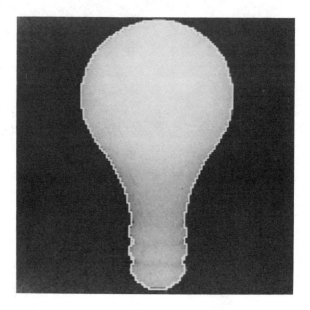

Figure 7.49: (b) Standard Results for Light Bulb

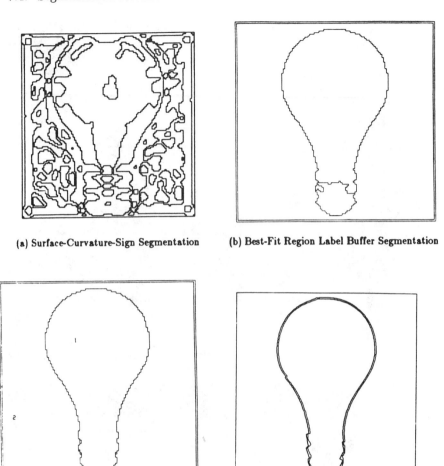

(a) Surface-Curvature-Sign Segmentation

(b) Best-Fit Region Label Buffer Segmentation

(c) Final Region Segmentation

(d) Edge Descriptions of Final Regions

Figure 7.50: Standard Results for Light Bulb

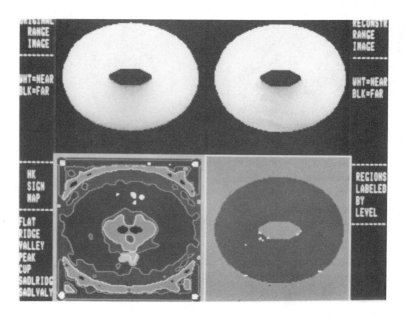

(a) Standard Results for Torus

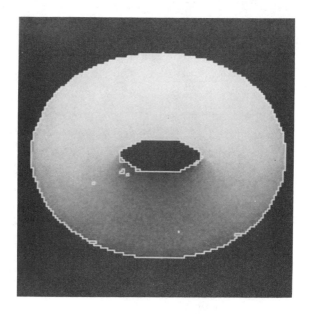

Figure 7.51: (b) Standard Results for Torus

(a) Surface-Curvature-Sign Segmentation

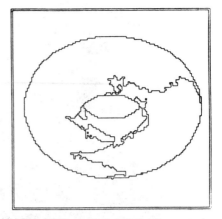

(b) Best-Fit Region Label Buffer Segmentation

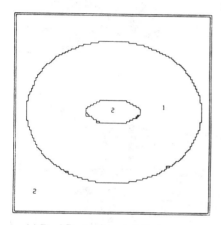

(c) Final Region Segmentation

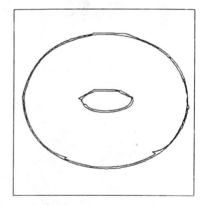

(d) Edge Descriptions of Final Regions

Figure 7.52: Standard Results for Torus

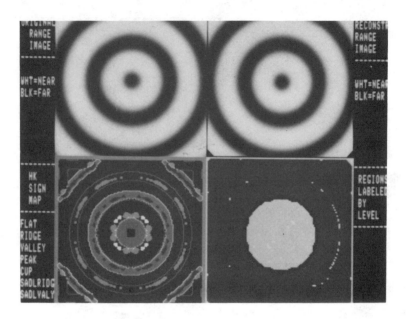

(a) Standard Results for Circular Waves

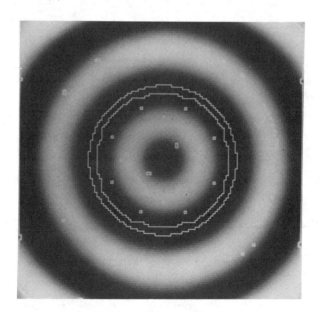

Figure 7.53: (b) Standard Results for Circular Waves

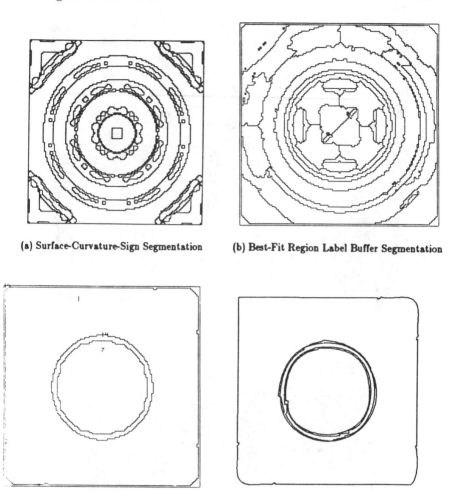

(a) Surface-Curvature-Sign Segmentation   (b) Best-Fit Region Label Buffer Segmentation

(c) Final Region Segmentation   (d) Edge Descriptions of Final Regions

Figure 7.54: Standard Results for Circular Waves

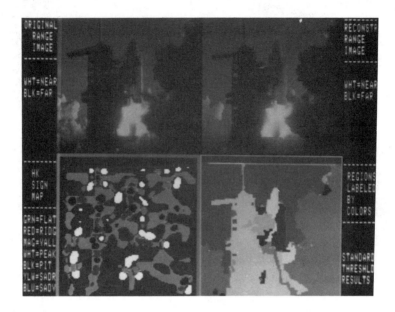

(a) Standard Results for Space Shuttle

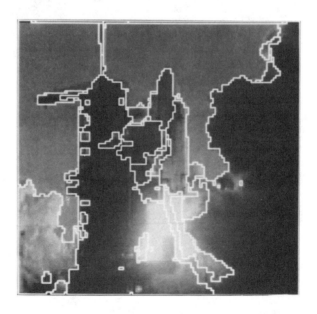

Figure 7.55: (b) Standard Results for Space Shuttle

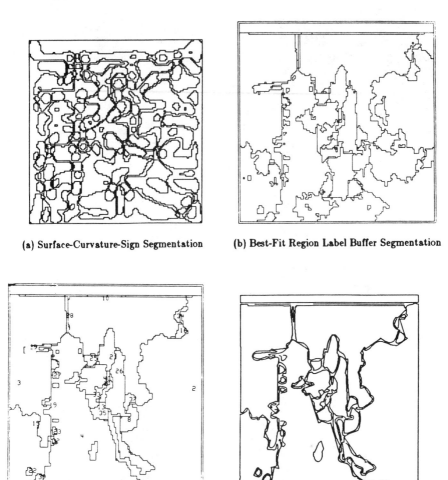

(a) Surface-Curvature-Sign Segmentation

(b) Best-Fit Region Label Buffer Segmentation

(c) Final Region Segmentation

(d) Edge Descriptions of Final Regions

Figure 7.56: Standard Results for Space Shuttle

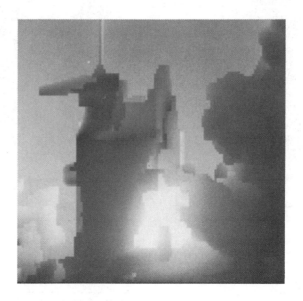

Figure 7.57: Reconstructed Image using Surface Normal Compatibility

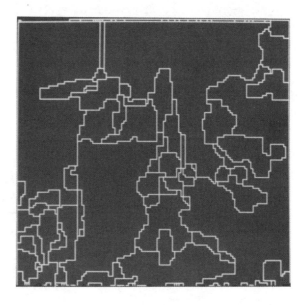

Figure 7.58: Best-Fit Segmentation using Surface Normal Compatibility

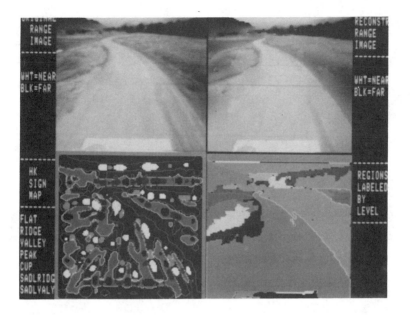

(a) Standard Results for Road Image

Figure 7.59: (b) Standard Results for Road Image

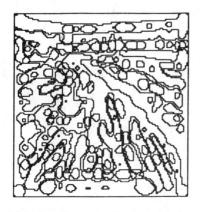

(a) Surface-Curvature-Sign Segmentation

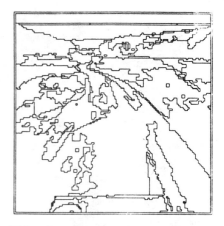

(b) Best-Fit Region Label Buffer Segmentation

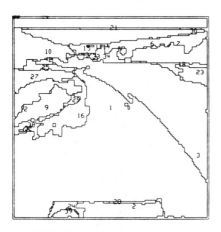

(c) Final Region Segmentation

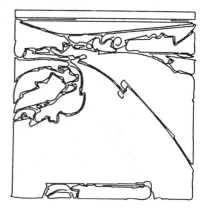

(d) Edge Descriptions of Final Regions

Figure 7.60: Standard Results for Road Image

Figure 7.61: Reconstructed Image using Surface Normal Compatibility

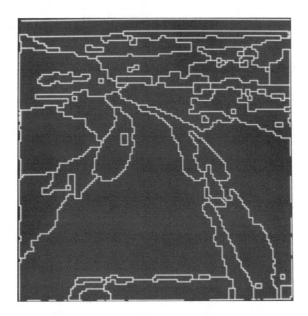

Figure 7.62: Best-Fit Segmentation using Surface Normal Compatibility

(a) Standard Results for USC Girl

Figure 7.63: (b) Standard Results for USC Girl

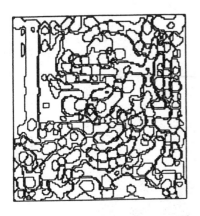

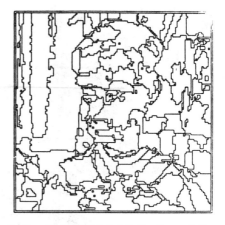

(a) Surface-Curvature-Sign Segmentation   **(b) Best-Fit Region Label Buffer Segmentation**

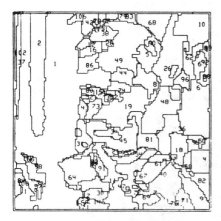

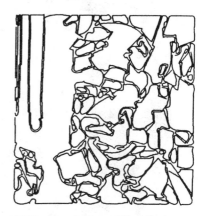

(c) Final Region Segmentation   **(d) Edge Descriptions of Final Regions**

Figure 7.64: Standard Results for USC Girl

Figure 7.65: Modified Algorithm Reconstruction for USC Girl

Figure 7.66: Modified Algorithm Segmentation for USC Girl
(Aggressive Error Tolerance Function w_A)

(a) Original Intensity Image of U-Mass House Scene (256x256)

Figure 7.67: (b) Standard Reconstruction for U-Mass House Scene

(a) Surface-Curvature-Sign Segmentation   **(b) Best-Fit Region Label Buffer Segmentation**

(c) Final Region Segmentation

Figure 7.68: Standard Results for U-Mass House Scene

(a) Standard Segmentation Results for House Scene

Figure 7.69: (b) Modified Threshold Segmentation for House Scene

(a) Modified Threshold Results for House Scene

Figure 7.70: (b) Modified Threshold Reconstruction for House Scene

Figure 7.71: Reconstructed Image using Surface Normal Compatibility

Figure 7.72: Best-Fit Segmentation using Surface Normal Compatibility

Chapter 8

Conclusions and Future Directions

The perception of surface geometry plays a key role in 3-D object recognition. It is proposed that general-purpose recognition of 3-D objects from 2-D images can be performed without complete reliance on special purpose features by matching perceived surface descriptions with stored models of objects. In range imagery, the perceived surface descriptions directly represent scene surface geometry. In intensity imagery, geometric surface descriptions are only available from other intermediate level processes, such as shape from shading. In either case, the first step in general-purpose object recognition is the *segmentation* of a digital image into regions that correspond to physical scene surfaces. If the pixels of a digital surface can be correctly grouped into surface descriptions that have meaningful interpretations based only on general knowledge of surfaces, this grouping process could provide an invaluable service to higher level recognition and model formation processes.

An algorithm for segmenting digital images that exhibit surface coherence properties into smooth surface descriptions has been presented in the previous chapters. This approach is *stimulus bound* in that it considers that the ultimate truth is the sensed image data, and hence the output of all processes should conform to the sensed values. Figure 8.1 shows the digital surface segmentation algorithm in a closed-loop control system format. Closed loop systems of this type use feedback to null the error signal to produce the desired output. The iterative region growing algorithm uses closed loop feedback to null the error image, which effectively binds the interpreted output symbols to the original stimulus signal.

Range images offer a simpler domain to study grouping processes for segmentation and scene analysis than intensity images because the range values at each pixel generally depend only on scene geometry, not on surface reflectances and scene illumination. Geometric image domain cues are physical scene domain cues in the range image context. The added complexity of illumination and reflection need not be considered. Since most of the problems of range image segmentation are also encountered in the

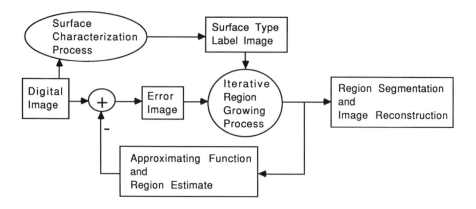

Figure 8.1: Digital Surface Segmentation Viewed as Closed Loop Feedback

more difficult intensity image segmentation, an effective solution to grouping problems should be useful to both areas. The experimental results of
Chapter 7 indicate good segmentation performance on range images and intensity images. The successes of the algorithm on both types of images are
due to the generality of the underlying digital surface model, which makes
no assumptions about the meaning of pixel values or the distribution of
pixel values except that they represent samples of a noisy piecewise-smooth
surface.

The surface-based approach to segmentation and early image understanding is promising. In the past, many image analysis and segmentation
techniques have focussed solely on discontinuity, or edge, detection. The
alternative dual approach of *continuity detection* has not received equal
attention in practice or in the literature. If one considers only the numbers of pixel available as evidence for supporting various hypotheses about
detected entities, the number of pixels representing continuity or spatial
coherence in an image is typically much larger than the number of pixels
representing discontinuity or spatial variation. In most edge detection approaches, an edge pixel is labeled as such based strictly on the pixel values
within an $N \times N$ window where N is as small as possible subject to the
noise properties in an image. In the digital surface segmentation algorithm,
a region pixel is grouped with a region in the image based on all the other
pixels in that region. The regions are grown as large as possible while still
satisfying all the compatibility constraints. In this sense, the statistical
decision that a group of pixels is a region that is well approximated as a
surface is supported by more evidence (more pixels) on average than the
statistical decision that a pixel is an edge pixel.

Edge detection may also be viewed as a method for reducing the dimensionality of the raw image data by focussing on the parts of the image

where the significant changes are taking place. One alternative to compressing image data into a relatively small set of edge pixels is to represent large smooth surface primitives in an image using small sets of function parameters. This text has stressed the power of continuity detection for image segmentation based on local and global surface properties and has (1) provided a theoretical framework for discussion of object recognition and image segmentation in terms of an underlying image model, (2) devised algorithms for image segmentation based on object recognition requirements, and (3) demonstrated a successful software implementation via experimental results on real data consisting of both range images and intensity images.

8.1 Range Image Understanding

The theoretical framework for range image understanding is summarized, and the fundamental concepts are italicized. Object recognition in range images is posed as a *generalized inverse set mapping* that maps a range image into a set of compatible image interpretations based on world knowledge. The largest geometric primitive element in a range image that is independent of object information is a *smooth surface primitive*. The *surface coherence predicate* is a logical predicate for stating the range image segmentation problem in the standard form [Horowitz and Pavlidis 1974] [Zucker 1976]. A signal plus noise model is proposed for *piecewise smooth digital surfaces* that allows a specific statement of the segmentation problem in terms of image regions and functional approximations.

Preliminary grouping for segmentation is based on concepts from the differential geometry of surfaces and curves. Just as curvature and speed characteristics uniquely specify the shape of 1-D smooth planar curves in 2-D Euclidean space, the *Weingarten mapping and the metric tensor* uniquely specify the shape of 2-D smooth surfaces in 3-D Euclidean space. *Visible-invariant surface characteristics* are quantities relevant to 3-D object recognition that are invariant to rotations, translations, and changes in parameterization. *Mean and Gaussian curvature* are two visible-invariant surface characteristics based on the Weingarten mapping and the metric tensor. The *sign-of-curvature paradigm* states that connected groups of pixels with constant mean and Gaussian curvature sign provide an initial segmentation of a range image that has visible-invariant properties. The sign-of-curvature paradigm only requires that the sign of the curvature function is correctly computed for most of the pixels in a region. The magnitude of curvature does not have to be estimated correctly.

The initial segmentation provides input to the *iterative region-growing* algorithm based on *variable-order surface-fitting*. This process is insensitive to grouping errors in the initial segmentation due to the *seed region extraction process* and the error tolerance function used with the iterative surface-fitting technique. A single final region-merging step joins adjacent surface primitives into smooth surface primitives based on geometric considerations. Such primitives are to be matched against geometric descriptions for image understanding or refined for model formation.

8.2   Algorithm Properties

Several capabilities and properties of the digital surface segmentation algorithm are summarized below.

1. The sign-of-curvature approach is unified, general, and independent of geometric dimension. In range image analysis (scalar 2-D images), flat surfaces are described explicitly as being flat, and arbitrary curved surfaces are described as being curved within the context of the same algorithm. In edge analysis (2-vector 1-D images), straight lines are described explicitly as being straight, and arbitrary curved edges are described as being curved. The method is generalizable to n-D m-vector images. It is assumed that a digital image possesses surface coherence so that the noisy piecewise-smooth surface image model is applicable, but no *a priori* assumptions about convexity, symmetry, or object shape are used.

2. The image description is driven by the content of the data, not by expected high-level models as is done in many other approaches as discussed in the literature survey of Chapter 1. Moreover, the exact same surface algorithm with the exact same set of thresholds is shown to be useful for segmenting and describing range images and intensity images. The exact same edge algorithm with the exact same set of thresholds is shown to be useful for segmenting and describing edges in a wide variety of images. The surface and edge algorithms are based on the same sign of curvature and variable order fitting concepts.

3. The segmentation algorithm allows for arbitrary four-connected image regions that are determined by the data during region growth. Blocky regions that can result from fixed-window-based segmentation methods are not encountered.

4. The parallel region growing approach allows logical association between non-adjacent regions that are part of the same physical surface without high-level knowledge. Isolated regions were given the same correct label as another surface in the coffee cup B image, the keyboard B image, and in the ring on polyhedron image (for surface normal compatibility results) as discussed in Chapter 7.

5. The final segmentation output is a rich, information-preserving data-driven description of an image. It allows reconstruction of a noise-

cleaned image that has almost all of the structural properties of the original image depending on the size of the smallest image regions and on the amount of surface coherence in the data. Step discontinuities and roof discontinuities between adjacent smooth surface primitives are enhanced in the final data description.

6. Image quality, or image surface coherence, can be roughly estimated by a simple noise estimation process at the first stage of the digital surface segmentation algorithm. The image quality measure predicts the success or failure of the standard set of input thresholds and automatically suggests more appropriate threshold levels.

No other known algorithm provides all the capabilities mentioned above in a unified manner, either heuristically or theoretically, and has been demonstrated on similar size test image database.

8.3 Final Data Description

The final data description of the digital surface segmentation algorithm contains a list of *smooth surface primitives*. Each smooth surface primitive consists of one or more polynomial surface primitives and has a support region bounded by edges that consist of smooth parametric edge-interval primitives. Each polynomial surface primitive is defined by at most fifteen coefficients over a given sub-region contained in the support region of the smooth surface primitive. The given sub-region may be represented either by a run-length code or by the bounding edges as described in Chapter 6. The surface fit errors (mean absolute, RMS, maximum) are also given for each polynomial surface primitive to indicate the quality of the approximation over each sub-region. Each smooth parametric edge-interval primitive consists of one or more vector polynomial edge-interval primitives. Vector polynomial edge-interval primitives are represented by at most ten coefficients, and each associated sub-interval of the smooth edge-interval is represented by its endpoints. The edge-interval fit errors (mean absolute, RMS, maximum) may also be given for each vector polynomial edge-interval primitive to indicate the quality of the approximation of the sub-interval. This type of representation may be considered as geometric data compression as opposed to other types of data compression based on statistics or differential codes. The primary goal is not the maximum reduction in the number of bits needed to represent the image even though that may occur, but rather an extraction of potentially meaningful surface region primitives.

Differential-geometric surface characterization provides an initial segmentation, or pixel grouping, for the region-growing algorithm based on local differences in the data, but it is also interesting in its own right. Although the Gaussian curvature function has received the most attention in previous literature, the mean curvature function is an interesting quantity in its own right as discussed in Chapter 3. The mean curvature uniqueness theorem states that the shape of graph surfaces is captured by the mean curvature function and a boundary curve. The mean curvature zero-crossings operator acts as a step-edge detector similar to the popular Laplacian zero-crossings edge operator. The mean curvature and Laplacian operators are both second-order elliptic differential operators, but mean curvature is only quasilinear whereas the Laplacian is linear. A mean curvature local-maxima operator acts as a roof-edge detector. It is also noted that the square-root metric determinant operator acts much like a Sobel edge detector, but it is also useful for estimating the 3-D surface area of range image regions and normalizing the curvature operators. The Gaussian curvature operator acts as a corner, cusp, bump, or dimple detector. The surface curvature characteristics for region growing are related to edge and corner detectors.

As mentioned above, the *stimulus bound* philosophy is an important aspect of the digital surface segmentation algorithm. Most decisions about the output quantities produced by the algorithm are checked against the original image data for verification. Each module anticipates the possibility of poor information from the lower-level module, and attempts to adjust its decisions based on feedback from the original data.

The dichotomies of Section 1.2 are summarized below. The input signals to the algorithm are digital surfaces, which may be intensity images or range images. The output symbols are the smooth surface primitives and their associated geometric data. The segmentation algorithm is primarily data-driven, but model-driven processes are needed for object recognition and image understanding. This early, low-level process creates a rich, surface-based description that is useful to later, higher-level processes. Local difference information is computed via partial derivative estimation and curvature computations and is used to provide global similarity information necessary for region growing using the original image data. Grouping errors are reduced via the seed region extraction process, and measurement errors are handled via iterative surface fitting. Statistical outliers are rejected based on the simple error tolerance threshold and also optionally the surface normal compatibility angle threshold. The experimental results in Chapter 7 show that it is possible to extract from an image those entities that are desirable to compute from an image without high-level object knowledge.

8.4   Future Directions

More research is needed in many areas related to the topics presented in this text. The higher levels of vision research require the most work. It is necessary to develop effective surface matching techniques and modeling schemes that enable object recognition given the output from the segmentation algorithm and the original image. The segmentation output provides enough information that arbitrary non-convex objects ought to be recognizable in range images without complete dependence on special purpose features with an appropriate surface matching algorithm. Very little work has be done on seven degree-of-freedom 3-D smooth surface matching. Research in qualitative and quantitative world model representations and model formation may be assisted by automatically generated polynomial surface primitives. It is hoped that possible that unified higher level processes can be developed that can handle range and intensity images separately and together.

Future research is also needed to improve some aspects of the segmentation algorithm. The current algorithm is sequential at the highest level where only one region is processed at a time. A parallel approach that maintained most aspects of the current algorithm but eliminated order dependence problems by working on all regions at once would be a welcome development. Chapter 4 mentioned various types of compatibility requirements that can be imposed during region growing. A theoretical treatment of the necessary thresholds for different types of compatibility based on noise statistics would also be useful.

The region description combination and region merging algorithms of Chapter 5 need the most improvement. Both algorithms in Chapter 5 are very simple and susceptible to errors. A better approach for maintaining the best-fit region label image during processing is preferable to the current type of post-processing. Such a step could make better use of the original image data. With respect to region merging, exact surface to surface intersections could be computed to replace the approximate techniques to determine exact orientation discontinuities to sub-pixel precision, and hopefully sub-pixel accuracy. However, the smooth surface intersections are difficult to locate accurately and reliably. It is interesting to note that the (x, y) points of the intersection of two graph surfaces lie on an algebraic polynomial planar curve with coefficients given by the difference of the parameter vectors of the graph surfaces. For intensity image segmentation, it will be especially important to develop clean and flexible ways to incorporate specific domain knowledge so that the final region descriptions correspond to physical scene surfaces.

Sensor integration is a key area for future research. Range images, intensity images, thermal images, and tactile images are all digital surfaces that can be processed using the surface-based segmentation algorithm. Multi-sensor integration of the individual outputs will increase the reliability and accuracy of the multiple image interpretation. If registered versions of images from m different types of sensors are available, the data should be arranged as a 2-D m-vector image. Each image is processed separately to create HK-sign maps. However, the region growing algorithm should grow separate surfaces in each image requiring compatibility in each image. Such an algorithm is a relatively simple generalization of the methods presented in Chapters 4 and 6.

The sign-of-curvature paradigm can also be applied to 3-D volumes embedded in 4-D space, or to similar entities in higher dimensional spaces. A sign-of-curvature algorithm is potentially useful for segmenting 3-D density images, such as those obtained from CAT scan sensors, or dynamic scenes (image sequences).

Intensity images with significant texture are not addressed by the digital surface segmentation algorithm because the surface coherence condition is not satisfied. An interesting area for future research is to take existing random field models and replace the current piecewise-constant underlying functions with piecewise-smooth functions and test the result on purely textured images and non-textured images.

In Chapter 2, the notions of quantitative segmentation and recognition error metrics were introduced. These preliminary ideas will be useful for system evaluation if they are refined and applied to different segmentation programs and object recognition systems. Without further work in this area, any claims that one segmentation algorithm is better than another will be necessarily subjective.

Derivative estimation is an area where the numbers can never be good enough. If surface curvature estimates can be improved, the initial HK-sign map segmentation could be improved, which would reduce the computational effort required by the iterative region-growing algorithm. Signal processing research may discover better methods of estimating partial derivatives from digital surface data. Performance analysis for the HK-sign map pixel labeling method should be included in such research to determine the accuracy of the pixel labels in different amounts of noise. The surface normal compatibility test also requires accurate derivative estimates from the raw data. Range imaging sensor improvements may alleviate some of the problems encountered with the noisy 8-bit images.

Future research might also include a post-processing analysis of the highest order surface functions based on the regions test that will indicate the accuracy of the highest order fit. If the regions test indicates that large regions of the fitted surface lie above or below the data, the surface region may need to be subdivided and refitted into smaller surface primitives. A complete evaluation of the applicability of other surface function types is another related research area.

For close to real-time applications, recursive least squares computations might be used to reduce the amount of computation and combine the region growing, surface fitting, and pixel compatibility tests by using an incremental update QR algorithm as discussed in Chapter 4 and Appendix C.

It has been shown that the segmentation of images into scene surfaces can be data-driven and need not involve higher level knowledge of objects. Range image object recognition systems will be much more flexible if this type of segmentation algorithm can be used since low-level algorithms would not require reprogramming from one application to another. The perceptual organization capabilities of the digital surface segmentation algorithm are also worthwhile capabilities for intensity image segmentation as shown in the experimental results. More research related to shape from shading concepts is needed to determine how higher level knowledge can be used in relating intensity-image smooth-surface primitives to real scene surfaces.

Appendix A

Surface Curvature Invariance Theorems

The rotation/translation and parameterization invariance properties of the mean and Gaussian curvature of a smooth surface were discussed in Chapter 3 without proof. Since these properties are the most important aspects of visible-invariant quantities and the direct proofs of these invariance properties are brief and straightforward, they are included here for reference.

A.1 Rotation and Translation Invariance

Theorem A.1: Mean curvature $H(u, v)$ and Gaussian curvature $K(u, v)$ are *invariant to rotations and translations* of the smooth surface represented by $\vec{x}(u, v) \in \Re^3$ where $(u, v) \in D \subseteq \Re^2$.

Proof: Let $\vec{x}'(u, v)$ be a rotated, translated version of the surface $\vec{x}(u, v)$. The affine transformation is written as

$$\vec{x}'(u, v) = \mathbf{U}\vec{x}(u, v) + \vec{t} \tag{A.1}$$

where the orthogonal (unitary) transformation matrix $\mathbf{U}$ is a real rotation matrix satisfying

$$\mathbf{U}\mathbf{U}^T = \mathbf{U}^T\mathbf{U} = \mathbf{I} = \text{Identity Matrix} \tag{A.2}$$

and $\vec{t}$ is a fixed translation vector. Since the rotation and translation are both assumed independent of the parameterization of the surface, the partial derivatives of the surface parameterization may be written as

$$
\begin{aligned}
\vec{x}'_u(u, v) &= \mathbf{U}\vec{x}_u(u, v) & \text{(A.3)} \\
\vec{x}'_v(u, v) &= \mathbf{U}\vec{x}_v(u, v) \\
\vec{x}'_{uu}(u, v) &= \mathbf{U}\vec{x}_{uu}(u, v) \\
\vec{x}'_{vv}(u, v) &= \mathbf{U}\vec{x}_{vv}(u, v) & \text{(A.4)} \\
\vec{x}'_{uv}(u, v) &= \mathbf{U}\vec{x}_{uv}(u, v)
\end{aligned}
$$

The first fundamental form coefficient functions are defined as inner products of the first partial derivative vectors.

$$
\begin{aligned}
E'(u,v) &= (\vec{x}_u'(u,v))^T \vec{x}_u'(u,v) && \text{(A.5)} \\
&= \vec{x}_u^T(u,v) \mathbf{U}^T \mathbf{U} \vec{x}_u(u,v) \\
&= \vec{x}_u^T(u,v) \vec{x}_u(u,v) = E(u,v).
\end{aligned}
$$

Similarly, $F(u,v) = F'(u,v)$ and $G(u,v) = G'(u,v)$. Hence, the E,F,G functions are invariant to rotations and translations and all intrinsic quantities that depend on these functions are also invariant.

The proof for the second fundmental form coefficients is much the same. The unit normal to the surface at each point is defined as

$$
\vec{n}(u,v) = \frac{\vec{x}_u \times \vec{x}_v}{\|\vec{x}_u \times \vec{x}_v\|} = \text{Unit Normal Vector.} \tag{A.6}
$$

Since rotation matrices preserve lengths and relative angles between vectors, we have

$$
\vec{x}_u' \times \vec{x}_v' = (\mathbf{U}\vec{x}_u) \times (\mathbf{U}\vec{x}_v) = \mathbf{U}(\vec{x}_u \times \vec{x}_v), \tag{A.7}
$$

which directly implies that

$$
\vec{n}'(u,v) = \mathbf{U}\vec{n}(u,v). \tag{A.8}
$$

The second fundamental form coefficient functions are defined via inner products of the second partial derivative vectors and the surface normal.

$$
\begin{aligned}
L'(u,v) &= (\vec{n}'(u,v))^T \vec{x}_{uu}'(u,v) && \text{(A.9)} \\
&= \vec{n}^T(u,v) \mathbf{U}^T \mathbf{U} \vec{x}_{uu}(u,v) \\
&= \vec{n}^T(u,v) \vec{x}_{uu}(u,v) = L(u,v).
\end{aligned}
$$

Similarly, $M(u,v) = M'(u,v)$ and $N(u,v) = N'(u,v)$. Hence, the L,M,N functions are also invariant to rotations and translations and therefore all quantities dependent on the first or second fundamental form matrices are invariant. Specifically, K and H depend only on the six E,F,G,L,M,N functions as expressed in equations (3.43) and (3.44) in Chapter 3. Therefore, mean and Gaussian curvature are invariant to arbitrary 3-D rotations and 3-D translations. ●

A.2   Parameterization Invariance

Mean and Gaussian curvature are also invariant to changes in the parameterization of a smooth surface. This type of invariance is equally important for visible-invariants because of the implicit reparameterization of surfaces in sampled range image projections from different views even under orthographic projections.

Theorem A.2: Mean curvature $H(u,v)$ and Gaussian curvature $K(u,v)$ are *invariant to changes in parameterization* of the smooth surface represented by $\vec{x}(u,v) \in \Re^3$ where $(u,v) \in D \subseteq \Re^2$ as long as the Jacobian of the parameter transformation is non-zero.

Proof: Suppose there are two parameters (η,ξ) and two differentiable functions $u = u(\eta,\xi)$ and $v = v(\eta,\xi)$ such that the composite surface parameterization $\vec{x}^*(\eta,\xi)$ over the domain $D^* \subseteq \Re^2$ describes exactly the same surface as $\vec{x}(u,v)$ over the domain D. Using the chain rule, the expressions for the partial derivative vectors can be written as

$$\vec{x}_u^*(\eta,\xi) = \vec{x}_\eta^* \eta_u + \vec{x}_\xi^* \xi_u \tag{A.10}$$

$$\vec{x}_v^*(\eta,\xi) = \vec{x}_\eta^* \eta_v + \vec{x}_\xi^* \xi_v. \tag{A.11}$$

The $E(u,v)$ function transforms as follows

$$\begin{aligned} E(u,v) &= \vec{x}_u \cdot \vec{x}_u = \vec{x}_u^* \cdot \vec{x}_u^* \\ &= \vec{x}_\eta^* \cdot \vec{x}_\eta^* \eta_u^2 + 2\vec{x}_\eta^* \cdot \vec{x}_\xi^* \eta_u\xi_u + \vec{x}_\xi^* \cdot \vec{x}_\xi^* \xi_u^2 \\ &= E^* \eta_u^2 + 2F^* \eta_u\xi_u + G^* \xi_u^2. \end{aligned} \tag{A.12}$$

Similarly, $F(u,v)$ and $G(u,v)$ transform as

$$F(u,v) = E^* \eta_u\eta_v + F^*(\eta_u\xi_v + \eta_v\xi_u) + G^* \xi_u\xi_v \tag{A.13}$$

$$G(u,v) = E^* \eta_v^2 + 2F^* \eta_v\xi_v + G^* \xi_v^2 \tag{A.14}$$

Thus, the E,F,G functions are *not* invariant to changes in parameterization of a smooth surface.

The term $EG - F^2$ is a common term in the denominator of the expressions for mean and Gaussian curvature. Several algebraic manipulations yield

$$EG - F^2 = (E^*G^* - F^{*2})(\eta_u\xi_v - \eta_v\xi_u)^2. \tag{A.15}$$

The second multiplicative term is the square of the determinant of the Jacobian matrix of the parameter transformation, known as square of the *Jacobian*. A common notation for the Jacobian is the following:

$$\frac{\partial(\eta,\xi)}{\partial(u,v)} = (\eta_u\xi_v - \eta_v\xi_u). \tag{A.16}$$

The second fundamental form coefficient functions are examined next. By definition of the normal vector to the surface, the tangent vectors $\vec{x}_u$ and $\vec{x}_v$ are always perpendicular to the normal vector.

$$\vec{x}_u \cdot \vec{n} = 0 \qquad\qquad \vec{x}_v \cdot \vec{n} = 0 \tag{A.17}$$

If these two zero functions are differentiated, the resultant derivative functions must also be zero. Using the inner product derivative rule, it is found that for sufficiently smooth surfaces

$$L(u,v) = \vec{x}_{uu} \cdot \vec{n} = -\vec{x}_u \cdot \vec{n}_u \tag{A.18}$$
$$M(u,v) = \vec{x}_{uv} \cdot \vec{n} = \vec{x}_{vu} \cdot \vec{n} = -\vec{x}_v \cdot \vec{n}_u = -\vec{x}_u \cdot \vec{n}_v$$
$$N(u,v) = \vec{x}_{vv} \cdot \vec{n} = -\vec{x}_v \cdot \vec{n}_v$$

Next, the chain rule is also applied to the partial derivatives of the normal vector:

$$\vec{n}_u^*(\eta,\xi) = \vec{n}_\eta^* \eta_u + \vec{n}_\xi^* \xi_u \tag{A.19}$$
$$\vec{n}_v^*(\eta,\xi) = \vec{n}_\eta^* \eta_v + \vec{n}_\xi^* \xi_v \tag{A.20}$$

The $L(u,v)$ function transforms as follows:

$$\begin{aligned} L(u,v) &= \vec{x}_u \cdot \vec{n}_u = \vec{x}_u^* \cdot \vec{n}_u^* \\ &= \vec{x}_\eta^* \cdot \vec{n}_\eta^* \eta_u^2 + 2\vec{x}_\eta^* \cdot \vec{n}_\xi^* \eta_u \xi_u + \vec{x}_\xi^* \cdot \vec{n}_\xi^* \xi_u^2 \\ &= L^* \eta_u^2 + 2M^* \eta_u \xi_u + N^* \xi_u^2 \end{aligned} \tag{A.21}$$

Similarly, the $M(u,v)$ and $N(u,v)$ functions are given by

$$M(u,v) = L^* \eta_u \eta_v + M^*(\eta_u \xi_v + \eta_v \xi_u) + N^* \xi_u \xi_v \tag{A.22}$$
$$N = L^* \eta_v^2 + 2M^* \eta_v \xi_v + N^* \xi_v^2. \tag{A.23}$$

Note that the same transformation occurs for both the E,F,G functions and the L,M,N functions. Since the transformations are exactly the same, this implies that

$$LN - M^2 = (L^*N^* - M^{*2})\left(\frac{\partial(\eta,\xi)}{\partial(u,v)}\right)^2. \tag{A.24}$$

Since $K = (LN - M^2)/(EG - F^2)$, the squared Jacobian term cancels out in the numerator and the denominator. Therefore, $K(u,v) = K^*(\eta,\xi)$ at corresponding points ($u = u(\eta,\xi)$ and $v = v(\eta,\xi)$).

More work is required to show that the mean curvature is invariant. The numerator of the mean curvature expression transforms as follows:

$$EN + GL - 2FM = (E^*N^* + G^*L^* - 2F^*M^*)\left(\frac{\partial(\eta,\xi)}{\partial(u,v)}\right)^2 \tag{A.25}$$

Since $H = (EN+GL-2FM)/(2(EG-F^2))$, it is clear that the squared Jacobian term will also cancel out in the numerator and denominator. Therefore, $H(u,v) = H^*(\eta,\xi)$ where $u = u(\eta,\xi)$ and $v = v(\eta,\xi)$. In summary, mean and Gaussian curvature are invariant to changes in the parameterization of a surface as long as the Jacobian of the parameter transformation is non-zero at every point on the surface. •

Note that Theorem A.2 shows that the mean and Gaussian curvature possess an invariance property that none of the fundamental form coefficient functions E,F,G,L,M,N possess.

Appendix B

Discrete Intrinsic Properties

There is at least one way to compute Gaussian curvature and other intrinsic surface properties from discrete surface data without using explicit partial derivative estimates [Lin and Perry 1982]. This technique originates in the Regge calculus of general relativity in which geometry is analyzed without coordinates, only metric information such as lengths. A discrete triangularization of a surface, a piecewise flat surface approximation, is needed to apply this technique, which works for arbitrarily spaced data points or data points on an equally spaced image pixel grid. Consider a particular vertex point $\vec{x}_k$ on the triangularized surface. In general, it may be a vertex of N different triangles. See Figure B.1 for an example of the geometry. The angle deficit shown in Figure B.1 occurs if one connecting shared edge between two triangles is dissolved and the triangles are pushed down onto a flat surface. The lengths of the sides of the i-th triangle are denoted a_i, b_i, c_i where c_i is the length of the side opposite the vertex point and where $a_{i+1} = b_i$. The angle deficit Δ_k at the vertex point $\vec{x}_k$ is given by

$$\Delta_k(\vec{x}_k) = 2\pi - \sum_{i=1}^{N} \theta_i \qquad \text{where} \quad \theta_i = \cos^{-1}\left(\frac{a_i^2 + b_i^2 - c_i^2}{2a_i b_i}\right). \qquad (B.1)$$

Surface Triangularization
about the point P

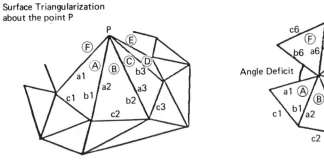

Figure B.1: Discrete Gaussian Curvature at Point using Angle Deficit

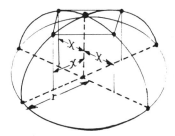

Figure B.2: Five Points on Hemisphere for Curvature Approximation

The Gaussian curvature function at every non-vertex point of the surface triangularization is zero whereas the Gaussian curvature function at a vertex point is infinite. When the Gaussian curvature function is integrated over a piecewise-flat surface area containing the vertex, the integral yields a finite smooth surface Gaussian curvature in the sense of distribution theory. Therefore, the Gaussian curvature function of the piecewise-flat surface surrounding the vertex point is given in terms of the angle deficit and the total area of surrounding triangles by the following expression:

$$K(\vec{x}) = \left(\frac{2\Delta_k}{\sum_{i=1}^{N} A_i} \right) \delta(\vec{x} - \vec{x}_k) \tag{B.2}$$

where the areas A_i of the triangles surrounding the vertex may be computed solely in terms of the lengths of the sides of the triangles as follows:

$$A_i = \sqrt{s(s - a_i)(s - b_i)(s - c_i)} \quad \text{where} \quad s = \frac{1}{2}(a_i + b_i + c_i) \tag{B.3}$$

and where $\delta(\cdot)$ is the Dirac delta function. This method is related to the smooth surface parallel transport formulation of Gaussian curvature mentioned in Chapter 3. Intrinsic surface area estimates are needed for the intrinsic Gaussian curvature estimates in this method. The differencing operations and the area computations in this method are quite unlike the local surface approximation method.

Accurate estimates of the Gaussian curvature $K_h = 1/r^2$ of a hemisphere of radius r can be obtained using only five points on the surface of the hemisphere using the following formulation:

$$\hat{K}_h(x, r) = \frac{2\pi - 4\cos^{-1}\left(1 - x^2/a^2(x, r)\right)}{x\sqrt{2a^2(x, r) - x^2}} \tag{B.4}$$

where the intermediate function $a(x)$ is given by

$$a(x, r) = \sqrt{2}r \cdot \sqrt{1 - \sqrt{1 - \frac{x^2}{r^2}}} \qquad (0 \le x \le r). \tag{B.5}$$

Gaussian Curvature Estimates for Unit Hemisphere based on
Five Symmetrically Spaced Points as shown in Figure B.2.

x	$\hat{K}$	% Error
0.0002	0.975231	-2.50%
0.0004	0.998412	-0.16%
0.0005	0.999415	-0.06%
0.001	0.99992	-0.01%
0.005	1.00000	0.00%
0.01	1.00000	0.00%
0.10	1.00000	0.00%
0.20	1.00007	+0.01%
0.30	1.00035	+0.04%
0.40	1.00116	+0.12%
0.50	1.00300	+0.30%
0.60	1.00672	+0.67%
0.70	1.01385	+1.4%
0.80	1.02755	+2.8%
0.90	1.05666	+5.7%
0.95	1.08714	+8.7%
0.97	1.10796	+10.8%
0.99	1.14454	+14.4%
1.00	1.20920	+20.9%

Figure B.3: An Example of Gaussian Curvature Estimates

The five points on the hemisphere are shown in Figure B.2. Four of these
points move from the north pole to the equator as a function of the variable
x which indicates distance from sphere center in the equatorial plane. The
results of an example calculation for $r = 1$ are shown in Figure B.3.

Despite these interesting results, the current computational method
based on least squares biquadratic surface fitting, as described in Chapter 3, is still used instead of this method. Intrinsic property computation
using surface fitting possesses noise sensitivity comparable to the discrete
intrinsic method discussed here, but is more computationally efficient and
can more easily incorporate the influence of additional neighboring pixels in
larger windows. Also, the local surface fit method can determine Gaussian
curvature as well as many other digital surface characteristics, both intrinsic *and* extrinsic. It is impossible to compute mean curvature and other
extrinsic surface characteristics in general with an approach of this sort if
only the lengths of the triangle sides are given because the embedding of
the piecewise-flat manifold in 3-D space cannot be determined from such
information.

Appendix C

Least Squares Surface Fitting

Least squares surface fitting and low-order polynomials were selected to demonstrate the feasibility and the capabilities of the region growing image segmentation approach based on iterative variable order fitting. Other types of approximation can be used, but linear least squares methods are the easiest and fastest type of approximation. Other types of functions might also serve in the place of low-order polynomials, but these are also the easiest and fastest to fit and evaluate.

If all regions of interest in an image were always regularly shaped, preferably rectangular, there would be no need to discuss least squares surface fitting because the description given in Chapter 3 for fitting surfaces to $N \times N$ windows of data would have been sufficient if the third and fourth order discrete orthogonal polynomials were also given. However, all image regions are not regularly shaped, and a data-driven algorithm should adapt itself to the regions in the data, not the other way around as is done in many fixed window techniques. Therefore, an approach is needed that is numerically stable over arbitrary regions and provide quick approximations.

Bartels and Jezioranski [1985] published an algorithm for least squares fitting using orthogonal polynomials in several variables over arbitrary discrete data sets. Their formalism is quite general, and also quite complicated, because it is formulated for arbitrary inner products and for any number of independent variables. It allows one to compute repeated least squares fits of surfaces to arbitrarily shaped regions in a very computationally efficient and numerically stable manner. The orthogonal basis functions are computed recursively using a three term recurrence relation that depends on the data. The coefficients for any fit are obtained then via inner products as in the local surface fitting approach of Chapter 3, not via singular value decomposition (SVD) or QR computations. The orthogonal polynomials used by this approach are customized for the data set and are not dependent upon the assumption of equally-spaced data points. This technique is interesting, but the expense of computing new orthogonal basis functions for each new image region does not really save any computations in the context of the iterative region growing algorithm because a new region is encountered at each iteration. In this appendix, an approach is presented that handles arbitrary regions using standard orthogonal polynomials that are dependent on the assumption of equally-spaced data points in images. This approach was used for all experimental results shown in Chapter 7 and did not present any numerical difficulties.

A least squares algorithm can be applied directly to image data using power basis functions $\{1, x, x^2, x^3, x^4\}$ to obtain the coefficients of the bivariate polynomial of interest. However, the finite word length of a digital computer may present numerical difficulties when higher order polynomials are used to approximate large regions if enough bits of precision are not available. To help avoid numerical problems, discrete orthogonal polynomials are used as basis functions for the least squares computation even though the region of the fit is not rectangular or regularly shaped. This approach poses a least squares problem in which the square matrix of the corresponding normal equations tends to be diagonally dominant in the sense that the larger numbers are on the diagonal with smaller numbers elsewhere. The min/max bounding box of a region and the center of mass of the region are used to specify the exact form of the discrete orthogonal polynomial basis functions. The coefficients obtained from fitting with orthogonal basis functions can be converted to provide the power basis coefficients of the sort used in the equations in Chapters 4 and 6. This conversion process requires longer word lengths to store the results accurately and is not recommended for numerical computations.

C.1   Discrete Orthogonal Polynomials

Let (x_{min}, y_{min}) and (x_{max}, y_{max}) represent the corners of the bounding min/max box that surrounds a closed, bounded, connected region of any shape. Let $n_x = x_{max} - x_{min} + 1$ and $n_y = y_{max} - y_{min} + 1$ denote the dimensions of the min/max box. Let (μ_x, μ_y) represent the center of mass for that region. The discrete orthogonal polynomial basis functions for fitting a surface to the image data in that region are given as follows:

$$\phi_0(x) = 1 \tag{C.1}$$

$$\phi_1(x, \mu) = x - \mu \tag{C.2}$$

$$\phi_2(x, \mu, n) = (x - \mu)^2 + \frac{(1 - n^2)}{12} \tag{C.3}$$

$$\phi_3(x, \mu, n) = (x - \mu)^3 + \frac{(7 - 3n^2)}{20}(x - \mu) \tag{C.4}$$

$$\phi_4(x, \mu, n) = (x - \mu)^4 + \frac{(13 - 3n^2)}{14}(x - \mu)^2 + \frac{3(n^2 - 1)(n^2 - 9)}{560} \tag{C.5}$$

where μ takes on the value μ_x or μ_y and where n takes on the value n_x or n_y. These polynomials are orthogonal with respect to the equal weight inner product over equally spaced data points. The normalization condition expressed here is that each polynomial has a leading coefficient of one.

In general, real orthogonal polynomials can be evaluated using a three-term recurrence relationship [Davis 1963] [Powell 1981] of the form

$$\phi_i(x) = (x - a_{i-1}(n))\phi_{i-1}(x) - b_{i-1}(n)\phi_{i-2}(x) \qquad (C.6)$$

where the constant coefficients $a_{i-1}(n)$ and $b_{i-1}(n)$, are precomputed given n and are defined in terms of inner products of the basis functions over the domain of the functions:

$$a_{i-1}(n) = \frac{<\phi_{i-1}, x\phi_{i-1}>}{<\phi_{i-1}, \phi_{i-1}>} \qquad b_{i-1}(n) = \frac{<\phi_{i-1}, \phi_{i-1}>}{<\phi_{i-2}, \phi_{i-2}>}. \qquad (C.7)$$

The inner product $< f, g >$ between two discrete basis functions over the interval X is notation to represent the sum

$$< f, g >= \sum_{x \in X} f(x)g(x). \qquad (C.8)$$

The specific form of the general recurrence relationship for equally-weighted least squares basis functions over equally spaced points is given by

$$\phi_i(x, \mu, n) = (x - \mu)\phi_{i-1}(x, \mu, n) - b_{i-1}(n)\phi_{i-2}(x, \mu, n). \qquad (C.9)$$

Although the recurrence relationship for the power basis about the mean argument value μ is computationally simpler $(x - \mu)^i = (x - \mu)(x - \mu)^{i-1}$, the relationship above allows the benefits of using orthogonal polynomials with only two extra computations per polynomial evaluation (a subtraction and a multiplication).

By expressing the most complicated polynomial used by the algorithm, simpler polynomials are easily obtained by letting the appropriate coefficients be zero. For each pixel p in the region of interest R, the three coordinates $x(p), y(p), z(p)$ for that pixel are plugged into the following equation to provide one equation for the least squares system to be solved.

$$z(x, y) = \sum_{i+j \leq m} c_{ij}\phi_i(x)\phi_j(y) \qquad (m \leq 4) \qquad (C.10)$$

$$= c_{00}\phi_0(x)\phi_0(y) + c_{10}\phi_1(x, \mu_x)\phi_0(y) +$$
$$c_{01}\phi_0(x)\phi_1(y, \mu_y) + c_{11}\phi_1(x, \mu_x)\phi_1(y, \mu_y) +$$
$$c_{20}\phi_2(x, \mu_x, n_x)\phi_0(y) + c_{02}\phi_0(x)\phi_2(y, \mu_y, n_y) +$$
$$c_{21}\phi_2(x, \mu_x, n_x)\phi_1(y, \mu_y) + c_{12}\phi_1(x, \mu_x)\phi_2(y, \mu_y, n_y) +$$
$$c_{30}\phi_3(x, \mu_x, n_x)\phi_0(y) + c_{03}\phi_0(x)\phi_3(y, \mu_y, n_y) +$$

$$c_{22}\phi_2(x,\mu_x,n_x)\phi_2(y,\mu_y,n_y)+$$

$$c_{31}\phi_3(x,\mu_x,n_x)\phi_1(y,\mu_y) + c_{13}\phi_1(x,\mu_x)\phi_3(y,\mu_y,n_y)+$$

$$c_{40}\phi_4(x,\mu_x,n_x)\phi_0(y) + c_{04}\phi_0(x)\phi_4(y,\mu_y,n_y).$$

The number of equations for a region R is the number of pixels $N_p = |R|$ in that region. Let us denote the $N_c \times 1$ vector of coefficients as $\vec{c}$ where $N_c = (m + 1)(m + 2)/2$ which means $N_c = 15$ for the biquartic surface. Also denote the $N_p \times 1$ vector of z values as $\vec{z}$, and the $N_p \times N_c$ matrix of $\phi_i(x)\phi_j(y)$ values as the matrix $\mathbf{\Phi}_{xy}$, then all N_p equations may be written down as a single matrix equation:

$$\vec{z} = \mathbf{\Phi}_{xy}\vec{c}. \tag{C.11}$$

C.2   Normal Equations

The least squares normal equations are formed by multiplying through by the transpose of the $\mathbf{\Phi}_{xy}$ matrix:

$$\mathbf{\Phi}_{xy}^T\mathbf{\Phi}_{xy}\vec{c} = \mathbf{\Phi}_{xy}^T\vec{z} \tag{C.12}$$

The normal equations represent a square $N_c \times N_c$ matrix equation. When the region R is nearly rectangular, the square normal matrix is nearly diagonal. Even when R is not rectangular, the diagonal terms are still generally the dominant terms in the matrix. The coefficient vector is solved for analytically as follows:

$$\vec{c} = (\mathbf{\Phi}_{xy}^T\mathbf{\Phi}_{xy})^{-1}\mathbf{\Phi}_{xy}^T\vec{z} \tag{C.13}$$

If the square matrix of the normal equations is singular, the unique Moore-Penrose (MP) pseudo-inverse can be used to return a coefficient vector which fits the degenerate data. The MP pseudo-inverse A^- of a matrix A may be calculated by computing the eigenvalue decomposition of the matrix $A = RDR^T$, inverting the non-zero eigenvalues of the diagonal matrix D to get D^-, and then multiplying terms to obtain $A^- = RD^-R^T$. Once the coefficient vector $\vec{c}$ has been solved for, the root mean square (RMS) error ϵ_{rms} can be computed conveniently as

$$\epsilon_{rms}^2 = \frac{1}{N_p}\|\vec{z} - \mathbf{\Phi}_{xy}\vec{c}\|^2 = \frac{1}{N_p}\vec{z}^T(\vec{z} - \mathbf{\Phi}_{xy}\vec{c}) \tag{C.14}$$

In practice, numerical methods are used to solve the least squares equation and the normal equations are not formed to solve for $\vec{c}$. For example, singular value decomposition (SVD) methods or QR decomposition methods can be used [Lawson and Hanson 1974] [Golub and VanLoan 1983]. In the iterative variable order surface fitting algorithm, the use of the QR updating method with a QR least squares solution allows the least squares problem

to be solved recursively when (1) adding new points to a region to create
the next region description and the next surface fit, or when (2) adding
new columns to the matrix for the next higher order surface fit [Golub and
VanLoan 1983] [Chen 1988]. The use of the orthogonal polynomials tends
to make the problem better conditioned so that several different numerical
methods can be used to solve these equations without difficulty.

C.3 Power Basis

Once the coefficient vector $\vec{c}$ and the fit error ϵ_{rms} have been computed,
equation (C.6) can be used to compute the value of z for any given (x, y)
pair. The power basis coefficients $\vec{a}$ can be computed so that the approximating polynomial may be expressed without involving the evaluation of
the discrete orthogonal polynomials. That is, the equation (C.6) above is
recast in the form of

$$z = \hat{g}(m, \vec{a}, x, y) = \sum_{i+j \leq m} a_{ij} x^i y^j \qquad (m \leq 4) \qquad \text{(C.15)}$$

$$= a_{00} + a_{10}x + a_{01}y + a_{11}xy + a_{20}x^2 + a_{02}y^2 + a_{21}x^2y + a_{12}xy^2 +$$

$$a_{30}x^3 + a_{03}y^3 + a_{31}x^3y + a_{22}x^2y^2 + a_{13}xy^3 + a_{40}x^4 + a_{04}y^4.$$

This is the form of the approximating polynomials used in Chapter 4.
The a_i coefficients are linear combinations of the c_i coefficients. Although
this transformation is numerically undesirable, the $\vec{c} \rightarrow \vec{a}$ transformation is
listed below to show the mathematical equivalence of the numerical compu-
tations and the analytic expressions used in Chapter 4. First, four constants
that occur in the expressions below are defined.

$$n_3^x = \frac{7 - 3n_x^2}{20} \qquad n_3^y = \frac{7 - 3n_y^2}{20} \qquad \text{(C.16)}$$

$$n_4^x = \frac{13 - 3n_x^2}{14} \qquad n_4^y = \frac{13 - 3n_y^2}{14} \qquad \text{(C.17)}$$

The fifteen coefficients are listed below:

$$a_{00} = c_{00} - (c_{10}\mu_x + c_{01}\mu_y) + c_{11}\mu_x\mu_y + \qquad \text{(C.18)}$$

$$c_{20}\phi_2(0, \mu_x, n_x) + c_{02}\phi_2(0, \mu_y, n_y) +$$

$$- (c_{21}\mu_y\phi_2(0, \mu_x, n_x) + c_{12}\mu_x\phi_2(0, \mu_y, n_y)) +$$

$$c_{30}\phi_3(0, \mu_x, n_x) + c_{03}\phi_3(0, \mu_y, n_y) +$$

$$- (c_{31}\mu_y\phi_3(0, \mu_x, n_x) + c_{13}\mu_x\phi_3(0, \mu_y, n_y)) +$$

$$c_{22}\phi_2(0, \mu_x, n_x)\phi_2(0, \mu_y, n_y) +$$

$$c_{40}\phi_4(0, \mu_x, n_x) + c_{04}\phi_4(0, \mu_y, n_y).$$

$$a_{10} = c_{10} - (c_{11}\mu_y + 2c_{20}\mu_x) + c_{12}\phi_2(0, \mu_y, n_y) + c_{30}(3\mu_x^2 + n_3^x) + \quad \text{(C.19)}$$
$$(2c_{21}\mu_x\mu_y) - c_{31}\mu_y(3\mu_x^2 + n_3^x) - 2c_{22}\mu_x\phi_2(0, \mu_y, n_y) +$$
$$c_{13}\phi_3(0, \mu_y, n_y) - c_{40}(4\mu_x^3 + 2\mu_x n_4^x).$$

$$a_{01} = c_{01} - (c_{11}\mu_x + 2c_{02}\mu_y) + c_{21}\phi_2(0, \mu_x, n_x) + c_{03}(3\mu_y^2 + n_3^y) + \quad \text{(C.20)}$$
$$(2c_{12}\mu_x\mu_y) + c_{31}\phi_3(0, \mu_x, n_x) - 2c_{22}\mu_y\phi_2(0, \mu_x, n_x)$$
$$-c_{13}(\mu_x(3\mu_y^2 + n_3^y)) - c_{04}(4\mu_y^3 + 2\mu_y n_4^y).$$

$$a_{11} = c_{11} - (2c_{21}\mu_x + 2c_{12}\mu_y) + 4c_{22}\mu_x\mu_y \qquad\qquad \text{(C.21)}$$
$$+c_{31}(3\mu_x^2 + n_3^x) + c_{13}(3\mu_y^2 + n_3^y).$$

$$a_{20} = c_{20} - (c_{21}\mu_y + 3c_{30}\mu_x) + 3c_{31}\mu_x\mu_y \qquad\qquad \text{(C.22)}$$
$$+c_{22}\phi_2(0, \mu_y, n_y) + c_{40}(6\mu_x^2 + n_4^x).$$

$$a_{02} = c_{02} - (c_{12}\mu_x + 3c_{03}\mu_y) + 3c_{13}\mu_x\mu_y \qquad\qquad \text{(C.23)}$$
$$+c_{22}\phi_2(0, \mu_x, n_x) + c_{04}(6\mu_y^2 + n_4^y).$$

$$a_{21} = c_{21} - (2c_{22}\mu_y + 3c_{31}\mu_x) \qquad a_{12} = c_{12} - (2c_{22}\mu_x + 3c_{13}\mu_y) \quad \text{(C.24)}$$
$$a_{30} = c_{30} - (4\mu_x c_{40} + c_{31}\mu_y) \qquad a_{03} = c_{03} - (4\mu_y c_{04} + c_{13}\mu_x) \quad \text{(C.25)}$$

$$a_{31} = c_{31} \qquad a_{22} = c_{22} \qquad a_{13} = c_{13} \qquad a_{40} = c_{40} \qquad a_{04} = c_{04} \qquad \text{(C.26)}$$

Given these equations, it is easy to see the need for added precision in the lower order a_{ij} terms compared to the c_{ij} terms. But given the $\vec{a}$ form, the equations for conversion to Bezier surface patch form in terms of Bernstein polynomials is presented in Faux and Pratt [1979]. The control points of the Bezier surface patch form have advantages in interpreting surface shape over polynomial coefficients, whether they are orthogonal or not. Bezier surface patches exhibit convex hull properties with respect to their control points and have advantages in certain very constrained types of surface matching.

In summary, a list of (x, y, z) coordinates is used to form the least squares matrix equation, and the equation is solved numerically to create the vector $\vec{c}$. The coefficient vector $\vec{c}$ for the discrete orthogonal polynomials is mathematically equivalent to the coefficient vector $\vec{a}$ for the standard power basis as stated in the conversion equations above. Conversions to other surface forms in the literature are often stated in terms of the power basis form.

In the notation used in Chapter 4, the least squares fitting procedure $L_{\hat{g}}(m_i^k, \hat{R}_i^k, g)$ accepts the original image g, a region $\hat{R}_i^k$, and a function type m_i^k. The original image defines a large set of (x, y, z) coordinates, and the region definition selects a certain subset of this data for the fit. As stated above, the biquartic case includes all lower order cases. For a planar surface, only c_{00}, c_{10}, c_{01} are allowed to be non-zero making Φ_{xy} an $N_p \times 3$ matrix. For the biquadratic surface, c_{11}, c_{20}, c_{02} coefficients are also allowed to be non-zero making Φ_{xy} an $N_p \times 6$ matrix. Bicubic surface fitting involves an $N_p \times 10$ matrix problem.

Appendix D

Equal Angle Increment Sampling

Most optical range imaging sensors [Besl 1988] do not directly produce rectangular Cartesian coordinates (x, y, z) on a regularly-spaced x, y Cartesian grid. The ideal equally-spaced orthographic-projection range images of the form $z(x, y)$ are seldom encountered in practice. Since all the theory in the text addressed such orthographic projection range images, a few words of explanation are in order. In this appendix, two types of "perspective projection" coordinate systems are treated that are useful for describing certain aspects of actual optical range imaging sensors that use equal angle increment (EAI) sampling. Even though orthographic depth measurements are obtainable from these sensors, the (x, y) locations of pixels are not regularly spaced. One reason for special projections is that it is convenient to use rotating mirrors with constant angular velocity to scan the direction of the optical range sensing operation for radar and triangulation techniques. Whenever the scanning mirrors rotate at a constant angular velocity, range samples are usually obtained at equal angle increments, not equal distance increments. For example, imaging laser radars developed at the Environmental Research Institute of Michigan (ERIM) use two mirrors that rotate in equal angle increments around orthogonal axes: a horizontal scanning mirror that rotates about the vertical axis and a vertical scanning mirror that rotates about a horizontal axis. Most of the real range images discussed in Chapters 3 and 7 were acquired using one of the ERIM imaging laser radars. Other range imaging sensors measure slant range as a function of azimuth and elevation [Milgram and Bjorklund 1980]. This type of device also normally uses equal-angle increments in azimuth and elevation.

Because the methods in the text are designed primarily for orthographic projection range images, it is important that the nature of "perspective projection" measurements is understood since many practical range imaging sensors do not fit the equal distance increment orthographic projection model exactly. Many range imaging sensors fall into one of the two categories of perspective models discussed below although other geometries of sensor optics are possible.

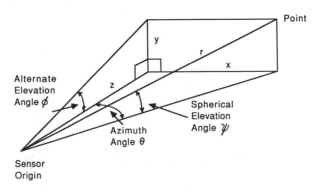

Figure D.1: Perspective Angle and Distances

Two types of equal angle increment (EAI) geometry found in range imaging sensors are analyzed below: the two orthogonal-axis (OA) angle coordinate system and the azimuth-elevation (AE) angle coordinate system. Forward and reverse mathematical transformations are listed and these two types of angular coordinate systems are compared to each other and to the Cartesian orthographic projection model.

D.1 Orthogonal-Axis (OA) Angles

An orthogonal-axis (OA) angle range imaging sensor measures range r to points in a scene as a function of a horizontal angle θ and a vertical angle ϕ. As shown in Figure D.1, the x direction is associated with the angle θ and the y direction is associated with the angle ϕ. The z direction is the direction where $\theta = \phi = 0$. This direction is typically the direction corresponding to the center pixel in a range image. The range imaging sensor is assumed to scan from θ_a to θ_b in the horizontal direction and from ϕ_a to ϕ_b in the vertical direction. Let $(x, y, z) = (0, 0, 0)$ be the effective point that rays from the range imaging sensor pivot about. Suppose that the range imaging sensor is measuring the range r to some point (x, y, z) while the horizontal mirror is set to position $\theta \in [\theta_a, \theta_b]$ and the vertical mirror is set to position $\phi \in [\phi_a, \phi_b]$. The (x, y, z) coordinates are formulated in terms of the (r, θ, ϕ) coordinates and vice versa.

No matter what angular model is chosen, the relationship

$$r^2 = x^2 + y^2 + z^2 \tag{D.1}$$

is always true. From the diagram in Figure D.1, it is clear that

$$x = z \tan \theta \qquad\qquad y = z \tan \phi. \tag{D.2}$$

Therefore, the range to the point (x, y, z) may be expressed as

$$r^2 = z^2 (1 + \tan^2 \theta + \tan^2 \phi). \tag{D.3}$$

This yields the transformation from (r, θ, ϕ) coordinates to (x, y, z) coordinates:

$$x(r, \theta, \phi) = \frac{r \tan \theta}{\sqrt{1 + \tan^2 \theta + \tan^2 \phi}}$$

$$y(r, \theta, \phi) = \frac{r \tan \phi}{\sqrt{1 + \tan^2 \theta + \tan^2 \phi}} \qquad \text{(D.4)}$$

$$z(r, \theta, \phi) = \frac{r}{\sqrt{1 + \tan^2 \theta + \tan^2 \phi}}$$

Note the symmetry between the horizontal and vertical angles. This symmetry is not present in the azimuth-elevation (AE) model. The inverse transformation is given by:

$$r(x, y, z) = \sqrt{x^2 + y^2 + z^2}$$

$$\theta(x, z) = \tan^{-1}(x/z) \qquad \text{(D.5)}$$

$$\phi(y, z) = \tan^{-1}(y/z)$$

Note that θ depends only on x and z and ϕ depends only on y and z. The six equations above completely specify the OA model.

Let us consider the behavior of range samples from the constant depth plane specified by $z(x, y) = h$. As a point moves incrementally in the x direction by a distance δx, the sensor angle θ changes as follows:

$$\delta\theta = \left(\frac{h}{h^2 + x^2} \right) \delta x \qquad \text{(D.6)}$$

Also, as a point moves incrementally in the θ direction by the angle $\delta\theta$, the x coordinate changes as follows:

$$\delta x = (h \sec^2 \theta) \delta\theta \qquad \text{(D.7)}$$

It is clear that incremental changes in one variable do not yield linear incremental changes in the other variable. Similar relationships hold for y and ϕ. The explicit functional relationships for $r(x, y)$ and $r(\theta, \phi)$ for the plane $z(x, y) = h$ are the following:

$$r(x, y) = \sqrt{h^2 + x^2 + y^2} \qquad \text{(D.8)}$$

$$r(\theta, \phi) = h\sqrt{1 + \tan^2 \theta + \tan^2 \phi} \qquad \text{(D.9)}$$

Since $\tan \theta \approx \theta$ to within 3% up to 17 degrees of arc, it is clear that the two perspective range images of the plane $r(x, y)$ and $r(\theta, \phi)$ will be very similar within a 34° × 34° field of view.

In Figure D.2, two surface plots for a plane at depth $z(x, y) = h$ are displayed. In the first plot, the expected constant depth surface is shown

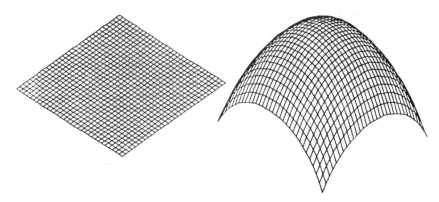

Figure D.2: Orthographic Cartesian Projection and OA Projection

under the standard Cartesian projection. In the second plot, the exact same surface is shown under the OA projection where the two angular coordinates are considered logically equivalent to the two (x, y) Euclidean coordinates. A 90 degree field of view was assumed. The warping of the surface increases at the larger angles.

D.2   Azimuth-Elevation (AE) Angles

The azimuth-elevation (AE) model is slightly different than the OA model. In the AE model, the horizontal rotation angle, known as the azimuth, is denoted as θ because it is identical to the θ in the OA model. The elevation angle ψ is not the same as the rotation angle ϕ in the OA model. The range r and x, y, z have the same meaning as above. The (r, θ, ψ) system is a spherical coordinate system where θ and ψ may be interpreted as longitude and latitude on the sphere. The key difference between the AE model and the OA model is that, although $r(x, y, z)$ and $\theta(x, z)$ are defined as above, the $\psi(x, y, z)$ angle is defined as follows:

$$\psi(x, y, z) = \tan^{-1}\left(\frac{y}{\sqrt{x^2 + z^2}}\right) \tag{D.10}$$

Note that ψ depends on all three x, y, z coordinates unlike ϕ in the OA model which depends only on y and z. This defines the transformation from (x, y, z) to (r, θ, ψ) coordinates. Given (r, θ, ψ), the (x, y, z) coordinates are computed using

$$
\begin{aligned}
x(r, \theta, \psi) &= r\cos\psi\sin\theta \tag{D.11}\\
y(r, \psi) &= r\sin\psi\\
z(r, \theta, \psi) &= r\cos\psi\cos\theta
\end{aligned}
$$

Note that y depends only on r and ψ in the AE model whereas it depended on all three r, θ, ϕ coordinates in the OA model. Note also that $z(r, 0, 0) = r$

and $r(0,0,z) = z$ as one would expect, and the same is true for the OA model. The x and y axes are not symmetrical in the AE model as they are in the OA model owing to the coupling between the azimuth and elevation angles.

Suppose again that a range image of the plane $z(x,y) = h$ is acquired using an AE type range imaging sensor. This means $r(x,y) = \sqrt{h^2 + x^2 + y^2}$ as before, but the function $r(\theta, \psi)$ is slightly different in that it contains an extra term that couples the θ and ψ directions:

$$r(\theta, \psi) = h\sqrt{1 + \tan^2 \theta + \tan^2 \psi + \tan^2 \theta \tan^2 \psi}. \qquad (D.12)$$

In this case, $r(x,y)$ is still approximately the same as $r(\theta, \psi)$ for small angles because the coupling term is a product of two small numbers yielding a much smaller number. However, the distortion near the limits of θ and ψ is worse for an AE type range imaging sensor than for a OA type range imaging sensor.

D.3   Summary of Models

Two types of range imaging sensor geometries (OA and AE) based on equal angle increment sampling have been analyzed. Six types of range image projections have mentioned in the above discussion and are labeled and summarized here:

1. Cartesian Orthographic Projection: $z(x,y)$

2. Cartesian Perspective Projection: $r(x,y)$

3. OA Orthographic Projection: $z(\theta, \phi)$

4. OA Perspective Projection: $r(\theta, \phi)$

5. AE Orthographic Projection: $z(\theta, \psi)$

6. AE Perspective Projection: $r(\theta, \psi)$

Each perspective projection allows direct recovery of z in the orthographic projection through an appropriate transformation:

$$z(x,y) = \sqrt{(r(x,y))^2 - (x^2 + y^2)} \qquad (D.13)$$

$$z(\theta, \phi) = \frac{r(\theta, \phi)}{\sqrt{1 + \tan^2 \theta + \tan^2 \phi}} \qquad (D.14)$$

$$z(\theta, \psi) = r(\theta, \psi) \cos \theta \cos \psi \qquad (D.15)$$

The problem with the orthographic OA and AE projections is that the digital surface $z(x,y)$ corresponding to the graph surface $z(\theta, \phi)$ and $z(\theta, \psi)$

are slightly different due to the equal angle increment sampling in the angular coordinates. To get a range image on an (x, y) grid, all three x, y, z coordinates should be computed for each angle pair:

$$x_{OA}(\theta, \phi) = z(\theta, \phi) \tan \theta \qquad x_{AE}(\theta, \psi) = z(\theta, \psi) \tan \theta \qquad (D.16)$$

$$y_{OA}(\theta, \phi) = z(\theta, \phi) \tan \phi \qquad y_{AE}(\theta, \psi) = \sqrt{z^2(\theta, \psi) + x_{AE}^2(\theta, \psi)} \tan \psi$$
$$(D.17)$$

An interpolation scheme could be used to resample the interpolated surfaces to obtain the desired equally-spaced sampled Cartesian orthographic projection $z(x, y)$. Since most range images of objects encountered so far use a small field of view, the range images have been processed directly without resampling and the results have been satisfactory. If an object surface matching algorithm were to use this data directly, it would have to account for a slight warping in the sensed surfaces using the current segmentation algorithm. In a practical system, it is proposed that (1) the segmentation algorithm runs on the raw data, (2) the segmented regions are converted to Cartesian (x, y, z) point lists, and (3) appropriate application surfaces are fitted to the x, y, z data to yield valid geometric representations of scene geometry.

Appendix E

A Metric Space of Image Regions

In this appendix, it is proved that the area of the symmetric difference of two connected finite-area regions in an image is a metric on the space of all connected regions of finite area in an image. The set of connected regions is denoted C^I as in Chapter 4. This region set along with the symmetric-difference size metric form a metric space. In such a mathematical framework, it is meaningful to discuss the "distance" between two region descriptions. A region distance metric allows one to quantitatively measure the quality of a region approximation just as the quality of a functional approximation is measured.

A metric space is a set X and a mapping $d : X \times X \to \Re^+$ that maps pairs of elements in X to non-negative reals and satisfies the following conditions for any $A, B, C \in X$:

$$d(A, B) \geq 0 \qquad \text{(Non-Negative)} \qquad (E.1)$$
$$d(A, B) = 0 \leftrightarrow A = B \qquad \text{(Positive Definite)}$$
$$d(A, B) = d(B, A) \qquad \text{(Symmetric)}$$
$$d(A, B) \leq d(A, C) + d(C, B) \qquad \text{(Triangle Inequality)}.$$

By defining a mapping $d(\cdot)$ for an existing set and proving that these four conditions hold, the analysis of that set may use the mathematics of metric spaces.

The region metric is defined using a set measure $m(\cdot)$. Let I be the universal set, the digital image. Let C^I be the set of connected finite-measure regions of interest. Let A be a subset of I and an element of the space C^I. The set measure $m(A)$ is defined to be the area of the set A for 2-D images. In a continuous domain I, $m(A) = \int_A dx dy$. In a discrete image domain I, $m(A) = |A| =$ the number of pixels in the region A. Hence, $m(A) = 0$ if and only if A is a set of measure zero. In the continuous domain, sets of measure zero are logically equated with the null set ϕ. For example, curves and points have no area. Hence, $m(A) > 0$ for any non-null connected set $A \in C^I$. Also, $m(A \cup B) = m(A) + m(B) - m(A \cap B)$.

The symmetric difference of two subsets A and B is defined as $A \Delta B = (A - B) \cup (B - A)$.

THEOREM E.1: The set C^I and the mapping $d(A, B) = m(A \Delta B)$ form a metric space.

Proof: The first condition is always satisfied because the symmetric difference of two sets is another set and all sets have non-negative area. The third condition is also satisfied due to the symmetry of the symmetric difference operator. The second condition is proved as follows: If $A = B$, then $A \Delta B = (A - B) \cup (B - A) = \phi$, which implies that $m(A \Delta B) = 0$. If $m(A \Delta B) = m(A - B) + m(B - A) = 0$, then non-negativity requires that $m(A - B) = 0$ and $m(B - A) = 0$ separately. This implies $A - B = \phi$ and $B - A = \phi$. Therefore, $A \subseteq B$ and $B \subseteq A$, which implies $A = B$.

The proof of the triangle inequality is more involved. Henceforth, $A \cup B$ is written as $A + B$ and $A \cap B$ as AB. The property that $A = AB + (A - B)$ disjointly yields the useful relationships

$$m(A) = m(AB) + m(A - B) \tag{E.2}$$
$$m(AB) = m(A) - m(A - B)$$
$$m(A - B) = m(A) - m(AB)$$

which express that the area of A consists of the part of A in B and the part of A not in B for any set B. This is needed in the proof. It must be shown that, for any set C,

$$m(A \Delta B) \leq m(A \Delta C) + m(C \Delta B). \tag{E.3}$$

An exhaustive expansion approach is used:

$$
\begin{aligned}
m(A \Delta B) &= m(A - B) + m(B - A) &\text{(E.4)}\\
&= m(A) + m(B) - 2m(AB)\\
&\leq m(A \Delta C) + m(C \Delta B) \quad (?)\\
&= m(A - C) + m(C - A) + m(B - C) + m(C - B)\\
&= m(A) + m(B) + 2m(C) - (2m(AC) + 2m(BC)).
\end{aligned}
$$

After canceling and rearranging the terms, the question becomes

$$m(AC) + m(BC) \leq m(C) + m(AB) \quad (?) \tag{E.5}$$

Each set is further decomposed into disjoint subsets. The set C is considered with the following disjoint decomposition:

$$C = (C - (A + B)) + (CB - A) + (CA - B) + ABC. \tag{E.6}$$

The preliminary lemma (E.2) mentioned above is used on the other sets.

$$m(AC - B) + 2m(ABC) + m(BC - A) \leq \tag{E.7}$$

$$m(C - (A + B)) + m(BC - A) + m(AC - B) + 2m(ABC) + m(AB - C).$$

Everything on the left-hand side cancels out leaving the following statement, which is obviously true, by the definition of the measure of area:

$$0 \leq m(C - (A + B)) + m(AB - C). \tag{E.8}$$

This proves the triangle inequality and completes the proof that the set C^I and the metric $m(A \Delta B)$ form a metric space. •

If the binary field $\{0,1\}$ is used with the metric space above, the measure $m(A)$ is also a norm. Let 1 times a set be the set and let 0 times the set be the null set.

$$
\begin{array}{lll}
m(A) \geq 0 & \text{(Non-negative)} & \text{(E.9)} \\
m(A + B) \leq m(A) + m(B) & \text{(Triangle Inequality)} & \\
m(\alpha A) = |\alpha| m(A) & \text{(Homogeneity)} & \\
m(A) = 0 \leftrightarrow A = \phi & \text{(Positive Definite)} &
\end{array}
$$

All of the properties are trivially satisfied by definition of $m(A)$ and the conventions for the sets in C^I. The triangle inequality is proved by observing

$$m(A + B) = m(A) + m(B) - m(AB) \leq m(A) + m(B). \tag{E.10}$$

Although there is nothing new presented in these results, the notions of norm and metric are useful for formulating questions about convergence, approximation quality, and segmentation quality. Although all questions are not resolved in this text, an apparently worthwhile mathematical framework for discussing such issues has been established. Although two dimensions are discussed above, the basic metric space concepts generalize to any dimension. It is interesting to note that when the regions A and B are represented as bit strings (bitmaps), the distance metric above is the Hamming distance between the bit strings: the number of bits where the bit strings differ.

Appendix F

Software Implementation

The experimental results were obtained using a range image segmentation system, an image processing system, and a software support environment developed by the author. The complete software system including the support environment consists of over 30,000 lines of commented C source code. The three primary programs of the image analysis system are (1) the digital surface characterization program (the simplest of the three), (2) the digital surface segmentation program (over 8200 lines), and (3) the surface region merging program with the edge description/segmentation option. These three programs represent about half of the total lines above. The purpose of this appendix is to briefly describe several key algorithms needed to implement the above programs. Many of these algorithms are supplied with commercial image processing systems that offer special hardware support for simple computationally intensive operations. An interesting aspect of this approach is that only a relatively small number of segmentation algorithm specific functions are required. Because several of these general-purpose modules have been mentioned in the text without any explanatory discussion, they are listed here with brief algorithm statements and descriptions.

F.1 Binary Image Contraction (Erosion)

The binary image contraction (erosion) operation for 3x3 windows maps a binary image into another binary image in which regions of the output image are smaller than the corresponding regions in the input image.

- **Algorithm Statement:** For each ON pixel in the input binary image, test each of the eight neighbors of that pixel in the input image. If any neighbor is OFF, turn that pixel OFF in the output binary image. Pixels that are OFF in the input binary image remain OFF in the output binary image.

The contraction operation can be accomplished very quickly on appropriate image processing hardware. It is useful for making a region smaller while maintaining most of the shape properties of the region.

F.2 Binary Image Expansion (Dilation)

The binary image dilation (expansion) operation for 3x3 windows maps a binary image into another binary image in which regions of the output image are larger than the corresponding regions in the input image.

- **Algorithm Statement:** For each OFF pixel in the input binary image, test each of the eight neighbors of that pixel in the input image. If any neighbor is ON, turn that pixel ON in the output binary image. Pixels that are ON in the input binary image remain ON in the output binary image.

Dilation is also achieved very quickly on appropriate image processing hardware. It is useful for making a region larger while maintaining most of the shape properties of the region.

F.3 Binary Image Connected Component Analyzer

The binary image connected component (connected region) analysis operation maps an input binary image into an output list of regions in which each region consists of a set of pixels that are connected to each other in some sense [Rosenfeld and Kak 1982] [Ballard and Brown 1982]. Four-connected regions have the property that any two pixels in a four-connected region can be connected by a string of four-connected pixels all belonging to the same region. One pixel p is four-connected to another adjacent pixel q if $|x(p) - x(q)| = 1$ and $|y(p) - y(q)| = 0$, or if $|x(p) - x(q)| = 0$ and $|y(p) - y(q)| = 1$. Only four-connected regions are of interest for surface-based algorithms. Eight-connected pixel chains were discussed Chapter 6 with respect to edge processing.

- **Algorithm Statement:** Set current label value to zero. Initialize label image (same size as binary image) with current label value. For each ON pixel in the input binary image as one scans the image left-to-right top-to-bottom, check the upper and left (four-connected) neighbors of that pixel.

    1. If the upper neighbor is ON and the left neighbor is OFF, give that pixel the label of the upper neighbor.

    2. If the upper neighbor is OFF and the left neighbor is ON, give that pixel the label of the left neighbor.

3. If the upper neighbor is OFF and the left neighbor is OFF, increment the current label value and give the new label value to that pixel.

4. If the upper neighbor is ON and the left neighbor is ON, give that pixel the label of the upper neighbor and, if the labels of the two neighbor pixels are different, record the logical equivalence of the two different labels in an equivalence table if not already recorded.

After all input image pixels have been checked, use the equivalence table to create a lookup table that maps old non-unique labels into a new set of unique labels with one label per four-connected region. Then, for each pixel in the label image, map the old value to the new value using the lookup table during a second pass over the label image. The number of unique non-zero labels is the number of regions in the binary image. Each region can be extracted by isolating all pixels of a given label. Region size is determined by computing the histogram of the label image with the unique labels.

Two sequential passes over the image pixels are required in this standard four-connected component algorithm. The connected component analysis algorithm is executed many times during the execution of the region growing algorithm. It is a key limiting factor to the speed of the current implementation on a general-purpose digital computer.

F.4   Separable Window Convolution

Window convolutions are required extensively for smoothing and differentiation in both the surface and edge characterization software. Only three procedures, two vector initialization procedures and one computation procedure, are required to perform both smoothing and differentiation on both surface and edge data. A binomial coefficient initialization procedure sets up any size vector of values to provide nearly Gaussian smoothing since a binomial distribution function is a good discrete approximation to a Gaussian distribution function. A binomial smoothing vector also provides central pixel weighting when used in conjunction with derivative operators as in the pre-smoothing operation described in Chapter 3. Equally-weighted least squares derivative operator vectors of any size are initialized by another procedure using operations described in Chapter 3. A single row vector convolution with transposed output procedure does all the actual window operator computations by applying a given smoothing or derivative window to the image data. Assuming physical memory for a temporary scratch image is available, the row vector convolution procedure takes the inner product of a row of image pixels with the window row vector and places the result in the image transpose position of the output image. Then the window column vector is used by the row vector convolution procedure on the transposed image to create another transposed image which is the desired result. This transposing allows use of a single row convolution procedure to achieve two-dimensional separable window convolutions. A pair of separate row and column convolution procedures that do not transpose the image can compute the result more efficiently on virtual memory systems at the minimal cost of a separate procedure. With three (or four) procedures, one can do arbitrary size rectangular window convolutions on arbitrary size rectangular images or edge vectors to accomplish smoothing or differentiation (low pass or high pass digital filtering).

F.5   Least Squares Fitting

As mentioned in Appendix C, several types of least squares fitting techniques are possible to solve the $m \times n$ matrix equation $Ax = b$. Once a basic least squares solver is chosen, it is possible to have a single procedure to do all surface fitting for any order and another procedure to do all edge fitting for any order. Univariate and bivariate polynomial evaluation procedures are required to compare polynomial properties to data properties.

F.6   3x3 Window Mapping

Edge refinement and region refinement operations on binary images can both be formulated in terms of a single mathematical operation that uses different lookup tables. Every 3x3 window in a binary image can be represented as an integer between 1 and 512. A 512-length lookup table of 9-bit numbers defines a mapping between all possible 3x3 windows that can exist in the data and the 3x3 windows that a human interpreter finds acceptable. A separate array of 512 elements must be defined for every type of operation to be performed. Generally, only a few values in the lookup table need to be altered from their original index value. Separate lookup tables were used for notch filling, burr trimming, and edge refinement. The operations provided by such a procedure are limited, but if an operation is useful, it can be provided quickly.

F.7   Image Booleans and Image Arithmetic

A software package for image processing would be complete without image boolean operators to do AND, OR, NOT, and XOR operations. Image arithmetic operators to do addition, subtraction, scaling, absolute values, square roots, squares, and other pixel operations are also needed. An image copy procedure, an assign-value-to-image procedure, and an image lookup-table mapping procedure must also be included.

F.8   Input, Output, Displays, and Conversions

Separate procedural are needed to get an image from disk, write an image
to disk, and to display an image on a video monitor. Interactive, almost
instantaneous displays were a critical part in the development of the digital
surface segmentation algorithm. By visually examining each step of the
algorithm as a picture, debugging and algorithm refinement were usually
fast and easy. Floating point images, integer images, byte images, and
bitmaps are used by the algorithm for different purposes. It is necessary
to have at least three different conversion procedures in order to do the
appropriate conversions.

F.9   Software Summary

This appendix is included to describe the basic software tools required to
implement the digital surface segmentation algorithm. Many of these tools
are provided on commercially available image processing systems, but few
vendors make products that can perform (1) binary image contractions
and dilations, (2) connected component analysis, (3) image polynomial
evaluation (evaluate a given function at each pixel), and (4) least squares
$Ax = b$ solutions in close to real-time. Once the base level of software is
available on a given system, the algorithm descriptions can be converted
to working software.

Appendix G

Iterative Region Growing Algorithm

In this appendix, the concepts of Chapter 4 are condensed into a "pseudo-code" description that captures the main ideas in a few pages. The pseudo-code description is not self-contained, but relies on definitions and material established in Chapters 3 and 4.

Given any arbitrary digital surface $g(x, y)$, the preliminary noise estimation and surface characterization algorithms are executed:

1. **Noise Estimation:** Compute scalar image quality measures ρ_1, ρ_2. Compare with results from other previously tested images. Estimate the relative quality of image and probable quality of output. If reasonable results are likely, estimate thresholds automatically and continue to execute algorithm. Otherwise notify user that image does not seem to possess surface coherence property.

2. **Surface Characterization:** Compute partial derivative estimates using default window sizes for given image quality. Use estimates to compute mean and Gaussian curvature. Use mean and Gaussian curvature to compute surface type label at each pixel: peak, pit, ridge, valley, saddle ridge, saddle valley, minimal, flat. Store labels in HK-sign map $\mathrm{sgn}_{HK}(x, y)$, an "initial-guess" coarse image segmentation.

Assuming that the data can be represented well as a piecewise-smooth surface function defined over the entire image, the segmentation algorithm executes as follows:

1. **Declarations:**
   Digital-Surface: $g(x, y)$;
   Surface-Order : $m \in F = \{1, 2, 3, 4\}$;
   Max-Surface-Order : $|F| = 4$ (Biquartic);
   Surface-Fit : $\{\ \vec{a} = \text{Parameters}, \ \sigma = \text{Fit Error}\ \}$;
   Fitted-Surface: $\hat{g}(m, \vec{a}, x, y)$;
   Surface-Type-Image : $\mathrm{sgn}_{HK}(x, y) \in \{1, 2, 3, 5, 6, 7, 8, 9\}$;
   Region-Label-Image : $\hat{l}_g(x, y) \in \{1, \ldots, \hat{N}\}$;

Surface-Fit-List : $\{\vec{a}_i\}$ where $i \in \{1, \ldots, \hat{N}\}$;
Reconstruction-Image : $\hat{g}(x, y)$;
Error-Image : $e(x, y) = |\hat{g}(x, y) - g(x, y)|$;
Current-Region, New-Region, Seed-Region, HK-Sign-Region:
Four-Connected Subsets of Image I, Elements of C^I.

2. **Initialization:**
   Error-Image = Big Error Value (1024);
   Reconstruction-Image = No Value (0);
   Region-Label-Image = No Label (0);

3. **Start-Iteration:**
   If Average Error in *Error-Image* < Threshold Error,
   Then GoTo **All-Done**;
   HK-Sign-Region = Next-Largest-Region(*Surface-Type-Image*);
   If Sizeof(*HK-Sign-Region*) < Threshold Size
   Then GoTo **Last-Chance**;
   Else *Seed-Region* = Extract-Seed-Region(*HK-Sign-Region*);
   Current-Region = *Seed-Region*;
   Surface-Order = 1 = Planar ($z = a + bx + cy$);

4. **Surface-Fitting:**
   Perform *Surface-Order* Fit to $g(x, y)$ Values in *Current-Region* to
   obtain *Surface-Fit*;

5. **Surface-Fit-Testing:**
   If *Surface-Fit* OK using RMS Error Test and Regions Test,
   Then GoTo **Region-Growing**;
   Else Increment *Surface-Order*;
   If *Surface-Order* > *Max-Surface-Order* ,
   Then GoTo **Accept-Reject**;
   Else GoTo **Surface-Fitting**;

6. **Region-Growing:**
   Find *New-Region* Consisting of Compatible Connected Neighboring
   Pixels where Compatibility means Pixel Value is Close to *Fitted-Surface* Value and Residual Error must be Smaller Than Current
   Value in *Error-Image*;
   (Optionally) Require Surface Normal Estimates from $g(x, y)$ Data at
   Compatible Pixel Values be Close to *Fitted-Surface* Normal;
   If Sizeof(*Current-Region*) – Sizeof(*New-Region*) < Threshold
   Then GoTo **Accept-Reject**;
   Else Set *Current-Region* = *New-Region*; GoTo **Surface-Fitting**;

7. **Accept-Reject:**
   If *Surface-Fit* Acceptable using RMS Error Test,
   Then GoTo **Accept-Surface-Region**;

Else Zero Out *Seed-Region* Pixels in *Surface-Type-Image*;
GoTo **Start-Iteration**;

8. **Accept-Surface-Region**:
   Zero Out *Current-Region* Pixels in *Surface-Type-Image*;
   Increment *Region-Label*;
   Label *Current-Region* Pixels in *Region-Label-Image*;
   Evaluate *Current-Region* Pixels in *Reconstruction-Image*
   using *Fitted-Surface*;
   Update *Current-Region* Pixels in *Error-Image* with Absolute
   Residual Errors;
   Add *Surface-Fit* to *Surface-Fit-List*;
   Label Connected Neighboring Pixels Close Enough to *Fitted-Surface*;
   Update *Error-Image* for Labeled, Close Enough, Neighboring Pixels;
   GoTo **Start-Iteration**;

9. **Last-Chance**:
   Surface-Type-Image = All Unlabeled Pixels Coalesced as One Type;
   Double Maximum Allowable RMS Fit Error;
   GoTo **Start-Iteration**;

10. **All-Done**:
    Surface-Fit-List Contains All Function Definitions;
    Region-Label-Image Contains All Region Definitions;
    Reconstruction-Image Contains Noiseless Version of Original Image;
    Error-Image Contains Best-Fit Error at Each Pixel;

Several relatively minor details of the algorithm as described in Chapter 4 have been omitted to keep this description as simple as possible while including all basic concepts.

References

1. ABDELMALEK, N.N. 1980. *L*1 solution of overdetermined systems of linear equations. *ACM Trans. Mathematical Software* **6**, 220-227.

2. ABELSON, H., AND DISESSA, A.A. 1980. *Turtle Geometry*. MIT Press, Cambridge, Mass.

3. AGIN, G.J., AND BINFORD, T.O. 1973. Computer description of curved objects. In *Proceedings of 3rd International Joint Conference on Artificial Intelligence* (Stanford, Calif., Aug. 20-23). pp. 629-640.

4. ANDERSON, R.L., AND HOUSEMAN, E.E. 1942. *Tables of Orthogonal Polynomial Values Extended to N=104*. Research Bulletin 297, Iowa State College of Agriculture and Mechanic Arts, Ames, Iowa. (April).

5. ASADA, H., AND BRADY, M. 1986. The curvature primal sketch. *IEEE Trans. Patt. Anal. Mach. Intell.* PAMI-8, 1 (Jan.), 2-15.

6. BALLARD, D.H. AND BROWN, C.M. 1982. *Computer Vision*. Prentice-Hall, Englewood Cliffs, N.J.

7. BARNARD, S. 1986. A stochastic approach to stereo vision. In *Proceedings of 5th National Conference on Artificial Intelligence*, (August 11-15, Phila, Pa.), AAAI, pp. 676-680.

8. BARROW, H.G., AND POPPLESTONE, R.J. 1971. Relational descriptions in picture processing. In *Machine Intelligence VI* (B. Meltzer and D. Michie, Eds.), American Elsevier, New York, pp. 377-396.

9. BARROW, H.G., AND TENENBAUM, J.M. 1978. Recovering intrinsic scene characteristics from images. Technical Note 157, SRI International (April).

10. BARROW, H.G., AND TENENBAUM, J.M. 1981. Computational vision. *Proc. IEEE* **69**, 5 (May), 572-595.

11. BARTELS, R.H., AND JEZIORANSKI, J.J. 1985. Least-squares fitting using orthogonal multinomials. *ACM Trans. Mathematical Software* **11**, 3 (Sept.), 201-217.

12. BEAUDET, P.R. 1978. Rotationally invariant image operators. In *Proceedings of 4th International Conference Pattern Recognition* (Kyoto, Japan, Nov. 7-10). pp. 579-583.

13. BESL, P.J. 1988. Active optical range imaging sensors. In *Advances in Machine Vision: Architectures and Applications*, (J.Sanz,Ed.), Springer-Verlag, New York.

14. BESL, P.J., AND JAIN, R.C. 1988. Segmentation via variable-order surface fitting. *IEEE Trans. Pattern Analysis Machine Intelligence* PAMI-10, 2 (March).

15. BESL, P.J., AND JAIN, R.C. 1986. Invariant surface characteristics for three-dimensional object recognition in range images. *Computer Vision, Graphics, Image Processing* **33**, 1 (January), 33-80.

16. BESL, P.J., AND JAIN, R.C. 1985. Three-dimensional object recognition. *ACM Computing Surveys* **17**, 1 (March), 75-145.

17. BESL, P.J., DELP, E.J., AND JAIN, R.C. 1985. Automatic visual solder joint inspection. *IEEE J. Robotics and Automation* **1**, 1 (May), 42-56.

18. BHANU, B. 1984. Representation and shape matching of 3-D objects. *IEEE Trans. Pattern Anal. Machine Intell.* PAMI-6, 3 (May), 340-350.

19. BHANU, B. AND HO, C.C. 1987. CAD-based 3D object representation for robot vision. *IEEE Computer* **20**, 8 (August), 19-36.

20. BLAKE A. 1984. Reconstructing a visible surface. In *Proc. of National Conference on Artificial Intelligence* (Austin, Tex., Aug. 6-10). American Association for Artificial Intelligence, pp. 23-26.

21. BLAKE, A. AND ZISSERMAN, A. 1987. *Visual reconstruction.* MIT Press, Cambridge, Mass.

22. BOEHM, W., FARIN, G., AND KAHMANN, J. 1984. A survey of curve and surface methods in CAGD. *Computer Aided Geometric Design* **1**, 1 (July), 1-60.

23. BOLLE, R.M., AND COOPER, D.B. 1984. Bayesian recognition of local 3-D shape by approximating image intensity functions with quadric polynomials. *IEEE Trans. Pattern Anal. Machine Intell.* PAMI-6, 4 (July), 418-429.

24. BOLLES, R.C., AND FISCHLER, M.A. 1981. A RANSAC-based approach to model fitting and its application to finding cylinders in range data. In *Proceedings of 7th International Joint Conference on Artificial Intelligence* (Vancouver, B.C., Canada, Aug. 24-28). pp. 637-643.

25. BOLLES, R.C., HORAUD, P., AND HANNAH, M.J. 1983. 3DPO: A three-dimensional part orientation system. In *Proceedings of 8th International Joint Conference on Artificial Intelligence* (Karlsruhe, West Germany, Aug. 8-12). pp. 1116-1120; Also In *Proceedings of 2nd International Symposium on Robotics Research,* (Hanafusa, H. and Inoue, H. Eds.), MIT Press, Cambridge, Mass, pp. 413-424.

26. BOLLES, R.C., AND HORAUD, P. 1986. 3DPO: a three-dimensional part orientation system. *Int. J. Robotic Res.* **5**, 3 (Fall), 3-26.

27. BRADY, M. 1982. Computational approaches to image understanding. *ACM Computing Surveys* **14**, 1 (Mar.), 3-71.

28. BRADY, M., PONCE, J., YUILLE, A., AND ASADA, H. 1985. Describing surfaces. In *Proceedings 2nd International Symposium on Robotics Research,* (Hanafusa, H. and Inoue, H. Eds.), MIT Press, Cambridge, Mass.

29. BRICE, C., AND FENNEMA, C. 1970. Scene analysis using regions. *Artificial Intelligence* **1**, 205-226.

30. BROOKS, R.A. 1981. Symbolic reasoning among 3-D models and 2-D images. *Artificial Intell.* **17**, (Aug.), 285-348.

31. BROOKS, R.A. 1982. Representing possible realities for vision and manipulation. In *Proceedings of Pattern Recognition and Image Processing Conference* (Las Vegas, Nevada, June 14-17). pp. 587-592.

32. BROOKS, R.A. 1983. Model-based three-dimensional interpretations of two-dimensional images. *IEEE Trans. Pattern Anal. Machine Intell.* PAMI-5, 2 (Mar.), 140-149.

33. CASASENT, D., VIJAYA-KUMAR, B.V.K., AND SHARMA, V. 1982. Synthetic discriminant functions for three-dimensional object recognition. In *Proceedings of Society for Photo-Optical Instrumentation Engineers Conference on Robotics and Industrial Inspection*, vol. 360, (San Diego, Calif., Aug. 24-27). SPIE, Bellingham, Wash., pp. 136-142.

34. CHEN, D.S. 1988. A data-driven intermediate level feature extraction algorithm. *IEEE Trans. Pattern Anal. Mach. Intell.* to appear.

35. CHERN, S.S. 1957. A proof of the uniqueness of Minkowski's problem for convex surfaces. *Am. J. Math.* **79**, 949-950.

36. CHIN, R.T., AND DYER, C.R. 1986. Model-based recognition in robot vision. *ACM Computing Surveys* **18**, 1 (March), 67-108.

37. COLEMAN, E.N., AND JAIN, R. 1982. Obtaining shape of textured and specular surfaces using four-source photometry. *Comput. Graphics Image Processing* **18**, 4 (Apr.), 309-328.

38. CONNOLLY, C.I. 1985. The determination of next best views. In *Proceedings of International Conference on Robotics and Automation* (St. Louis, Mo., Mar. 25-28). IEEE-CS, New York, pp. 432-435.

39. DAHLQUIST, G., AND BJORK, A. 1974. *Numerical Methods.* Prentice-Hall, Englewood Cliffs, N.J. (Translated by N. Anderson).

40. DANE C. 1982. An object-centered three-dimensional model builder. Ph.D. dissertation, Comp. and Info. Sci. Dept., Moore School of Electr. Eng., Univ. of Penn., Philadelphia, Pa.

41. DANIEL, W. 1978. *Applied Nonparametric Statistics.* Houghton-Mifflin, Boston, Mass.

42. DAVIS, L.S. 1975. A survey of edge detection techniques. *Computer Graphics Image Processing* **4**, 248-270.

43. DAVIS, P.J. 1963. *Interpolation and Approximation.* Chapter 10: Orthogonal Polynomials. Dover, New York.

44. DIZENZO, S. 1983. Advances in image segmentation. *Image and Vision Computing* **1**, 4 (November), 196-210.

45. DOUGLASS, R.M. 1981. Interpreting 3-D scenes: a model-building approach. *Comput. Graphics Image Processing* **17**, 2 (Oct.), 91-113.

46. DRESCHLER, L., AND NAGEL, H.H. 1981. Volumetric model and 3D-trajectory of a moving car derived from monocular TV-frame sequences of a street scene. In *Proceedings of 7th International Joint Conference on Artificial Intelligence* (Vancouver, B.C., Canada, Aug. 24-28), pp. 692-697.

47. DUDA, R.O., AND HART, P.E. 1972. The use of Hough transform to detect lines and curves in pictures. *Comm. ACM* **15**, 11-15.

48. DUDA, R.O., NITZAN, D., AND BARRETT, P. 1979. Use of range and reflectance data to find planar surface regions. *IEEE Trans. Pattern Anal. Machine Intell.* PAMI-1, 3 (July), 254-271.

49. EICHEL, P.H. 1985. Sequential detection of linear features in two-dimensional random fields. Ph.D. dissertation, EECS Dept., Univ. of Mich., Ann Arbor.

50. FANG, T.J., HUANG, Z.H., KANAL, L.N., LAMBIRD, B., LAVINE, D., STOCKMAN, G., AND XIONG, F.L. 1982. Three-dimensional object recognition using a transformation clustering technique. In *Proceedings of 6th International Conference Pattern Recognition* (Munich, West Germany, Oct. 19-22). pp. 678-681.

51. FAUGERAS, O.D. 1984. New steps toward a flexible 3-D vision system for robotics. In *Proceedings of 7th International Conference Pattern Recognition* (Montreal, Canada, July 30-Aug.2). pp. 796-805.

52. FAUGERAS, O.D., AND HEBERT, M. 1986. The representation, recognition, and locating of 3-D objects. *Int. J. Robotic Res.* **5**, 3, Fall, 27-52.

53. FAUGERAS, O.D., HEBERT, M., PAUCHON, E., AND PONCE, J. 1985. Object representation, identification, and positioning from range data. In *Proceedings 2nd International Symposium on Robotics Research*, (Hanafusa, H. and Inoue, H. Eds.), MIT Press, Cambridge, Mass., pp. 425-446.

54. FAUGERAS, O.D., HEBERT, M., AND PAUCHON, E. 1983. Segmentation of range data into planar and quadric patches. In *Proceedings of 3rd Computer Vision and Pattern Recognition Conference* (Arlington, Va.), pp. 8-13.

55. FAUX, I.D., AND PRATT, M.J. 1979. *Computational Geometry for Design and Manufacture.* Ellis Horwood, Chichester, U.K.

56. FELDMAN, J.A., AND YAKIMOVSKY, Y. 1974. Decision theory and artificial intelligence. I. A semantics-based region analyzer. *Artificial Intelligence* **5**, 349-371.

57. FISHER, R.B. 1986. From surfaces to objects: recognizing objects using surface information and object models. Ph.D. dissertation. Artificial Intelligence Department, University of Edinburgh, Scotland, UK.

58. FOLEY, J.D., AND VAN DAM, A. 1982. *Fundamentals of Interactive Computer Graphics.* Addison-Wesley, Reading, Mass.

59. FU, K.S., AND MUI, J.K. 1981. A survey on image segmentation. *Pattern Recognition* **13**, 3-16.

60. GEMAN, S. AND GEMAN, D. 1984. Stochastic relaxation, gibbs distributions, and bayesian restoration of images. *IEEE Trans. Pattern Anal. Machine Intell.* PAMI-6, 6 (November), 721-741.

61. GENNERY, D.B. 1979. Object detection and measurement using stereo vision. In *Proceedings of 6th International Joint Conference on Artificial Intelligence* (Tokyo, Japan, Aug. 20-23). pp. 320-327.

62. *GEOMOD User Manual and Reference Manual 1983.* Structural Dynamics Research Corporation (SDRC), Milford, Ohio.

63. GIL, B., MITICHE, A., AND AGGARWAL, J.K. 1983. Experiments in combining intensity and range edge maps. *Comput. Vision, Graphics, Image Processing* **21**, (Mar.), 395-411.

64. GILBARG, D., AND TRUDINGER, N. 1983. *Elliptic Partial Differential Equations of Second Order*. 2nd Ed. Springer-Verlag, New York.

65. GOAD, C. 1983. Special purpose automatic programming for 3D model-based vision. In *Proceedings of the Image Understanding Workshop* (Arlington, Va., June 23) DARPA, pp. 94-104.

66. GOLUB, G.H. 1965. Numerical methods for solving least squares problems. *Numerische Mathematik* **7**, 3, 206-216

67. GOLUB, G.H., AND VAN LOAN, C.F. 1983. *Matrix Computations*. Johns Hopkins Univ. Press, Baltimore, Md.

68. GRIMSON, W.E.L., AND LOZANO-PEREZ, T. 1984. Model-based recognition and localization from sparse range or tactile data. *Int'l. J. Robotics Research* **3**, 3, 3-35.

69. GRIMSON, W.E.L., AND PAVLIDIS, T. 1985. Discontinuity detection for visual surface reconstruction. *Computer Vision, Graphics, and Image Processing* **30**, 316-330.

70. GROGAN, T.A., AND MITCHELL, O.R. 1983. Partial shape recognition using Fourier-Mellin transform methods. *Optical Society of America Winter '83 Topical Meeting on Signal Recovery and Synthesis with Incomplete Information and Partial Constraints*, (January), pp. ThA19-1:ThA19-4; see also Ph.D. disseration, Purdue University 1983.

71. GUISTI, E. 1978. On the equation of surfaces of prescribed mean curvature: existence and uniqueness without boundary conditions. *Inventiones Mathematicae* **46**, 111-137.

72. GUZMAN, A. 1968. Computer recognition of three-dimensional objects in a visual scene. MAC-TR-59 (Ph.D. dissertation), Project MAC, MIT, Cambridge, Mass.

73. HALL, E.L., TIO, J.B.K., MCPHERSON, C.A., AND SADJADI, F.A. 1982. Measuring curved surfaces for robot vision. *Computer* **15**, 12 (Dec.), 42-54.

74. HAMPEL, F.R., RONCHETTI, E.M., ROUSSEEUW, P.J., STAHEL, W.A. 1986. *Robust statistics: the approach based on influence functions*. Wiley, New York.

75. HANSON, A.R., RISEMAN, E.M., AND NAGIN, P. 1975. Region growing in textured outdoor scenes. In *Proceedings of 3rd Milwaukee Symposium on Automated Computation and Control*, pp. 407-417.

76. HARALICK, R.M. 1984. Digital step edges from zero-crossings of second directional derivatives. *IEEE Trans. Pattern Anal. Machine Intell.* PAMI-6, 1 (Jan.), 58-68.

77. HARALICK, R.M., AND SHAPIRO, L.G. 1985. Image segmentation techniques. *Computer Vision, Graphics, Image Processing* **29**, 100-132.

78. HARALICK, R.M., AND WATSON, L. 1981. A facet model for image data. *Computer Graphics Image Processing* **15**, 113-129.

79. HARALICK, R.M., WATSON, L.T., AND LAFFEY, T.J. 1983. The topographic primal sketch. *Int. J. Robotics Res.* **2**, 1 (Spring) 50-72.

80. HEBERT, M., AND KANADE, T. 1985. The 3-D profile method for object recognition. In *Proceedings of Computer Vision and Pattern Recognition Conference* (San Francisco, Calif., June 9-13), IEEE-CS, New York, pp. 458-463.

81. HEBERT, M., AND PONCE, J. 1982. A new method for segmenting 3-D scenes into primitives. In *Proceedings of 6th International Conference Pattern Recognition* (Munich, West Germany, Oct. 19-22). pp. 836-838.

82. HENDERSON, T.C. 1983. Efficient 3-D object representations for industrial vision systems. *IEEE Trans. Pattern Anal. Machine Intell.* PAMI-5, 6 (Nov.), 609-617.

83. HENDERSON, T.C., AND BHANU, B. 1982. Three-point seed method for the extraction of planar faces from range data. In *Proceedings of Workshop on Industrial Applications of Machine Vision* (Research Triangle Park, N.C., May). IEEE, New York, pp. 181-186.

84. HERMAN, M. 1985. Generating detailed scene descriptions from range images. In *Proceedings of International Conference on Robotics and Automation* (St. Louis, Mo., Mar. 25-28). IEEE-CS, New York, pp. 426-431.

85. HOFFMAN, R. 1986. Object recognition from range images. Ph.D. dissertation, Computer Science Department, Michigan State University, East Lansing, Michigan.

86. HOFFMAN, R. AND JAIN, A.K. 1987. Segmentation and classification of range images. *IEEE Trans. Pattern Anal. Machine Intell.* PAMI-9, 5 (Sept.), 608-620.

87. HORAUD, P., AND BOLLES, R.C. 1984. 3DPO's strategy for matching three-dimensional objects in range data. In *Proceedings of the International Conference Robotics.* (Atlanta, Ga., Mar. 13-15). IEEE-CS, New York, pp. 78-85.

88. HORN, B.K.P. 1977. Understanding image intensities. *Artificial Intell.* 8, 2 (Apr.), 201-231.

89. HORN, B.K.P. 1984. Extended Gaussian images. *Proc. IEEE* 72, 12 (Dec.) 1656-1678.

90. HOROWITZ, S.L., AND PAVLIDIS, T. 1974. Picture segmentation by a directed split-and-merge procedure. *Proceedings 2nd International Joint Conference Pattern Recognition*, pp. 424-433.

91. HSIUNG, C.C. 1981. *A first course in differential geometry.* Wiley-Interscience, New York.

92. HUECKEL, M. 1973. A local operator which recognizes edges and lines. *J. Assoc. Comp. Mach.* 20, 634-647.

93. IKEUCHI, K., AND HORN, B.K.P. 1981. Numerical shape from shading and occluding boundaries. *Artificial Intell.* 17, (Aug.), 141-184.

94. IKEUCHI, K., HORN, B.K.P., NAGATA, S., CALLAHAN, T., AND FEIMGOLD, O. 1983. Picking up an object from a pile of objects. MIT Artificial Intelligence Lab Memo 726. Cambridge, Mass.

95. IKEUCHI, K. 1981. Recognition of 3-D objects using the extended Gaussian image. In *Proceedings of 7th International Joint Conference on Artificial Intelligence* (Vancouver, B.C., Canada, Aug. 24-28). pp. 595-600.

96. INOKUCHI, S., NITA, T., MATSUDAY, F., AND SAKURAI, Y. 1982. A three-dimensional edge-region operator for range pictures. In *Proceedings of 6th International Conference Pattern Recognition* (Munich, West Germany, Oct. 19-22). pp. 918-920.

97. INOKUCHI, S., AND NEVATIA, R. 1980. Boundary detection in range pictures. In *Proceedings of 5th International Conference Pattern Recognition* (Miami, Fla., Dec. 1-4). pp. 1031-1035.

98. ITTNER, D.J., AND JAIN, A.K. 1985. 3-D surface discrimination from local curvature measures. In *Proceedings of Computer Vision and Pattern Recognition Conference* (San Francisco, Calif., June 9-13), IEEE-CS, New York, pp. 119-123.

99. JARVIS, R.A. 1983. A perspective on range finding techniques for computer vision. *IEEE Trans. Pattern Analysis Mach. Intell.* PAMI-5, 2 (Mar), 122-139.

100. KAJIYA, J.T. 1986. The rendering equation. em Computer Graphics **20**, 4 (August), 143-150.

101. KANADE, T. 1981. Recovery of the three-dimensional shape of an object from a single view. *Artificial Intell.* **17**, (Aug.), 409-460.

102. KANADE, T. 1980. Survey: region segmentation: signal vs. semantics. *Computer Graphics Image Processing* **13**, 279-297.

103. KIM, H.S., JAIN, R.C., AND VOLZ, R.A. 1985. Object recognition using multiple views. In *Proceedings of International Conference on Robotics and Automation* (St. Louis, Mo., Mar. 25-28). IEEE-CS, New York, pp. 28-33.

104. KNOLL, T.K., AND JAIN, R.C. 1986. Recognizing partially visible objects using feature-indexed hypotheses. *IEEE J. Robotics Automation* RA-2, 1 (March), 3-13.

105. KUAN, D.T., AND DRAZOVICH, R.J. 1984. Model-based interpretation of range imagery. In *Proceedings of the National Conference on Artificial Intelligence* (Austin, Tex., Aug. 6-10). American Association for Artificial Intelligence, pp. 210-215.

106. LANGRIDGE, D.J. 1984. Detection of discontinuities in the first derivatives of surfaces. *Comput. Vision, Graphics, Image Processing* **27**, 3 (Sept.), 291-308.

107. LAWSON, C.L., AND HANSON, R.J. 1974. *Solving least squares problems.* Prentice-Hall, Englewood Cliffs, N.J.

108. LEVINE, M.D., AND NAZIF, A.M. 1985. Dynamic measurement of computer generated image segmentations. *IEEE Trans. Patt. Anal. Mach. Intell.* PAMI-7, 2 (March), 155-164.

109. LIANG, P. 1987. Representation and recognition of surface shapes in range images. Ph.D. dissertation. Dept. of Electrical Eng., University of Pittsburgh, Pittsburgh, PA.

110. LIN, C., AND PERRY, M.J. 1982. Shape description using surface triangularization. In *Proceedings of Workshop on Computer Vision: Representation and Control* (Rindge, N.H., Aug. 23-25). IEEE-CS, New York, pp. 38-43.

111. LIPSCHUTZ, M.M. 1969. *Differential Geometry.* Mc-Graw Hill, New York.

112. LITTLE, J.J. 1983. An iterative method for reconstructing convex polyhedra from extended Gaussian images. In *Proceedings of the National Conference on Artificial Intelligence* (Washington, D.C., Aug. 22-26). American Association for Artificial Intelligence, pp. 247-250.

113. LUENBERGER, D.G. 1984. *Linear and Non-linear Programming (2d.Ed).* Addison-Wesley, Reading, Mass.

114. LYNCH, D.K. 1981. Range enhancement via one-dimensional spatial filtering. *Comput. Graphics Image Processing* 15, 2 (Feb.), 194-200.

115. MARIMONT, D.H. 1984. A representation for image curves. In *Proceedings of the National Conference on Artificial Intelligence* (Austin, Tex., Aug. 6-10). American Association for Artificial Intelligence, pp. 237-242.

116. MARR, D. 1976. Early processing of visual information. *Phil. Trans. Royal Soc. Lond. B 275*, 483-524.

117. MARR, D. 1982. *Vision.* Freeman, New York.

118. MEDIONI, G., AND NEVATIA, R. 1984. Description of 3-D surfaces using curvature properties. In *Proceedings of the Image Understanding Workshop* (New Orleans, La., Oct. 3-4). DARPA, pp. 291-299.

119. MILGRIM, D.L. 1977. Region extraction using convergent evidence. *Computer Graphics Image Processing* 11, 1-12.

120. MILGRIM, D.L., AND BJORKLUND, C.M. 1980. Range image processing: planar surface extraction. In *Proceedings of 5th International Conference Pattern Recognition* (Miami, Fla., Dec. 1-4). pp. 912-919.

121. MINKOWSKI, H. 1897. Allgemeine lehrsatze uber die konvexen polyeder. Nachrichten von der Koniglichen Gesellschaft der Wissenschaften, Mathematisch-Physikalische Klasse, Gottingen, pp. 198-219.

122. MISNER, C.W., THORNE, K.S., AND WHEELER, J.A. 1973. *Gravitation.* W.H. Freeman, San Francisco, Calif. (Box 14.1, Item 7).

123. MITICHE A., AND AGGARWAL, J.K. 1985. Image segmentation by conventional and information-integrating techniques: a synopsis. *Image and Vision Computing* 3, 2 (May), 50-62.

124. MITICHE, A., AND AGGARWAL, J.K. 1983. Detection of edges using range information. *IEEE Trans. Pattern Anal. Machine Intell.* PAMI-5, 2 (Mar.), 174-178.

125. MOKHTARIAN, F., AND MACKWORTH, A. 1986. Scale-based description and recognition of planar curves and two-dimensional shapes. *IEEE Trans. Patt. Anal. Mach. Intell.* PAMI-8, 1 (Jan.) 34-43.

126. MUERLE, J.L., AND ALLEN, D.C. 1968. Experimental evaluation of techniques for automatic segmentation of objects in a complex scene. In _Pictorial Pattern Recognition_ (Cheng et al., Eds.), Thompson, Washington, pp. 3-13.

127. NACKMAN, L.R. 1984. Two-dimensional critical point configuration graphs. _IEEE Trans. Pattern Anal. Machine Intell._ PAMI-6, 4 (July), 442-449.

128. NACKMAN, L.R. 1982. Three-dimensional shape description using the symmetric axis transform. Ph.D. dissertation, Comp. Sci. Dept., Univ. of N.C., Chapel Hill, N.C.

129. NEVATIA, R., AND BINFORD, T.O. 1973. Structured descriptions of complex objects. In _Proceedings of 3rd International Joint Conference on Artificial Intelligence_ (Stanford, Calif., Aug. 20-23). pp. 641-647.

130. NEVATIA, R., AND BINFORD, T.O. 1977. Description and recognition of curved objects. _Artificial Intell._ 8, 1, 77-98.

131. NEWMAN, W.M., AND SPROULL, R.F. 1979. _Principles of Interactive Computer Graphics, 2d Ed._ McGraw-Hill, New York.

132. NITZAN, D., BRAIN, A.E., AND DUDA, R.O. 1977. The measurement and use of registered reflectance and range data in scene analysis. _Proc. IEEE_ 65, (Feb.), 206-220.

133. OHLANDER, R. 1975. Analysis of natural scenes. Ph.D. dissertation, Dept. of Comp. Sci., Carnegie-Mellon Univ., Pittsburgh, Pa.

134. ONEILL, B. 1966. _Elementary Differential Geometry._ Academic Press, New York.

135. OSHIMA, M., AND SHIRAI, Y. 1983. Object recognition using three-dimensional information. _IEEE Trans. Pattern Anal. Machine Intell._ PAMI-5, 4 (July), 353-361.

136. OSSERMAN, R. 1969. _A survey of minimal surfaces._ Dover, New York.

137. PALMER, S. 1983. The psychology of perceptual organization: a transformational approach. _Human and Machine Vision_ (Beck et al., Eds.), Academic Press, New York, pp. 269-340.

138. PAVLIDIS, T. 1972. Segmentation of pictures and maps through functional approximation. _Computer Graphics Image Processing_ 1, 360-372.

139. PEET, F.G. AND SAHOTA, T.S. 1985. Surface curvature as a measure of image texture. _IEEE Trans. Pattern Anal. Machine Intell._ PAMI-7, 6 (November), 734-738.

140. PONCE, J., AND BRADY, M. 1985. Toward a surface primal sketch. In _Proceedings of International Conference on Robotics and Automation_ (St. Louis, Mo., Mar. 25-28). IEEE-CS, New York, pp. 420-425.

141. PONG, T.C., SHAPIRO, L.G., WATSON, L.T., AND HARALICK, R.M. 1984. Experiments in segmentation using a facet model region grower. _Computer Vision, Graphics, and Image Processing_ 25, 1-23.

142. POPPLESTONE, R.J., BROWN, C.M., AMBLER, A.P., AND CRAWFORD, G.F. 1975. Forming models of plane-and-cylinder faceted bodies from light stripes. In _Proceedings of 4th International Joint Conference on Artificial Intelligence_ (Tbilisi, Georgia, USSR, Sept.). pp. 664-668.

143. POTMESIL, M. 1982. Generating three-dimensional surface models of solid objects from multiple projections. IPL-TR-033, Ph.D. dissertation, Image Proc. Lab, RPI, Troy, NY.

144. POTMESIL, M. 1983. Generating models of solid objects by matching 3D surface segments. In *Proceedings of 8th International Joint Conference on Artificial Intelligence* (Karlsruhe, West Germany, Aug. 8-12). pp. 1089-1093.

145. POTMESIL, M. 1987. Generating octree models of 3D objects from their silhouettes. *Computer Vision, Graphics, Image Processing*, **40**, 1, 1-29.

146. POWELL, M.J.D. 1981. *Approximation theory and methods.* Cambridge University Press, Cambridge, UK.

147. PREWITT, J. 1970. Object enhancement and extraction. In *Picture Processing and Psychopictorics*, B. Lipkin and A. Rosenfeld, Eds., Academic Press, New York, pp 75-149.

148. PREWITT, J.S.M., AND MENDELSOHN, M.L. 1966. The analysis of cell images. *Ann. N.Y. Acad. Sci.* **128**, 1035-1053.

149. REEVES, A.P., PROKOP, R.J., AND TAYLOR, R.W. 1985. Shape analysis of 3-D objects using range information. In *Proceedings of Computer Vision and Pattern Recognition Conference* (San Francisco, Calif., June 19-23), IEEE-CS, New York, pp. 452-457.

150. RISEMAN, E.M., AND ARBIB, M.A. 1977. Computational techniques in the visual segmentation of static scenes. *Computer Graphics and Image Processing*, **6**, 221-276.

151. ROBERTS, L.G. 1965. Machine perception of three-dimensional solids. *Optical and Electro-Optical Information Processing.* J.T. Tippett et al., Eds., MIT Press, Cambridge, Mass. pp. 159-197.

152. ROCK, I. 1983. *The logic of perception*, MIT Press, Cambridge, MA.

153. ROSENFELD, A. 1978. Iterative methods in image analysis. *Pattern Recognition* **10**, 181-187.

154. ROSENFELD, A., AND DAVIS, L.S. 1979. Image segmentation and image models. *Proc. IEEE* **67**, 5 (May), 764-772.

155. ROSENFELD, A., AND KAK A. 1982. *Digital Picture Processing*, vols. 1 and 2. Academic Press, New York. (1st Ed. 1976)

156. ROSENFELD, A., AND THURSTON, M. 1971. Edge and curve detection for visual scene analysis. *IEEE Trans. Computers* **C-20**, 562-569.

157. ROSENFELD, A., HUMMEL, R.A., AND ZUCKER, S.W. 1976. Scene labeling by relaxation operations. *IEEE Trans. Systems, Man, Cybernetics* **6**, 6, 420-433.

158. SADJADI, F.A., AND HALL, E.L. 1980. Three-dimensional moment invariants. *IEEE Trans. Pattern Anal. Machine Intell.* PAMI-2, 2 (Mar.), 127-136.

159. SARRAGA, R.F. AND WATERS, W.C. 1985. Free-form surfaces in GM-Solid: goals and issues. In *Solid Modeling by Computers* (M.Pickett and J.Boyse,Eds.), Plenum Press, New York. pp. 187-209.

160. SATO, Y., AND HONDA, I. 1983. Pseudodistance measures for recognition of curved objects. *IEEE Trans. Pattern Anal. Machine Intell.* PAMI-5, 4 (July), 362-373.

161. SCHMITT, F., BARSKY, B., AND DU, W. 1986. An adaptive subdivision method for surface-fitting from sampled data. *Computer Graphics* **20**, 4 (August), 179-188.

162. SETHI, I.K., AND JAYARAMAMURTHY, S.N. 1984. Surface classification using characteristic contours. In *Proceedings of 7th International Conference Pattern Recognition* (Montreal, Canada, July 30-Aug.2). pp. 438-440.

163. SHAHRARAY, B. AND ANDERSON, D.J. 1985. Uniform resampling of digitized contours. IEEE Trans. Pattern Anal. Machine Intell. PAMI-7, 6 (November), 674-681.

164. SHAPIRO, L.G. and HARALICK, R.M. 1981. Structural descriptions and inexact matching. *IEEE Trans. Pattern Analysis Mach. Intell.* PAMI-3, 5, 504-519.

165. SHIRAI, Y., AND SUWA, M. 1971. Recognition of polyhedra with a range finder. In *Proceedings of 2nd International Joint Conference on Artificial Intelligence* (London, U.K., Aug.). pp. 80-87.

166. SMITH, D.R. AND KANADE, T. 1985. Autonomous scene description with range imagery. *Computer Vision, Graphics, Image Processing* **31**, 322-334.

167. SNYDER, W., AND BILBRO, G. 1985. Segmentation of three-dimensional images. In *Proceedings of International Conference on Robotics and Automation* (St. Louis, Mo., Mar. 25-28). IEEE-CS, New York, pp. 396-403.

168. SUGIHARA, K. 1979. Range-data analysis guided by junction dictionary. *Artificial Intell.* **12**, 41-69.

169. SVETKOFF, D.J., LEONARD, P.F., SAMPSON, R.E., AND JAIN, R.C. 1984. Techniques for real-time 3D feature extraction using range information. In *Proceedings of The Society for Photo-Optical Instrumentation Engineers Conference on Intelligent Robotics and Computer Vision*, vol. 521, (Cambridge, Mass., Nov. 5-8).

170. TENENBAUM, J.M., AND BARROW, H.G. 1976. IGS: a paradigm for integrating image segmentation and interpretation. In *Proceedings 3rd International Conference Pattern Recognition*, pp. 504-513.

171. TERZOPOLOUS, D. 1985. Computing visible surface representations. AI Memo No. 800, MIT Artif. Intell. Laboratory, Cambridge, Mass. (March). see also Multiresolution computation of visible surface representations. Ph.D. dissertation, MIT, Cambridge, Mass., 1984.

172. TERZOPOULOS, D. 1983. Multilevel computational processes for visual surface reconstruction. *Comput. Vision, Graphics, Image Processing* 24, 52-96.

173. TOMITA, F., AND KANADE, T. 1984. A 3D vision system: generating and matching shape descriptions in range images. In *Proceedings of the*

International Conference Robotics. (Atlanta, Ga., Mar. 13-15). IEEE-CS, New York, pp. 186-191.

174. TSUJI, S., AND TOMITA, F. 1973. A structural analyzer for a class of textures. *Comput. Graphics Image Processing* 2, 216-231.

175. TURNEY, J.L., MUDGE, T.N., AND VOLZ, R.A. 1985. Recognizing Partially Occluded Parts. *IEEE Trans. Pattern Anal. Mach. Intell.* PAMI-7, 4 (July), 410-421.

176. VEMURI, B.C., MITICHE, A., AND AGGARWAL, J.K. 1986. Curvature-based representation of objects from range data. *Image and Vision Computing,* 4, 2 (May), 107-114.

177. WALLACE, T.P., AND WINTZ, P.A. 1980. An efficient three-dimensional aircraft recognition algorithm using normalized Fourier descriptors. *Comput. Graphics Image Processing* 13, 96-126.

178. WALTZ, D.L. 1975. Understanding line drawings of scenes with shadows. *The Psychology of Computer Vision,* McGraw-Hill, New York, pp. 19-91. also, Generating semantic descriptions from drawings of scenes with shadows. AI-TR-271, MIT Artificial Intelligence Lab, Cambridge, Mass., (Nov. 1982).

179. WATSON, L.T., LAFFEY, T.J., AND HARALICK, R.M. 1985. Topographic classification of digital image intensity surfaces using generalized splines and the discrete cosine transformation. *Comput. Vision, Graphics, Image Processing* 29, 143-167.

180. WESZKA, J.S. 1978. A survey of threshold selection techniques. *Comput. Graphics Image Processing* 7, 259-265.

181. WITKIN, A.P. 1981. Recovering surface shape and orientation from texture. *Artificial Intell.* 17, (Aug.), 17-45.

182. WITKIN, A.P., AND TENENBAUM, J. 1983. The role of structure in vision. *Human and Machine Vision.* (Beck et al., Eds.), Academic Press, New York, pp. 481-543.

183. WONG, R.Y., AND HAYREPETIAN, K. 1982. Image processing with intensity and range data. In *Proceedings of Pattern Recognition and Image Processing Conference* (Las Vegas, Nevada, June 14-17). pp. 518-520.

184. WOODHAM, R.J. 1981. Analysing images of curved surfaces. *Artificial Intell.* 17, (Aug.), 117-140.

185. WOODHAM, R.J. 1977. A cooperative algorithm for determining surface orientation from a single view. In *Proceedings of 6rd International Joint Conference on Artificial Intelligence,* pp. 635-641.

186. YASNOFF, W.A, MUI, J.K., AND BACUS, J.W. 1977. Error measures for scene segmentation. *Pattern Recognition* 9, 217-233.

187. ZUCKER, S.W. 1976. Region growing: childhood and adolescence. *Computer Graphics Image Processing* 5, 382-399.

188. ZUCKER, S.W., AND HUMMEL, R.A. 1981. A three-dimensional edge operator. *IEEE Trans. Pattern Anal. Mach. Intell.* PAMI-3, 3, 324-331.